UML AND C++

A PRACTICAL GUIDE TO OBJECT-ORIENTED DEVELOPMENT
Second Edition

RICHARD C. LEE
Lucent Technologies

WILLIAM M. TEPFENHART
AT&T

An Alan R. Apt Book

Prentice Hall

Upper Saddle River, New Jersey 07458

Library of Congress Cataloging-in-Publication Data
Lee, Richard C., 1956–
    UML & C++: a practical guide to object-oriented development / Richard C. Lee,
William M. Tepfenhart.
      p. cm.
    Includes bibliographical references and index.
    ISBN 0-13-029040-8
    1. Object-oriented programming (Computer science) 2. Computer software—
Development. 3. C++ (Computer program language) 4. UML (Computer science)
I. Tepfenhart, William M. II. Title.
QA76.64 .L449 2001
005.1'17—dc21   00-051636

Vice president and editorial director, ECS: **Marcia J. Horton**
Publisher: **Alan R. Apt**
Associate editor: **Toni D. Holm**
Editorial assistant: **Amy Todd**
Senior marketing manager: **Jennie Burger**
Production editor: **Carlisle Communications**
Executive managing editor: **Vince O'Brien**
Managing editor: **David A. George**
Art director: **Heather Scott**
Cover art and design: **John Christiana**
Art editor: **Adam Velthaus**
Manufacturing manager: **Trudy Pisciotti**
Manufacturing buyer: **Dawn Murrin**
Vice president of production and manufacturing, ESM: **David W. Riccardi**
Creative director: **Carole Anson**

The author and publisher of this book have used their best efforts in preparing this book. These efforts inlcude the development, research, and testing of the theories to determine their effectiveness. The author and publisher make no warranty of any kind, expressed or implied, with regard to the documentation contained in this book.

Printed in the United States of America.

10 9 8 7 6 5 4 3 2 1

ISBN 0-13-029040-8

Prentice-Hall International (UK) Limited, *London*
Prentice-Hall of Australia Pty. Limited, *Sydney*
Prentice-Hall Canada Inc., *Toronto*
Prentice-Hall Hispanoamericana, S.A., *Mexico*
Prentice-Hall of India Private Limited, *New Delhi*
Prentice-Hall of Japan, Inc., *Tokyo*
Pearson Education Asia Pte. Ltd., *Singapore*
Editora Prentice-Hall do Brasil, Ltda., *Rio de Janeiro*

CONTENTS

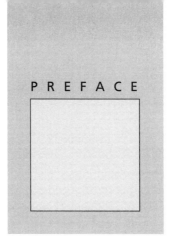

P R E F A C E

Preface to Second Edition

> *A xioms in Philosophy are not axioms until they are proved upon our pulses: we read fine things but never feel them to the full until we have gone the same steps as the author.*
>
> John Keats (1795–1821), Letter to
> J. H. Reynolds, May 3, 1818

UML and C++: A Practical Guide to Object-Oriented Development continues to be aimed at busy professional software analysts and developers who work on large systems, especially those who need to integrate their new systems with legacy systems. If you do not have time to take a class yet and get up-to-speed on object-oriented (OO) technology using Unified Modeling Language and C++, this book is a self-teaching guide for you. It will help you understand the differences between OO analysis, OO design, and OO programming. Our goals in the first edition were to:

- Teach you to build an object-oriented application using C++ and make the right trade-off decisions to meet your business needs;
- Clarify the basic concepts associated with object-oriented technology;
- Supply sufficient depth in coverage for students and practitioners entering the field to get them up to speed;
- Expose some of the myths surrounding OO technology while focusing on its practicality as a software engineering tool;
- Give you a "recipe" or step-by-step guide to do all of the steps of object-oriented technology;

- Advocate the view that OO, rule-based concepts, fuzzy logic, multimedia, and data modeling integrated into a single model can address the current and future business challenges for information technology organizations;
- Provide a practical approach to analysis, design, and programming in the OO technology.
- Show how to implement OO technology using C++ (though not an object-oriented language it is an extremely powerful multi-paradigm language); and
- Balance theory with application practices in the existing literature.

This, the second edition, has extended those goals to include:

- Give a practical approach for the development of use cases as part of OO analysis;
- Provide greater coverage of UML diagramming; and
- Introduce key C++ libraries that provide important functionality supporting implementation of an OO model in C++.

In addition, the second edition made improvements on the following topics:

- Dynamic behavior modeling
- Implementation of the state model
- Class projects

As always, you do not have know computer science or advanced mathematics to understand the important object-oriented concepts and issues in depth. Even the programming chapters do not require a background in C++; they illustrate how working code in C++ is produced.

Object-Oriented Technology

WE are software developers of large systems. We believe that OO technology is the most important software evolution (revolution) of the 1990s. It is changing the way we build software and the way applications intercommunicate over worldwide networks and across multi-vendor computers. Moreover, the OO model is changing the way we design business processes and the way we think about an enterprise. Most enterprises need redesigning today in order to meet future business challenges.

Business process redesign is one of the most important functions of an information technology organization. A model that captures the business processes, procedures, policies, and rules facilitates design. Tools that translate the model into an operational system speed the implementation of the redesign. When the market or business condition changes, these systems should be regenerated to reflect these changes by updating the model and using these tools. Information science (engineering) has taken us further and faster than any other approach in previous decades. However, it needs constant updating through even better, more refined methods to meet our business needs and challenges through OO modeling and OO programming. More and more people believe that OO technology will put a dent into the software crisis, meaning that the mechanisms of OO will become for software what the bolts and beams are for the construction design and what the chip is for computer hardware design. This belief stems from the following:

- The proficiency of a higher-level OO model should provide the software designer with real-world, programmable components, thereby reducing software development costs.
- Its capability to share and reuse code with OO techniques will reduce time to develop an application.
- Its capability to localize and minimize the effects of modifications through programming abstraction mechanisms will allow for faster enhancement development and will provide more reliable and more robust software.
- Its capability to manage complexity allows developers to address more difficult applications.

The collection of OO concepts is a tool set for modeling reality. This OO tool set gives developers the best means of managing the complexity. Certain OO concepts help developers produce flexible and maintainable software.

Why Unified Modeling Language?

As practitioners of OO technology, we know that all of the methods, if practiced properly, result in the same or a similar model. For many years, the number of different modeling language notations were impediments to progress and we adopted UML before it was widely accepted or supported by modeling tools. The wide acceptance of UML has eliminated these problems—different modeling language notations and scarcity of modeling tools—for the most part.

Underlying the reason for the success of the Unified Modeling Language is that it gives us all the drawing icons necessary to capture most of the concepts or *mechanisms* that we find valuable in solving real business problems. Also, it provides all of the necessary diagrams that are vital for documenting our models. In addition, it is a living language that gives us the ability to extend the notation for mechanisms not yet defined by the distinguished group of Grady Booch, James Rumbaugh, and Ivor Jacobson at Rational Software Corporation.

Why C++?

It is a misconception that C++ is exclusively an OO programming language. It is a multi-paradigm language that supports a number of programing paradigms, including procedural, abstract data type, and OO. We show you how to map your OO model into the C++ constructs using the OO paradigm in C++. We also show you how to use other non-OO concepts of the language in the context of OO design to help you meet your business needs.

C++ is our language of choice for two practical reasons. First and foremost, most developers have to address real constraints: interfacing to legacy systems and technical limitations on databases, storage, and performance. C++ gives developers multiple paradigms that they can tune as needed. Second, vendors supplying tools and compilers have put their money on C++.

Our Approach to Object-Oriented Technology

WE are not OO purists, nor are we theorists. We are developers who are willing to use any good idea that will help us achieve two very critical business goals: lower development costs and reduce time-to-market for enhancements. We believe that these technical objectives—reliability, maintainability, and flexibility—are critical to meeting these business goals.

Our approach to using OO technology is to manage the complexity of developing software so that it is reliable, maintainable, and flexible. Managing complexity is the key to achieving these objectives and, thus, our business goals. To manage complexity in complex problem domains, we find that the developers are required to know how objects, classes, relationships, and rules fit into the object paradigm. When we model most complex problem domains, we find objects, classes, and many relationships among objects. In addition, we need to capture the rules (policies) within that domain. Thus, we have to use very rich static modeling techniques to capture the data (object) relationships.

Many OO experts consider relationships as "bad" because they violate the encapsulation principle. From our perspective, it helps us manage the complexity of the problem domain and helps us to achieve our business goals. We gladly use it and we look for more mechanisms and language support in this area. In Chapter 9 on declarative semantics, we write that rules and policies should be captured as an integral part of our model and not in special subsystem extensions.

Using mechanisms to help us model complex problem domains is consistent with our choice of UML as our modeling language and C++ as our programming language. Both UML and C++ allow us to define any needed mechanism that helps us to build more manageable software.

We discuss behaviors (dynamic and static) and polymorphism for capturing the procedural aspects of the model. The use of a finite state machine or some other state model helps us manage procedural complexity while addressing timing, synchronization, and interrupts. These areas are generally ignored or overlooked by most OO books. We do not address these issues in depth, but we lay the foundation so the reader can make use of the semantics added to UML.

We believe the key to success in building large OO systems requires that developers/ programmers know more than what is taught in most OO books. Building large systems requires using mechanisms promoted by some OO experts but not accepted by all. Professional developers need to at least understand how these aspects of the problem domain can be handled before they can be a productive team member. This book will not make you an expert. You still need experts/consultants to develop the system. By applying the 80/20 rule, this book provides the 80% that can make you productive and understand how the experts solve the difficult 20%.

In this book we do not cover the latest trends or fads in OO technology, including object design patterns and distributed object computing. Although they are interesting, we are not convinced that they contribute significantly to our goal of providing a practical framework for enabling developers new to OO programming to get up to speed as soon as possible. Design patterns are proven techniques that enhance good OO practices and were not intended to be a paradigm by themselves. We still believe that learning the basic fundamentals of OO is essential to the correct application of design patterns. Distributed computing is being made as transparent to application developers as possible via well-written middleware. We expect that the infrastructure vendors will eventually make this technology issue transparent to the application domain.

Finally, we do not agree with most experts that OO technology is a mature technology. We believe it is in its infancy; what impresses us is how much we can accomplish with such an infant technology. Object-oriented technology has the enormous potential to help us manage complexity that did not exist with the earlier technologies (procedural, functional, rule-based, etc.).

Organization of the Book

WE take the reader through our rationale in applying OO techniques and methods. These are not a set of absolute laws. Our goal is to make you think about good OO concepts and good design principles when developing software and programming in C++. In the case study, we take a project through all of the steps of OO analysis, design, and coding, using specific OO techniques and applying fundamental OO concepts. The design is implemented in C++ with performance enhancements techniques of C++.

This book was originally written to be a self-teaching guide that should be read in sequential order. We have kept this aspect of the book the same. Each chapter discusses a major step of our approach to OO technology. Most chapters conclude with a step-by-step guide or recipe. We hope the reader will use these steps as a guide only; always rely on common sense rather than following prescribed steps blindly.

Chapter 1 provides the reasons why companies are interested in OO and why a software professional should understand OO.

Chapter 2 addresses the business of software and the need to manage complexity.

Chapter 3 describes how to find the basic terminology and key concepts in OO technology.

Chapter 4 describes how to employ use cases to bound the domain to relevant objects.

Chapter 5 describes how to find potential objects, the first step employing OO technology.

Chapter 6 describes how to differentiate between "real" objects and "false" objects by identifying attributes (data) and services associated with the object.

Chapter 7 demonstrates how to capture an object's behavior.

Chapter 8 describes how to identify and describe dynamic behavior.

Chapter 9 describes the various relationships (generalization/specialization, link, object aggregation, etc.) that are available for organizing all objects in a system.

Chapter 10 describes how to incorporate declarative facts into the OO model about object knowledge and a rule-based mechanism for their implementation.

Chapter 11 describes how we can make objects into classes to take advantage of the mechanisms of C++.

Chapter 12 addresses some design issues with OO system development.[1]

Chapter 13 provides C++ basics necessary to perform OO programming using C++. (Readers who are familiar with C++ can skip this chapter.)

Chapter 14 teaches you how to implement a class, which is a template for creating objects.

Chapter 15 introduces the C++ libraries for use in the subsequent chapters.

Chapter 16 teaches you how to implement the behavior specifications developed in Chapter 6.

Chapter 17 teaches you how to implement the dynamic behavior developed in Chapter 8.

Chapter 18 addresses how to create and destroy objects using the class mechanism of C++.

Chapter 19 addresses how to implement generalization/specialization (one of the key OO concepts) by using the class derivation mechanism of C++.

Chapter 20 addresses how to implement other relationships not supported by C++.

Chapter 21 introduces the two case studies.

Chapter 22 presents a case study based on the Breakout game.

Chapter 23 presents a case study for a microwave oven.

Appendix A presents a summary of the Unified Modeling Language.

Use of this Book as a Text

THIS book arose out of industrial courses attended by competent programmers who knew nothing about OO and C++. This material was taught in two courses of 1 week in duration. The first course covered the material of the first 13 chapters and the second course covered the remainder of the material. At the end of the second course, the students had a fully functional program that reflected the design achieved at the end of the first course. The case study at the end of this book was the project implemented by the students in this course. This book continues to support this instructional context.

At present, one of the authors teaches a one-semester course that covers the first 13 chapters of the book to university students who already know C++. He continues to

---

[1] Design is very complex and is a separate topic from object-oriented technology.

teach this material in conjunction with a project, depending upon the project rather than homework to reinforce the concepts. Use of a significant project allows the student to apply the concepts as they are learned. Following the whole process of performing an OO analysis and design for a project seems to work much better than a large number of discrete, unrelated homework problems. A significant analysis and design model can be completed in one semester. A second semester is necessary to implement the model.

The selection of a project of suitable scale enables a student to master all of the key concepts. Bill Tepfenhart, the instructor, assigns a large adventure game as a project and allows students to develop their own theme for it. Completed projects typically consist of more than 100 classes and just as many relationships. The games typically incorporate many different kinds of terrain, weapons, monsters, treasures, and characters. Some of the games have a complexity equivalent to many commercially available products.

A reasonable project team consists of three or four students. A larger team tends to spend too much time coming to agreement on the game theme and a smaller team tends to get overwhelmed. This team size has the further advantage that individual team members get a taste of what it is really like to work as part of a development team. They have to work on it weekly in order to complete the project within an allotted time frame.

Following is a suggested schedule of course activities. It assumes a standard 15-week schedule with a final exam given in week 15. A key feature of this schedule is that it allows generous time up front to define the game and develop the use cases. Lectures lead the activities being performed by the individual teams by as much as 3 weeks. This has been found to be advantageous because it helps prevent students from making some common mistakes, such as confusing object state with attributes of objects.

TABLE A-1   Schedule of Classes for OO Analysis and Design

Week	Chapters	Project Activities
1	1,2	Form teams
2	3	Develop game idea
3	4	Start writing use cases
4	5	Continue writing use cases
5	6	Continue writing use cases
6	7	Identify objects and their attributes
7	8	Identify object static behaviors
8	9	Identify dynamic behavior
9	10	Identify relationships
10	11	Review model
11	12	Design
12	12	Design
13	Review	Finish project
14	—	Class presentations

xxiv   PREFACE TO SECOND EDITION

Acknowledgments

WE owe so much to many people. The impetus of this book came from the thousands of students who have taken Richard Lee's class, his friends, and his many colleagues. He appreciates their persistence and their encouragement, ignoring the perils to his personal life.

Because we are developers (not researchers, academics, or writers), we have leveraged off the work of OO researchers (who originated all of the ideas) and OO writers (who presented these ideas to us in earlier writings). We simply apply these ideas to building real applications in a useful way. To all of the originators of the ideas, concepts, mechanisms, and techniques, and to the greater object-oriented writers before us, we acknowledge and thank you; without you, this book would not have been possible.

Theories and ideas are wonderful; however, to practitioners, experience is the best teacher. We could not have produced this book without our experiences in applying OO technology and the methods to real projects. We thank our many bosses, present and past, who had the courage to let us do leading-edge (and many times bleeding-edge) software development. Without their support, we would not have been able to test what we have written.

Richard Lee thanks the multitude of people who have worked for him and were the pioneers in applying the ideas written in this book on real projects. They shared with him both the excitement and the misery of being "first" to apply OO technology to large projects in their respective companies. (Or was it their stupidity to follow his lead to take challenges that no one else in the company wanted?) To all of you, Richard owes his thanks.

William Tepfenhart thanks his co-workers, past and present, each of whom has contributed to his understanding of computer science. He thanks Bill Case, Freid Elliot, and Dayton Eden, who allowed him to transition from writing FORTRAN models of physical systems to artificial intelligence models for reasoning about physical systems. He thanks his colleagues who broadened his modeling repertoire to include objects, relations, and rules.

The second edition wouldn't have been possible without the help of the following individuals:

- Terrance Cleary, AT&T Labs
- Dan Dvorak, Jet Propulsion Laboratory
- John Eddy, AT&T Labs
- Bruce Handelman, AT&T
- Rolf Kamp, AT&T
- David Lundin, pcorder.com
- David Simen, AT&T

These people contributed a significant amount of time and effort reviewing the manuscript. Their comments and insights into the material are truly appreciated.

A lot of credit goes to our managers Dick Machol, Raj Warty, Moses Ling, and Raj Dube at AT&T and Lucent Bell Laboratories, for their support. If they had not allowed us to use computer tools and the computer resources off-hours, then we wouldn't have been able to complete this book. Also, thanks goes to the management at Monmouth University, who supported Bill for the second edition. However, do not construe this as being a book approved by AT&T or Lucent Bell Laboratories. This is our private view of OO technology, based largely on Richard Lee's 35 years in the software development business and his experiences with OO technology. William Tepfenhart provided as many excellent "recipes" and organized the material so developers can quickly become contributing members of a development team.

Finally, we acknowledge and appreciate the valuable input from our reviewers: Rex Jaeschke, chair of the ANCI C committee and independent consultant and author, and Robert Taylor, Taylor Computing. As authors, we are perfectly happy to take the blame for all errors, omissions, inaccuracies, falsehoods, fuzzy thinking, and any good qualities of this book. We welcome all constructive comments. We happily will ignore destructive ones.

Richard C. Lee
William M. Tepfenhart

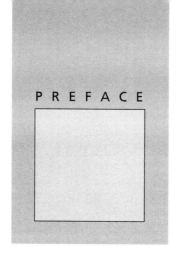

P R E F A C E

Preface to First Edition

A xioms in Philosophy are not axioms until they are proved upon our pulses: we read fine things but never feel them to the full until we have gone the same steps as the author.

John Keats (1795–1821), Letter to
J. H. Reynolds, May 3, 1818

UML and C++: A Practical Guide to Object-Oriented Development is for busy professional software analysts and developers who work on large systems, especially those who need to integrate their new systems with legacy systems. If you do not have time to take a class yet and get up-to-speed on object-oriented (OO) technology using Unified Modeling Language and C++, this book is a self-teaching guide for you. It will help you understand the differences between OO analysis, OO design, and OO programming. Our goals are to:

- Teach you to build an object-oriented application using C++ and make the right trade-off decisions to meet your business needs;
- Clarify the basic concepts associated with object-oriented technology;
- Supply sufficient depth in coverage for students and practitioners entering the field to get them up to speed;
- Expose some of the myths surrounding OO technology while focusing on its practicality as a software engineering tool;
- Give you a "recipe" or step-by-step guide to do all of the steps of object-oriented technology;

■ Advocate the view that OO, rule-based concepts, fuzzy logic, multimedia, and data modeling integrated into a single model can address the current and future business challenges for information technology organizations;

■ Provide a practical approach to analysis, design, and programming in the OO technology.

■ Show how to implement OO technology using C++ (though not an object-oriented language it is an extremely powerful multi-paradigm language); and

■ Balance theory with application practices in the existing literature.

You do not have know computer science or advanced mathematics to understand the important object-oriented concepts and issues in depth. Even the programming chapters do not require a background in C++; they illustrate how working code in C++ is produced.

Object-Oriented Technology

WE are software developers of large systems. We believe that OO technology is the most important software evolution (revolution) of the 1990s. It is changing the way we build software and the way applications intercommunicate over worldwide networks and across multi-vendor computers. Moreover, the OO model is changing the way we design business processes and the way we think about an enterprise. Most enterprises need redesigning today in order to meet future business challenges.

Business process redesign is one of the most important functions of an information technology organization. A model that captures the business processes, procedures, policies, and rules facilitates design. Tools that translate the model into an operational system speed the implementation of the redesign. When the market or business condition changes, these systems should be regenerated to reflect these changes by updating the model and using these tools. Information science (engineering) has taken us further and faster than any other approach in previous decades. However, it needs constant updating through even better, more refined methods to meet our business needs and challenges through OO modeling and OO programming. More and more people believe that OO technology will put a dent into the software crisis, meaning that the mechanisms of OO will become for software what the bolts and beams are for the construction design and what the chip is for computer hardware design. This belief stems from the following:

■ The proficiency of a higher-level OO model should provide the software designer with real-world, programmable components, thereby reducing software development costs.

■ Its capability to share and reuse code with OO techniques will reduce time to develop an application.

■ Its capability to localize and minimize the effects of modifications through programming abstraction mechanisms will allow for faster enhancement development and will provide more reliable and more robust software.

■ Its capability to manage complexity allows developers to address more difficult applications.

The collection of OO concepts is a tool set for modeling reality. This OO tool set gives developers the best means of managing the complexity. Certain OO concepts help developers produce flexible and maintainable software.

Why Unified Modeling Language?

AS practitioners of OO technology, we know that all of the methods, if practiced properly, result in the same or a similar model. Different modeling language notations can be impediments to progress. We are interested in results that help us produce more maintainable software at less cost and in a more timely manner. Unified Modeling Language gives us all the drawing icons necessary to capture most of the concepts or *mechanisms* that we find valuable in solving real business problems. Also, it provides all of the necessary diagrams that are vital for documenting our models. Finally, it is a living language that gives us the ability to extend the notation for mechanisms not yet defined by the distinguished group of Grady Booch, James Rumbaugh, and Ivor Jacobson at Rational Software Corporation.

Why C++?

IT is a misconception that C++ is exclusively an OO programming language. It is a multi-paradigm language that supports a number of programing paradigm, including procedural, abstract data type, and OO. We show you how to map your OO model into the C++ constructs using the OO paradigm in C++. We also show you how to use other non-OO concepts of the language in the context of OO design to help you meet your business needs.

C++ is our language of choice for two practical reasons. First and foremost, most developers have to address real constraints: interfacing to legacy systems and technical limitations on databases, storage, and performance. C++ gives developers multiple paradigms that they can tune as needed. Second vendors supplying tools and compilers have put their money on C++.

Our Approach to Object-Oriented Technology

WE are not OO purists, nor are we theorists. We are developers who are willing to use any good idea that will help us achieve two very critical business goals: lower development cost and reduce time-to-market for enhancements. We believe that these technical objectives—reliability, maintainability, and flexibility—are critical to meeting these business goals.

Our approach to using OO technology is to manage the complexity of developing software so that it is reliable, maintainable, and flexible. Managing complexity is the key to achieving these objects and, thus, our business goals. To manage complexity in complex problem domains, we find that developers are required to know how objects, classes, relationships, and rules fit into the object paradigm. When we model most complex problem domains, we find objects, classes, and many relationships among objects. In addition, we need to capture the rules (policies) within that domain. Thus, we have to use very rich static modeling techniques to capture the data (object) relationships.

Many OO experts consider relationships as "bad" because they violate the encapsulation principle. From our perspective, it helps us manage the complexity of the problem domain and helps us to achieve our business goals. We gladly use it and we look for more mechanisms and language support in this area. In Chapter 9 on declarative semantics, we write that rules and policies should be captured as an integral part of our model and not in special subsystem extensions.

Using mechanisms to help us model complex problem domains is consistent with our choice of UML as our modeling language and C++ as our programming language. Both UML and C++ allow us to define any needed mechanism that helps us to build more manageable software.

We discuss behaviors (dynamic and static) and polymorphism for capturing the procedural aspects of the model. The use of a finite state machine or some other state model helps us manage procedural complexity while addressing timing, synchronization, and interrupts. These areas are generally ignored or overlooked by most OO books. We do not address these issues in depth, but we lay the foundation so the reader can make use of the semantics added to UML.

We believe the key to success in building large OO systems requires that developers/programmers know more than what is taught in most OO books. building large systems requires using mechanisms promoted by some OO experts but not accepted by all. Professional developers need to at least understand how these aspects of the problem domain can be handled before they can be a productive team member. This book will not make you an expert. You still need experts/consultants to develop the system. By applying the 80/20 rule, this book provides the 80% that can make you productive and understand how the experts solve the difficult 20%.

In this book we do not cover the latest trends or fads in OO technology, including object design patterns, the standard template library, and distributed object computing. Although they are interesting, we are not convinced that they contribute significantly to our goal of providing a practical framework for enabling developers new to OO programming to get up to speed as soon as possible.

Finally, we do not agree with most experts that OO technology is a mature technology. We believe it is in its infancy; what impresses us is how much we can accomplish with such an infant technology. Object-oriented technology has the enormous potential to help us manage complexity that did not exist with the earlier technologies (procedural, functional, rule-based, etc.).

Organization of the Book

WE take the reader through our rationale in applying OO techniques and methods. These are not a set of absolute laws. Our goal is to make you think about good OO concepts and good design principles when developing software and programming in C++. In the case study, we take a project through all of the steps of OO analysis, design, and coding, using specific OO techniques and applying fundamental OO concepts. The design is implemented in C++ with performance enhancements techniques of C++.

We have written and designed this book to be a self-teaching guide that should be read in sequential order. We have adopted a method that Richard has used for years teaching OO concepts and basic skills; we do not advocate this as a method for building OO systems. Each chapter discusses a major step of our approach to OO technology. Most chapters conclude with a step-by-step guide or recipe. We hope the reader will use these steps as a guide only; always rely on common sense rather than following prescribed steps blindly.

Chapter 1 provides the reasons why companies are interested in OO and why a software professional should understand OO.

Chapter 2 addresses the business of software and the need to manage complexity.

Chapter 3 describes how to find the basic terminology and key concepts in OO technology.

Chapter 4 describes how to find potential objects, the first step employing OO technology.

Chapter 5 describes how to differentiate between "real" objects and "false" objects by identifying attributes (data) and services associated with the object.

Chapter 6 demonstrates how to capture objects behavior.

Chapter 7 describes how to identify and describe dynamic behavior.

Chapter 8 describes the various relationships (generalization/specialization, link, object aggregation, etc.) that are available for organizing all of the objects in the system.

Chapter 9 describes how to incorporate declarative facts into the OO model about object knowledge and a rule-based mechanism for their implementation.

Chapter 10 describes how we can make objects into classes to take advantage of the mechanisms of C++.

Chapter 11 addresses some design issues with OO system development.[1]

Chapter 12 provides C++ basics necessary to perform OO programming using C++. (Readers who are familiar with C++ can skip this chapter.)

Chapter 13 teaches you how to implement a class, which is a template for creating objects.

---

[1]   Design is very complex and is a separate topic from object-oriented technology.

Chapter 14 teaches you how to implement the behavior specifications developed in Chapter 6.

Chapter 15 addresses how to create and destroy objects using the class mechanism of C++.

Chapter 16 addresses how to implement generalization/specialization (one of the key OO concepts) by using the class derivation mechanism of C++.

Chapter 17 addresses how to implement other relationships not supported by C++.

Chapter 18 introduces a case study example demonstrating how to use the method in Chapters 4–17.

Chapter 19 presents one team's approach to performing the object analysis of the case study.

Chapter 20 presents a second team's approach to performing the object analysis of the case study.

Chapter 21 demonstrates how the object model arrived at in Chapter 20 is translated into an object design and implemented in C++.

Acknowledgments

WE owe so much to many people. The impetus of this book came from the hundreds of students who have taken Richard Lee's class, his friends, and his many colleagues. He appreciates their persistence and their encouragement, ignoring the perils to his personal life.

Because we are developers (not researchers, academics, or writers), we have leveraged off the work of OO researchers (who originated all of the ideas) and OO writers (who presented these ideas to us in earlier writings). We simply apply these ideas to building real applications in a useful way. To all of the originators of the ideas, concepts, mechanisms, and techniques and to the greater object-oriented writers before us, we acknowledge and thank you; without you, this book would not have been possible.

Theories and ideas are wonderful; however, to practitioners, experience is the best teacher. We could not have produced this book without our experiences in applying OO technology and the methods to real projects. We thank our many bosses, present and past, who had the courage to let us do leading-edge (and many times bleeding-edge) software development. Without their support, we would not have been able to test what we have written.

Richard Lee thanks the multitude of people who have worked for him and were the pioneers in applying the ideas written in this book on real projects. They shared with him both the excitement and the misery of being "first" to apply OO technology to large projects in their respective companies. (Or was it their stupidity to follow his lead to take challenges that no one else in the company wanted?) To all of you, Richard owes his thanks.

William Tepfenhart thanks his co-workers, past and present, each of whom has contributed to his understanding of computer science. He thanks Bill Case, Freid Elliot, and Dayton Eden, who allowed him to transition from writing FORTRAN models of physical systems to artificial intelligence models for reasoning about physical systems. He thanks his colleagues who broadened his modeling repertoire to include objects, relations, and rules.

We thank Barry Peiffer, David Siemen, John Eddy, and Dan Dvorak for sharing their time and feedback. Steve Ruder did an excellent job as technical editor.

A lot of credit goes to our managers Dick Machol, Raj Warty, Moses Ling, and Raj Dube, for their support. If they had not allowed us to use computer tools and the computer resources off-hours, we wouldn't have been able to complete this book. However, do not construe this as being a book approved by AT&T or Bell Laboratories. This is our private view of OO technology based largely on Richard Lee's 30 years in the software development business and his experiences with OO technology. William Tepfenhart provided many excellent "recipes" and organized the materials so developers can quickly become contributing members of a development team.

Finally, we acknowledge and appreciate the valuable input from our reviewers: Rex Jaeschke, chair of the ANCI C committee and independent consultant and author, and Robert Taylor, Taylor Computing. As authors, we are perfectly happy to take the blame for all errors, omissions, inaccuracies, falsehoods, fuzzy thinking, and any good qualities of this book. We welcome all constructive comments. We happily will ignore destructive ones.

Richard C. Lee
William M. Tepfenhart

CHAPTER

1

The Information Management Dilemma

D ouble, double toil and trouble;
Fire burn, and cauldron bubble

William Shakespeare, *Macbeth*

Currently, there is a great deal of excitement and interest in object-oriented techniques in business and in the information technology (IT) industry. In the midst of all the ballyhoo, most practitioners in software engineering need to understand what the ballyhoo is all about.

The Problem

CORPORATIONS are becoming information-based organizations that depend on a continuous flow of data for virtually every aspect of their operations. Information is becoming more and more crucial to all business decisions and opportunities. Even corporations that historically have not been information-focused are now heavily dependent upon it. However, the volume of information is increasing faster than the capacity to process it and make sense of it. Thus, corporations are drowning in their own data.

The problem is that:

- Software project costs are going up and hardware costs are going down.
- Software development time is getting longer and maintenance costs are getting higher, while at the same time hardware development time is getting shorter and less costly.
- Software errors are getting more frequent as hardware errors become almost non-existent.
- Software is developed using a rigidly structured process that is inflexible.

This is confirmed by studies, as shown in Table 1-1 and Table 1-2.

It is clear that our present software methods result in systems that are very expensive to maintain. Corporations are spending most of their money in testing and maintaining the system. Unfortunately, the present methods are not effective in requirements analysis and design stages where the cost of correction is very low. Furthermore, Table 1-2 shows that 85% of our errors are made during the requirements analysis and design. Improving these two steps is the most cost-effective way of improving the quality of software.

TABLE 1-1   Software Project Costs by Development Phase[a]

Work Step	%
Requirements	3
Design	8
Programming	7
Testing	15
Maintenance	67

[a]   Source: Butler Bloor

TABLE 1-2   Costs of Correcting Software Errors[a]

Software Development Phase	% of Dev in $	Errors Intro in %	Errors Found in %	Relative Cost to Correct
Requirements Analysis	5	55	18	1.0
Design	25	30	10	1.0–1.5
Code and Unit Test	10			
Integration Test	50	10	50	1.0–5.0
Validation and Documentation	10			
Operational Maintenance		5	22	10–100

[a]   Source: Hughes DoD Composite Software Error History

Modern Corporations Are Headed Toward Disaster

If we combine these software problems with the increasing rate of change in business conditions today, one has a recipe for disaster. A corporation's accounts receivable may be in good shape today, but decisions based on the output of incorrect software can threaten the ability of a business to be financially strong tomorrow.

Today, much of the corporate software is obsolete long before delivery, and it is incapable of evolving to meet future business needs. In a study of MIS organizations by the Standish Group, software projects were characterized by resolution, restarts, cost overruns, time overruns, and content deficiencies.

The Standish Group found that there were three basic categories of projects: Success, Challenged, and Impaired. Successful projects deliver full functionality on-time and on-budget. Challenged projects deliver, but less than full functionality, over-budget, and late. Impaired projects are canceled during development. The bottom line: only 16.2% of projects are successful. The majority of projects, 52.7%, are challenged. The remaining 31.1% get canceled before they are able to deliver. It is estimated that the cost of challenged and impaired projects for 1995 was $140 billion.

Many projects are started with the wrong goals and find themselves having to start over again from the beginning. Starting over does not support delivering at the original delivery date. The Standish Group found that for every 100 projects that start, there are 94 restarts. This does not mean that all of those restarts are for individual projects — some projects have multiple restarts.

Approximately 28% of projects exhibit cost overruns of 150% to 200% of their original cost estimate. The average cost overrun across all companies is 189% of the original estimated cost. Table 1-3 illustrates the distribution of cost overruns. It doesn't take too many 200% cost overruns to put a small company out of business. Unfortunately, small businesses tend to have larger cost overruns, with an average of 214%.

The figures for time overruns are equally dismal. The average overrun for the same 28% of projects is 222% of the original time estimate. The figures for time overruns are given in Table 1-4. In this day and age, when getting a product to market quickly is a major goal, a 200% overrun can seriously impact a company's competitive edge.

TABLE 1-3   Cost Overruns

% Cost Overrun	% of Responses
< 20%	15.5%
21–50%	31.5%
51–100%	29.6%
101–200%	10.2%
201–400%	8.8%
> 400%	4.4%

TABLE 1-4   Time Overruns

Time Overruns	% of Responses
< 20%	13.9%
21–50%	18.3%
51–100%	20.0%
101–200%	35.5%
201–400%	11.2%
> 400%	1.1%

TABLE 1-5   Delivery of Features

% of Features (Functions)	% of Responses
< 25%	4.6%
25–49%	27.2%
50–74%	21.8%
75–99%	39.1%
100%	7.3%

A common joke about delivering software is, "Do you want it on time or fully functional?" Unfortunately, the Standish Group has the data to show that this is not a joke. The typical project does not deliver full functionality. Table 1-5 illustrates the percent of responding projects, with their delivered percentage of functionality.

What Does the Customer Want?

THE customer wants a solution (system) that:

- Meets functional requirements
- Adapts to the rapidly changing business environment
- Fits the run time (time/space) constraints

The customer wants software that is:

- Maintainable
- Developed within budgeted resources (time/space/material/people)
- Designed with appropriate longevity in mind

Because our classical development methods (structured methods, data modeling, ad-hoc, etc.) have not met our customers' needs, object-oriented consultants have told corporation managers that the use of object-oriented technology will meet these needs better than the classical methods. Now that we understand the reason why businesses are excited about object-oriented technology, let us see why leading-edge software engineers are excited about this technology.

Why Object-Oriented Is Important to Developers

IN the 1960s, software developers were building small and relatively simple applications/systems. They used some very simple languages (assembly language, FORTRAN, and COBOL) that were designed specifically for their use. Developers used no method other than their own "creativity." Programming was considered a creative activity, and developers were hired based on their independent spirit. Unfortunately, this led to spaghetti code and the famous GOTOs in code that are a horror to maintain.

In the 1970s, Al Constantine and Ed Yourdon came up with a method of developing software that used the function as its building block. This method, known to most developers as structured analysis and design, helped developers organize the software by functions. At the time, this seemed very natural because organizations were organized functionally. Most computer systems and applications were written for a specific functional organization, so the applications became an extension of that organization.

This seemed like a better way to build software, especially if you did modular programming in addition to structured analysis and design. Modular programming eliminated the unmanageable GOTOs. Structured analysis and design helped developers manage only the functions. However, it did very little to help developers manage data.

Despite being developed for "business applications," structured analysis and design was better suited for "scientific applications." In most scientific applications, functions are very stable; most of them are determined by laws of nature that rarely change. In business applications, however, the functions are human-defined and are subject to change at any time.

Although structured analysis and design was successfully applied to many scientific applications, it led to large maintenance organizations in business applications. For many of these applications, software professionals had to continuously change the building blocks (i.e., change the functions). Changes at such a fundamental level require basically rebuilding the application/system; thus, software professionals recognized the need for other methods of developing software.

In the 1980s, Peter Chen (who developed the entity-relationship diagram) and Ed Codd (designer of the relational database) provided developers with the foundation for a new way of developing software that was based on a collection of data items, called an entity, as its building block. This discovery seemed appropriate for the foundation of a new methodology for software development for business applications because software professionals and researchers at that time believed that data was the most stable part of the "business application."

As a result of the widely held belief that entities were stable and because relational databases had an excellent mathematical basis, most companies in the 1980s began using data-modeling methods to develop software. However, data-modeling methods had the converse weakness of structured methods. Structured methods did help developers manage the data, but data-modeling methods did not help developers manage the functions. The theory was that all of the functions could be defined by using language constructs that were consistent with first-order predicate calculus. Unfortunately, most of the problems that needed to be solved could not be done using first-order predicate calculus.

Now there is a need for a software development method that addresses the weaknesses of earlier methods. Earlier methods used only one view of the system as their building block and did not readily accommodate other views. For example, structured analysis and design focused on the function as the building block of a system. Data organization is very weakly supported in the data flow diagrams. Similarly, in the data analysis method (entity-relationship diagram) the building block was an entity, but the functions needed to satisfy the system requirements were virtually ignored in the method. Neither method deals well with capturing dynamic behavior. Declarative semantics (rules) and exception-handling mechanisms were totally ignored.

The object-oriented method is the only method we know that provides software developers with a paradigm that supports all views of a system equally well, and it does so in an orthogonal manner. As a result, the developer can manage the complexity of the situation.

In object-oriented programming, the application (system) is a dynamic network of collaborating objects. With the addition of rules to the paradigm in an orthogonal manner, declarative semantics can be integrated with the procedural semantics into one system.

From a pragmatic point of view, the object-oriented method allows software developers to manage the complexity of the problem domain and its supporting technology. When developers can manage more aspects of the problem domain, they can produce more flexible and more maintainable software.

■ ■ SUMMARY

AT the present time, we are facing a crisis in terms of software development. This crisis spans cost, time to market, errors, and functionality. The earlier in the software development process that errors are identified, the greater the cost savings. Object-oriented approaches provide advantages that can reduce cost, the time required to develop a product, and errors, and provide flexibility in the development process.

CHAPTER

2

Managing Complexity: Analysis and Design

*W*hat *cannot be cured must be endured.*

Francis Rabelais

In the early 1960s, developers used no method other than their own creativity. Performance and using less core (memory) were the major constraints. Writing spaghetti code and using the infamous GOTOs were accepted ways to increase performance and use less core. Most programs were neither large nor complex by today's standards. However, even then developers had difficulty remembering all of the information they needed to know to develop, debug, and maintain their software.

For example, when one of the authors first started in this field in the early 1960s, he wrote some mission-critical software for his employer. This code is still in use today. About 10 years ago, his former employer called him and asked him to help them make modifications to this code. The employer's programmers had studied the code, but could not figure out how the software worked. As his former employer succinctly put it, "We know that the program works as we have been using it for 20 years, but when we study the code we cannot figure out how you made it work." His former employer sent the author the code for him to study. After a couple of weeks, he concluded that he could not help his former employer design the modification as he also did not know how he got it to work 20 years ago. Thus, his former employer had no choice but to leave the code untouched and make the modifications at a different level with code that was comprehensible.

In the late 1960s and early 1970s, higher-level languages (COBOL, FORTRAN, ALGOL) were introduced to help solve some of these problems. These languages certainly helped automate the management of local variables and did implicit matching of arguments to parameters.

In conjunction with these new languages, developers used a more structured method to design and develop software. Remember structured analysis and design? Remember modular programming? These techniques raised the expectations of what a computer could do in our user community. As developers attempted to satisfy their user community by trying to solve more complex problems using the computer, the tasks became so large and complex that even the best programmers could not comprehend them. So we moved programming from being a creative individual activity to a structured team activity.

When this happened, we observed that a program we expected one programmer to write in 3 years could not be written by *three* programmers working for 1 year. It is this phenomenon that led to Fred Brooks's memorable phrase: "The bearing of a child takes 9 months, no matter how many women are assigned." Of course, software complexity was the main reason behind the nonlinear behavior of the development effort.

In imperative programming, the interconnections between software components are very complicated, and a large amount of information has to be communicated among the various team members to get it correct.[1] The key question is, "What brings about this complexity?" Sheer size alone cannot bring about complexity, for size itself is not a hindrance to the concept of partitioning the software into many pieces. In fact, the method of structured analysis and design assumed that large programs differ from small program only in size. If size was the issue, structured analysis and design would have solved the difficulty.

Unfortunately, the aspect of software development using the imperative-programming model that makes it among the most complex tasks for humans is its high degree of *coupling*. Coupling refers to the dependence of one portion of code on either another section of code and/or some data storage. A high degree of coupling is an inherent aspect of imperative programming.

In designing imperative programs, we partition our program into subroutines (essential tasks). However, if these subroutines are useful to other parts of the program, there must be some communication of information either into or out of these subroutines. Remember that data is not managed. Thus, a complete understanding of what is going on usually requires knowledge of the subroutine and all the routines that use it. This is poor *cohesion*. Cohesion refers to how well a set of code and its associated data fit together. This is especially true when you consider the data that may be needed. In most imperative-programming languages, variable names (means of accessing data) can be shared only if they are in a common pool.

In brief, much of the complexity of imperative programming came from the high degree of coupling and poor cohesion in the way we built the software.[2] It is now

---

[1] F. Brooks Jr. has addressed this topic in "The Mythical Man-Month."

[2] Data modeling is still imperative programming because most of the functions/transactions are still written using a procedural language. Moreover, rule-based systems (i.e., artificial intelligent systems) also have coupling and cohesion issues.

apparent to us that using classical methods in software development will almost always result in systems being built with poor cohesion and high coupling; this makes the system inflexible and unmaintainable. In our opinion, there needs to be a better method to develop software that gives developers a chance to meet their customers' needs. To be able to accomplish this, developers cannot use the same building blocks (functions, entities, or rules) as used in classical methods. They need to use a more powerful abstraction mechanism as the building block for software. This abstraction mechanism is a *class*. The class will serve as our blueprint for manufacturing *objects* that will be the building blocks for systems.

Abstraction Mechanism

TO understand how the object-oriented paradigm uses the abstraction mechanism to manage complexity, we will first review the various ways that software engineers/ programmers have used abstraction prior to the object-oriented paradigm. From a historical perspective, object-oriented use of the abstraction mechanism may be a natural progression of abstracting for functions, to modules, to abstract data types, and then to objects.

Functions

With the advent of imperative-programming languages, functions and procedures became the early abstract mechanisms widely used to write programs. Functions allowed tasks that were used in many places, even in different applications, to be collected in one place and reused. Procedures allowed programmers to organize repetitive tasks in one place. Both of these abstractions prevented code from being duplicated in several places.

Functions and procedures also gave programmers the ability to implement information hiding. One programmer writes a function or a set of functions that will be used by many other programmers. Other programmers do not need to know the exact details of the implementation; they only need to know the interface. Unfortunately, abstract functions are not an effective mechanism for information hiding. They only partially solve the problem of multiple programmers making use of the same names.

To illustrate this, we will look at how we write a set of functions to implement a simple stack. First, we establish our visible interfaces: init (initialize the stack), push (place something on the stack), and pop (take an item off the top of the stack). After defining the interface, we need to select some implementation technique such as an array with top-of-stack pointer, a linked list, and so on. We elect to implement the stack by using an array and proceed to code the functions. It is easy to see that the data contained in the stack itself cannot be made local to any of the functions because all of the functions need to use it; therefore, the variable must be shared.

In imperative-programming languages, such as COBOL, or C prior to the introduction of static modifier, the only choices for keeping data are local variables and global variables. As a result, the stack data must be maintained in global variables if we want the data to be shared by all of the functions. Unfortunately, there is no way to limit the accessibility or visibility of global variable names.

Let's assume that we have named the array for our stack *stackarray*. All other programmers working on the project who use our functions must know about stackarray, since they must not create a variable using the same name. This is true even though the data is used only by the stack functions written by us and should not be used outside these functions. Similarly, the names init, pop, and push are now reserved and cannot be used by other programmers on the project for other purposes, even if that portion of code has nothing to do with the stack.

In advanced imperative-programming languages such as ALGOL and Pascal, the block-scoping mechanism offered a slightly better control over name visibility than just local and global names. However, this mechanism did not solve the information-hiding problem just presented. To solve this problem, a different abstract mechanism had to be developed.

Modules

A module is an abstract mechanism that is useful for creating and managing name spaces.[3] In its basic form, a module gives the programmer the ability to divide the name space into two parts: public and private. The public part is accessible to everyone, while the private part is accessible only within the module. Variables (data), functions, procedures, and types can all be defined in either part of the module. This abstract mechanism was popularized by David Parnas, and he gave us the following guidelines for using modules:

1. The designer of the module must provide the intended users with all of the information needed to use the module correctly, and nothing more.
2. The designer of the module must provide the implementor with all of the information necessary to complete (code) the module, and nothing more.

These guidelines are similar to the way the military handles secret documents via the "need to know." If you do not need to know some information, you do not have access to it. This explicit and intentional concealment of information is information hiding, which is the second principle of the object-oriented paradigm.[4]

The module, as an abstract mechanism, solves our information-hiding problem. We can now hide the details of the stack. Note that a module enforces the first two principles of object-oriented paradigm, namely encapsulation and information hiding. When a mechanism does this, it isolates one part of the system, namely the module, from all other parts of the system. When this is done, we increase the maintainability of the software produced because the isolation allows code to be modified or extended and bugs to be fixed without the risk of introducing unnecessary or unintended side effects.

However, a module has a major shortcoming. Let's look at the stack problem again. What if a user wants to use two or more stacks? We cannot handle this with a

---

[3] A name space is a mechanism for managing the visibility and names of program elements (e.g., function, attribute, and class names).

[4] The principles of the object-oriented paradigm are discussed in the next chapter.

module. As a mechanism, the module does not allow us to perform **instantiation**, which is the ability to make multiple copies of the data areas. This idea of instantiation is the sixth principle of the object-oriented paradigm.

For a better example of why instantiation is an important and desired capability, consider the following situation. We need to develop a new type of number called *complex*. We define the arithmetic operations (addition, subtraction, multiplication, etc.) for complex numbers and functions to convert a conventional number (integer, float, double, etc.) to a complex number. If we were to use module as the way to capture our new type of number complex, we would have a small problem — we can manipulate only one complex number at a time. A complex number system with such a restriction would not be very useful.

Abstract Data Types

An abstract data type is a programmer-defined data type that can be manipulated in a manner similar to the programming language predefined data types. Like a predefined data type, an abstract data type corresponds to a set (perhaps an almost infinite set) of legal data values and a number of functions that can be performed on these values. Programmers can create instances of this abstract data type by assigning legal values to the variables. Furthermore, one can use the functions to manipulate the values assigned to the variables. In brief, an abstract data type mechanism must be able to:

1. Extend a programming language by adding programmer-defined type(s).
2. Make available to other code a set of programmer-defined functions that are used to manipulate the instance data of the specific programmer-defined type.
3. Protect (hide) the instance data associated with the type and limit the access to the data to only the programmer-defined functions.
4. Make (unlimited) instances of the programmer-defined type.

Modules, as defined previously, can address only items 2 and 3 directly. With appropriate programming skills, some of the other capabilities may be addressed. However, packages found in languages such as Ada and CLU are a much better example of an implementation of the abstract data type mechanism.

Thus, we can solve our instantiation problem for the stack and for complex numbers by using an abstract data type mechanism.

Classes/Objects

MANY people consider Smalltalk "the object-oriented language." They would define a class as being a different name for an abstract data type and an object as an instance of an abstract data type. Technically, one can argue that they are correct; however, it is our opinion that this definition leaves out the most important part of object-oriented programming. Today, object-oriented programming has expanded on the idea of abstract data types and added to them some very important innovations that help us better manage complexity. It is these additional innovations that gives object-oriented technology all of its power.

Message Passing

Object-oriented programming added several new ideas to the concept of abstract data types. First is the idea of *message passing*. In object-oriented programming, an action is initiated by a service request (message) sent to a specific object, not as in imperative programming by a function call using specific data. On the surface, this may appear to be just a change of emphasis. The imperative-programming style places primary importance on the functions, while the object-oriented style places primary importance on the object (value). For example, do you call the push function with a stack and a data value, or do you ask a stack to push a value onto itself?

If this is all there is to message passing, it would not be a very powerful mechanism. However, message passing gives us the ability to overload names and reuse software; this is not possible using the imperative-programming functional call style. Implicit in message passing is the idea that the interpretation of a message can vary with objects in different classes. That is, the behavior (response that a message will elicit) depends on the class of the object that receives the message. Thus, our push function can mean one thing to our stack object, but mean a very different thing to another object—a mechanical arm object, for example.

In object-oriented programming, names of functions are unique only within a class. We can use simple, direct, and meaningful names for our functions across classes, leading to more readable and more understandable code. This also provides for better cohesion at the implementation level than does a conventional imperative-programming language.

Generalization/Specialization and Polymorphism

In addition to message passing, object-oriented programming added two more mechanisms to abstract data types: generalization/specialization[5] and polymorphism. Generalization/specialization allows classes to share the same code. This reduces the code size and provides for more maintainable software. In addition, it helps us by giving us good cohesion and a lower degree of coupling in our implementation. Polymorphism allows the shared code to be tailored to fit the specific circumstances of each of the individual classes. These mechanisms work together to support the independence (low degree of coupling) of individual components (objects) that support an incremental development process (good cohesion).

As useful as generalization/specialization and polymorphism are in helping us organize (or structure) our classes and objects[6], these mechanisms only help us manage

---

[5] Generalization/specialization is implemented by using inheritance in many object-oriented languages, including C++. If it helps, you may consider the two terms to be synonymous. However, in the design chapter (Chapter 12), we will discuss inheritance as a different concept.

[6] Thus, they also help us manage complexity.

relationships that are heritable. In reality, we certainly have heritable relationships with our children, parents, grandparents, etc. However, we also have other types of relationships that need to be managed. For instance, married people have spouses that cannot be modeled by using generalization/specialization and/or polymorphism (even though many married people may wish that they could polymorph their other half). Moreover, in most organizations people work in teams to get a job done, and there is a hierarchical structure of people that makes up the organization. Again, these structures cannot be modeled by using the few mechanisms that we have discussed. Therefore, the need exists for more mechanisms to enable the object-oriented paradigm to accurately model our perception of reality.

Additional Relationships

IN the previous section, we were introduced to one type of relationship, namely, generalization/specialization. However, this type of relationship is not adequate for us to model our perception of reality. For example, we cannot capture the marriage relationship or the supervisor-subordinate relationship by using generalization/specialization. Instead, we need additional mechanisms to help us model these concepts.

Associations

Let us look at an instance of marriage more closely. Assume that Joe is married to Jane. From Joe's perspective, the marriage relationship captures the fact that Jane is his wife and provides a set of "wifely" services to Joe. Similarly, from Jane's perspective, the marriage relationship captures the fact that Joe is her husband and provides a set of "husbandly" services to Jane. Thus, it is very common to have role names (husband, wife) associated with a relationship (marriage). In some sense, the role names help us define what services are expected to be accessible via that relationship. For example, if Jane is also Joe's supervisor at work, a second relationship (supervisor-subordinate) must be established to capture the "subordinate" services of Joe. This second relationship is necessary to maintain the semantic consistency of the relationship. Joe can stop being Jane's subordinate at work and stay married to Jane. This kind of relationship, in which one object knows about another object for specific services, is called a *link*.

If we define marriage as being only between two persons of different genders, then we need to categorize people into two categories (classes): Male and Female. Note that Joe, an object, is an instance of Male and that Jane, another object, is an instance of Female. Now, since all marriage links are between one object of the class Male and another object of the class Female, we can capture all the marriage links by using a higher-level concept called an *association*. An association describes a group of links with common structure and common semantics. All links in an association must connect objects from the same class to objects from a second class. Note that from an object-oriented perspective, the common semantics means that services provided by each object in the same class are the same. Also, remember that providing the same service does not mean that the behavior is identical. For instance, if we define "mow the lawn" as one of the services of husband, then every male object must have a "mow the lawn" service. However, the method that each male object uses to mow the lawn can be very different (polymorphism). Specifically, Joe can actually mow the lawn himself, while Jack may pay one of his kids to mow the lawn, and Jim may use a professional lawn-mowing company.

With the marriage relationship, one can argue that not only is the behavior (how the service is provided) different, but also the services provided by each partner are different for each marriage. This is certainly more likely to be true today than when people had fixed concepts associated with the roles of husband and wife. If this is correct, we would not be able to abstract each of the marriage links into a group; we would require a unique template for each group of links with different services. That is, each marriage would be a different association.

Associations are bidirectional; thus, it is common to give a name to an association in each direction. In our marriage example, from Female's direction it is husband and from Male's direction it is wife. By the way, it is common practice to name a relationship with the same name as the class with which it is associated. This practice is not recommended as it captures no semantic meaning (poor cohesion). This is effective only if there is only one association between the classes; if there is more than one association, a better convention should be used. For example, consider the relationship between a person and a company. It is very common for a person to be both an employee and a stockholder of a company, especially now with an increase of employee-owned companies. To model these two different relationships accurately, we would create two associations between the class Person and the class Company. One association would represent the employer/employee relationship and the second would represent the ownership relationship.

In theory, associations may be binary (between two classes), ternary (among three classes), or higher. In practice, however, the vast majority of associations are binary or ternary; we have only rarely used the higher forms. Higher-order associations are very difficult to draw, implement, and to think about; they should be avoided if possible.

The notion of association is not a new concept; it has been widely used for years in database modeling. However, very few programming languages explicitly support the association mechanism. Nevertheless, we believe that we should model an association as a separate abstraction that contains information that depends on two or more classes rather than a single class.

Some would argue that capturing an association as a separate abstraction violates the encapsulation principle of a class. However, there is information that we need to model that naturally transcends a single class. In the marriage relationship, for example, the marriage date and the church where the ceremony is held are examples of information that naturally transcends either class of Female and Male.

Not capturing an association accurately will cause programs to contain hidden assumptions and dependencies that will make them hard to maintain. For instance, in our employer/employee example, a person's salary is not really information about a Person. Consider the case in which you need to model a person who has two or three jobs with different employers.

Conceptually, and especially during analysis, we recommend that a link should be treated as an object. Because an object has attributes (i.e., may store information) and provides services, a link has the potential to store data and provide services. In our marriage relationship, for example, the attributes could be date of marriage and the church where the ceremony was held. Although associations (and aggregations) are not directly supported by present-day programming languages, our goal should be to demonstrate the usefulness of these mechanisms and to encourage the development of programming languages that will support these mechanisms that help us manage complexity.

Aggregation

From the preceding examples, we can see that an association is a very weak relationship. People regularly change employers. In fact, management talks about people needing to change careers and employers many times during their working career. Furthermore, marriage in the United States is certainly not permanent, as evidenced by subsequent marriages and divorced single parents.[7] Thus, an association is like a "Hollywood marriage" — it can be changed very rapidly.

But there are other relationships, like a car with its parts or a purchase order with its line items, that do not allow changes as easily. Furthermore, these specialized forms of an association have special properties. We would like to have another relationship mechanism to capture these more specialized forms of an association because the special properties need to be enforced. The new mechanism is called *aggregation*.[8] In this mechanism, an object that represents the whole is associated with a set of objects representing its components. A good example of a relationship that is probably best modeled by an aggregation is a bill-of-material and all of its associated line items.

Aggregation contains the following properties:

Transitivity. Transitivity is the property that if object A is a part of object B and object B is a part of object C, then object A is a part of object C. In our example, consider the possibility that a line item may have sub-line items. By transitivity, the sub-line items are also part of the bill-of-material.

Antisymmetricity. Antisymmetricity is the property such that if object A is a part of object B, then object B cannot be a part of object A. Again using our example, a line item may not be part of a sub-line item.

---

[7] In most situations, we would model marriage as an association. In some societies, the marriage is permanent, with no divorce.

[8] This is also called the whole-parts, assembly-parts, or part-of relationship. In terms of a modeling mechanism, we can define an aggregation as relating an assembly class to a set of component classes. Aggregation reduces complexity by letting us treat many objects as one object and giving us a better mechanism than a link to model specific domain entities (e.g., purchase order, cars, assemblies).

Finally, some of the attributes and/or methods of the assembly usually propagate to its components as well. In our example, the bill-of-material usually has an order number that is also used by all of the line items and sub-line items.

There are at least two difficulties in dealing with aggregations. First, the components must all be of the same semantic domain.[9] For example, a computer terminal is composed of a CRT, keyboard, cables, etc. However, a terminal is also made of glass, silicon, steel, and plastic. The "made_of" decomposition of the terminal is not the same as the "composed_of" decomposition; it would be incorrect to mix components in these two decompositions. The second difficulty has to do with "optional components." For example, a car normally has door handles as part of the car. If all the door handles got removed, is the car still a car? Now, we need to be careful; it seems like a car still exists. However, it is true that car handles are optional, but what about tires? The logic can then be extended to include every part of a car. But if every part is optional, then a car may exist with no parts. We will see that we can allow only a certain amount of flexibility when we define the aggregation using conditional components.

Behavior

RELATIONSHIP mechanisms give us a way to organize classes/objects in both peer-to-peer (association) and hierarchial (generalization/specialization and aggregation) structures. This structure portion of the model is called the static model by many object-oriented experts. We would prefer to use James Martin and James Odell's term and call it the *structure analysis*.

However, a structure analysis of an application/system is not adequate; we also need to do a *behavior analysis*. Behavior analysis is the process we use to look at how each object (class) provides its services (i.e., the methods).

With the class/object mechanism, we create the conceptual building blocks of our model. The class mechanism, like a blueprint, defines the data structure and provides an index for the system functions. Services (functions and procedures) are tied to a specific class, and an object (as well as its associated data) can only be manipulated by the functions that are associated with the class of which the object is an instance. Without classes and objects, we can neither define any data nor use any methods (code).

When we specify "how a service is provided," we are defining "how a class of objects will perform that service." From an analysis perspective, there are two types of behavior: static and dynamic

Static Behavior

In static behavior, the operation (code) within the method will not be affected by any external or internal events (actions). A good example of static behavior is the "square

---

[9]   In a later chapter, we will see how we can identify this situation by identifying the different kind of aggregations.

root" service for Number. If one requests the "square root" service from the number 4, which is an instance of Number, the result will always be 2. It is 2, today. No external or internal action can cause the method of Number to change the result of computing the square root. If there were only static methods in reality, we would have a very nice model by just managing the structure portion of the model. In fact, writing the method (code) would be easy, as we would be using the same techniques we used in imperative programming.

Dynamic Behavior

If all behaviors in the world were static, it would not be interesting. Fortunately, we live in a dynamic world. For example, look at how a loan agent will respond to your asking, "What is the prime loan interest rate?" The answer to this question can change almost hourly. Similarly, how does the airline reservation clerk answer your question, "What is the lowest fare from New York to San Francisco for January 15?" This answer may change as you are trying to make a decision on the telephone. These are two examples of dynamic behavior. The reasons for these changes in behavior may be captured by letting an object exist in many different states. Then an object's response can be based on its state. This kind of behavior is not handled very well by using the imperative-programming technique. Such methods are better captured by using another mechanism called a finite-state machine.

To better understand the concept of states, let us look at the reservation process in an airline reservation system. When a request comes in, a reservation is created and moves to the requested state. While in the requested state, if there are seats, it can confirm the reservation; however, if there are no seats, it puts the reservation on the wait list. When a confirmed reservation is canceled, the reservation is moved to the canceled state. If the person shows up and flies at the given time, the reservation is moved to the used state, and when the plane lands, the reservation is moved to the archived state. A similar scenario holds for a reservation on the wait list. Thus, the Reservation object could have the following states: Requested, Wait-listed, Confirmed, Cancelled, Used, and Archived. A change of state may occur when a service of the object is requested. When a method associated with a service changes the state of the object, the state is recorded in the data portion of the object. Usually, there is a finite set of sequences of state changes that is allowed with an object. The complete set of sequences is called the lifecycle of the object. Because all possible sequences of state changes are usually programmed using a finite-state machine mechanism, we need a way of capturing this information in a graphical form. One such mechanism is the fence diagram. Figure 2-1 illustrates a fence diagram that shows the lifecycle of the Reservation object.

This fence diagram shows the state and the transitions (movement from one state to another state) that are possible. However, it does not show what will cause the object to change its behavior or state, nor does it show what action (operations performed) is taken when the change of state is recognized. A better model for capturing these additional two aspects of dynamic behavior is a state transition diagram. In the Unified Modeling Language (UML), a state diagram shows (1) state, (2) transition, (3) event,

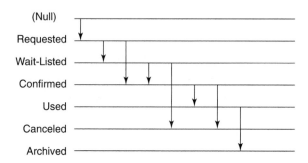

FIGURE 2-1   Reservation fence diagram.

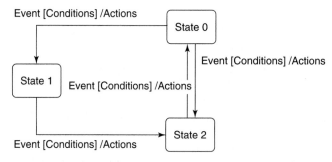

FIGURE 2-2   State transition diagram.

(4) condition, and (5) action. The full description of the major components of a state transition diagram follows:

> **State:** Mode of behavior of the object.
>
> **Transition:** Represents the movement from one state to another state. The transition logically is modeled as taking no time (i.e., the object moves from one state to another state instantly). A transition has two parts: transition condition and transition action.
>
> **Event:** Technically, an event is an occurrence at a point in time. Each event represents an incident or indication that a progression is to happen. An event can incorporate arguments that further define the event.
>
> **Condition:** When a transition condition is satisfied, the object moves from one state to another state. A condition can be the receipt of an external/internal signal, a variable's reaching an absolute or relative value, or the receipt of a time signal. The condition is also known as a *guard*.
>
> **Action:** Operation (algorithm) executed by the object when it moves from one state to another state. Actions may include sending a signal to another object and triggering a transformation.

Figure 2-2 illustrates a template for a state transition diagram. In Figure 2-3, we illustrate a state transition diagram for the Reservation object.

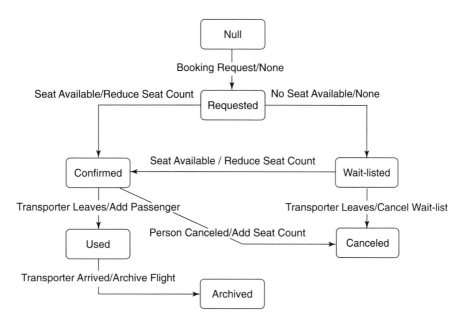

FIGURE 2-3 State transition diagram for the reservation object.

UML has added some additional semantics to the dynamic model that address (1) interrupt handling (history state), (2) ongoing operations within a state that take time to complete (activities), (3) timing constraints (timing mark), (4) processes in threads (tasks), and (5) synchronization. These additional elements will be covered in a later chapter.

Rules

WITH the addition of relationships (inheritance, aggregation, and association), object-oriented technology added some powerful mechanisms for specifying the data semantics of any application domain. The use of classical techniques for specifying static behavior and the use of finite state machines for specifying dynamic behaviors are powerful mechanisms for capturing the procedural semantic. However, one of the weaknesses of current object-oriented methods is the lack of mechanisms to support declarative semantics. In most object-oriented methods, declarative semantics (i.e., rules) are left to the inventiveness of the analyst/developer. If we assume that the purpose of the new method is to help us manage complexity by giving us mechanisms that model the full semantics of the problem domain, then we need to add mechanisms that handle rules (or declarative semantics) to our repertory.

For the novice, declarative semantics addresses the issues of global control description and business rules. Because most declarative semantics are explicitly specified in rules, we will focus on the issue of rules. The types of rules we are interested in capturing are: (1) control rules, (2) business rules, (3) exception-handling rules, (4) contention rules, and (5) triggers.

In a later chapter, we will look at a new language, R++, that extends C++ to give us some of the capabilities required to handle some of the rules types just listed. In a sense, R++ extends C++ to give us the additional mechanisms necessary to support full functional semantics (i.e., support for both procedural and declarative semantics).

Complex Systems

WE now have previewed the major mechanisms available via the object-oriented paradigm to manage complexity. There are other mechanisms that are more properly included in an advanced object-oriented book, of which several are currently available in the market.

Before we can determine if a paradigm helps manage complexity better than other paradigms, we must first understand the characteristics (attributes) of complex applications or systems. Studies have identified five key attributes of complex application/systems. They are as follows:

- Complex systems take the form of a hierarchy. A complex system is composed of interrelated subsystems that have their own subsystems, and so on, until some lowest level of elementary components is reached.
- The choice of which components in a system are primitive is relatively arbitrary and is largely up to the discretion of the observer of the system.
- Intracomponent linkages are generally stronger than intercomponent linkages.
- Hierarchical systems are usually composed of only a few different kinds of subsystems in various combinations and arrangements.
- A complex system that works is invariably found to have evolved from a simple system that worked.

A good example of a complex system is a human being. Let us compare the mechanisms available in the object-oriented paradigm to the mechanisms that a biologist uses to analyze a human being. In biology, the building block (primitive component) is the cell, which is made from a membrane, cytoplasm, and the nuclei. Similarly, in the object-oriented paradigm, the primitive component is an object that has two subcomponents: data and function. Cells are joined together to form organs; similarly, objects are joined together via relationships to form subsystems. Organs are organized in some hierarchical manner to form biological systems; subsystems are joined via various relationships to form systems/applications.

In a human being, the "cell" and the "organ" behave in both a static (same every time) and a dynamic (not necessarily the same) manner. Object-oriented technology includes techniques to capture the dynamic behavior of both an object and a subsystem. Furthermore, a human may actually change its behavior completely by actually providing different services. Similarly in object-oriented technology, there are techniques/mechanisms to migrate an object of one type to another type. Moreover, additional techniques/mechanisms are still being developed to support other concepts necessary to model our perception of reality.

■ ■ SUMMARY

INITIALLY software development was an artistic endeavor that relied heavily upon the skills and technical abilities of the individual. As software grew in complexity, such a free-wheeling approach was no longer acceptable. The introduction of high-level languages helped solve some of the problems associated with complexity, but these languages were not enough. The rise of more formality in software development was supported by the introduction of formal methods:

- Structured programming
- Modular programming
- Imperative programming
- Object-oriented programming

As a result of these major trends, modern developers have a number of abstraction mechanisms in their toolbox that they can use as needed. These mechanisms include:

- Functions and procedures
- Modules
- Abstract data types
- Classes/objects

Classes/Objects is only the latest mechanism and, assuredly, will not be the last.

The classes/objects abstraction mechanism has several key concepts associated with it:

1. **Message passing.** An action is initiated by a service request (message) sent to the specific object.
2. **Generalization/specialization.** Allows classes to share the same code.
3. **Polymorphism.** Allows the shared code to be tailored to the specific class.
4. **Relationships.** Mechanism by which objects know about each other.
   - **Associations.** A relationship among objects.
   - **Aggregations.** An object is composed of other objects.

5. **Behavior.** The services that an object provides.
   - ■ **Static behavior.** Behavior that is independent of the current state of the object.
   - ■ **Dynamic behavior.** Behavior that differs according to the state of the object.
6. **Rules.** A declarative mechanism for addressing the issues of global control description and business rules.

Object-Oriented Programming

> *We hear desperate cries for a silver bullet—something to make software costs drop as rapidly as computer hardware costs do. But as we look to the horizon of a decade hence, we see no silver bullet. There is no single development in either technology or in management technique that promises even one order of magnitude improvement in productivity, in reliability, and in simplicity.*
>
> F. Brooks Jr., The Silver Bullet,
Essence and Accidents of Software Engineering

Maintainable, flexible, and reliable software is difficult to produce. Software systems are complex and, as suggested by Brooks, complexity is a part of the essence of the system. No process of abstraction can eliminate complexity in its entirety. However, we believe that we can create mechanisms that help us manage these complexities. Furthermore, we believe some difficulties are not "accidents"; they arise as a consequence of the way that software is constructed. It is our belief that changing the way we construct software will ameliorate these so-called "accidental" difficulties.

What Is Object-Oriented Programming?

Not a Silver Bullet

Programming a computer is, and will always be, one of the most difficult tasks ever undertaken by humans. Even with the advent of many tools, a proficient programmer must have intelligence, logic, the ability to find and use abstractions, experience, and creativity. Object-oriented programming is not the silver bullet or holy grail for which the managers of software development organizations are looking. However, object-oriented programming is more than simply a collection of new features added to an existing programming language; it is an advanced paradigm.

An Advanced Paradigm

Object-oriented programming is an advanced programming paradigm. Paradigm is defined as "a set of theories, standards, and methods that together represent a way of organizing knowledge." This is the expanded definition of the word given in Thomas Kuhn's book, *The Structure of Scientific Revolution*. Developers have been using other paradigms such as imperative programming (C, Pascal, Cobol, Ada), logic programming (Prolog, C5), and functional programming (FP, ML).

The programming language we use directly influences the way we view (model) reality. In the 1970s when we were using programming languages such as C, Pascal, and PL/1, we used an imperative-programming paradigm for modeling reality—the structured method. In the 1980s, when we were using SQL and 4GL with relational databases, we used a data-modeling paradigm for modeling reality—entity-relationship diagrams. Today we are programming using C++, Java, Smalltalk, and Objective C. We use the object-oriented paradigm to model reality.

For a compiler, the difference between an imperative language such as C and an object-oriented language such as C++ is only the addition of a few keywords and data types. However, making effective use of these facilities requires developers to shift their perception to an entirely different approach for modeling and problem solving. Object-oriented programming is a new way of thinking about what it means to compute, how we organize our information inside a computer system, and how we describe our view (model) of reality.

Basic Object-Oriented Programming Concepts

THE most fundamental concept/mechanism of object-oriented programming is an *object*. Because this is a book for developers, we will define an object as a software unit consisting of the attributes (data) and the methods (code) that act on those data. The data is not directly accessible to the users of the object. Access to the data is granted only via the methods, or code, provided by object (i.e., function calls to its methods), as shown in Figure 3-1. This defines the first principle of the object-oriented paradigm—encapsulation.

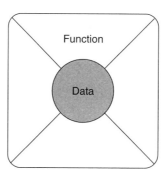

FIGURE 3-1   Object has data encapsulated by functions.

Encapsulation. The object contains both the data and the methods (code) that will manipulate or change that data.

The services of an object define how other objects gain access to its methods. Each object advertises the public services it is willing to provide to all objects. It also provides other services (protected and private) that are restricted only to specific other objects. We will discuss this in depth later. The idea of providing services defines the second principle of the object-oriented paradigm—information hiding.

Information Hiding. The object that contains the attributes (data) defines what services (functions) are available to the other objects. In fact, other objects have neither access nor knowledge of the data (attributes) or how (method/code) a service is provided.

Let us define an agent as an object that provides services and a client as an object that uses one or more of these services.[1] Before a client may use an agent's services, an interface must be defined. This interface definition is called the prototype of the service. The prototype is made from two parts: (1) the name of the service (called the selector by some experts), and (2) the arguments for the service (called the signature by some experts). Every object must define its prototype for each service it plans to provide. The set of defined prototypes is the protocol of the object (or, alternatively, it is the object's interface). The protocol defines how a client may invoke (or request) the services of this object.

A good example of an object and its interface is the icon system that we all use in a windowing system. A very common action in this system is to select an icon and then use a pull-down menu to get all of the services that we can choose for that icon. Thus, in an object-oriented system, the icon is really an object and the menu defines the object interface (or protocol).

One object can use the public service of another object by using the message-passing mechanism (paradigm) to send a message that conforms to the prototype of the service. If

---

[1]   An agent may also be called a server. An agent may be better term during analysis, as a server may then be reserved to mean the actual object that does the work.

object 1 (the client) wants to use a service of object 2 (the agent), the client sends a message to the agent requesting the specific service of the agent. Note that the message must be directed to a specific object and contain the name of the requested service. Furthermore, the message may contain additional information (arguments) needed by the agent to perform the requested service.

For example, in the programmer's parlance, object 1 makes a function call to the service (function) that belongs to object 2 and passes all the appropriate parameter values needed by the function call. Since we stated that message passing is implemented by a function call in C++, it is fair to ask in what sense a message-passing mechanism is different from a function-call mechanism. Certainly, in both cases there is an implicit request for action and there is a set of well-defined operations that will be performed to fulfill the request. However, there are three important distinctions.

First, in a message-passing mechanism, each message is sent to a designated receiver (agent). In the imperative-programming paradigm, a function-call mechanism has no designated receiver (agent). This distinction supports encapsulation.

Second, the interpretation of the message (method or set of operations/code used to fulfill the service request) depends on the receiver and can vary with different receivers. This distinction is necessary to support information hiding and polymorphism, which we will explain later. This leads to the third principle of the object-oriented paradigm—message passing.

> **Message Passing.** An object may communicate with another object only via the message-passing mechanism.

Each message must be sent to a designated receiver, and the interpretation of the message depends on the receiver.

Third, in the object-oriented paradigm, the specific receiver of any given message is not usually known until run time, so the determination of which method to invoke cannot be made until then. Thus, there is late binding between the message (service request/function call) and the method (code fragment) that will be used to fulfill the request for action. This can be contrasted to the early binding (compile or link time) of the function call to the code fragment in the imperative-programming paradigm.

The support for late binding defines the fourth principle of the object-oriented paradigm—late binding.

> **Late Binding.** Support for the ability to determine the specific receiver and its corresponding method (code) to be executed for a message at run time.

From a client's perspective, it is the agent that provides the service. It is possible that the agent actually delegates the work to a third object. This leads to the fifth principle of the object-oriented paradigm—delegation.

> **Delegation.** Work is passed, via message passing, from one object (client) to another object (agent) because, from the client's perspective, the agent has the services that the client needs. Work is continuously passed until it reaches the object that has both the data and the method (code) to perform the work.

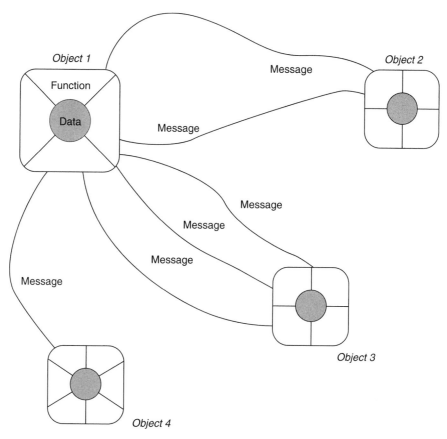

FIGURE 3-2 Message passing among objects.

Delegation is sometimes referred to as the perfect bureaucratic principle. Consider, for example, a corporation or a governmental organization. The chairperson of the board sends a service request (message) to the chief operating officer to build a new plant in Texas. From the perspective of the chairperson of the board, it is the chief operating officer's responsibility to provide the service. However, we all know that the chief operating officer has neither the skills nor the knowledge (information) to actually build a plant in Texas. So the chief operating officer has a method that delegates the work to the head of projects. The head of projects has a method that delegates the work to the chief engineer who has the staff to build a plant in Texas. In fact, the chief engineer's method delegates specific tasks to the appropriate heads of various disciplines to build the plant. It is the specific engineers who have the knowledge and the skills to design the plant to be built.

Here we see the fifth principle of the object-oriented paradigm applied. The work is delegated to the object that has the information (data) and the skills (method) to perform the task. The bureaucratic part comes from the fact that both the chief operating officer and the head of projects advertise the service "build a new plant," even though neither one has the information or the skills to perform the task. However, they have access to resources (objects) that can perform the task, so they can then take the responsibility for performing the task.

What got delegated is the authority to get the work done; responsibility cannot be delegated. From the chairperson of the board's perspective, it is the responsibility of the chief operating officer to fulfill the request to build a new plant in Texas. Similarly, from the chief operating officer's perspective, it is the responsibility of the head of projects to fulfill the request to build a new plant in Texas. When the head of projects accepts this request, he/she has accepted the responsibility from the chief operating officer to perform the work. However, neither the chief operating officer nor the chairperson knows how the work will be done. This is applying the information-hiding principle.

Now let us look at some other object-oriented concepts. Categorizing helps us organize the complex world in which we live. We can make certain assumptions about an object that is in a particular category. If an object is an instance of the category (class), it will fit the general pattern for that category. This leads us to the sixth principle of the object-oriented paradigm—class/instance/object.

> **Class/Instance/Object.** All objects are instances of a class. Instances can be created (instantiated) or destroyed (deleted) at run time.

How the object provides a service is determined by the class of which the object is an instance. Thus, all objects of the same class use the same method (code) in response to a specific service request (function call). Earlier we discussed the prototype of a service and the protocol as it relates to an object. Now with the concept of a class, we see that the prototypes and the protocol are really defined for a class and that they are applicable to every object that is an instance of that class.

Not only do we organize our objects into categories (classes), but we also arrange our categories into a hierarchy from the general to the specific. This leads us to the seventh principle of the object-oriented paradigm—generalization (without polymorphism).

> **Generalization Without Polymorphism.** Classes can be organized by using a hierarchial inheritance structure. In the structure, the subclass will inherit the attributes, the relationships, and the methods from the superclass that are higher in the tree. An abstract superclass is a class that is used to create only subclasses. Thus, there are no direct instances of that class.

However, there are always exceptions to the rule. In order to handle exceptions to the rule within our hierarchal structure, we define the seventh principle of the object-oriented paradigm—generalization with polymorphism, a modification of the sixth principle.

> **Generalization With Polymorphism.** Classes can be organized by using a hierarchal inheritance structure. In the structure, the subclass will inherit the attributes, relationships, and methods from the superclass that is higher in the tree. However, a subclass may create its own method to replace a method of any of its superclasses in providing a service that is available at the superclass level when an instance of that subclass is the agent.

For the subclass, its method will *override* the superclass method for providing the same service.

Although generalization is a powerful concept, there are relationships between objects that cannot be captured using this concept. This leads us to the eighth principle of the object-oriented paradigm—relationships.

> **Relationships.** Collaborations[2] between objects to provide a service to a client are usually captured by an association relationship, which is technically called a **link**.

Later in this book, we will discuss an aggregation relationship; a link is sufficient here, as an aggregation is really a link with special properties.

Object-Oriented Programming Languages

BEFORE we can discuss C++, we should look briefly at the programming paradigms and the variety of languages used in object-oriented technology. This will give us a better perspective as to why we have chosen C++ for this book.The programming paradigms and languages are:

Object-based Programming

Object-based programming is a programming style that uses encapsulation and objects. The methods and attributes are hidden within the object, and each object is uniquely identified. There is no support for the class mechanism, inheritance, relationships, dynamic behavior, and rules. Ada is an example of an object-based language.[3]

Class-based Programming

Class-based programming includes all of the mechanisms of object-based languages as well as the mechanisms for classes and instances. CLU is an example of a class-based programming language.

Object-oriented Programming

Object-oriented programming includes all of the mechanisms for class-based programming as well as mechanisms to support inheritance and self-recursion. Smalltalk is an example of an object-oriented programming language.

Advanced OO Programming

Advanced OO Programming includes all of the mechanisms for object-oriented programming and includes capabilities to support multiple inheritance, association, aggregation, and dynamic behavior. C++ and Java are examples of advanced OO programming languages.

---

[2] The definition of the different kinds of relationships (i.e., association, aggregation, link, generalization, specialization) will be explained in depth in later chapters.

[3] Visual Basic is also an example of an object-based programming language.

Leading-edge Object-Oriented Programming

Leading-edge OO programming includes all of the mechanisms of an advanced OO programming style as well as mechanisms for supporting implementation of rules. R++ is an example of such a leading-edge programming language.

Why C++?

THE C language was developed by Dennis Ritchie in the early 1970s as a system implementation language and was used to build UNIX. The design philosophy of the C language is as follows:

- Make it portable.
- Keep the language small and simple.
- Make it fast.
- Trust the programmer.
- Do not prevent the programmer from doing what needs to be done.

With the use of the UNIX systems and because it was a terse and small language, C became widely used as a general-purpose programming language.

C++ was created by Bjarne Stroupstrup in the early 1980s. Bjarne had four main goals in the design of the language:

1. Make C++ compatible with C.
2. Extend C with a class construct similar to the class construct of Simula 67.
3. Support strong typing.
4. Retain the design philosophy of the C language.

To achieve these goals, C++ retained much of the C language, including a rich set of operators, nearly orthogonal design, terseness, and extensibility.

For us, the selection of C++ for our development language was largely determined by these goals. First, we wanted a programming language that preserves the design philosophy of C, as we do not believe that developing software will ever be so easy that all you need is an "object-oriented language." Second, we wanted a language that will facilitate interfacing our new systems to legacy systems.

The technical capabilities of C++ helped make our decision easy:

1. C++ is a highly portable language, as there is now an ANSI standard for C++. Also, there are compilers for the language on nearly every different computer and operating system.
2. A C++ program can be fast, as it does not incur the run-time expense of type checking and garbage collection of most "pure object-oriented" languages.
3. C++ does not require a graphical environment and is relatively inexpensive to buy.
4. C++ is a marriage of low-level (assembly language) and high-level (object-oriented constructs). The developer may write code at the appropriate level to accurately

model the particular solution and still maintain machine-level implementation details.

5. C++ is a multi-paradigm language that gives the developer a range of choices to design and code a solution. We will use these choices to demonstrate techniques that work, rather than insisting on paradigmatic dogma.

In brief, one may view C++ as a professional developer's object-oriented language alternative to "pure object-oriented" languages such as Smalltalk, Objective C, Eiffel, and so on. The language trusts the programmer and does not prevent the programmer from extending the language to support useful abstract mechanisms and also using non-object-oriented techniques when appropriate. Furthermore, it is an extension of a programming language that has been used to write a large number of applications on a wide range of machines.

These capabilities are important from a practical point of view because we know of very few commercial systems that live up to the "pure concepts of object-orientation" as defined by the object-oriented pundits. For most of the systems we built, we needed to go beyond the "pure concepts" to produce systems to meet the limitations of time, resources, and budgets, and/or to interface with legacy systems written in imperative-programming languages such as C. There is no better language, other than a multi-paradigm language, to give leading-edge developers a way to use their creativity and experience in a controlled context to solve real problems, meet business constraints, and still exact the benefits of the promised new technology.

When we discuss rules, we will look at R++, a leading-edge programming language from AT&T Labs and Lucent Bell Laboratories.

Ways of Organizing Reality

IN prior years, software developers have used various paradigms (ways of viewing or modeling reality) to organize and manage software. However, each of the earlier paradigms supported modeling a specific view of a system. The four essential views of a system are as follows:

- **Data/Entity View**
  Entity-relationship diagram

- **Function View**
  Functional decomposition (structured techniques)

- **Behavioral View**
  State transition diagrams (state charts)

- **Control View**
  Rule-based Systems

Major software methodologies have been developed using one of these views as a fundamental building block.

For example, structured analysis and design is based on using the functional view as the essential building block of its paradigm of reality. In this model, the computer is a data manipulator. It has some set of instructions that will cause it to go into memory and pull values (data) out of various slots (memory addresses), transform them in some manner, and then store the results back in another slot. Although fairly accurate of the way a computer works, this model does not reflect the way most people go about solving problems. This has been called the pigeon-hole model of computation.

The relational database (data analysis) methodology is based on the data/entity view of reality. In this model, the computer is a data manager that organizes data into collections (called entities) that are the building blocks of the system. The computer then manipulates the data within the entities to get the information it needs to process. However, this methodology was silent on how the computer was to take advantage of the entity in processing the data. Thus, most practitioners who used this methodology for data analysis still used the pigeon-hole model of computation for processing the data.

The finite state machine (statemate) methodology is based on the behavioral view of reality. In this model, the computer is a state manager. It organizes the processing based on the state of the system. The state is the building block of this system, and the data that gets manipulated is state-dependent. This methodology does not address data management. Moreover, in designing the functions and actions of this methodology, practitioners continued to use the pigeon-hole model of computation.

The rule-based system (part of artificial intelligence systems) is based on a control view of reality. In this model, the computer is an inference engine that executes a set of rules (if-then statements). In theory, the sequence in which the rules were executed was not material. However, in practice, most of us were not able to find rules that were truly decoupled. Because there was no structure to organize the rules, there was also very poor cohesion. Furthermore, rule-based systems did not help us manage the data and did not support procedural concepts.

Nearly all of these methodologies are still based on the pigeon-hole model of computation, and all are very weak in modeling alternate views of the system. In brief, a rich enough methodology to manage the information about a complex problem domain did not exist.

Software engineers and software researchers have been trying for at least 30 years to improve the techniques for building software applications/systems. Attempts to address this issue have come from innovations in programming languages and from various structured approaches to application development. That is, we used structured methods, 4GLs, CASE tools, prototyping techniques, and code generators to address this issue.

The extent to which these efforts have succeeded is questioned in many reports. These reports show that structured methods impaired both the productivity of the developers and the quality of the end product. Furthermore, in very complex applications, 4GLs may actually degrade productivity and, due to the restrictiveness of high-level languages, cause the switch to 3GL coding.

It was time for software professionals to understand why they were having these difficulties when,

■ Software became the predominant cost of delivering and maintaining a system, and
■ Not even the most skilled programmers could produce resilient and correct code.

To gain understanding, computer scientists began to research software development.

It has taken software researchers all this time to understand how difficult it is to build "good" software. In their research, they have found software difficult to build for the following reasons:

- The complexity of problem domain
- The difficulty of managing the development process
- The flexibility possible through software
- The problem of characterizing the behavior of a continuous system

In this book, we address mainly the first reason. The last reason is discussed in our case study. We also discuss the proper use of the flexibility of object-oriented techniques in the case study and the flexibility of C++ in the coding sections. Managing the development process is outside the scope of this book.

Simulation Model of Computation

THE problem-solving view of object-oriented programming is very different from the pigeon-hole model used in imperative programming. In the object-oriented paradigm, we never used any of the conventional terms such as *assignments*, *variables*, or *memory addresses*. Instead, we use terms such as *objects*, *messages*, and *services*. We have a universe of well-behaved objects that courteously ask each other to perform services for themselves. We have a community of helpers that assist us in solving problems.

The idea of creating a universe of helpers is very similar to a style of computer simulation called "discrete event-driven simulation." In this style, the user creates models of various elements of the simulation and describes how they interact with each other. Then, via some discrete event, the elements are set in motion.

This is almost identical to the way we do object-oriented modeling/programming. We define various objects in the universe that will help us solve the problem as well as how they interact with each other, and then we set them in motion. As a result, we consider object-oriented programming as using a simulation model of computation instead of a pigeon-hole model of computation.

This simulation model also provides the designer/programmer with a better metaphor for problem solving. When we think in terms of services and methods (how to provide the service), we can bring a wealth of experience, understanding, ideas, and intuition from our everyday lives. In contrast, most of us have very little insight into how to structure a program that thinks about problem solving in terms of pigeon holes or slots containing values.

Object-Oriented Way of Organizing Reality

TO illustrate how the object-oriented paradigm helps us manage complexity, let us apply this modeling technique to a real-world situation. First we will describe the situation and then we will discuss how we would use the object-oriented paradigm to capture the situation.

In this example, we have a family with a father (John), a mother (Jane), two sons (Peter and Paul), and two daughters (Elizabeth and Mary). John is an actor and Jane is a dentist. All the children are students and the family dog is Lassie. Their family physician is Alice. This family owns a house in the suburbs. Although mowing the family lawn is normally a chore for the father, it can also be a paid chore for any one of the children. However, working within the neighborhood is Jack, a professional lawn mower.

One morning, Jane notices that the lawn needs mowing, so she mentions to John that it is time to mow the lawn. John agrees and says that he will mow the lawn this evening. Later that evening, John comes home and is exhausted from a long day at the studio and decides to pay one of his children to mow the lawn. He looks for one of his children; he sees Mary first. He asks Mary to mow the lawn for five dollars. Mary agrees; however, Mary knows that Jack, a professional lawn mower, is willing to mow the lawn for four dollars. So Mary calls Jack to mow the lawn for four dollars, and Jack agrees to mow the lawn. Jane comes home later that evening and she sees the lawn mowed. Thinking that John mowed the lawn, Jane compliments John on the excellent condition of the lawn.

Now let us do an object-oriented analysis of this situation. There are the following tangible objects in our model: John, Jane, Peter, Paul, Elizabeth, Mary, Lassie, the family lawn, Jack, and Alice. Jack, the professional lawn mower, advertises a lawn-mowing service. John, as the father of the house, also provides a lawn-mowing service that is limited to the family lawn. Each of the children also provides a lawn-mowing service, for a specific price.

The prototype of the lawn-mowing service is not the same for each of the objects. For example, the prototype for Jack's lawn-mowing service may have the name (selector) "mow the lawn" and the arguments (signature)—address of the lawn, whom to bill, billing address. The four children's prototype for "mow the lawn" service may look similar to Jack's, as the children are willing to mow any lawn for cash. The children's prototype may have the name "mow the lawn," and the arguments address of the lawn, money (in form of cash). Finally, John will only mow the family lawn as his chore. John's prototype may have the name "mow the lawn" and no arguments. John had a default value for the lawn to be mowed, namely the family's lawn, when Jane asked him to mow the lawn. He also knew that he would not get paid for mowing the family lawn.

Jane, the client, solves the problem of getting the lawn mowed by finding an appropriate agent, John, to whom she passes a message containing her service request for action. In order for John to process the message, Jane's message must follow the protocol/prototype that John has defined for the service. Because Jane sent a message that John can interpret (i.e., the message is consistent with a prototype within the protocol that John has advertised), John must have a method (some algorithm or set of operations) to perform the requested service ("mow the lawn").

In this case, John behaves in a dynamic manner. If he is not tired at the end of the day, he mows the lawn himself; if he is tired, however, he asks one of his children to mow the lawn. Alternatively, if John always mows the lawn himself, as Jane apparently assumed, then John's behavior would be considered static. In either scenario (whether John used a dynamic or static method for his behavior), when John accepted the message, he accepted the responsibility to satisfy Jane's request. Similarly, when Mary accepted the request from John to "mow the lawn" for five dollars, Mary accepted the responsibility to satisfy John's request.

Jane did not know, and probably did not want to know, the particular method that John used to provide the service "mow the lawn." She was very content that the lawn was mowed when she got home. If she would have investigated, however, Jane would have found that Jack mowed the lawn for four dollars. Similarly, John did not know the particular method that Mary used to mow the lawn. This is the client's view of the principle of information hiding.

In the object-oriented paradigm, the agent's service is defined to the client in terms of responsibilities. Jane's request for action (i.e., service from John) must indicate only the desired outcome (mow the lawn). John is free to pursue any technique that achieves the desired results and is not hampered by interference from Jane. It is John's responsibility to define how he will provide for the requested service by defining the method to provide the service.

John's method was an algorithm based on whether or not he was tired at the end of the day. As we know, on this particular day, he delegated the work to mow the lawn to his daughter, Mary. Furthermore, Mary subsequently delegated the work to Jack.

From this example, we see another principle, all too human, in message passing. The first thought of every client and agent is to find someone else to perform the work. This is the application of the principle of delegation. Of course, objects cannot always respond to a message by asking another object to perform an action. If this was allowed, there would be an infinite circle of requests, like a bureaucracy of paper pushers, each passing papers to some other member of the organization. At some point, at least a few objects need to perform some work other than passing the request to some other object. These ideas are used in our mowing the lawn example. From Jane's perspective, her husband John has provided the service "mow the lawn," which is the reason she compliments John for the excellent condition of the lawn. From John's perspective, it was Mary who mowed the lawn. John, then, may also thank Mary for the excellent job that she did. But, in fact, if the behaviors or methods (how we provide the services) were not hidden (information hiding) from Jane, she would have known that Jack mowed the lawn.

To better understand the message-passing mechanism, let us look at a different scenario. John could have sent his message "mow the lawn" to one of his sons. Let us assume that he sent it to Peter instead of Mary. Peter's behavior or method is different from Mary's. Specifically, he needs all five dollars to pay for the gasoline to get to tomorrow's ball game. So, Peter mows the lawn himself. John and Jane had a choice of which person to request the service (or send the message). However, the client must send the message to a designated receiver, and the designated receiver must provide the service. If Jane had called Alice, the family physician, to mow the lawn, she would have been in error because Alice does not provide a lawn-mowing service. If Alice understands the message, she would probably send back an error message "physicians do not mow lawns." More likely, this would result in an invalid message for the recipient.

Now let us look at some other object-oriented concepts. Although Mary may have never dealt with Jack, she has some ideas about the behavior that she can expect from Jack when she requests his service. This is due to the fact that Jack is a professional lawn mower and she has information about lawn-mowing professionals. Because Jack is an instance of the category (class) **LawnMower,** he will fit the general pattern for lawn mowers. We can use the word **LawnMower** to represent the category of all lawn mowers. This is an application of the class/instance/object principle.

Mary has additional generic information about Jack that goes beyond his being an instance of the class **LawnMower**. She also has generic information about Jack because Jack is also in the class **HouseCareProfessional**. She knows that Jack will come to the house to do the mowing, just as the other housecare professionals such as the rug cleaner and the gardener. This is different from the class **HealthCareProfessional,** who usually does not make house calls. Furthermore, Mary knows Jack is also in the class **SmallBusinessOwner**, and as such he will ask for money as part of the service and will give a receipt, just as would any other small business owner. Mary has organized her knowledge of Jack in terms of a hierarchy of classes.

The generalization tree with Mary's organization is shown in Figure 3-3. We use the UML notation in this illustration. Generalization/specialization (inheritance) is shown as a solid line from subclass to superclass with a triangular head on the superclass end. Instantiation of a class is shown with a dashed line from the instance to the class with a triangular head on the class end. Classes and instances are shown as rectangles. Instances are distinguished from classes by underlining the name.

Jack is an instance of the class **LawnMower**, but the **LawnMower** is a specialized form (subclass) of the class **HouseCareProfessional**. Furthermore, **HouseCareProfessional** is a subclass of the generalized form (superclass) of **SmallBusinessOwner**, and Mary can continue up the hierarchy to **OrganicMatter** via **Human** and **Mammal**. Thus, there is a lot of generic information that Mary has about Jack that is not directly attributed to Jack being in the class **LawnMower**. This is due to the fact that Mary assumes that the knowledge of a more general class applies to a specialization of that class. Mary's classification of Jack is the application of the generalization with polymorphism principle.

Generalization (inheritance) works in a manner for which every parent wishes. The children (subclasses) inherit all the attributes (knowledge) and all the methods (behavior) of the parent (superclass). In addition, children can have additional attributes (smarter than the parent) and have additional methods (can do more than parent). This is what we call the "good child" form of specialization. Unfortunately, not all children are "good children."[4] We need a way of modeling the "bad child." Let us look at this next.

We know that mammals reproduce by giving birth to children; certainly humans do and so does the dog Lassie. However, Phyllis, the female platypus, reproduces by

---

[4] This is not a moral judgement about good and bad. In fact, we appreciate the fact that this paradigm supports bad children.

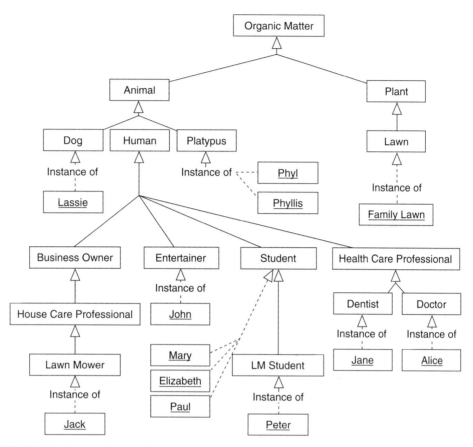

FIGURE 3-3 Generalization/specialization—hierarchy for the lawn-mowing example.

laying eggs instead of giving birth. Thus, the subclass **Platypus** provides the service of reproduction in a different manner than do the rest of the mammals.

If we want to capture this fact and still use our generalization hierarchy, we must have a way of handling the exceptions to the general rule. We do this by providing a way for the subclass to provide a different method for a service that is defined in the superclass (parent class). In our example, the superclass **Mammal** has defined a service called "reproduce." The method for the service "reproduce" is to give birth to live children. **Platypus** is a subclass of **Mammal**. In the "good child" form of specialization, Phyllis would reproduce by giving birth to live children. However, Phyllis is a "bad child"; she has chosen to reproduce by laying eggs. In this form of specialization, called generalization with polymorphism, Phyllis provides her own method (i.e., laying eggs) for the service "reproduce." Thus, Phyllis will use a different method of providing the service "reproduce" than Lassie. Phyllis is an example of the need to modify the generalization without polymorphism principle.

In our example, we need to use generalization with polymorphism. Mary and all of the other students will respond to the "mow the lawn" message by delegating any request that pays over five dollars to Jack, as he will mow the lawn for four dollars. However, Peter is an exception, as he will always respond to the "mow the lawn" request by doing it himself. Thus, we must use generalization with polymorphism to capture Peter's behavior (see Figure 3-3).

Let us look more closely at the method that Mary uses to "mow the lawn." For Mary to call Jack to mow the lawn, Mary has to have access to Jack. Normally, this is done when Jack sends flyers around the neighborhood advertising his service. Mary sees the flyer and puts Jack's name and telephone number into her diary. Although this action may seem innocuous, Mary has established a relationship with Jack. At the instant Mary put Jack's name into her diary, she decided to consider using his service when the occasion arises. A connection was established between Mary and Jack. In fact, the reason why Jack sends out the flyers is to establish relationships that will add to his customer base. Every person who reads the flyer and saves Jack's name, telephone number, and kind of service has established a relationship with Jack. We can name that relationship from two perspectives: (1) from Jack's perspective, all the people who keep the flyer information are customers, and (2) from these people's (and Mary's) perspective, Jack is a professional lawn mower.

This kind of relationship, where one object knows about another object for specific services, is called a *link*. Let us presume that the neighborhood is called FunTown and that we have a category (class) of people called **FunTowner**. Because Jack is an instance of **LawnMower** and every one of his customers is an instance of **FunTowner**, we can capture this link at a higher-level concept called *association*. An association describes a group of links with a common structure and common semantics. All links in an association must connect objects from one same class to objects from a second same class. Thus, if we have a second person, Joan, who also is an instance of **LawnMower** and every one of her customers is an instance of **FunTowner**, we have a second link that belongs to the same association.

Associations are bidirectional. It is common to give a name to an association in each direction. In our example, from **LawnMower**'s direction, it is customer, and from the **FunTowner**'s direction, it is lawnmower.[5] Without the association, there would be no vehicle for Mary to access the services of Jack.

Table 3-1 summarizes the key object-oriented concepts using the "mowing the lawn" example.

---

[5] In actuality, a link is implemented via pointers from one object to another object(s). A *pointer* is an explicit reference to an object; thus an association is implemented in a class as a class pointer attribute to the other class. For example, in the data portion of a class **FunTowner,** there may be a data member *lawnmower* that points to a **LawnMower** object. Conversely, the data portion of class **Lawn Mower** may contain a data member *customer* that points to a set of **FunTowner** objects that are the customers.

TABLE 3-1   OO Concepts with Examples

OO Concept	Explanation/Example
Client	Requestor of the service (i.e., sender of the message—Jane)
Agent (server)	Agent to whom the message is sent (i.e., John)
Object	Jane, John, Mary, Lassie
Message sending	Mary's request to John to "mow the lawn"
Signature	Additional information (arguments) needed to carry out the request (i.e., amount to be paid)
Responsibility	John's responsibility to satisfy Jane's request
Attributes	Name, age, etc.
Services	John and Jack both provide the service "mow the lawn"
Method	This is the operation(s) of providing the service, which is hidden from the client
Collaboration	Object that helps another object in performing the method (i.e., Jack helps Mary in providing the "mow the lawn" service)
Class	Mammal, BusinessOwner
Instance	Same as an object
Inheritance	LawnMower is a specialized form of a HouseCare Professional. HouseCare Professional is a Human, which is a specialized form of Mammal.
Polymorphism	Phyllis laying eggs
Subclass	Subclass will inherit attributes and methods from its superclass(es) (i.e., Human will inherit all the attributes and methods of Mammal)
Superclass	Dentist is a subclass of the superclass HealthCare Professional.
Abstract superclass	Class used to create only subclasses (i.e., Mammal)

■ ■ SUMMARY

THE principles of the object-oriented paradigm are as follows:

1. **Encapsulation.** An object contains both the data and the methods (code) that will manipulate or change the data.
2. **Information hiding.** The services of an object define how other objects have access to its methods and, therefore, its data. Each object advertises public services that it is willing to provide to other objects.
3. **Message passing.** An object (client) may communicate with another object (agent) only via the message-passing mechanism. A client requests a service of an agent by sending a message that matches a predefined protocol that the agent defines for that service.

4. **Late binding.** The specific receiver of any given message will not be known until run time, so the determination of which method to invoke cannot be made until then. Remember inheritance with polymorphism.

5. **Delegation.** Work is passed, via the message-passing mechanism, from one object (client) to another object (agent) because from the client's perspective the agent has the services that the client needs. Work is continuously passed until it reaches the object that has both the data and the method (code) to perform the work. Delegation is sometimes called the perfect bureaucratic principle.

6. **Class and objects.** All objects are instances of a class. How an object provides a service is determined by the class of which the object is an instance. Thus, all objects of the same class use the same method (code) in response to a specific service request.

7. **Inheritance and polymorphism.** Classes can be organized by using a hierarchal inheritance structure. In the structure, the subclass will inherit the attributes and the methods from the superclass(es) higher in the tree. However, a subclass may create its own method to replace the method of any of its superclasses in providing a service that is available at the superclass level. When the subclass is the agent for that specific service, the method of the subclass will override the method of the superclass(es) for providing the same service.

8. **Relationships.** Association and aggregation are used to capture the collaboration between objects necessary to provide a service to a client.

C H A P T E R

4

Bounding the Domain

T he boundary lost the line invisible that parts the image from reality.

William Wordsworth

T he previous chapter introduced the object-oriented way of organizing reality. Organizing all of reality for modeling is not a simple activity, even if one does it the object-oriented way. Practically speaking, one does not attempt to organize all of reality. One usually deals with modeling a specific application domain. That is, one has to select a manageable domain within which the model will be developed. This chapter identifies two methods for capturing this bounding of domain: use cases and contracts.

Use cases capture the functional requirements and the value propositions[1] of a proposed system with its associated high-level processes (i.e., those processes that are outside of the system boundary) that are needed to achieve these specific value propositions.[2] Contracts articulate the services (operations) provided by the system (application software) to achieve these value propositions. One of the key values of producing use cases and contracts is that they ease discussions between stakeholders and analysts/developers. They are typically written using business terms that are natural to the majority of stakeholders.

---

[1] The value propositions are the reasons why the system is being built. They identify the value that various features provide to the business.

[2] The authors have also used them to capture the performance characteristics/requirements of the system from a usage perspective. Capturing these parameters are useful for performance testing.

Introduction to Use Cases

IVAR JACOBSON, in *Object-oriented Software Engineering: A Use-Case Driven Approach*, established a scenario based approach for establishing a boundary on the domain called the Objectory method. This method focused on identifying the important elements of a domain in terms of how they contributed or behaved while providing a service. He called each scenario, a "use case because it described a use of the system.[3]

Various authors define use cases differently:

- A use case specifies a sequence of actions, including variants, that a system performs and that yields an observable result of value to a particular actor (Jacobson, Booch, Rumbaugh 1999).
- A use case is a description of all of the possible sequences of interactions among the system and one or more actors in response to some initial stimulus by one of the actors (Rumbaugh 1994).
- A use case is a collection of possible sequences of interactions between the system under discussion and its external actors, related to a particular goal (Cockburn 2000).

The common threads in all of these definitions are actors and sequences of interactions. In this approach, several concepts are important: the goal, the system, the actor, the use case, and use case bundle.

The *goal* is the business value to the "user(s)" of the system who usually initiate the interaction with the system.
The *system* is the application with all of its associated hardware that will be used by the "users."
An *actor* is external entity that interacts with a system.
A *use case* is a description of an interaction that achieves a useful goal for an actor.
A *use case bundle* is a collection of use cases that are highly correlated with some activity or organizing business element. A use case bundle gives us a way to organize our use cases into collections that will help us better understand the functionality of the system that we are developing.

System

Historically, systems have been understood utilizing three basic models: black box, white box, and transparent box. Each successive model, as illustrated in Figure 4-1, provides increasing detail into the internals and implementation of the system. The black box model, shown as the solid boundary, emphasizes the value the system provides and where it fits into the rest of the business computing environment. It presents the system without concern about how it provides the business value. Here the key concepts are the users of the system (including other systems) and the value the system provides to each user.

---

[3] The use of the system is assumed to achieve some useful goal for the user of the "system." Thus, use cases try to capture the value proposition from an external view. Namely, the goal is to capture the value proposition from the user's perspective.

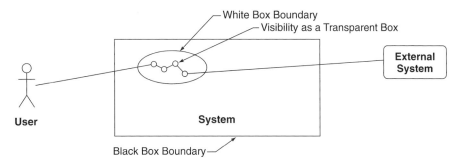

FIGURE 4-1 **Visibility into the internals of a system according to the black box, white box, and transparent box models.**

The white box model, shown as the oval, presents the system in terms of what specific business functions the system provides. This model emphasizes how objects in the system map to business processes. We can use a white box model to capture the detailed, essential use cases that are both primary and secondary. A white box model does not concern itself with the hardware or software architecture.

The transparent box model, shown as the very small circles, presents the internals of the system and how they contribute to the business functionality. Each circle represents an internal element, whether it be source code or device. In this model, technology entities employed within the system are included as well as details about how they work together to provide the business functionality.

In the design of use case cases, we are supposed to view the system as a black box. But experience has shown us that it is sometimes necessary to at least take a white box view to determine the sequence of interactions between an actor and the system. This helps us define the use case. Furthermore, when we are doing low-level concrete use cases, we probably have to take a transparent view of the system.

Actors

The use case model divides the world into two parts: the system and the users (the external entities that use it). Actors are a mechanism for categorizing the users (usually a physical entity) of the system who share a set of common interactions to achieve a goal or set of goals. An actor can be a user, an external system, or a device. An actor can make a service request of the system, be requested to provide a service, and interact with the system through a complex dialog of service requests between the actor and the system. It is the usage of a set of common iterations in a like manner to achieve a goal that is the key to the categorization. Thus, an actor is a representation[4] of any entity that can initiate an action on the part of the system or receive a request for an action from the system. An actor can be characterized by requests that it initiates to the system or the requests to which it can respond. In a real sense, the complete set of requests/responses

---

[4] In a standard use case, an actor's instance is the initiator. The initiator is the entity that starts a series of interactions with the system. In addition to the initiator, a use case may have participating actors that are entities that did not initiate the interaction.

for all actors establishes a boundary on the domain of which the system can be aware. That is, a system can never respond to aspects of a domain for which it has not been designed (i.e., it will not process request [inputs] for which it has not been designed).

Occasionally, a number of actors may share common requests that they all invoke on the system. Rather than explicitly associate the same set of requests with each actor, we can introduce a generalized actor that encompasses those common requests. The other actors are treated as specializations and inherit the ability to perform those requests from the generalization.

Use Cases

A **scenario** is a little story that outlines some expected sequence of requests and responses between a user(s) and the system. It is used to convey how a specific user[5] employs the system to achieve some useful goal. Writing a scenario is a simple game of "what happens next." Most scenarios are simple; there is only one logical sequence of operations from the initial state. Other scenarios are more complicated, with multiple exception cases (things going wrong) or different interaction paths (options).

A use case is closely related to a scenario.[6] Figure 4-2 illustrates a simple use case diagram for a course registration system.[7]

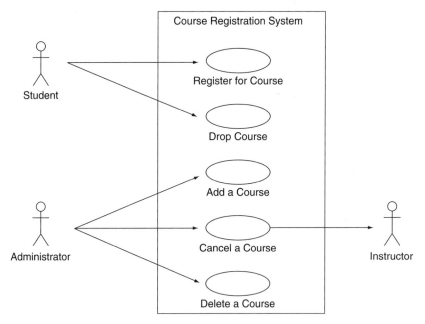

FIGURE 4-2   Simple use case diagram.

---

5   A specific user is an instance of an actor. For example, Joe is a user. Joe is an instance of the actor: user.

6   A use case is the generalized form of a family of scenarios. Thus a scenario is a specific instance of a use case.

7   A detailed discussion about use case diagrams appears later in this chapter.

It describes a system in terms of sequences of interactions between various actors and the system (i.e., a specific use cases captures all the scenarios that begin with the same request to achieve the same user goal). Also, it is a formal way of describing all the interactions between the actors and the system to achieve the business goals of the system. The actor that initiates the use case is called the initiation actor. In most interactions, the dialog may result in the interaction of the system with other actors; these actors are called participating actors. The interaction assumes that the system is a black box and uses domain elements as actors that interact with the system in a request/response manner. A use case identifies the preconditions that must exist for it to be valid, the post-conditions that define the state of the system after the use case has concluded, detailed business (non-technology-dependent) that is performed, business exceptions that may arise, and business constraints that apply to the system in reacting to a specific actor request.

In capturing the functional aspects of the system, one of the difficulties in generating a useful discussion of a system is keeping the description at a consistent level of abstraction. For use cases to be successfully developed, it is necessary to know the dimension of the functional description that one is attempting to capture. Then one can determine the level of detail in the information that should be captured.

In one dimension, we can distinguish between high-level and low-level functional descriptions of a system. A high-level description provides general and brief descriptions of the essence of the business values provided. It is not concerned with how the business values are achieved. A low-level description provides business details showing the exact order of activities, tasks, or alternatives.[8]

In a second dimension, we can distinguish between primary and secondary functions of the system. Primary functions are the essential business functionalities of the system—the functions provided to users that constitute the reason for which the system exists. The secondary processes deal with the rare and exceptional cases.[9] These are the functions that are necessary to deliver a robust system.

Finally in a third dimension, we can distinguish between the essential and the concrete functions of the system. The essential use cases are business solutions that are independent of implementation (hardware and software), while the concrete use cases are design-dependent. The distinction between essential and concrete is the distinction between black box and transparent box models.

Relations among Use Cases.   A typical use case outlines some sequence of interactions between the initiator of a service request to the system and the system. It often happens that some sequences of interactions are common across multiple use cases. In this situation, we can extract these common sequences as a use case. We then include the use case[10]

---

[8]   A high-level description of Shakespeare's Romeo and Juliet is that it is a love story. A low-level description includes the kinds of details about the story as presented in study guides. Neither level description is actually the story.

[9]   It can be argued that secondary processes are not rare or occasional if one includes within this category processes such as backing up data or downloading needed data from other systems. Such processes may not be the primary reason for building the system, but are essential processes that are almost always required. We consider those cases to be primary cases.

[10] This is like a common subroutine that is used by many routines.

so formed within the use cases from which they were extracted. When this situation exists, we say that each of the "multiple" use cases includes the common use case (i.e., we can have an include relationship between use cases). The includes relationship allows us to localize in one use case a common sequence of activities among several use cases. This has the advantage that when changes occur in this common sequence, it only needs to be changed in one place.

In addition, we can have the situation in which several use cases are identical with the exception of one or two specific subsequences of interactions. In this case, we can extract the common core (base use case) and treat the use cases that differ as extensions[11] of this base use case. Thus an extend relationship exists between an extension and the core. This allows us to capture in an easy form those situations where the sequences captured in several use cases may differ as the result of a simple conditional at the end of the sequence.

Finally, in the development of a high-level use cases, it is often the case that it can encompass several detailed and extended use cases. The relationship that exists between the high-level use case and the detailed and the extended use case is a generalization/specialization relation.

Subject of Description.   As stated previously, a use case can be classified in three different dimensions:

1. Primary vs. secondary
2. Essential vs. concrete
3. High-level vs. low-level

A use case description of a system will emphasize one of each pair of factors. Several groupings are commonly used to scope the level of detail captured in use cases:

- Primary, essential, high-level
- Primary and secondary, essential, low-level
- Primary, concrete, low-level
- Primary and secondary, concrete, low-level

Generating a full, detailed functional description of a system will involve successively producing the various kinds of use cases starting from the top and working downward. Descriptions of these common kinds of use cases follow.

At the most abstract level are the primary, essential, high-level use cases. They basically define how the system supports the business processes involved in attaining the business value propositions. These use cases usually only define the functions that will be performed by the system; they do not clearly define the inputs and outputs (i.e., interfaces or the services associated with the system or actors) of the "processes" or process owners. Nor do they define how the process will perform its work. They are useful in getting a high-level understanding of the workflow. In addition, they give us an order

---

[11] This is like subclassing, in which you are only allowed to add code to the parent routine.

of magnitude on the number of detailed use cases (primary and secondary, essential, low-level) that will be produced and a framework to identify the critical success factors for the project.[12] For example, we can use these use cases to prioritize the features according to business value and estimate usage based on the value proposition. If rare and unusual use cases or reliability are critical to our system design, secondary use cases should also be developed to help size the problem.[13]

To understand a very large and complex system, we may require the development of essential and low-level use cases (both primary and secondary). When we do this, several use cases may be required to provide the details that are summarized in one primary, essential high-level use case. We use these use cases to capture the interfaces needed to support the business goals. They can be used to capture the sequence of interactions (service request/events) between the system and all of the actors; however all of the interfaces are described in a technology-independent manner. Use cases written at this level are the minimum level needed to write an interface contract for the system.

However, for some contracts, more specific details (i.e., technology-dependent constraints) are needed. In these cases, primary, concrete, and low-level use cases are developed. In the primary, low-level, and concrete use cases, not only is the sequence of interactions captured, but technology-based design decisions are included.[14] Finally, when our system also has critical, rare, and unusual functions or has robustness as a key requirement, we will develop both primary and secondary, low-level concrete use cases. When we take use cases to this degree of detail, we deal with the initialization, recovery, and secondary use cases that are necessary for a robust system.

Information Captured.   One of the reasons for employing a use case approach to bounding our system is the ease with which information can be identified. Use cases can capture the following set of information:[15]

- Actors

    A use case will identify all actors that participate in it. In some situations, there won't be an actor explicitly identified (a common situation with supporting use cases), and this must be noted.[16]

- Relationships with other use cases

    A use case description will identify the relationships (generalization/specialization, include, and extend relationships) that use cases have with each other.

---

[12] The critical success factor in a lot of re-engineering process efforts may not be the system; it is the successful deployment of the new business processes to the users!

[13] These use cases are not usually sufficient to write an interface contract for the system.

[14] This is an encroachment upon architecture and/or design. Yes, theory is perfect, but practice is more useful.

[15] The authors have also extended this to include usage data that will help them tune for performance on large systems.

[16] The purpose of use cases is to capture the interaction between actors and the system. In the situation addressed here, the actor that is participating is implicitly identified from the use case that includes it. Included use cases can be incorporated into several use cases, each of which deals with different actors. It is for this reason that we state that a use case might not explicitly identify an actor.

■ Preconditions

A use case may require specific conditions to hold in order for it to be successfully invoked. All such conditions must be identified. In some cases, systems are intended to exhibit modality in behavior. That is, they are expected to operate in different modes and exhibit different behaviors for different modes. A pre-condition will identify the mode required and any other conditions that must hold for the use case to be valid. This includes information such as the action requested, confirmation of user identity, values that must hold, and any other factor that affects successful conclusion of the use case.

■ Details[17]

A use case describes the details about how a system provides some service. The details of a use case identify the details of the sequences of interactions. The details are captured as step-by-step interactions among domain objects. Each step provides sufficient detail to identify which entities are involved, what each entity does, and the result of the step. This can be accomplished using text or sequence diagrams.

■ Postconditions

The execution of a use case is intended to bring about some desired computation or state. The postconditions identify exactly what results are expected from execution of the use case. This includes any side-effects produced — such as any objects created and all objects destroyed. We recommend that the following be specified:

■ Instance creation or destruction
■ Relations (association and aggregation) formed or broken
■ Value changes in variables
■ State changes (including final state)

■ Exceptions

Every action performed in a use case is susceptible to error. Desired data may not be located, computations might be aborted, and connectivity may be lost. It is necessary to identify all possible errors that can occur in the use case. In addition, it is useful to identify the specific actions to be taken to recover. Hence, for each exception we wish to know the circumstance in which it can occur and the action that should be taken.

■ Constraints

It is also necessary to identify all constraints that might apply to the use case. Such constraints can be on the values being manipulated, resources allocated to it, and resource allocations to various steps. There are usually the invariant conditions (i.e., the conditions that must always be true). The invariant conditions must hold at the beginning (precondition) of the service (operation) and at the end (postcondition) of the service (operation). Violation of these constraints can also give rise to errors, and these errors should be identified as an exception.

---

[17] The details section is not developed for high-level use cases.

■ Variants/Alternatives

It is also necessary to identify all variations that might apply to the use case. These are usually the variations that are not covered by independent use cases. Usually these variations are either easily handled or they are considered as part of another use case.

Of course, the actual information that is captured in a specific use case will vary according to several factors. In particular, it will vary on whether it is (1) high-level or low-level and (2) essential or concrete. Table 4-1 summarizes the information that is typically developed for common kinds of use cases that are developed.

Table 4-1 correlates information with the various kinds of use cases. It can be used to guide the development of a use case. For example, the development of high-level, primary, essential use cases requires that one identify:

■ The essential business information (i.e., establish the business value proposition),
■ The preconditions that must apply for the use case to complete,
■ The post-conditions that are promised, and
■ any constraints or variations that might exist.

According to Table 4-1, one will not be identifying relationships among use cases, details, or exceptions, as this information is not appropriate for this kind of use case.

TABLE 4-1   Information Associated with the Different Kinds of Use Cases[a]

	High-Level Primary Essential[b]	Low-Level Primary & Secondary Essential	Low-Level Primary Concrete	Low-Level Primary & Secondary Concrete
Actors	B	B	B,T	B,T
Relations		R		R
Preconditions	E	E	E	E
Details	H	H	D	D
Postconditions	E	E	E	E
Exceptions		A		A
Constraints	A	A	A	A
Variants	A	A	A	A

[a] Key to table entries: B—essential business information; T—essential technological information; R—essential information describing relationships among primary and secondary, extending, and included use cases; E— essential information; H — high-level information about the interaction between system and actors; D—detailed concrete information that applies to use cases that are not generalizations; A—information included as appropriate for the specific use case (not all use cases will have exceptions, constraints, or variations).

[b] Included or extending use cases follow the guidelines for the kind of use case to which they are related.

Use Case Bundles

Use case bundles are collections of use cases that are highly correlated with some activity or organizing business element. They make sense only when the business value being provided by a system necessitates significant functionality such as might be found in a fly-by-wire aircraft system, computer aided design (CAD) program, or software for a telecommunications switch.[18] To facilitate understanding, a domain can be partitioned into smaller units such that we gain insight into the whole domain by studying the parts. Some basic criteria for bundling use cases into a package are described in the following list. It is highly likely that the wording of the simple descriptions of the use cases will clearly indicate which of the criteria is best for establishing use case bundles.

- Same Actor-Same State

  An extremely simple package is achieved by bundling together all use cases initiated by the same actor in the same state of the system. Since a large system can have a number of different states from which different actors make requests. Such a packaging scheme will often result in a balanced set of bundles that encompass a reasonable number of use cases each.

- Common Entities

  Many times it makes more sense to bundle according to the use cases that deal with the same entities. In this case, multiple actors may be involved in managing different aspects of the same entity. For example, a web-based store front may have a component of the software that deals with customer orders. In this case, we may have actors that input those orders (customers), actors that bill against orders (credit card transaction system), actors (shipping clerks) that ship orders, and actors who wish to tailor the inventory to best support customers (managers). The one thread that binds all of these actors together is "orders" and "order management." Bundling together all of these use cases makes sense, particularly when there is another entity (such as "product" and "product management") that is the focus of many actors as well. Such bundling focuses on common elements.

- Specific Workflow

  Alternatively, a system that supports actors in doing their jobs can be bundled using workflow. In this situation, a bundle describes a set of activities that are performed by a single actor in the course of performing some aspect of his or her job. The use cases describe different paths through the workflow. This approach to bundling use cases is similar to the viewpoints approach.[19]

---

[18] Systems that have extensive user interfaces occasionally fall into this category. Visual editing and multimedia programs in which one can place many business objects, establish relationships among them, edit the model, validate the model, and distribute the model among many individuals are complex enough that there are many sequences of events that can occur.

[19] The viewpoints approach is based on viewing a system from an ethnographic studies perspective. It emphasizes how an individual works to solve a problem.

Documenting Use Cases

AN important aspect of use cases is documenting them in a fashion that provides greater understanding of the domain. Because a picture is worth a thousand words, a highly useful and informative way to document use cases is to use the UML notation.

Use Case Diagram

A use case diagram shows how use cases are related to each other and to actors. An example use case diagram is illustrated in Figure 4-3. An actor is illustrated as a stick figure person, even in external system situations. Individual use cases are represented as ovals labeled with the name of the use case. Lines connect actors with the use case they initiate or connect the use cases with the participating actors from which the system makes requests. If the interaction is unidirectional, the line is terminated by an arrow. The direction of the arrow is from the requestor to the provider of a service. In the example, the bank manager makes a request of the system, which makes a request of the account database.

In some situations, the interaction is bidirectional and the link is illustrated as a double-headed arrow. In this case, the actor can generate a request of the system or it can request the actor to take some action. This might be the case in which the manager wants to monitor specific accounts for specific activities and the system generates alerts

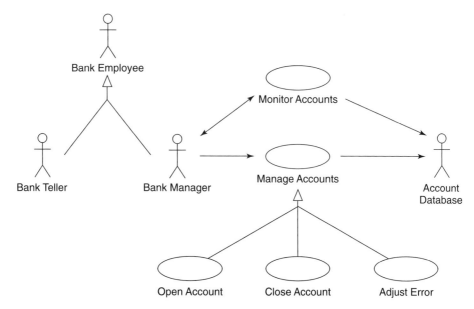

FIGURE 4-3 An example use case diagram illustrating actor generalization/specialization, use case generalization/specialization, and bi-directional interaction between a use case and an actor.

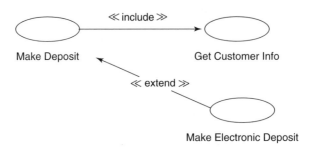

FIGURE 4-4   Representing the <<extend>> and <<include>> relations between use cases in UML.

requesting manager attention when specific events occur. The system may perform periodic queries against the account database to identify when the event occurs.

Use case and actor generalizations/specializations that were previously identified are also documented in use case diagrams. The relationship is illustrated with a triangle at the end of a line. The lines originate at the specializations and point with the triangle toward the generalization. In the example, the actor bank employee is a generalization of the specialization actors bank teller and bank manager. The idea here is that some use cases (look up account balance, change customer address, etc.) can be performed by either a bank manager or a bank teller.

UML has a mechanism for illustrating supporting use cases; i.e., a notation for the extends and includes relationships. A dashed arrow is drawn between the supporting use case and the use case that it supports with the arrow labeled by the kind of relationship being represented. The direction of the arrow indicates the direction of the relationship. For use cases that extend another, the arrow points from the extending use case. The arrow points toward the included use case. This is illustrated in Figure 4-4. The Make Deposit use case includes the Get Customer Info use case. The Make Electronic Deposit extends the Make Deposit use case by adding functionality.

Sequence Diagram: Documenting the Details

The details of a use case can be documented utilizing sequence diagrams.[20] A sequence diagram shows the order in which messages are exchanged between the actor(s) and the system. The sequence diagram has the participants represented by rectangular boxes. From that rectangular box, there is an extended vertical, dashed line. Message exchanges between participants are illustrated as directed arrows and are labeled by the message being communicated. The sequence of messages is read from the top down. Thus, time elapses from top to bottom. When the dashed line is

---

[20] Sequence diagrams are discussed further in Chapter 7.

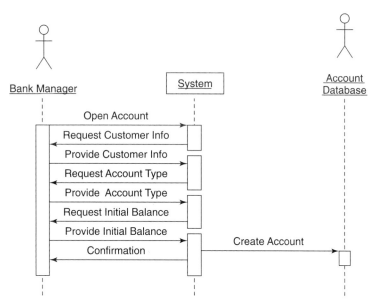

FIGURE 4-5 Sequence diagram illustrating the detailed interaction between the system and actors for the Open Account use case.

replaced with a rectangle, this means that the object is active and using resources during that time period.

An example of a sequence diagram capturing the open account use case is illustrated in Figure 4-5. This example shows how a bank manager requests the system to create a new account. The system asks for information about the customer, which the bank manager provides. The system then requests the bank manager to identify the type of account, which the bank manager provides. The system requests the initial balance information, which the bank manager provides. Once all of the information has been acquired, the system requests the account database to create a new account. The bank manager is then informed by the system that an account has been successfully created.

Textual Description

In addition to graphical representations of use cases, it is common practice to use textual descriptions of individual use cases. A textual description contains the information identified in the previous section. A typical template is illustrated in Figure 4-6. The key value of textual descriptions is that more information is captured than in graphical descriptions. As a result, most practitioners use a combination of use case diagrams to provide an overview of the system, sequence diagrams to capture the interactions, and textual descriptions to capture the pre-conditions, postconditions, exceptions, invariant conditions, and variations.

Use Case Name

Description: A one- or two-sentence description of the use case.

Actors: Identifies the actors participating in the use case.

Includes: Identifies the use cases included in it.

Extends: Identifies the use case that it may extend.

Preconditions: Identifies the conditions that must be met to invoke this use case.

Details: Identifies the details of the use case.

Postconditions: Identifies the conditions that are assured to hold at the conclusion of the use case.

Exceptions: Identifies any exceptions that might arise in execution of this use case.

Constraints: Identifies any constraints that might apply.

Variants: Identifies any variations that might hold for the use case.

Comments: Provides any additional information that might be important in this use case.

FIGURE 4-6   Template for documenting use cases.

Guidelines for Developing Use Cases

THIS section presents a set of practices the authors have found useful in developing use case descriptions. The guidelines are presented here to help avoid analysis paralysis. Analysis paralysis occurs when the analyst is unable to write any scenarios or creates too many detailed scenarios. The purpose of use case modeling is to understand the external behavior of the system. The later stages will be much easier if the up-front requirements are clear and unambiguous.

The following sections provide guidelines for problem areas that many people encounter when trying to develop use case descriptions. The basic areas are:

- Avoiding Analysis Paralysis
- Identifying Actors
- Identifying High-level and Essential Use Cases
- Establishing Use Case Bundles
- Developing Use Case Details
- Identifying Supporting Use Cases
- Developing Boundary Use Cases

Avoiding Analysis Paralysis

The following guidelines are specifically targeted to avoid analysis paralysis:

1. Write two or three of the most common simple transactions first.
2. Try to create more "abstract" scenarios when two or three scenarios look very similar.
3. Be cautious of creating more than 30 use cases to cover the fundamental system actions.

4. Additional use cases for unusual events should be chosen with care and kept to a manageable number.

5. Perform the analysis in an incremental fashion. First develop a primary, high-level, essential use case model. Second, use that model to develop a primary and secondary, low-level, essential use case model. Third, use the resulting model to guide development of the primary, low-level, concrete use cases. Finally, use that model to develop primary and secondary, low-level, concrete use cases.

6. Within a model, develop it iteratively. Provide very brief descriptions initially and then refine them.

Identifying Actors

It is critical to identify all external entities that will interact with the system. Each external entity is an actor. As actors are identified, they must be documented. In particular, we must identify all of the responsibilities that each has to fulfill using the system or must provide to the system. This helps identify the set of actions that the actor will take with regard to the system. Some guidelines follow:

1. Identify the actors first, then document their responsibilities. This prevents us from getting too involved in documenting one actor and forgetting others.

2. Focus efforts on actors that initiate actions on the system. These are the easiest actors to identify and, if not identified here, are likely to remain missed for a long time. Other actors from which requests are made will show up later in the process if missed here.

3. Identify the different roles that a single individual might take with respect to the system and introduce actors for each role. This helps identify different modes of operation that the system might have to exhibit.

It is often difficult to identify all actors that interact with a system. In this section, four high-level categories of users are discussed to help give a systematic way of identifying actors:

■ Users

Although we can think of a specific individual as a user, we want to view these individuals with respect to the role that they play with respect to the system. Thus, a person who adds data, uses the data, and generates reports is acting in three different roles that will be reflected as three different actors. It is easy to overlook individuals who employ the system. Given the large variety of roles for possible users, we can only give a short list of use subcategories that may be helpful:

- ■ Targeted end-users
- ■ Administrators
- ■ Managers
- ■ Customers[21]

---

[21] The authors have worked on systems in which the customer required (demanded) an interface that would enable them to gain insights into the system and how the users employ it. Despite the cost and effort in creating those interfaces, most of them were never used by anyone other than system testers.

Each of these subcategories can describe different individuals and encompass multiple actors to capture the various roles of each individual.

■ Applications

All external applications (both individual processes and software systems) that interact with the system are actors.[22] For the moment, we must ignore machine boundaries because they have not been established. This means that applications that will eventually run on the same platform as our system are treated as external applications from the perspective of our system boundaries.

Care must be taken to establish if different processes of a given external system are directly involved, as each of those will be a separate actor. Do not include processes within the hypothetical system being described (even if you think they will be there) because the purpose here is to establish the application domain. That is, we wish to draw a boundary between the application and the outside world.

■ Devices

Identify all devices that interact with the system. Normally, this does not include things like monitors, keyboards, mice, and other standard user interface types of devices.[23] Instead, we are talking about external sensors and actuators.

■ External Events (e.g., Cron)

As we are building more real-time and asynchronous interactive systems, the recognition of external events as potential actors is becoming more important. For example, it is a common situation that a system activity is initiated by the passage of time. As a result, time can be treated as though it were an actor. The authors call that actor Cron after the UNIX mechanism for invoking functionality at particular times.[24] While Cron may be implemented as a timer within the completed system, the timer is still driven by a clock external to the program. Cron can be used to capture periodic activities and timeouts. If more than one periodic trigger is needed, then multiple Cron actors can be introduced.

These categories are to be used to help identify actors in a system manner. These categories are common enough across systems that using them as a trigger will allow discovery of actors.

---

[22] This does not include the services of the operating system or the framework. Instead, we are talking about business applications that the system may need to interact with to accomplish its business goals.

[23] User interface devices are important if one is developing user interface frameworks. Generally, one can assume that an appropriate set of framework classes will handle the interaction with these devices. It is recognized that some people treat devices as interfaces to actors. This practice allows a single sensor to serve several different roles with respect to the system.

[24] Cron is named after the titan Cronus, the son of Uranus and Gaea. He was the Greek god of fate.

Identifying High-level and Essential Use Cases

From a modeling perspective, a use case must capture the series of interactions between an actor and the system that achieves some useful business goal for the initiator of the interaction. The identification of responsibilities of the actors is a good base from which to find reasons for the actor to interact with the system. For all actors, ask the following questions:

- What are the processes that they participate in that achieves some business goal?
- How in the process do they use the services of the system to complete their tasks in achieving the goal?
- What are the fundamentally different processes that they participate in?
- What is the initial event that starts the process?
- What is the event that starts the series of interactions with the system?

Each process that will achieve a useful business goal is definitely one use case. The other fundamentally different processes in which they participate usually result in other use cases. Although the standard practice of documenting use cases is to start from the external event to the system, in certain circumstances, one may want to document the use case from the external event to the actor.

For documenting the use cases identified, one can simply construct a table[25] of (1) the name of the use case, (2) the initiating actor, (3) the service request to event (action) that an actor initiates, (4) a short description, and (5) the business goal of that initial service request or event. This table is used to develop the use cases. There will be at least one use case for each event; but in certain circumstances, more than one use case may be needed to capture the necessary information.

While it is our goal to identify all use cases that each actor can initiate, it is often the case that some uses of the system will be overlooked. As a result, this table will be updated with new entries as the use case model is further developed in later steps.

Some simple guidelines for performing this step follow:

1. When identifying the use cases, give a descriptive name and a one- or two-sentence description of each. Name use cases based upon the goal the actor is attempting to achieve and, if necessary, to distinguish variations in the circumstance in which it is invoked. Use a verb to start the name of the use case. The one- or two-sentence description serves to identify the approximate interaction that is to be captured in the use case. All of this information should appear as separate columns in the table.

2. Do not jump ahead and use the template described in a later step of this approach as your sole mechanism for documenting these use cases. It is necessary to get a good overview of the use cases (such as provided in a table) to accomplish the next steps.

---

[25] The authors also add economic value to the customer, frequency of use, and usage distribution to this table to help prioritize the use cases (corresponding to feature) and to size performance requirements.

3. Do not introduce too much detail in the basic descriptions. It is normal for a description to seem trivial by the time one completes documenting a use case. The value of keeping it simple is to give us a mental nudge when we are bogged down in details later.

4. It is important to distinguish the service request or event notification the actor is initiating from the manner (action) in which the actor invokes the request or event notification. In many cases, the same service request can be invoked in multiple fashions: by keystrokes, menu items, or buttons. However, the resulting activities of the system are identical. It is this later component that we are attempting to capture in use cases.

5. Avoid technology-dependent use cases[26] (load, save, startup, and shutdown) at this point in time. We are still addressing business use cases. There is not enough information available to effectively identify appropriate behavior. These use cases will be the last ones to be developed because we must wait until sufficient details are known to identify what information must be initialized during startup and preserved during shutdown.

6. Identify general activities first. These general activities constitute high-level use cases that are actually defined by a set of low-level use cases.[27] The low-level use cases are where the specific activities are identified. (Example, managing accounts is a high-level use case, while adding an account, updating an account, and deleting an account are low-level use cases that establish detailed activities for managing an account.)

7. Immediately document actors identified as a result of describing a use case. These actors will need to be documented in terms of what actions they are required to provide.

8. If multiple actors can initiate the same set of actions, introduce an abstract actor of which all the others are specializations. This simplifies development of the use cases later and also provides insight into various degrees of access to system functionality that various individuals are provided.

Establishing Use Case Bundles

This activity is optional and should only be performed if one is dealing with a very large-scale system that involves hundreds of use cases.[28] Getting a handle on them all can be a daunting task. The goal is to partition the use cases into meaningful packages that can be understood. Each package constitutes a context.

---

[26] According to some experts, there are various kinds of use cases. For the use case experts, we are working on essential use cases and not on real use cases at this time.

[27] There is great controversy over which use cases need to be documented. We suggest that you use common sense instead of following some insane rules with a million exceptions. The use case is to help us bound the business domain and ease design. Do document the use cases that are consistent with these goals.

[28] Even with 30 use cases, it is not unusual for the context diagram to span multiple pages. The placement of use cases on the various pages can follow the same guidelines presented here.

In this activity, we must adopt a set of criteria that produces an effective organization of the use cases. The criteria identified in the section where context was introduced should be considered. Some things to keep in mind when selecting criteria by which to develop bundles follow:

- No use case bundle should contain an excessive number of use cases (such as might result from describing the whole system). This defeats the purpose of partitioning the domain in the first place.

- It is also not particularly useful to have bundles that only contain one or two use cases. Again, this defeats the purpose of partitioning the use cases. We won't be able to see the forest for all of the trees.

- The bundles have to make sense from a domain perspective. It doesn't help to have disparate use cases bundled together without some underlying aspect of the domain unifying them all.

Developing Use Case Details

Once we have identified the use cases and organized them into meaningful bundles, we can begin to develop detailed descriptions of each use case. Work with one bundle at a time, as documented in your context diagram. Often, if these cases are well-developed, some members of a development team can proceed with other analysis activities while the remaining bundles are being documented.

We suggest using the template illustrated in Figure 4-6. It captures all of the information associated with use cases, organizes that information in a fashion consistent with how details are identified, and provides a comments section where additional information can be recorded. Use of this template helps assure that all use cases are documented in exactly the same fashion. Some basic guidelines follow:

1. When filling out the template, do not leave portions of the document blank that you have established do not apply. An appropriate notation should appear in that portion—this lets others know that it has actually been considered.

2. Start each use case on a new page. In actual practice, use cases get rewritten many times before they become stable. Starting a new use case on a new page allows us to print only the changed case without getting the following use cases disorganized or killing an extra tree by printing out all of the use cases.

3. Think of the use case description from the actor's perspective.

4. Emphasize interactions (service requests) and events between the system and the actor without decomposing the internal processing of the system.

5. Discussion of internal processing or design decision may be necessary and is permissible (by our practical use of this technique) to find participating actors, but it should be done with the understanding of the consequences (i.e., early design commitment) and must be documented in the details section.

6. Variations of the use case that will not be covered with independent use cases should also be documented in the variant section.

Additional Details for Primary and Secondary, Essential, High-level Use Cases.   As stated previously, use cases are easiest to develop in an iterative fashion. In each iteration, the goal is to provide greater detail about the use case. If one is using the template just presented, the first few passes will concentrate on the top half of the template. In particular, we focus on the following sections of the template: Actors, Includes, Extends, Preconditions, and Postconditions. This allows us to develop details and get them in a steady state before we tackle the lower half of the template, which is closely related to the upper half. Some guidelines to following during the early iterations follow:

1. Start simple and slowly introduce complexity. Focus first on the simple case where everything is perfect and no problems exist. It is not a bad idea to give a very brief set of details initially for each use case, focusing only on course features. This allows one to identify supporting use cases that simplify the process by extracting common details into other use cases.

2. Worrying about screens can lead to difficulty in writing the use case. Often, one gets about halfway through the use case and then starts describing what some screen looks like. The description can go on for pages if the screen layout is complex. Instead, one should only identify the objects present on the screen. Even then, only focus on those that apply to the use case. Don't worry about the layout of the buttons and fields on the screen. It is the interaction with the screen that is important in the use case. That can be done as a figure in the comment section of the use case description or in a separate description from the use case.

3. Including lots of ifs and jumps in the details interferes with understanding the domain. Almost everyone has heard of spaghetti code, but using ifs and jumps in use cases leads to spaghetti text. The problems are the same between spaghetti code and spaghetti text—no one can understand what is intended (not even the author).

4. It is important to label each step appearing within the details section of the template with a number. This allows us to make cross-references to that step in other sections of the use case (and across use cases). This is extremely significant when it comes to identifying exceptions and constraints.

Additional Details for Primary and Secondary, Concrete, Low-level Use Cases. When dealing with primary and secondary, concrete, low-level use cases, we are introducing details that border on design. At this point, we are looking into the structure of the system rather than the system itself. For example, some messages may be translated into service requests on domain objects that are captured within the system. If we have an account object, then we may include within the use case details a statement to the effect that the account object is sent an update message. Some guidelines that apply for these use cases follow:

1. The development of these use cases should only be attempted by individuals with significant design skills. An extremely common problem encountered is for a poor design to be specified in these use cases.

2. Frequent use of the word system in each detailed description indicates another problem. Usually, there is an element missing from the design. This missing element is often a control object that manages an interaction among many different objects. If these control objects are not introduced into the model, the result is a bloated system object that has to manage interactions among hundreds of objects.

3. For each step in the details section, identify what errors or alternatives can occur. Each error is examined in terms of what actions should be taken to keep the model consistent. The information necessary to identify what actions should be taken is often clear from the context in which the error occurs.

4. Capture exceptions in a table that includes three columns: the step in which the error occurs, a label for the error, and the actions that should be performed. As was the case with the details section, it is useful to number each step in the actions to be performed (starting at 1 for each exception).

5. If the detail section of a use case includes another use case, identify all of the exceptions that the included use case can throw for that step. This allows the including use case to identify the error condition to which it must react. Of course, these exceptions will be identified in the exceptions section of the description for the included use case.

Identifying Supporting Use Cases

Supporting use cases are use cases that are included in other use cases or extend another use case. We are concerned with three types different kinds of use cases: included, extending, and generalizing. Some guidelines for identifying and using supporting use cases follow:

1. View includes as a relation that identifies a use case that acts like a subroutine to other use cases. Typically, included use cases will not have actors that initiate them. We can consider these use cases as inheriting actors.

2. The preconditions section of the use case description should identify what information is required for this use case to execute normally. If we are writing a "save" use case, one piece of information that might be required is the filename.

3. In some cases, a number of use cases all share a common structure with the exception of some minor additional steps. These cases can be simplified as an extension of a common core use case. In this case, the use case exploits the details of another use case and identifies where the additional details are incorporated.

4. The precondition section of a use case that extends another identifies the condition that determines if the extension should be invoked.

5. In some cases, the same general activity may take place in several use cases, but have significantly different details depending upon the entities that participate in them. Even though generalizations should have been identified earlier than this point, it is still a good idea to examine the use cases to determine if new generalizations can be added.

Developing Boundary Use Cases[29]

The most common situation encountered among people writing use cases for the first time is that they immediately start writing use cases for starting and stopping the system. The main problem is that they don't even know what the system is to do, yet they are worried about what initialization activities have to take place. Some guidelines to establish when boundary use cases should be developed follow:

1. Initialization activities are highly design-dependent. If one is developing essential use cases, then there will not be sufficient information to identify what actions should be performed during startup and shutdown. These events should not be developed for essential use cases.

2. If one is developing concrete use cases, the boundary use cases should only be addressed once all of the essential and secondary use cases have been developed. At this point, one has sufficient detail to identify if connections to external actors should be created during initialization or not; whether specific structural details have to be constructed, and so on.

Contracts

CONTRACTS are a mechanism that was introduced by Bertrand Meyers in the development of Effiel to develop reliable, extensible, and reusable software modules. The idea has been adopted by others in the development of the BON method for object-oriented analysis and design.

The basic idea is that a contract is a formal agreement that expresses the rights and obligations between a client and a provider of a service. The contract establishes the conditions under which a service is provided. It identifies what conditions (precondition) the client must satisfy for the request to successfully complete and what the provider of a service guarantees for a result (postcondition) if the precondition was met. It can be summarized as follows:

> If a calling routine promises to call our service with the precondition satisfied, then the service (method) promises to return a final state in which the postcondition is satisfied.

The reliability concept of contracts is based on the following principles:

- A software system or software element is not correct or incorrect per se.

  A software system or element can only be consistent or inconsistent with its specification.

  Correctness should actually be applied to the software and its specification.

---

[29] The authors use the term *boundary* to indicate an activity that occurs at the beginning and end of system activities.

- For a program to be correct, any execution of it starting in the state where the precondition is true will result in a state where the postcondition is true.
- The precondition states the properties that must hold before the service is called. Meeting the postcondition is the obligation of the caller.
- The postcondition states the properties that must hold after the service has executed. This is the obligation of the method being executed.
- Under no circumstances shall the body of the service (method) ever test for the preconditions. This prevents unnecessary defensive programming.
- Assertions are not an input-checking mechanism. A precondition is a software routine to software routine specification. It will not handle human errors.
- Assertions are not control structures. Assertions are not used for flow control. A run-time assertion violation is a bug in the program.
- Every feature appearing in a precondition must be available to every client; i.e., the client must be able to validate each feature of a precondition.
- Invariant conditions must be satisfied by both the constructors and all of the methods.

The use of contracts changes development from a defensive programming activity to a trusted programming activity.

A simple example for computing the square root of a number illustrates the use of contracts. The conventional approach taken in defining a subroutine for computing the square root captures two separate tasks: (1) finding and returning the square root when passed a non-negative number and (2) returning something reasonable when passed a negative number. The first task is well understood. The second task, though, is not. The key problem is that the supplier doesn't know what constitutes a reasonable result from the perspective of the requester.

In a perfect world, preconditions and postconditions would be all that is necessary is establish guaranteed services. However, the real world is another matter. For example, connections between two machines are lost, resources are unavailable, or a signal is received from hardware. The situations in which a service provider is unable to meet its obligations is termed a failure.

The contractual approach for dealing with failures is for the service provider to raise an exception that identifies the failure. This provides a consistent error-handling approach from the service provider's perspective. The exception is then handled by the client in a fashion that is appropriate for the specific client. As a result, various clients can deal with the exception in their own way.

The development of use cases identified preconditions and postconditions. These are the same preconditions and postconditions that will be used in specifying a contract. The preconditions establish the conditions that must be met by the client prior to requesting the service. The postconditions establish the result of the operation provided by the service provider assuming the precondition has been met. The operation identifies what transformation, function, or service is provided. The exceptions section of the use case description identifies the failures that the service provider admits can occur while providing a service.

From the perspective of understanding the system, the use of contracts is especially useful. The contracts identify the specific services the system will provide, what the requester of a service must assure to get the service, and what exceptions will be raised when the system fails. In short, it defines the system interface.

Recommended Approach

THIS chapter has presented use cases and contracts as a means for bounding the business domain. The recommended approach is:

1. Develop a primary, essential, high-level use case model.
2. If the business domain is not well understood, use the model of step 1 to develop a primary and secondary, essential, low-level use case model.
3. If the technology is not well understood, use the model of step 2 to develop a primary, concrete, low-level use case model.
4. If reliability is an issue, use the models of step 2 and step 3 to help develop a secondary, concrete, low-level use case model.

In developing any of these use case models, the following guidelines are recommended:

1. Write two or three of the most common, simple transactions first.
2. Try to create more "abstract" scenarios in which two or three scenarios look very similar.
3. Be cautious of creating more than 30 use cases to cover the fundamental system actions.
4. Additional use cases for unusual events should be chosen with care and kept to a manageable number.
5. Within a model, develop it iteratively. Provide very brief descriptions initially and then refine them.

Once use cases have been identified, use them to establish system-level contracts. In the contracts, identify (1) the preconditions, (2) the postconditions, (3) the operation, and (4) exceptions.

Example

The lawn-mowing example of the previous chapter was presented to demonstrate how a real-world situation could be modeled using an object-oriented way of organizing reality. Knowing or having the ability to model such a situation is not sufficient reason for building a system. It is necessary to establish a business value that justifies the initial development of this model and its transformation into a system. So what kind of business value can be established to justify a system that describes how a family deals with the situation of mowing the lawn?

In this chapter, we will generalize this situation into a home-care system. The goal of this home-care system is to acquire better insight into how and why a family spends its money.[30] The system may include other home-care activities like painting the walls, fixing the plumbing, adding extensions, replacing appliances, and other common activities. In terms of our stated business value for the system, this allows the system to capture how the home is maintained. One practical subsystem may be to track the breakage situations that cost money to repair.

In the design and implementation of this model, we will use a simulation approach to the design of the system[31]. For a standard simulation, there is one key actor: a simulation clock. The simulation clock drives the system from a time-dependent aspect. However, we want our system to also react to asynchronous events. To handle these asynchronous events, we will add another daemon called asynchronous event daemon.

This is how the two actors (or event generators) work:

- The simulation clock is a periodic timer that periodically sends a message to the system indicating the current simulation increment. The system responds to this event by informing all active objects in the simulation to perform the actions appropriate for the current time in the simulation.
- The asynchronous event daemon sends an event notification to the system when an event occurs. Anything can register an event with the asynchronous event daemon. The system responds by having all the system parts examine the environment to determine if some action needs to be taken.

For example, if the laundry is done every day at 9 P.M.; the simulation clock can be used to initiate the correct behavior. Similarly, if the washing machine breaks down (causes an event), the asynchronous event daemon can be used to notify the system. (Note that this system is very inefficient as it will still need to be observed.)

In the previous chapter, it was stated that the mother, Jane, noticed that the lawn needed mowing. Does this make Jane an actor with respect to our system? Actually, Jane is a part of our system in the sense that she is one of the objects that participates in the system. Does this make the lawn one of our actors since we could say that the lawn told Jane that it needed cutting? We could take this perspective, but that decision could lead to

---

[30] Because this is an example that we don't have to sell to management or actually implement, we are free to establish the business domain however we wish. Neither of the authors would actually want to go to management and explain that we want to implement a lawn-mower simulation.

[31] The simulation clock and the examine surroundings daemon are both examples of actors (Cron) that correspond to external events, namely the passage of time. This allows us to focus on what happens as a result of time passing without worrying about how it is implemented within the system. We also won't have spontaneous events getting generated by the system without an external source creating the conditions for creation of the event. Spontaneous events are rather difficult to explain and code.

the situation in which everything around the house is an actor, with the possible exception of the family members. We decided to have the lawn send an event to the asynchronous event daemon. Then we will assert that it was the receipt of an event (i.e., a message) from the asynchronous event daemon that caused Jane to look at the grass, observe that it was too tall and, hence, decide that it needed mowing. This, of course, assumes that Jane was outside at the time she received the message to examine her surroundings. [32]

These two actors together can drive the simulation in nonrepetitive fashion. That is, the effects of these two actors can combine. For example, the clock simulation can schedule John to activate his conditional lawn-mowing lawn service, which is state-dependent on every Saturday at 2:35 P.M. But we can also use the asynchronous event handler to change John's state by sending an event on a rainy Saturday that will prevent John from mowing the lawn that day.

To make the model effective for use cases, we will add two more actors[33]:

- Observer
- Director

The observer subscribes to and gets updates on the status of the simulation. The director sends commands to the system to control the evolution of the simulation.

Based on the preceding description, we have four actors: (1) simulation clock, (2) asynchronous event daemon, (3) observer, and (4) director. We have also identified the basic functional response of the system to messages from these actors. Now we will define them in more detail.

The functional responses of the system due to messages from the simulation clock:

- Tick:
  - The system responds by running the simulation forward one increment of simulation time.
  - The system forwards simulation information requested by the observer to the observer.

The functional response of the system due to messages from the asynchronous event daemon:

- Look:
  - The system responds by having all self-directed objects examine their surroundings and respond to any situation that they may identify by assigning and scheduling work.

---

[32] If Jane had been inside the house at the time, she might have noticed that the carpet needed vacuuming.

[33] We can also argue that a good reason for separating the two roles is that it might be possible to replace the human who is fulfilling the role of director with an external program (scenario generator). Likewise, the observer might be replaced by a system that collects data from the simulation for use in statistical studies of simulation results.

The functional responses of the system due to messages from the observer,[34]

- Subscribe:
  - The system stores the subscription so that it can start forwarding state change information to the observer.

The functional responses of the system due to messages from the director:

- Set:
  - The system sets the appropriate simulation variable.

These messages are used to trigger the primary high-level essential use cases.

The use case diagram for our use cases is given in Figure 4-7. As can be seen from the figure, we have kept the number of use cases to a minimum while capturing the key details of the system.

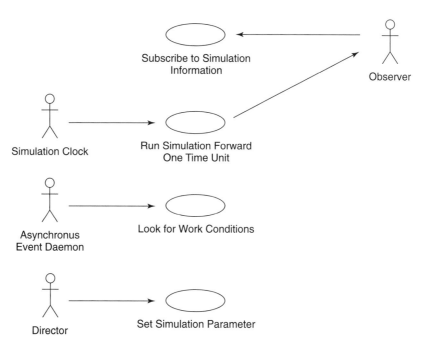

FIGURE 4-7 Use case diagram for the primary, high-level, essential use cases of the lawn mower example.

---

[34] We could add a start and stop message to be sent from the observer to the system for starting and stopping the simulation. These messages would have the effect of sending a start and stop message to the simulation clock and the observe surroundings daemon.

Look for Work

Description: This use case establishes what work is to be performed within the simulation as a result of simulated people observing the simulated surroundings.

Actors: Asynchronous Event Daemon

Preconditions: None

Details:

1. The Asynchronous Event Daemon sends a Look message to the system.
2. Every person at the home looks in the immediate surroundings for something that is not in a correct state (Check environment).
3. If a work item is identified, the work item is scheduled to be performed (Schedule work).

Postconditions: Any work items within the location of a person is scheduled to be addressed.

Comments: If we allow the observer to start and stop the simulation, then a pre-condition would be that the simulation is running.

FIGURE 4-8   Textual description of the Look for Work use case.

Run Simulation Forward One Time Unit

Description: This use case details how the simulation is kept current with the simulation time.

Actors: Simulation Clock, Observer

Preconditions: Sufficient real-time has passed from last update.

Details:

1. The Simulation Clock sends a Tick message to the system.
2. Every object computes its current state taking into account the change in simulation time.
3. The system forwards state change information to the Observer.

Postconditions: The model has been updated to reflect the new simulation time.

Comments: If we allow the observer to start and stop the simulation, then a pre-condition would be that the simulation is running.

FIGURE 4-9   Textual description for the Run Simulation Forward One Time Unit use case.

The use cases are documented textually as well. We use Table 4-1 to identify the information captured in the text. The use case descriptions are given in Figure 4-8 through Figure 4-11 The description identifies the case, provides a very high-level description of it, identifies the actors involved, the pre-conditions, the details, the post-conditions, and any comments. Those areas that do not apply (pre-conditions) are not left blank, but are filled in with appropriate notations so that we know that this aspect has been considered. In this case, we do not have any pre-conditions that must hold for the message to be handled.

Set Simulation Parameter

Description: This use case allows the simulation to be tailored based on user-settable parameters.

Actors: Director

Preconditions: None

Details:

1. The Director sends a message to the system identifying a simulation parameter and a value.
2. The System sets the simulation parameter to the new value.

Postconditions: A value of a simulation parameter is changed and the simulation continues taking into account the new value for the parameter.

Comments: Example parameters might include the real clock time between simulation clock ticks (e.g., 3 seconds must pass between ticks); the simulated time increment for the simulation clock (e.g., each tick corresponds to 1 hour), or tailor what is to occur in a simulation (e.g., it is supposed to rain on Saturday).

FIGURE 4-10   Textual description for the Set Simulation Parameter use case.

Subscribe To Simulation Information

Description: This use case describes how the system is informed about what simulation information the Observer wants from the simulation.

Actors: Observer

Preconditions: None

Details:

1. The Observer sends a Subscribe message to the system.
2. The system configures itself so that all information of the requested type is passed to the observer.

Postconditions: The system is configured to forward specific information to the observer.

Comments: None

FIGURE 4-11   Textual description for the Subscribe to Simulation Information use case.

Now that we have the simulation of Time Forward use case and the Look for Work use case, how do we develop the use case associated with mowing the lawn? The use cases that deal specifically with mowing the lawn are essential, low-level use cases that further define how the high-level functionality is achieved. We can model the mowing the lawn scenario described in the earlier chapter with three essential low-level use cases: (1) Check the Lawn, (2) Schedule Mowing the Lawn, and (3) Mowing the Grass.

If we consider the Check Environment step, we should recognize that there are quite a few specialized use cases for this high-level use case. In particular, there are different surroundings that can be examined and the examination requires that a person be in the appropriate location to observe the need. Thus, for example, when we are outside of the house, we may want to "check the lawn"; however, when we are inside the house, we may want to "check the carpet." Hence, we introduce a generalization use case, Check Environment, of which Check the Lawn is a specialization along with other use cases (for example, Check the Carpet).

The Check the Lawn use case captures the situation where Jane notices that the lawn needs cutting. This is now a specialized version[35] of Check Environment. Furthermore, the Look for Work use case will include the Check Environment use case.

In the model, Schedule the Work is also a use case that has a specialized version for the lawn by Schedule Mow the Lawn. This is done by Jane by requesting John to mow the lawn, whereby he agrees to schedule mowing the lawn that evening.

The third use case, Mow the Lawn, captures how the lawn gets mowed. It covers the details about how the father, John, involves the children, and the professional lawn mower, Jack. This is a specialization of the Take Corrective Action use case. (There are a number of other use cases of a similar nature, for example, Vacuum the Floor).

Of course, the pre-condition for the Take Corrective Action use case is that a work item has been identified. This generalization is included in the Look for Work use case to provide the functionality where a work task is scheduled to be performed once it has been identified.

A portion of the use case diagram for our system is illustrated in Figure 4-12. It shows how the Asynchronous Event Daemon triggers the Look for Work use case. This use case includes the Check Environment use case, which is a generalization for the Check the Lawn and Check The Carpet use cases. The Look for Work use case also includes the Take Corrective Action use case, which is a generalization for the Mow the Lawn and Vacuum the Carpet use cases.

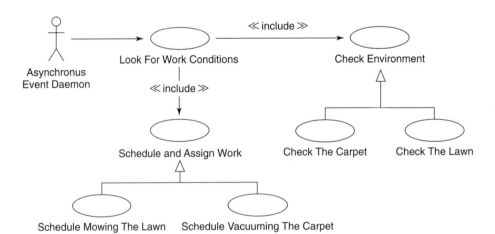

FIGURE 4-12 Portion of the use case diagram for the primary, low-level, essential use cases detailing the low-level use cases associated with the high-level use Look for Work Conditions use case.

---

[35] It should be noted that this use case is one of several specialized use cases that can potentially occur when we examine our surroundings in the Look for Work use case.

Check the Lawn

Description: This use case deals with the situation in which a person observes the lawn to determine if it needs mowing.

Actors: System

Specializes: Check Environment

Includes: None

Extends: None

Preconditions: Person must be in the vicinity of the lawn.

Details:

1. The system sends a message to the person to check the lawn.
2. The person looks at the height of the lawn.
3. If the height is greater than some value, the lawn needs mowing, otherwise it doesn't.
4. The person sends a message identifying the need to mow the lawn.

Postconditions: The need to mow the lawn is established (either it does or it doesn't).

Exceptions: None

Constraints: None

Variants: None

Comments: Should have a threshold for the height of the grass to be particular to the person.

FIGURE 4-13   **Textual description of the Check Lawn Primary Low-Level Essential use case.**

These use cases must be documented so that our understanding of what the system is doing is captured. Again, we can turn to Table 4-1 to identify the information that should be captured in primary, low-level, essential use cases. The information that we have to capture includes the name of the use case, a high-level description, any use case relationships, the preconditions, the details, the postconditions, constraints, and variants. Again, the template is employed for a textual description. An example textual description for the Check the Lawn use case is given in Figure 4-13. The other use cases discussed previously are left as an exercise for the reader.

The Check the Lawn use case demonstrates a tricky point about use cases. In particular, this is a use case that is a specialization of a use case that is included within another use case. A question arises concerning the actor that triggers it. Specifically, who is the actor? Ultimately, in this specific example, this use case is triggered as a result of a message received by the Asynchronous Event Daemon.

■ ■ SUMMARY

THIS chapter has introduced use cases as a means of bounding a domain. The fundamental concepts associated with use cases have been defined, namely the goal, system, the actors, use cases, and use case bundles. They can be summarized as follows:

The *goal* is the business value to the "user(s)" of the system who usually initiates the interaction with the system.

The *system* is the application, with all its associated hardware, that will be used by the "users." There are three standard views of the system: black box, white box, and transparent box. Use cases employs the black box view of the system in analysis.

An *actor* is external entity that interacts with a system. An actor can be a user, an external system, or a device. An actor can make a service request of the system, be requested to provide a service, and interact with the system through a complex dialog of service requests between the actor and the system.

A *use case* is a description of an interaction that achieves a useful goal for an actor. The actor that initiates the use case is called the initiation actor. In most interactions, the dialog may result in the interaction of the system with other actors; these actors are called participating actors. The interaction assumes that the system is a "black box" and uses domain elements as actors that interact with the system in a request/response manner. A use case identifies the preconditions that must exist for it to be valid, the postconditions that define the state of the system after the use case has concluded, detailed business (non-technology-dependent) that are performed, business exceptions that may arise, and business constraints that apply to the system in reacting to a specific actor request.

A *use case bundle* is a collection of use cases that are highly correlated with some activity or organizing business element. A use case bundle gives us a way to organize our use cases into collections that will help us better understand the functionality of the system that we are developing.

The various relationships that a use case may hold with other use cases have been introduced. As will be shown in the next chapter, use cases and contracts help us identify objects that will be part of our model.

CHAPTER

5

Finding the Objects

I *have a cat named Trash . . . if I were trying to sell him (at least to a computer*
scientist), I would not stress that he is gentle to humans and is self-sufficient,
living mostly on field mice. Rather, I would argue that he is object-oriented.

Roger King, *My Cat Is Object-Oriented*

The previous chapter presented use cases as a means of scoping a domain. The
material of that chapter was not directly associated with object orientation other
than the fact that UML provides a graphical representation for use cases. Use cases
apply to many different paradigms.

This chapter describes the first real step in our method for building an OO model.
We begin at a logical starting point—finding the objects.[1] We cover many different techniques for identifying objects in this chapter. The goal here is not to master all of them,
but to provide a solid background by which developers can direct their efforts. We recommend one technique, recognizing that it isn't the newest, most comprehensive, or
trendy approach. Instead, we concentrate on presenting a technique that is easy to
apply for someone new to the object-oriented paradigm.

---

[1] We are not really finding objects; we are actually finding categories and types (analysis concepts) that will
be implemented using classes and pure abstract classes.

Object-Oriented Analysis: Model of an Application Domain

WHEN we analyze systems, we create models of application domain of interest to our business. The model can be very specific and highly specialized (i.e., vendor ledger system), or can cover a whole enterprise. In either case, the model represents an aspect of reality and is built in a manner that helps us manage the complexity and understand the business reality. The model is always much simpler than reality, just as any toy model is simpler than the real thing. For example, a toy fire truck is much simpler than a real fire truck. Even sophisticated airplane models are simpler than real airplanes. In our case, however, if the model is rich enough, we can manipulate the model to help us invent or redesign our businesses.

With traditional analysis methods, we model the world using functions or behaviors as our building blocks. We have seen some of the weaknesses of such a modeling paradigm. With object-oriented analysis, we model reality with objects as our building blocks, hoping to eliminate the shortcomings of a modeling paradigm based on functions. In the object-oriented paradigm, we describe our world using the object categories (classes) or object types (pure abstract class or Java interface). We assign attributes (data variables) and services (operations, functions, methods) to these object categories (classes). We also define relationships (inheritance, association, and aggregation) between the classes. Then, we model the behavior of the world as a sequence of messages that are sent between various objects that are instances of the various object categories or object types. By using this form of analysis, we can more easily design and program the software in an object-oriented manner to achieve the benefits of flexible and maintainable software.

Building the OO Model

IN traditional textbooks, building the OO model is considered the requirements phase of the project. What makes this phase very confusing to developers is that two very distinct but related activities are taking place simultaneously: problem analysis (domain analysis) and business solution description (product description).

There are at least two reasons to keep these activities nonsequential and nonmutually exclusive. First, a large number of product developments require little or no problem analysis. Usually, problem analysis is applied only to new, difficult, or yet unsolved problems. Companies usually do not waste time or resources on a problem that is already well understood. Second, when doing problem analysis, most teams initiate the problem analysis. When some part of the problem or problem domain is well understood, the teams start to work on the business solution description to solve that part of the problem. This back-and-forth process gives the team an effective way of monitoring its own progress.

The goal of problem analysis is a relatively complete understanding of the problem and the constraints on the possible business solutions. The goals of business solution description are a correct, complete, unambiguous, verifiable, consistent, modifiable, traceable, organized, concise description of the business solution that is understandable to the customer/user/buyer. This does not mean that the goals of a business solution description are always met, but one should come close.

In problem analysis, the developers/analysts/system engineers acquire knowledge of the problem (and the problem domain) at hand and identify all of the possible constraints on the problem's solution. Much of the time is spent interviewing users and business/domain experts and brainstorming ideas. During this period, there is considerable expansion of information and knowledge about the problem to be solved. The issues that need to be addressed during this activity are (1) finding a way of trading off constraints, and (2) finding ways to organize the plethora of information and knowledge acquired.

In a business solution description, the developers/analysts/system engineers make some of the difficult decisions on constraint trade-offs and describe the external behavior of the product to be built. In this activity (1) ideals are organized, (2) conflicting views are resolved, and (3) inconsistencies and ambiguities are eliminated.

The end result of problem analysis and business solution description should be a model that:

- Organizes the data into objects and classes, and gives the data a structure via relationships of inheritance, aggregation, and association
- Specifies local functional behaviors and defines their external interfaces (service prototypes)
- Captures control or global behavior (event trace diagrams)
- Captures constraints (limits and rules)

In our version of object-oriented analysis, we do not differentiate between problem analysis and business solution description; we build a model of reality that should capture both. This is consistent with the idea that a good and effective method should have seamless steps and preferably no transformation from one step to another. The first step in this method is finding the objects.

Identification of Objects

IDENTIFYING objects (and classes)[2] is the most important and difficult step in any object-oriented method. Identifying them is important because the requirements specification, design, and code will use them as the building blocks; mistakes in properly identifying them will have an impact on the extensibility and maintainability of the software. Identifying them is difficult (at least for most beginners) as it requires in-depth knowledge and skill in the object-oriented paradigm and the ability to apply it to the applications. It typically takes 3 months to 1 year of practice for the necessary skills to mature, but can take longer depending on the person's attitude (toward object orientation), aptitude, and amount of on-the-job training/experience.

In theory, identifying objects and classes should not be difficult. We deal with objects and classes every day of our lives. For example, a child's toy (a toy fire truck or

---

[2] Technically, a class is also an object. In the next few chapters, we will treat a class like an object. For the experienced reader, we are really interested in finding classes and not instances of a class in this chapter.

a doll) is merely a model of a real world entity (a truck or a person). The toy fire truck has attributes that are either constant (i.e., height, width, color) or variable (i.e., battery level and relative state of newness or disrepair), as well as services (i.e., move forward, move backward, turn on siren). It also has exception conditions such as battery drained, broken wheel, etc.

Making mental models and using abstractions are standard human approaches for dealing with the complexity of everyday life. Therefore, if software professionals understand their application domain, identifying objects and classes requires merely capturing the relevant models/abstractions of the application domain needed to solve the problem. Then why is identification still so difficult?

The biggest problem is that developers have been taught and have been practicing a much less natural and less powerful approach to software development—the functional approach (structured analysis and functional decomposition). As mentioned earlier, due to the limitations of computers and programming languages, developers needed to use a paradigm that mimicked a computer. This resulted in a functional approach to modeling reality that focused on the procedural step-by-step operations.

With human inertia, it is now very difficult for experienced developers to break this habit, especially because functional approaches are unnatural (until the skill is developed) and developers have spent years honing that skill. Furthermore, thinking in terms of objects in everyday life may appear to be easy and natural, but thinking about software development analogies in terms of objects will take some time. When developers first apply an object-oriented method, they are often unsure of what constitutes a software object or class. Even when they know the definition, they are not always sure that something meets the definition of an object or a class.

This difficulty has provoked a philosophical debate and much confusion. There are basically two fundamentally different views of how objects and classes came to being: empiricist and phenomenalist. The empiricist view says that they are out there just waiting to be perceived. According to Betrand Meyers, "the objects are just there for the picking." Therefore, developers must be blinded to them because they are too accustomed to functional decomposition and are still trying to use functions as their building blocks.

The phenomenalist view says that objects come from both the world and our consciousness through a dialectical process. Other phenomenalists suggest that real-world objects are a reflection of social relations and human thinking processes.

We are members of the phenomenalist school. Not only do we believe that objects come from our consciousness, but we must also now "objectify" the world to get maximum benefit from this new technology. It is this "objectifying" that makes object identification difficult, even for experienced object-oriented analysts.

Over the past 10 years, object-oriented practitioners and researchers have developed many techniques (often indirect) to combat this issue. These techniques were based on the assumption that there is a mapping (hopefully, one-to-one) between things that neophytes can identify as well as objects and/or classes that neophytes have difficulty recognizing. This allows the object-oriented neophytes to do useful work while acquiring the skills and experiences to make the full paradigm shift to the object-oriented approach.

Different methodologists have their own favorite approaches, and many of these techniques are tightly coupled to a few approaches. Most books and articles discuss only a small number of these identification techniques, and some approaches are rarely taught. Some of the techniques are well suited for object-oriented design,[3] but are less useful during object-oriented domain analysis (i.e., requirements analysis). Some techniques are safe in the sense that they identify minimally false objects and are easy to use, but will identify only the obvious objects and classes.

Because there is not necessarily an easy one-to-one mapping between objects and classes with "other things," all of these techniques have shortcomings, namely, that using these techniques may produce false-positive identification and that none of these techniques provide a complete list of objects.[4] We believe that there neither is nor will be a technique that will help us find all of the objects and only all of the objects. This is consistent with our phenomenalist view; we believe that we will mature our perception of reality via a dialectical process because the real world of objects is a reflection of social relations and our thinking processes. As with most things, it is the responsibility of your management and yourself to manage this risk.

These techniques then give us a list of potential objects, albeit an incomplete list, and may be divided into two categories: current and traditional. Current techniques are the most effective and state-of-the-art, although they require significant training and experience to be used effectively. Traditional techniques are usually highly indirect and are easy to use and misuse, especially for beginners. Miscellaneous techniques are limited in scope, but useful given the right situation.

Current Techniques

CURRENT techniques rely on experience and knowledge of the domain to be captured in the object model. They cover the range from using the things to be modeled to extending existing models of the domain.

Using the Things to be Modeled

This is the preferred method of experienced object-oriented software engineers. It recognizes that the application domain entities need to be identified before identifying the corresponding objects and classes. This technique is advocated by such noted authors as Coad and Yourdon (1991), Shlaer and Mellor (1992), and so on.

This technique is highly effective because it is natural, direct, and reliable. Unfortunately, it tends to help only in finding the terminators and other tangible objects that are the easiest entities to identify. Abstract classes are not readily identified using this technique. Furthermore, this technique requires that the user makes the paradigm shift to the object-oriented mindset. Although this paradigm shift should be the ultimate goal, on-the-job training may be very expensive.

---

[3] In our definition of design, we mean modeling the technology domain.

[4] For example, all of the abstractions of concepts or ideas that need to be modeled as objects.

The steps of this technique are to:

1. Identify individual or group things, such as persons, roles, organizations, locations, logs, reports, forms, etc. in the application domain that is to be modeled.
2. Identify the corresponding objects and classes.

Using the Definitions of Objects and Classes

This technique assumes that the most effective approach is a direct approach and that the software engineer has experience in identifying objects and classes. The technique is very simple; the developer uses object abstraction, knowledge of the application domain, and the definition of class to intuitively identify them. This is the same way experienced developers would recognize functional and process abstractions.

This is a direct and effective approach that provides the best partitioning of the requirements into classes. When used properly, this technique produces the fewest false-positive identifications. This technique has no limitations, but it requires a significant paradigm shift for the developer.

This paradigm shift requires significant training, practice, intuition, and experience, which usually takes at least 6 months of on-the-job training. Moreover, there are no tricks or tools to help in this technique; the tools are designed only to document the results.

Using Object Decomposition

This technique assumes that many objects and classes are aggregates of component objects and classes. Furthermore, it assumes that decomposition is a good way to identify the component objects and classes and that you have some of these aggregate objects or classes identified.

The steps of this technique are:

1. Find the aggregate objects or classes.
2. Use object decomposition to identify their component objects or classes.

This technique is a natural way to deal with aggregates; unfortunately, not all objects and/or classes are aggregates or components of an aggregate. Furthermore, real-world aggregates normally physically contain their components; and because of this property, novices often nest the implementation components within this aggregate when an association relationship may be a better model of the implementation components. This can lead to both subtle modeling issues and technical issues such as recompilation, reuse, and maintenance.

Using Generalization

Generalization assumes that objects are identified prior to their classes, that every object is an instance of some class, and that the commonalities among objects can be used to generalize classes.

The steps of this technique are:

1. Identify all objects.
2. Look for two or more objects that share the same attributes and services.
3. Generalize these common aspects to form a class.
4. To continue finding classes, see "Using Subclasses."

The primary benefit of this approach is that it promotes reuse and supports the development of one or more classification hierarchies.

Using Subclasses

When using subclasses, we skip finding objects and directly start identifying classes. It assumes that separate classes often contain common resources (i.e., attributes, services, methods, etc.) and that they can be changed into subclasses that inherit the common resources from a common superclass.

The steps of this technique are:

1. Identify classes that share common resources (i.e., attributes, methods, service name, aggregation relationship, association relationship, etc.).
2. Factor out the common resources to form a superclass (parent), and then use inheritance for all classes that share these resources to form simpler subclasses.

The key benefit of this technique is reuse, but it has some serious drawbacks. When misused, it leads to unmaintainable and opaque classes that reuse randomly unrelated resources that do not logically belong to subclasses of the same superclass. It also may produce inappropriate or excessive inheritance coupling.

Using Object-Oriented Domain Analysis

This technique assumes that an object-oriented domain analysis (OODA) of an application in the same problem domain has been done previously. Given the OODA, the steps of this technique are:

1. Analyze the results of the given OODA (in the same domain).
2. Reuse (with or without modification) objects or classes from the OODA.

This technique supports reuse and tends to maximize cohesion in classes and minimize message and inheritance coupling. If one assumes that the previous OODA is solid, this technique also naturally gives a "reality check" on the current project because the objects and classes should be the similar to the ones in the OODA. Thus, considerable time and effort could be saved if the original OODA is relevant and complete. Unfortunately, this technique has limitations.

Today, finding adequate and relevant OODA is not easy. Most systems have either incomplete OODA or no OODA model at all. For reuse to be effective, the problem domain must be well documented and understood by the developers. Tailoring for performance and other business constraints in a specific project may lower reuse. Finally, although it is easier to reuse than to reinvent, the not-invented-here (NIH) syndrome of many developers must be successfully overcome.

Reusing an Application Framework

This technique assumes that at least one OODA has been done to create an application framework of reusable classes. An application framework is a reusable domain-specific template of classes and/or subassemblies and all of its associated classes that implement some common capabilities. Because it is domain-specific, it usually applies specifically to applications that are in the same domain.

The steps of this technique are:

1. Identify one or more relevant application frameworks in the same application domain.
2. Reuse both objects (instances of classes) and classes from previously developed frameworks. Note that some of the classes may need to be modified to be reused in your specific application.

This technique may be considered an enhancement of the OODA technique just described; thus, it has all of the advantages and limitations of that technique. Moreover, it has additional limitations. Your current developers must be able to identify one or more relevant application frameworks that have been previously developed and stored in a repository. Most likely, not all of the needed classes will be in the application framework(s) examined.

One concern with application frameworks is the NIH (not invented here) syndrome. This syndrome translates into a general belief that if the application framework wasn't developed locally, then it can't take into account all of the concerns of the local team. This concern is not totally unfounded. In particular, application frameworks often contain both analysis and design classes. Unfortunately, it is not easy to distinguish between the two. A result of this is that the analysis may be unnecessarily limited.

Reusing Class Hierarchies

This technique assumes that a reuse repository with relevant reusable class hierarchies has been developed. To use this technique, the steps are:

1. Look for classes in the reuse repository that can be reused, either with or without modification.
2. After identifying the classes, attempt to reuse the associated class hierarchy.
3. After modifying the classes, attempt to create new abstract classes by grouping common attributes and methods.
4. If the classes are parameterized, supply the generic formal parameters.

This technique has the same advantages as using OODA. In addition, this technique maximizes the use of inheritance and is a natural fit for Smalltalk (an OO language). As with all techniques, it has additional limitations beyond those for OODA. The existing classification hierarchies may not be relevant to the current application. Existing classes may need to be parameterized, or new subclasses may need to be derived.

Reusing Individual Objects and Classes

If a reuse repository with relevant reusable objects and classes has been developed, we can reuse specific objects and classes.

The steps of this technique are:

1. Look for relevant objects and classes in the reuse repository that can be applied to the application.
2. If necessary, modify the objects and/or classes.
3. Supply generic, formal parameters to parameterize classes as necessary.

This technique has some very serious shortcomings that will be discussed later in this book.

Using Subassemblies

This technique assumes that developers are incrementally developing subassemblies using a recursive development process. This technique is similar to function decomposition; instead of a function, take an object and decompose it into other objects (subassemblies). Continue the decomposition until there are only terminal objects (i.e., do not need to send messages to other objects at a lower level) at the leaves of the decomposition.

The steps of this technique are:

1. Identify all of the objects (classes) at the current level that must remain temporarily incomplete because they depend on one or more as yet unidentified objects or classes.
2. Develop a skeleton specification/design for the methods of the temporarily incomplete object using either: (1) narrative English, (2) an object-oriented specification language such as OOSDL, or (3) a program design language (PDL).
3. Create the appropriate child subassemblies (objects) at the next lower level to handle the messages for the incomplete objects at the higher level.
4. Do step 1 at the current level that has the new subassemblies.

This technique has several advantages. It supports incremental identification of objects/classes. It also identifies all the subassemblies in an application domain. It is very similar to functional decomposition, so there is less culture shock for developers trained in the structured methodology. However, there are limitations to this technique; it identifies only assembled objects. Thus, one must have some other technique to identify fundamental components of the subassemblies.

Using Personal Experience

This technique will eventually become more popular and may be the most viable of all the techniques given as developers gain more experience in using the object-oriented methodology. It assumes that the developers have previously designed one or more relevant classes in the application domain. To build the new models, the developers reuse some of the objects and classes that have been developed on the previous projects.

The steps of this technique are to:

1. Find objects and classes that correspond to ones found in previous models that are in the same application domain.
2. Modify the classes as necessary to support the present project.

By building on one's experience, this technique provides a reasonable "reality check" on the current project. Thus, the quality of the classes and objects may be substantially improved, as they are based on classes and objects that are already built and tested. It is also very natural to want to leverage off the application experience of the developer.

However, there are drawbacks. This technique assumes relevant previous experience, which is not always present. This is especially dangerous when the previous experience is based on functional decomposition projects; the developers have a tendency to identify suboptimal classes. In such a situation, past experience may be of limited value and may possibly even be misleading. Moreover, this technique is very informal, and different developers may identify substantially different objects and classes given the same starting information; thus, it is a highly subjective technique. Also, it may not minimize the message and inheritance coupling.

Traditional Techniques

TRADITIONAL techniques focus more on discovering a domain model rather than using existing domain models. We feel that it is a good practice for an individual learning object-modeling techniques to understand and apply these techniques before using current techniques.

Using Nouns

Pioneered by Russell J. Abbott and popularized by Grady Booch, this technique was widely used between 1983 and 1986 and was included in many object-oriented development methods. This technique, when coupled with use cases, is particularly easy. In many cases, objects are identified as the use cases are written.

The steps of this technique are as follows:

1. Obtain (i.e., from a requirement document) or explicitly author a narrative English text that represents an informal description of the problem to be solved. If use cases were used to scope the domain, then they can serve as the narrative text.

The text should use the words of the application domain (i.e., use the terms of the domain experts).

2. Use the nouns, pronouns, and noun phrases to identify objects and classes (find the "real-world" objects and classes). Singular proper nouns (Jim, he, she, employee number 5, my workstation, my home) and nouns of direct reference (the sixth player, the one-millionth purchase) are used to identify objects. Plural nouns (people, customers, vendors, users, employees) and common nouns (everyone, a player, a customer, an employee, a workstation) are used to identify classes.

3. Verbs (pay, collect, read, request) and predicate phrases (are all paid, have simultaneously changed) are used to identify the services.

This technique has many advantages. Narrative languages (English, Chinese, French, German, Japanese, etc.) are well understood by everyone on a project and can be an effective communication medium for both technical and nontechnical project staff. Moreover, there usually is one-to-one mapping from nouns to objects or classes.

Using nouns requires no learning curve; the technique is straightforward and well defined, and does not require a complete paradigm shift for the beginner. Moreover, this technique does not require a prior OODA; you can apply it to an existing requirement specification written for structural analysis and/or any other methodology.

This technique has some shortcomings, however. For one thing, this is an indirect approach to finding objects and classes. Nouns are not always classes or objects in the problem domain. Many sentences in a functional specification are in the wrong form for easy identification of the objects and classes, for example, "roll back the transaction" or "the software will compute the average salary." In many cases, the nouns, especially subjects of sentences, refer to (1) an entire assembly or a computer software configuration (i.e., CICS), (2) a subassembly or a software component, (3) an attribute, or (4) a service. Later, we will discuss these shortcomings and how we can address them.

Using Traditional Data Flow Diagrams

This technique is the result of many software developers and managers who had invested a large sum of money in expensive CASE tools that supported data flow diagrams (DFDs). In their need to make a transition from functional decomposition requirements analysis methods (i.e., structured analysis) to object-oriented design, they wanted a "Holy Grail" that would protect their investment and make the transition easier. This technique was first published by Ed Seidewitz and Mike Stark of NASA's Goddard Space Flight Center.

This technique is comprised of the following:

■ Terminators on context diagrams (CDs)
■ Data stores on DFDs
■ Complex data flows on DFDs

Before you use this technique, a structure analysis must be completed and all of the CDs and DFDs must be written.

To use this technique, do the following:

1. Map each terminator on the CDs to an object to encapsulate the interface.
2. Identify one class to encapsulate the interface of each set of similar or identical "terminator" objects.
3. Map each data store on the DFDs to an object.
4. Map data stores that contain more than one data field to an aggregate object.
5. Map all or part of the data transformation associated with the data store to a service of the object, and, thus, of the class.
6. Map complex data flows (i.e., record with numerous fields) to an object.
7. Identify subtransformations associated with the parts of the data flow and then map these subtransformations to services of the object.

The major benefit of this technique is that it requires no paradigm shift by the analysts and developers. If the original DFDs are well constructed, false-positive identification of objects and classes are rare. Finally, there are a lot of projects that already have the CDs and DFDs.

Unfortunately, the shortcoming is also directly related to not making the paradigm shift. Nearly all of the DFDs were originally written for functional decomposition, and they have a tendency to create a top-heavy architecture of classes.

With functional decomposition, there is a tendency to assume that the stem is an assembly of subassemblies at the appropriate level. Moreover, one tends to assign services at the corresponding level where the subassembly was found. This may cause objects to be identified in the wrong subassembly. Although false-positive identification of objects and classes is rare, not all of the objects or classes are identified. The rareness of false-positive identification is totally dependent on the quality of the original DFDs. This is still an indirect method of finding objects and classes; it is based on data abstraction and not on object abstraction.

In many instances, an object or class contains more than one data store. Thus, their attributes may be mapped to objects and classes while their associated objects and classes remain unidentified.

Because the DFDs represent functional decomposition, pieces of an object may be scattered across several DFDs assigned to different persons. Thus, different variants of the same object may be redundantly and independently identified.

Finally, transforms are not required to be a service of an object. Therefore, transforms are often compound operations that need to be assigned to multiple objects. If the objects are not properly identified, this leads to fragmented objects and classes.

Using Class-Responsibility-Collaboration (CRC) Cards

This technique was developed by Rebecca Wirfs-Brock and others. These developers observed that identifying objects and classes is a human activity that can be stimulated by the use of small pieces of paper (i.e., CRC cards or Post-it Notes) to represent the objects/classes. It was found that by letting the developers handle the CRC cards, developers with experience, creativity, and intuition can often identify new objects/ classes by noticing holes in the current set of cards. Thus, the cards served both as a vehicle to document the previously identified objects and classes and to stimulate the developers into finding iteratively and incrementally new objects and classes not currently documented.

For the classical version of this technique, do the following:

1. On a CRC card, document the name of the class and list both the responsibilities (i.e., which services it provides) and collaborators (i.e., objects/classes it needs to fulfill its responsibilities).
2. Identify missing objects and/or classes that should be added to the existing set of CRC cards. Specifically, look for responsibilities that cannot be allocated to existing classes and collaborators that have not yet been assigned to a class.

For the modern version of this technique, do the following:

1. On a Post-it Note, document the name and list the responsibilities of the class.
2. Position all of the classes on a white board and draw association arcs between the classes to represent the collaborators.
3. Identify missing objects and/or classes that should be added to the existing set of classes. Look for attributes and services that cannot be allocated to the current classes.

For a use case version of this technique, do the following:

1. Start the effort as a brainstorming session for classes.
   - Identify some candidate classes by writing down a list of some of the "nouns" from the problem domain.
   - Pick the nouns that have some responsibilities and write them on the cards (Post-it Notes).
   - Write a short description of the class for guidance.
2. Use your use cases to generate scenarios for the system.
   - Assign a class to a participant.
   - Act out the scenario and discover the actual responsibilities of each of the classes.
   - Look for attributes and services that cannot be allocated to the current classes.
   - Add missing classes to handle these situations as you run through the scenarios.
   - Update the Post-it Notes as to class name, responsibilities, and collaborators, as you go through the scenarios.
3. Position all of the classes on a white board and draw association arcs between the classes to represent the collaboration.

Some guidelines for using this technique follow:

- Limit the size of the group to three to six participants.
- Scenarios must be concrete and specific (i.e., use cases must be expanded and real).
- Create a discard pile (not the garbage can; you may want to resurrect a discarded class).
- Record each scenario (we like to use sequence diagrams).
- Use a single pen to make changes (this ensures that everyone agrees before changes are made).
- Turn all objections into a concrete scenario (if you cannot show a scenario; it is not real).
- You can consider yourself done when you have a model that can handle all of the use cases.

This technique is inexpensive and easy to use. Little effort is invested in making the classes, and they can be easily discarded. Also, the method stimulates communication and is not intimidating to beginners.

Historically, this technique is better suited for thinking about and designing objects and classes than for identifying them. You must already have objects and classes in order to use this technique to identify additional objects and classes. Finally, the developers must have significant experience, creativity, and intuition for this technique to be consistently successful. However, the revised version based on use cases described previously is very effective. It addresses many of the shortcomings of the original method.

Recommended Approaches

WHICH approach to use depends on the situation and the experience of your team. There is no one approach or one technique that will be suitable for all, especially when you take into consideration time to market and cost. In spite of this caveat, we present here the most common preferences. If you have tested relevant application frameworks as well as their associated repository, the "reusing application frameworks" technique is the best approach. If the frameworks do not exist, then there should be a separate effort using OODA.

However, for the novice, this book presents a different approach that uses many of the aforementioned techniques (proven to be more usable by novices to this new object-oriented paradigm).

We will start by doing the following:

1. Because most analysts/developers are still given a requirements document in narrative English (native language) that uses the terms of the domain expert, it is not unreasonable to use the "Using Nouns" technique of Abbott/Booch with the caveat that this technique is used to find potential objects and will not find all of the objects.

2. Identify all "potential objects" in the problem domain by interactive dialog with the domain expert. Remember that both we and the domain expert are dealing with objects every day. Furthermore, domain experts make mental models and use abstraction to deal with the complexity of their respective businesses. We want to capture the objects that are in the mental model of the domain experts. If we can do this, we can deliver software to the marketplace faster and enhance that software package faster because it is consistent with the mental model of the domain experts. The goal of this step is to identify all the objects that the domain experts would identify.

3. Use the "Using the Things to be Modeled" technique to elicit more potential objects. In an attempt to find objects, some object-oriented pundits have suggested this technique as a way to trigger our recognition of "potential objects." The categories given by three leading teams of well-known experts are shown in Table 5-1, Table 5-2, and Table 5-3.

4. As a guide to help eliminate some potential false problem domain objects, apply the following definition test. An object can be considered as:

   - Any real-world entity
   - Important to the discussion of the requirements
   - Crisply defined boundary

TABLE 5-1   Categories According to Coad and Yourdon

Categories	Explanation
Structure	"Kind-of" and "part-of" relationships
Other systems	External systems
Devices	
Events remembered	A historical event that must be recorded
Roles played	The different role(s) that users play
Locations	
Organization units	Groups to which the user belongs

TABLE 5-2   Categories According to Shlaer and Mellor

Categories	Explanation
Tangible	Cars, telemetry data, sensors
Roles	Mother, teacher, programmer
Incidents	Landing, interrupt, collision
Interactions	Loan, meeting, marriage
Specification	Product specification, standards

TABLE 5-3   Categories According to Ross

Categories	Explanation
People	Humans who carry out some function
Places	Areas set aside for people or things
Things	Physical objects
Organizations	Collection of people, resources, facilities, and capabilities having a defined mission
Concepts	Principles or ideas not tangible, per se
Events	Things that happen (usually at a given date and time), or as steps in an ordered sequence

A real-world entity attempts to keep the analysis in the problem domain and helps to eliminate implementation objects (design objects) such as stacks, keyboards, and programming languages. The phrase "important to the discussion of the requirements" helps exclude some of the objects that are not relevant to the present problem. For example, the space shuttle is a real-world entity, but it is hard to believe that it is important to our "mow the lawn" problem domain. The "crisply defined boundary" comes from Booch and helps to exclude verb phrases such as "going to the store" from being considered as an object.

5. If you have done use case analysis, consider doing these additional steps:
   - Use the use cases to generate scenarios.
   - Use the scenarios to find missing classes.
   - Record scenarios.

Example

Let us return to our lawn-mowing example and apply our approach. In step 1, we apply the "using nouns" technique. Following is the statement of the lawn-mowing example with nouns underlined.

> We have a family with a father, John, a mother, Jane, two sons, Peter and Paul, and two daughters, Elizabeth and Mary. John is an actor and Jane is a dentist. All the children are students and the family dog is Lassie. Their family physician is Alice. This family owns a house in the suburbs of New York City and though mowing the family lawn is normally a chore for the father, it can also be a paid chore for any one of the children. However, working within the neighborhood is Jack, a professional lawn mower.

If we now apply our domain knowledge, step 2, we may add lawn mower as a generalization of professional lawn mower, lawn as a generalization of family lawn,

TABLE 5-4   Initial List of Potential Objects for Lawn Mower Example

List of Potential Objects/Classes	
John	Jane
Peter	Paul
Elizabeth	Mary
Lassie	Family lawn
Jack	Alice
Family	Children
Lawn mower	Physician
Professional lawn mower	Family physician
Dentist	Actor
Mother	Father
Daughter	Son
New York City	Dog
Students	Family dog
House	Suburb
Chore	Paid chore
Office	Studio
Neighborhood	Lawn
"Mowing the lawn"	Is_married

and dog as a generalization of family dog. In addition, we may add studio as a place where John works and office as a place where Jane and Alice practice their professions. In step 3, we may add "is_married" relationship and "mowing the lawn" to the list. Table 5-4 illustrates a typical result of applying the combined technique. This may have left us with some "false positives"—for example, "mowing the lawn" might be better modeled as a service than as an object.

■ ■ SUMMARY

THE standard four steps that we recommend are:

1. Given a requirements document in narrative English (native language) that uses the terms of the domain expert, use the "Using Nouns" technique of Abbott/ Booch with the caveat that this technique is used to find potential objects and it will not find all of the objects.

2. Identify all "potential objects" in the problem domain by interactive dialog with the domain expert. We want to capture the objects that are in the mental model of the domain experts.

3. Use the "Using the Things to be Modeled" technique to elicit more potential objects.

4. As a guide to help eliminate some potential false problem domain objects, apply the following definition test. An object can be considered as (1) any real-world entity, (2) that is important to the discussion of the requirements, and (3) has a crisply defined boundary.

When you get more experience, we suggest the following steps for finding a list of potential objects/classes:

1. Underline all of the nouns in the requirements document or use cases.

2. Filter the list of nouns to identify things outside the scope of the system. These are usually "external objects" to which the system interfaces. These external objects will be useful for the context diagram, but it is helpful to keep these objects in the context diagram. Technically, they are not objects in the final model of the application/system, so are not objects that we want to refine. We can then eliminate them from our list of potential objects as part of the application/system.

3. Usually several different nouns, or noun phrases, are used to describe the same thing (concept or idea). A single term must be selected, and the alternative eliminated. For example, the "workplace" and the "office" are probably the same concept in nearly all problem domains. If a different term is used to describe the same physical thing in a different semantic domain, (i.e., to capture a different concept), you need to capture both concepts. An example of this is if you used "mother" and "dentist" as problem domain terms that apply to Jane in our lawn-mowing example. However, each term captures a different concept, so these terms represent two different potential objects. Specifically, "mother" captures a concept that has to deal with the parenting semantic domain, while "dentist" captures a concept in a work/healthcare semantic domain.

4. Sometimes the same noun is used to capture two different concepts; a new term(s) must be created to ensure that each concept, or "thing," is captured. For example, consider the term "floor." There are two concepts that we can capture using this word: (1) we can refer to a floor as part of a room and, (2) we can refer to a floor (or a level) in a building. These are two separate concepts (or ideas), and they may not be represented by the same object. Remember that an object is a way of capturing a concept or idea.

5. Use the category list given by our experts to check if there are other concepts or ideas that we should add to the list.

6. As a guide to help eliminate some potential false problem domain objects, apply the following definition test: an object can be considered as (1) any real-world entity, (2) that is important to the discussion of the requirements, and (3) has a crisply defined boundary.

7. If you have use cases, you may want to use our modified version.

Identifying Responsibilities

> *P*resent themselves as objects recognized, in flashes, and with glory not their own.
>
> William Wordsworth

In the first step of our method, we created a list of "potential objects." Now we need to determine if these potential objects are "real objects" that we want to put into our model. Thus, the second step in our method is to determine if there is any responsibility for these objects in our application/system.

Before we can do this, however, we have to know what an object is and what we mean by responsibility.

What Is an Object?

In Chapter 3, we defined an object from a developer's perspective as it relates to the production of software. In Chapter 5, we provided a different definition for use in finding objects in the problem domain. Now we want to use a more technical definition, from the problem-domain perspective, to help us eliminate "false objects" from the list of potential objects. A domain analysis view or definition of an object is:

Object. An object is an abstraction of something in the problem domain, reflecting the capabilities of a system to keep information about it, interact with it, or both.

Humans have always formed concepts in order to understand the world. Each concept captures a particular idea or understanding that we have of the world in which we live. As we acquire and organize more concepts, we use them to help us make sense of and reason about things in our world.

An object is one of those things to which we apply our concepts. Examples include invoice, employee, paycheck, train, train engine, boxcar, passenger car, dining car, computer, computer keyboard, joystick, screen, icon on a screen, mouse pad, organization, department, office, and the process of writing this line. Note from the examples that a train is composed of a train engine, boxcar, passenger car, and dining car. Thus, an object may be composed of other objects. These objects, in turn, may be composed of other objects, and so on. For example, the passenger car is composed of doors, seats, windows, and so on. Another example is a machine that is composed of subassemblies that are made from other subassemblies. Moreover, the object may be a real thing (e.g., train, car, computer) or an abstract thing (e.g., process, marriage, time).

In object-oriented analysis and design, we are interested in an object for its business services. Remember that the way an object-oriented system works is by one object requesting the service of another object via the message-passing paradigm. Thus, from an external (or system) perspective, an object is defined by its public services; that is, an object is defined by the services that it advertises. So, technically, the protocol defines the class/object. However, we know as software developers that the protocol (collection of prototypes) alone is not adequate. During analysis, we expect to identify the business data and the associated business methods necessary to support the defined business services. For analysis, then, an object is an encapsulation of business attribute values (data) and their associated business methods (how services are provided). To preserve encapsulation and information-hiding principles, an object also defines an external view of its public methods for access by other objects. This external view is its public business services. These public services are defined via prototypes and are the only vehicle by which another object may access its methods and thus its data. According to Wirfs-Brock (1990), responsibility is the set of public services that an object provides and the associated data necessary to provide the services.

For most people, however, it is more natural to be able to relate attributes (i.e., data) to an object than to define its services, so we will look at identifying both attributes and services for an object together as one step.

What Is an Attribute?

THINGS in the real world have characteristics. For example, a person can be described by her or his height, weight, hair color, eye color, and so on. Each characteristic that is common to all instances of the object/class is abstracted as a separate attribute. For example, Joe is 6′ tall, weighs 175 pounds, and has red hair and brown eyes, while James is 5′10″ tall, weighs 160 pounds, has black hair and green eyes. For a person, potential attributes are height, weight, hair color, and eye color. Note that the characteristics that are abstracted into attributes are highly problem-dependent. Consider the "person" object. Most of us can come up with a large number of characteristics for a "person" conceptually. When we limit our abstraction of a person to a specific problem domain or to a specific problem, we reduce the number of applicable characteristics.

Thus, for the purposes of analysis, an attribute is an abstraction of a single characteristic that is applicable to the business domain and is possessed by all of the entities that were themselves abstracted as objects. From a technical perspective, an attribute is some variable (data item or state information) for which each object (instance) has its own value. Each attribute must be provided with a name that is unique within the object/class. Because each attribute may take on values, the range of legal values allowed for an attribute should also be captured.

According to some object-oriented authors, there are four types of attributes: descriptive, naming, state information, and referential. State-information attributes are used to keep a history of the entity; this is usually needed to capture the states of the finite state machines used to implement the dynamic aspect of behavior. Referential attributes are facts that tie one object to another object and are used to capture relationships. However, capturing states and relationships using attributes is an implementation issue. In this book, states and relationships will be represented pictorially, and not as part of the attribute list of an object or class. In this chapter, we will address only descriptive attributes and naming attributes.

Descriptive Attributes

Descriptive attributes are facts that are intrinsic to each entity. If the value of a descriptive attribute changes, it means only that some aspect of an entity (instance) has changed. From a problem-domain perspective, it is still the same entity. For example, if Joe gains 1 pound, from nearly all problem-domain perspectives, Joe is still a person. More importantly, Joe is still the same person as he was before he gained 1 pound.

Naming Attributes

Naming attributes are used to name or label an entity. Typically, they are somewhat arbitrary. These attributes are frequently used as identifiers or as part of an identifier. If the value of a naming attribute changes, it only means that a new name has been given to the same entity. In fact, naming attributes do not have to be unique. For example, if Joe changes his name to James, that is all that is changed; his weight, height, etc. are still the same.[1]

What Is a Service?

A service may be defined as work done for others. In a sense, the services of an object are the advertised or public work that an object is willing to perform when requested by another object via the message-passing paradigm. These services are defined by prototypes.

---

[1] During analysis in the early days, many developers also required a unique naming attribute that was used as a key to map objects into a relational database. Better support for object-oriented technology exists today, so this requirement is no longer needed.

The prototype is made from two parts: (1) name of the service (called the selector by some experts), and (2) the arguments for the service (called the signature by some experts). Thus, every object must define its prototype for each service it plans to provide.

The defined collection of prototypes is the protocol of the class/object, which is the object's interface (i.e., all of its advertised services). The selector (i.e., the name of the service) should be externally focused. For example, a service of a local restaurant may be "changing bills for coins."[2] The "changing bills for coins" is defining a service from the user's perspective, while naming the service "changing coins for bills" is an internal perspective of the service. Naming services is very difficult because we want names that reflect an external perspective and are consistent with the semantic domain in which the object resides.

What Is a Method?

TECHNICALLY, a method is a detailed set of operations that an object performs when another object requests a service.[3] However, a behavior by definition is a set of actions that an object is responsible for exhibiting—so alternatively, a method specifies a behavior of an object. A method is similar to a function in functional decomposition. However, there are some very important differences. Remember that these methods can only be accessed via the message passing paradigm and each method may only use its own data and data passed to it via its argument list.[4] Perhaps most importantly, these services should be specified to a level of depth that is consistent with the semantic domain in which the object resides.

Identifying Attributes

THE key issue here is what data do we believe the object is responsible for knowing and owning. The following questions must be asked about each potential object:

- How is this object described in general?
- What parts of the general description are applicable to this problem domain?
- What is the minimal description needed for this application?

If you take the Eastern or Taoist approach to object-oriented analysis, you will design your system by asking only the first two questions. You will not be concerned with the specific application that you are implementing. We have found that with this approach, there is a tendency to produce a more flexible and robust model from a busi-

---

[2]   The reason that the restaurant provides the service may be because it gets a lot of loose change from tips and the bank does not accept coins for deposit.

[3]   Conversely, a service of an object defines how another object may have access to a specific behavior (method/function).

[4]   In a later chapter we will see that it also has access to other data via services of other objects with which it has relationships.

ness perspective. You will then be able to respond to changes in the marketplace more quickly. This flexibility is usually at the expense of performance and space utilization.

If you ask all three questions and look only at the present application (Western approach), you will tend to produce a fine-tuned, high-performing system with good space utilization that makes more effective use of the hardware. However, it will be at the expense of having less reusable classes/objects and having less flexibility to respond to the marketplace.

Attributes are rarely fully described in a requirements document. Fortunately, they seldom affect the basic structure of the model. You must draw upon your knowledge of the application domain and the real world to find them.

Because most guidelines for identifying attributes do not help differentiate between false attributes and real attributes, Rumbaugh (1991) has offered the following suggestions to help eliminate "false" attributes:

1. **Objects**. If the independent existence, rather than just the value, of the attribute is important, then the attribute is an object and there needs to be a link to it. For example, consider a Person object. Is the address or city in which the person lives an attribute or another object? If, in your application, you do not manipulate the address without knowing to which person the address belongs, then it is an attribute. However, if you manipulate the address as an entity by itself, then the address should be an object with a link between it and the person.

2. **Qualifiers.** If the value of an attribute depends on a particular context, then consider restating it as a qualifier. For example, an employee number is not really an attribute of a Person object. Consider a person with two jobs. It really qualifies as a link "employs" between the company object and the person object.[5]

3. **Names**. A name is an attribute when it does not depend on the context. For example, a person name is an attribute of Person. Note that an attribute, as in a person's name, does not have to be unique. However, names are usually qualifiers and not attributes. As such, they usually either define a role in an association or define a subclass or superclass abstraction. For example, parent and teacher are not attributes of Person. Both are probably roles for associations. Another example is male person and female person. There are two ways to capture this: consider gender as an attribute of Person or make two subclasses.[6]

4. **Identifiers**. Make sure not to list the unique identifier that object-oriented languages need to unambiguously reference an object. This is implicitly assumed to be part of the model. However, do list the application domain identifiers. For example, an account code is an attribute of Account, while a transaction identification is probably not an attribute.

---

[5] If is not important to the application that a person has a second employer, then making it an attribute of the Person object may be satisfactory.

[6] Technically, making two subclasses is the most accurate model. However, if we never have services or relationships that are gender-specific, then it is appropriate to make gender an attribute during implementation.

5. **Link attributes**. If the proposed attribute depends on the presence of a link, then it is an attribute of the link and not of the objects in the link. Make the link an associative object and make the proposed attribute one of its attributes. For example, let us assume that Jim is married to Mary. The date of their marriage is an attribute of the is_married association and not an attribute of Jim or Mary.

6. **Fine Details**. Omit minor attributes that do not affect the methods.

7. **Discordant attributes**. An attribute that seems completely unrelated to all other attributes may indicate that the object may need to be split into two objects. A class should be coherent and simple (i.e., must represent a concept that operates in a single semantic domain).

To aid you in finding attributes, we suggest you begin by using the adjectives and possessive phrases in the requirements document. For example, *red* car, the *40-year-old* man, the *color* of the truck, and the *position* of the cursor. Then, after identifying a few attributes, you should ask the preceding questions to identify more attributes.

Specifying Attributes

COAD and Yourdon (1991) stated it very well when they said, "Make each attribute capture an atomic concept." Atomic concept means that an attribute will contain a single value or a tightly-related grouping of values that the application treats as a whole. Examples of attributes include individual data items (such as age, salary, and weight) and composite data items (such as legal name, address, and birth date).

Issues on normalization, performance, object identification, and keeping recalculable information should be left to design and implementation. However, the form of the data (character, integer, string, color, etc.) should be specified. Its range, constraints, and invariants should also be captured. We recommend capturing constraints and invariants using declarative semantics. See later chapters for discussions on rules.

Because identifying attributes is difficult, Shlaer and Mellor (1992) have offered properties to which an attribute must adhere. We have added an additional property, identified in this list as Property Zero.

> **Property Zero:** An attribute must capture a characteristic that is consistent with the semantic domain in which this object (as a concept or idea) resides. For instance, consider the object Programmer. A characteristic of a programmer may be the years of experience in writing computer programs. However, age is probably not an attribute of Programmer; it is probably an attribute of Person, which is a different object from Programmer. Now if we make the dangerous assumption that all programmers are also people, then we can create a Human Programmer object by having it inherit the programmer's attributes (e.g., years of writing computer programs) from the Programmer object and the human attributes (e.g., age) from the Person object. Thus, Human Programmer is a composite of two objects.

Property One: An instance (entity) has exactly one value (within its range) for each attribute at any given time. For example, we can choose eye color as an attribute of the Person object with the range of black, brown, blue, and green. If we discover that a person, Carey, which should be an instance of Person, has one green eye and one brown eye, then we cannot assign both green and brown as the eye color of Carey.[7]

Property Two: An attribute must not contain an internal structure. For example, if we made name an attribute of Person, then we are not interested in manipulating the given name and the family name independently in the problem domain.

Property Three: An attribute must be a characteristic of the entire entity and not a characteristic of its composite parts. For example, if we specify "computer" as an object that is composed of a terminal, keyboard, mouse, and CPU, the size of the screen is an attribute of terminal and not computer.

Property Four: When an object is an abstraction of a concept that interacts with other objects (especially tangible objects), the attribute of the object must be associated with the concept and not the other objects. For example, let us assume we want to transfer oil from a holding tank to a separator tank, and we define an Oil Transfer object to capture the concept about the body of liquid that moves. Then, if we assign the attribute gallon to the object Oil Transfer, it must represent the number of gallons that are transferred. It may not be used to represent the number of gallons in the holding tank or in the separator tank.

Property Five: When an object has a relationship with another object, especially an object of the same kind (class), the attribute must capture the characteristics of the object, and not the relationship or the other object(s) in the relationship. For example, if we add salary as an attribute and spousal relationship to Person, we cannot use the spouse's pay as the value for the salary attribute of a nonworking spouse, and the date of their marriage is not an attribute of either spouse.

Identifying Services

ACCORDING to Coad and Yourdon (1991), services may be categorized as either algorithmically simple and algorithmically complex. Within each of these categories, services can be broken down into various types. Each category and its types are given in Table 6-1 and Table 6-2. Coad and Yourdon believe that 80–90% of the services will be algorithmically simple. We believe that the number is closer to 60%.

Algorithmically simple services are not usually placed in an object-oriented model. Every class/object is assumed to have these services. This makes the model simpler and will aid in reading large and complex models. In this step, we are only interested in identifying those algorithmically complex business services that must be provided by the object.

---

[7] This can be easily solved by having the eye color as an attribute of an object Eye and have Person own (have a referential attribute to) two eyes. This requires that the model be changed, but the change is for the better — the model more accurately reflects the reality of the domain.

TABLE 6-1   Algorithmically Simple Services

Create	Creates and initializes a new object
Connect	Connects an object with another object
Access	Gets or sets attribute values
Disconnect	Disconnects an object from another object
Delete	Deletes an object

TABLE 6-2   Algorithmically Complex Services

Calculate	Calculations that the object is responsible for performing on its values
Monitor	Monitors that the object is responsible for in order to detect or respond to external system or device or internal object
Query	Computes a functional value without modifying the object

To aid us in finding services, we should use the verbs in our requirements document. Typically, an English sentence is in the form "subject—action verb—object." *In this case, the verb is usually defining a method that must be provided by the object of the sentence.*[8] For example, "A person hit the ball." The tendency as a novice is to define a "hit" service for the Person object. In OD, the sentence is used to define a "receiving a hit" service for the Ball object. For the Person object to hit the Ball object, the Ball object must have a prototype service within its protocol to receive the "hit" message request from Person.

After using the verbs to identify services (application-specific case), we should consider generalizing the service name for the domain. Remember that the name should be given from an external perspective (user of the service). We want to use as generic a word as possible to give us an opportunity to find abstract classes, which are the most difficult objects/classes to discover.

Specifying Services

SPECIFYING the service is done by defining the prototype for the service. Remember from Chapter 3 that the prototype is made from the name of the service and the signature of the service. The name chosen should reflect either an external item or a user's view of

---

[8]   In the object-oriented paradigm, interaction between objects is via message passing.

the service. The signature is a list of arguments that need to be passed to the object for it to perform the named service. This is the additional data that an object does not have and expects to be given by the calling object.

Normally, it is good practice to specify no more arguments than what is necessary for the specific object to perform (execute) its method associated with the service. However, because we are trying to capture concepts and not technical definitions, the argument list may be adjusted to take advantage of polymorphism later. So during this step, the name of the service should be considered very carefully, and we can be a little more lax about the arguments.

Recommended Approach

OUR approach for identifying responsibilities is:

1. Identify attributes
   a. Look at all of the adjectives and possessive phrases in the requirements document.
   b. Ask the following questions:
      1. How is this object described in general?
      2. What parts of the general description are applicable to this problem domain?
   c. If you want to follow the Western school, ask also the question:
      1. What is the minimal description needed for this application?
   d. Use Rumbaugh's suggestions to eliminate false attributes.

2. Specify attributes
   a. Make each attribute an "atomic concept."
   b. Eliminate attributes that are calculable or derivable from the basic attributes.
   c. Eliminate attributes that address normalization, performance, or object identification during this step.
   d. Test that the attribute adheres to all of the properties suggested by Shlaer and Mellor and that as a group the attributes are in the same semantic domain (good cohesion).

3. Identify services
   a. Look at the verbs in a requirements document. Remember that the verb usually defines the services of the object of the sentence.
   b. Look at the user scenarios, which usually indirectly identify a lot of services.
   c. Look at each feature, which usually requires services from many objects.

4. Specify services
   a. Give a name to the service that is externally (relative to itself) focused.
   b. Define the signature of the service by identifying its argument list.

Example

Let us return to our lawn-mowing example. In this example, we have very few adjectives that would help us define attributes for the potential objects we identified in step 1a. However, we are dealing with objects that we all know, as well as with a problem domain that we can all readily understand. So we can start with step 1b, question number 1. Let us start with the eight Person objects: John, Jane, Peter, Paul, Elizabeth, Mary, Jack, and Alice. Examples of descriptive attributes that Person objects probably have are birth date, height, weight, hair color, eye color, and gender; naming attributes are Given-Name and SocialSecurityNumber (see Table 6-3).

Before moving to question 2, we have to decide on the problem domain. We can decide that we want to define our problem domain to cover everything. If that is true, our attribute list would have to be extended to cover the area of a person's health, employment, taxes, investments, social relationships, and so on. It will probably make the object very large, and neither maintainable nor usable to any application, unless it has unlimited CPU and space resources. (There goes management's idea of one class/ object definition for all usage.) However, it is not as bad as all that. Normally, every business is bound by the kind of domain for which they are in business.

Let us now limit our domain to home owner property care. We are interested in capturing applications like mowing the lawn, fertilizing the lawn, seeding the lawn, trimming the bushes, cleaning the pool, carpet cleaning, house painting, roof repair, gutter cleaning, chimney-sweeping, and so on.

If we think very carefully about the problem domain, we will probably realize that none of the attributes we have identified are applicable to our problem domain of "home owner property care." However, from the requirements description, we can see that the schedule of a person's time is useful, and some state information (is Dad tired or not?) may be needed.

Furthermore, because family physicians are not within the domain of "home owner property care," we can drop Alice and FamilyPhysician from our list of potential objects. With similar logic, we can probably drop Studio, Dentist, Actor, Student, and Suburb from the list. It is also probably safe to drop Father, Mother, Son, and Daughter

TABLE 6-3   Attributes and Values for a Selection of Objects in the Lawn Mower Example

Attribute Name	John	Jane	Peter	Paul
Birth date	9/12/50	2/24/52	8/30/79	3/5/81
Height	5'8'	5'10"	6'2"	6'6"
Weight	110 lbs	160 lbs	210 lbs	195 lbs
Hair color	gray	white	black	blond
Eye color	blue	grey	green	black
Gender	male	female	male	male
Name	John Doe	Jane Doe	Peter Doe	Paul Doe
SSN	123-45-6789	234-56-7899	345-67-1234	456-78-0123

from the list,[9] especially in these modern days of equal opportunities of chores for all. We have kept Lassie and Dog on the list, because a dog may be an alternative to chemical fertilizer. The house is needed for other applications such as house painting. We are not sure about Chore and PaidChore. We suspect that we will need LawnMower, ProfessionalLawnMower," and FamilyLawn for our application.

After applying question 2, our revised attribute list now looks as follows:

For John, Jane, Peter, Paul, Elizabeth, and Mary, there is one attribute: schedule.[10]

For Jack and ProfessionalLawnMower, the attributes are address, telephone number, and schedule.

For Lassie and Dog, there is one attribute: schedule.

For House, the attributes are address, telephone number, last painted date, last roof repaired date, and so on.

For the FamilyLawn, the attributes are height of grass, last seeded, last fertilized, and so on.

For Chore and PaidChore, no attributes were found.[11]

Now, we are ready for question 3; our application is "mowing the lawn." If we restrict ourselves only to our application, we would eliminate the following potential objects from consideration: Lassie, Dog, Chore, PaidChore, and House.

After applying question 3, our revised attribute list now looks as follows:

For John, Jane, Peter, Paul, Elizabeth and Mary, there is one attribute: schedule.

For Jack and ProfessionalLawnMower, attributes are address, telephone number, and schedule.

For FamilyLawn, there is one attribute: height of grass.

In applying question 3, we have eliminated objects (and if we had a lot of attributes, probably some attributes) that are applicable to the general problem domain, but not applicable to our specific application.

In Tao philosophy, the focus is on the path rather than on the destination or, in our terminology, the process rather than the goal. When we translate this into object-oriented modeling, the Tao philosophy tells us to focus on capturing the objects in the problem domain rather than on the objects that will help us solve the immediate problem. It is the belief of the Taoist that focusing on the goal will cause you to ignore valuable information, while focusing on the process will let the path show you the way. Translated to object-oriented technology, focusing on the specific problem or application will cause you to ignore important concepts and, as a result, will make your classes (objects) less reusable.

If you are trying to produce flexible and reusable software, you should apply an Eastern or Taoist philosophy to problem solving and object-oriented modeling. In Eastern

---

[9] This is actually incorrect. We will see in a later chapter that we need to use the father-child relationship. However, because "parenting" is a different semantic domain than "home owner property care," we have a tendency to eliminate these objects during this step.

[10] Schedule could easily be complex enough that it should be modeled as an object with a link to the person.

[11] Amount of pay could be an attribute of PaidChore.

philosophy, we would not have asked question 3. We would expect that the proper modeling of the problem domain would automatically also contain our business solution to our application. This kind of philosophy is based on experimentation versus our classical Western thinking, which is based on planning.

Step 2 for attributes is left to the reader.

Now let us perform steps 3 and 4 for services. Because we have contrived a very simple example, the only service is "mow the lawn." If we look at people in general, the number of services that they provide is endless; but we do not want to capture all of these services. If we were to only consider services in the domain of "home owner property care," we will have added services such as house painting, lawn fertilizing, lawn seeding, house cleaning, gutter cleaning, sweeping the sidewalk, trimming the bushes, and raking the leaves. However, when we get back to our specific application, we are back to one service: "mow the lawn."

Thus, we have the following objects with a "mow the lawn" service: John, Peter, Paul, Elizabeth, Mary, Jack, and ProfessionalLawnMower.

Note that the family lawn already has a changeHeight or setHeight "height of grass" service because it is algorithmically simple.

As useful as the Eastern philosophy is in helping us perform better object specification, we still do not want to include in our final model objects or services that are not needed for our specific application. So when all is said and done, we still need to apply the following test to ensure that we have only the necessary (but at this time, it probably is not sufficient) objects.

Tests:

1. The object must provide some service for some other object in the application/system or an external interface service to some external object.
2. In general, the object must have multiple attributes. There are cases in which an object will have no attributes and will only provide services.[12]

Sometimes it is useful to keep an object (an abstraction) that may help us in organizing our structural model, which captures the relationships between objects. In such an instance, the only services of that object may be its constructor and destructor.

■ ■ SUMMARY

OUR approach for identifying responsibilities is:

1. Identify attributes
2. Specify attributes
3. Identify services
4. Specify services

---

[12] However, this kind of object should be rare and is usually not discovered during this step.

CHAPTER

7

Specifying Static Behavior

$$\nabla^2 \psi = -\frac{2\mu}{h}(E - V)\Psi$$

Time Independent Schroedinger Equation

In the second step of our method, we created a list of "real objects." In the process of finding these "real objects," we identified attributes and services of these objects. However, during that step, we took an external view of the service. More specifically, we did not concern ourselves with how the object will provide (perform) the service. In the third step in our method, we need to capture how each object provides the services identified in step 2. In the process of specifying these services, we may also identify additional services that must be provided by other objects.

What Is Behavior?

In the previous chapter, we defined a service as "work done for others."[1] Behavior can be defined as the set of actions that an object is responsible for exhibiting when it provides a specific service. Another object may access a specific behavior of an object only via the appropriate service. This behavior is usually captured as a method (function) in the object.

---

[1] Technically, an object can provide services to itself. This is quite common for complex objects.

A behavior is defined when the following are specified: (1) all of the inputs (arguments to the service), (2) all of the outputs, and (3) how (from a domain perspective) the object will provide the service. Behavior can be either static or dynamic (see chapter 2). In this chapter, techniques for capturing static behavior will be addressed. Techniques for capturing dynamic behavior will be addressed in chapter 8.

In static behavior, the set of actions is captured by the operations (code) within the method. By definition, the operations within the method will not be affected by any external or internal events[2] (actions). A good example of static behavior is the "square root" service for Number. If one requests the "square root" service from the number 4, which is an instance of Number, the result will always be 2. There is no external or internal action that would cause the method of Number to change the algorithm for computing the square root and thus providing a different result.

The most natural way to document behavior[3] is to use any natural language. Unfortunately, all natural language is rich in ambiguities and inconsistencies. When it is spoken, some clarification is provided by intonation, hand movements, and body language. In many situations, especially in specification, even spoken words will not alleviate the ambiguities or inconsistencies. The problem is that natural language is a set of atomic elements (words) that lack well-defined semantics (consistent and unambiguous definition in the problem domain). Thus, the resulting collection of words that form sentences or paragraphs becomes ambiguous or inconsistent; thus, the behavior descriptions written in natural language become inconsistent and ambiguous.

One solution is to build a shell around the natural language with well-defined semantics. This technique is used in every field of endeavor. For example, in accounting, words such as *ledger*, *debit*, and *credit* have very precise and well-defined semantics. Similarly, in the computer world, words such as *input*, *output*, *bit*, and *byte* have well-defined semantics.

When we construct a shell around the English language to provide a richer set of semantically clear constructs, this is really modeling. The purpose of a model is to provide a richer, higher-level, and more semantically precise set of constructs (usually words) than those of the underlying natural language. The model is designed to reduce ambiguities and inconsistencies, manage complexity, facilitate checks for completeness, and improve understandability. Associated with each of the models are techniques for capturing the behavior (function/method) of the model. Thus, the following techniques for documenting behavior are based on a relatively formal underlying model.

Techniques for Specifying Static Behavior

THERE are at least two ways of specifying static behavior:[4] (1) giving the before and after conditions on its execution and (2) decomposing the service into a series of activities and tasks that can be mapped to basic operations of the class or as a service class to other objects.

---

[2]   If they were true, we would model this with dynamic behavior.

[3]   For example, how the object will provide the service.

[4]   This is called operation specification in UML.

From a formal language perspective, the first way is preferred. In fact, UML uses this technique for operation specification, of which static behavior is a special case. However, we have found that analysts had a great deal of difficulty in recognizing the necessary preconditions and postconditions. Furthermore, this technique neither helps us to understand the business nor to find additional services that are not identified in our process. Thus, we prefer to perform a business service analysis, which is the second way of specifying static behavior.

A service is comprised of a series of activities that perform the work of that advertised service. The discrete activities are, in turn, composed of tasks. Thus, an activity is a set of tasks that is organized and proceduralized to accomplish a specific subgoal. The tasks and activities are interdependent, and there is a well-defined flow of control between them. The definition of the behavior is the identification of the activities and tasks that are to be performed in support of the named service.

In capturing activities and tasks, the following questions should be answered:

- How are they performed?
- Why are they performed?
- What are their interrelationships?

For use in control specification and design, the following additional information should be gathered:

- Is it part of a transaction (if you are using the transaction paradigm)?
- Timing
- Frequency
- Volume
- Variants
- Business rules on verification and validation
- Processing algorithms
- Saved and/or stored data
- Reports
- Control points and check points, if any
- Error detection, correction, and recovery

The steps are very simple. Begin with the service trigger,[5] document all of the manual and mental steps that must be performed, document every decision point, document each test and calculation or change to the attribute, and document all possible results from a decision point. Finally, consider exceptions and special cases.

The following three points of caution are appropriate:

1. Be careful with modeling manual processes. The ideal behind the object-oriented paradigm is that the object that has the data does the work. So, many manual processes

---

[5] The service call from some other object. The other object is usually an external object.

should not be done by a conceptual human object in the system; these are done by the object itself. For example, a purchase order can fill itself. This may seem a little unnatural to a novice, but the purchase order has all the data needed to process itself. Similarly, a check in most banking applications will basically process itself.

2. In many situations, only the activities are in the same semantic domain as the object—the tasks are in a different semantic domain. In such a situation, the task needs to be modeled as services supplied by other objects. These other objects are usually related to the present object either through inheritance or aggregation. Capturing each service in the correct object is critical to having low coupling and good cohesion in the model. Remember that low coupling and good cohesion of objects lead to reusable and flexible software.

3. Operations allowed as part of service specification in an object are bounded. Operations can only change data that the object owns (i.e., its attributes), and have access only to the object's data and data passed to it via the argument list. Furthermore, an object can only access services of other objects that it knows about. In the next chapter,[6] we will discuss how an object knows about another object.

Techniques for Specifying Control

FINDING the services and describing each one as a sequence of actions that produce the intended result is one of the issues that is not well addressed in most object-oriented books or courses. We will attempt to give the reader some guidelines in this area.

We believe that just as we have borrowed techniques for documenting behavior from other methodologies, we need to borrow a technique from an existing method (McMenamin and Palmer, 1984) to help us specify the behavior of objects and capture the necessary services that will meet all the requirements. This method was adopted and modified by Jacobson (1992) for capturing requirements in object-oriented analysis in his Objectory method.

The steps described by McMenamin and Palmer are very simple:

1. List all of the external and internal events to which the application/system needs to respond. The users and the interface system(s) are external to the system. A good way to get a list of external events is to perform a task analysis for the users and the external systems. In the terminology of the Objectory method, this would be called identifying the actors.

2. For each event, usually a message, determine how and in what sequence the necessary messages will be passed among objects to satisfy the request. This particular series of interactions among objects is called a scenario. A scenario shows a single execution of the application/system in time. When the scenario requires

---

[6] These constraints are consistent with the encapsulation and information-hiding principles of the object-oriented paradigm. Fundamental to building good-quality systems is the fact that the services of each object must be in the same semantic domain.

specific sequencing and synchronization beyond what is provided as part of the services of objects in the scenario, a task object should be created to capture the scenario controls. A scenario is equivalent to a transaction in many applications. Thus, a task object is commonly used to capture the control aspects of a transaction.

3. Capture these sequences by drawing a sequence diagram for each scenario and its variations. These scenarios, or sequences of messages, are useful for understanding the application/system and for integrated testing. This step is different from both McMenamin and Palmer and Jacobson's Objectory method. In structured methods, usually a state machine for the whole system is designed to capture the scenarios; similarly, in the Objectory method, a state model is used to represent the system. This makes sense, for both of these methods are used in the early part of this method before decomposition. We are using this technique after detail analysis (domain analysis) of the application/system in order to verify the validity of the domain analysis in addressing the specific application. This is a critical difference; we believe that using scenarios to validate our domain model is a better way to develop reusable classes than to start the modeling process for the application, as originally suggested by McMenamin and Palmer.

4. Capture the details of how each service is provided. By thinking through each scenario, the analyst/developer can specify precisely what must be done in each of the object services. Then the details of the actions that need to be taken within a service are captured. Again, this is different from the classical method, which would have taken a system view. We are now taking a decomposed view of the system in terms of objects rather than functions.

5. If you haven't already done so, consider modeling the scenarios as use cases to reduce the number of scenario diagrams.

Techniques for Documenting Control

Activity Diagrams

This technique uses processes or tasks as its building block.[7] The response is captured as a series of processes that operate on a set of data. From a technical perspective, one can argue that the activities and tasks are captured as "processes" (i.e., bubbles on the diagram) in lower-level diagrams. If we were performing functional decomposition, this would be correct. However, in object-oriented analysis, it is not always correct to

---

[7] An activity diagram has always been a fuzzy item. It was intended originally to capture the processes at a higher level. It was used at a pre- or co-use case level. Activity is not OO, just like use cases. It is probably better to introduce activity as a way to document the process at the "domain"/business level. Then the activities or processes within which the "system will be used" will need to be objectified. Actually, you do not need everything to be OO. What must be OO is the system and the parts that interface with the system.

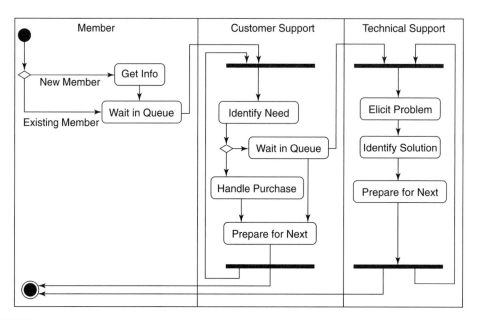

FIGURE 7-1   The UML notation for a generic activity diagram.

map every activity or task to a service of an object. Often we will map a task to an object.[8]

An activity diagram describes how activities are coordinated. Some authors consider activity diagrams to be a better mechanism for showing essential dependencies among activities performed by various entities.

The UML notation for an activity diagram is illustrated in Figure 7-1. The solid circle represents the entry point. The diamond represents decision points. The rounded rectangles identify tasks that are to be performed. Arrows identify transitions from one task to the next. The solid lines are sychronization bars that identify synchronization for ends of tasks (flows into the bar) and starts of tasks (flows out of the bar). Activities that are performed by different individuals can be expressed using partitions called **swimlanes**.

Collaboration Diagram[9]

A collaboration diagram shows the flow of control emphasizing the structural relationships among the instances in the interaction, as well as the messages passed among them. It shows the objects and links that exist just before the service begins and also

---

[8]   Mapping a task to an object is one technical solution. A more correct approach would be to re-engineer the process so that it could be mapped to the service of a single object.

[9]   The term in UML is collaboration diagram, but earlier OO writings have used other terms. Many older sources refer to this diagram as an object interaction diagram.

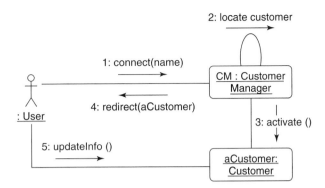

FIGURE 7-2 The UML notation for a collaboration diagram.

the objects and links created (and possibly destroyed) during the performance of the service.[10]

A message from one object to another is indicated by a label consisting of a sequence number, the name of the service requested, and the arguments list with an arrow showing the message-flow direction. In UML, there are additional options to handle synchronization with other threads of control, nested procedural calling sequences, concurrent threads, iteration, and possible conditional expressions. A collaboration diagram is illustrated in Figure 7-2.

Sequence Diagram[11]

A sequence diagram shows the flow of control by time ordering and emphasizes the passing of messages as they unfold over time. It shows the sequence of messages that implement a service or transaction. This technique uses objects as its building block. In this analysis technique, you trace the response of an event as a series of messages between objects. Each message is a request for services from another object. In using this technique, one must already have some idea about the objects that are in the system. This is one reason why we identify objects as the first step of our object-oriented method.

The UML notation for sequence diagrams is illustrated in Figure 7-3. A straight vertical line is used to represent an object. An event (external service request) is used to label the diagram. A service call to another object is represented by a direct arrow with the prototype of the service call as its label.

---

[10] A collaboration diagram is much like the sequence diagram that follows. However, it captures additional information about how the objects are related to each other. The incorporation of additional detail is good, but it is harder to follow. While we prefer the use of collaboration diagrams, it is often the case that people do not read them as carefully as they deserve.

[11] Sequence diagrams were previously known as event trace diagrams and have origins predating object-oriented methodologies.

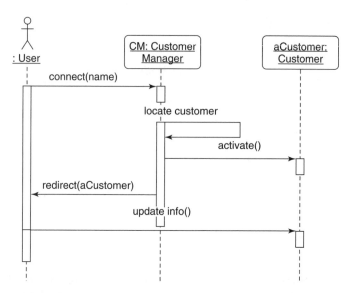

FIGURE 7-3   UML notation for a sequence diagram.

Techniques for Documenting Static Behavior

Preconditions and Postconditions

In UML specifications, the recommended way of specifying preconditions and postconditions is via textual specification. The textual specification would have the following sections: service name, inputs, output(s), elements of the object modified, preconditions, and postconditions. We recommend adding invariant conditions to the list, if you choose this technique.

Flowcharting

A flowchart is the oldest technique for specifying a method/function. There are a large number of object-oriented methods that use this technique and have highly specialized notations for documenting the behavior.

   A generic flowcharting technique is described. A rectangle is used to capture the calculation or operations, and the diamond is used to capture the decision. Flow of control is shown via arrows. Words are placed on arrows from a diamond (decision point), as each arrow from the diamond represents one of the possible results.

Data Flow Diagrams

Data flow diagrams (DFDs) are an integral part of a number of methods (e.g., Rumbaugh). Each specific method uses a slightly different notation. A generic notation is described. Data flow (i.e., information) is represented by a labeled arrow. Operations (actions or transformations) are represented by labeled bubbles. Information sources or sinks are represented by labeled boxes. Attributes (stored information) are represented by a double horizontal line. The keywords *and* and *or* are used to link data flows.

Structured English

Structured English is also used with some methods. This method is widely used by system engineers who have no formal training in computers.

The generic guidelines for using structured English are as follows:

1. Use command verbs to describe operations, transformations, or actions.
2. Use attribute names for data to be manipulated.
3. Use prepositions and conjunctions to show logical relationships.
4. Commonly understood (semantically precise) mathematical, physical, business, and technical terms may be used.
5. Mathematical equations as well as illustrations such as tables, diagrams, and graphs may also be used for clarification.
6. Words other than those just listed should be used sparingly and only to help document the behavior.
7. Sentence or paragraph structures must be simple with single-entry, single-exit constructs. The constructs should consist only of the following:
   - Sequence: actions that occur in a specified time sequence.
   - Concurrence: more than one action taking place simultaneously.
   - Decision: a branch in the flow of actions is made based on the results of a test.
   - Repetition: the same action(s) are repeated until some specified limit or result is reached.

Examples are given in Figure 7-4. Words that appear in all capitals are attributes (i.e., data) and lines that are indented represent subordination.

```
1. Sequence Example
     Find INTEREST DUE as
          RATE x INSTALLATION PERIOD x PRINCIPAL.
     Next, subtract INTEREST DUE from ACCOUNT BALANCE.
     Next, issue REMAINING BALANCE as ACCOUNT BALANCE.
2. Concurrency Example
     Calculate NAVAID DISTANCE as great circle distance from
          AIRCRAFT POSITION to NAVAID POSITION.
     Calculate ALT DIFFERENCE as
          AIRCRAFT ALTITUDE—NAVAID ALTITUDE.
3. Decision Example
     If AMOUNT REQUESTED is greater than LIMIT,
     then:
          return "NOT APPROVED"
     else:
          subtract AMOUNT REQUESTED from LIMIT.
          Next, return "APPROVED"
     endif:
4. Repetition Example
     For each member of selected Accounts:
          ask each account to change its INTERESTRATE to NEWINTERESTRATE.
     endfor:
```

FIGURE 7-4 Examples of structured English.

Recommended Approach

ALTHOUGH the use of process flow diagrams may be more familiar to most of us, we do not recommend it. When they are used, analysts and developers have a tendency to map activities onto services of objects and to use the analysis as the specification of services. This is very bad practice because many of our activities violate the encapsulation and information-hiding principles of object-oriented technology. When these principles are violated, a system with high coupling and poor cohesion is created. A highly coupled system of objects with poor cohesion means that software is less maintainable and less flexible. We believe that the improper use of process flow diagrams will cause the development of poor software.

We recommend using the existing method of McMenamin and Palmer to specify the behavior of objects. The steps are very simple:

1. List all of the external and internal events to which the application/system needs to respond.
2. From each event, usually a message, determine how and in what sequence the messages will be passed between objects necessary to satisfy the request.
3. Capture these sequences by drawing a sequence diagram for each scenario and its variations. These scenarios or sequence of messages are useful for understanding the application/system and for integrated testing.
4. (Added by the authors) If you haven't already created a use-case model, create a use-case model for the scenarios. This is almost always necessary for large systems, as the number of actual scenarios or sequence diagrams would be overwhelming.
5. Capture the details of "how each service is provided." By thinking through each scenario, the analyst/developer can specify precisely what must be done in each of the object services. Then, the details of the actions to be taken within a service are captured using structured English.[12]

Example

Based on earlier analysis, we have the following objects with a mowTheLawn service: John, Peter, Paul, Elizabeth, Mary, Jack, and ProfessionalLawnMower. Remember that we are assuming that the family lawn already has a change or set heightOfGrass service

---

[12] Although there are advantages and disadvantages to all three techniques of documenting the behavior, we recommend using structured English for the following reasons: (1) In many organizations the analysis is performed by noncomputer scientists/programmers and, for them, structured English is easier to understand than either data flow diagram or flow charts. (2) DFDs and flowcharting should be used with a computer aided software engineering (CASE) tool. Unfortunately, most CASE tools today do not provide satisfactory end-to-end support. (3) Furthermore, today, CASE tools for object-oriented methods are neither easy to use nor conducive to the way we really do analysis and design. (4) Many of us still assume that when we use DFDs or flowcharts, we can revert back to functional decomposition. When we do this, we negate the benefits of going to object-oriented technology. Again, most CASE tools have not enforced the additional semantic constraints on DFDs and flowcharts that are really implied by using these same techniques for documenting object (class) behavior.

OBJECT NAME	John

SERVICE: "mowFamilyLawn (no arguments)"
If MYCONDITION is equal to "tired,"
then:
for each child in selected Children
ask each child to "mow the lawn" for five dollars.
if answer is "yes,"
then:
remove "mowFamilylawn" from SCHEDULE.
return;
else:
endif:
endfor:
perform mowing the lawn.
else:
perform mowing the lawn.
endif:

FIGURE 7-5 Service provisions of John for mowing the lawn.

because it is algorithmically simple. The definition of service for mowTheLawn for each object is shown in Figure 7-5 using structured English.

For this model to work, we will need an external object (Cron job) that will periodically (i.e., every 15 minutes) ask each object, including John, to start the service/task that is on its schedule. This is a very common external event; many services are called based on a predetermined schedule. Let us presume that John's mowTheLawn service has scheduled the actual mowing (mowFamilyLawn service) to occur at 7 P.M. when John comes home. When John comes home, he will immediately perform the mowFamilyLawn service. Figure 7-4 defines the mowFamilyLawn service.

We have not refined the actual mowing the lawn. We have also assumed that John has a way of contacting all of his children. We will show how contacting his children can be accomplished in a later chapter.

OBJECT NAMES	Paul, Elizabeth, Mary

SERVICE: mow the lawn (ADDRESS_OF_LAWN, DOLLAR_AMOUNT)
if DOLLAR_AMOUNT is less than five dollars,
then:
get SCHEDULE for evening (7p.m.–9p.m.)
Next, if SCHEDULE has open slot,
then:
place mowLawn in slot.
associate ADDRESS_OF_LAWN with mowLawn.
return "yes, I will mow lawn this evening."
else:
return "no, I cannot mow the lawn."
endif
else:
get Jack's TELEPHONE NUMBER from Telephone Book.
ask Jack to mow the lawn (ADDRESS_OF_LAWN, self, ADDRESS)
if Jack's response is "yes,"
then:
return "Yes, I will mow lawn this evening."
else
return "No, I cannot mow the lawn."
endif:
endif;

FIGURE 7-6 CRC card for Paul, Elizabeth, and Mary in the lawn-mowing example.

OBJECT NAME	Peter

SERVICE: "mow the lawn (ADDRESS_OF_LAWN, DOLLAR_AMOUNT)"
get SCHEDULE for evening (7p.m.–9p.m.)
Next, if SCHEDULE has open slot,
then:
place mowLawn in slot.
associate ADDRESS_OF_LAWN with mowLawn.
return "Yes, I will mow the lawn this evening."
else:
return "No, I cannot mow the lawn."
endif

FIGURE 7-7 CRC card for Peter in the lawn-mowing example.

Now, let us look at the mowTheLawn service for the children. All of the children, with the exception of Peter, will delegate any lawn-mowing request that pays over five dollars to Jack, who will mow any lawn for four dollars. Their service is defined in Figure 7-6. Peter always mows the lawn, regardless of the pay. His service is defined in Figure 7-7.

The children have a mowLawn service instead of a mowFamilyLawn service, as the children will mow any lawn. Because of this flexibility, we needed to associate a lawn address with that service. In the case of John, we did not do this as John will only mow the family lawn. Also, for the children to be able to get access to Jack, it is assumed they have access to his telephone number via the telephone book. In a later chapter, we will discuss the various vehicles by which one object has access to another object's services. The definition of the mowTheLawn service for Jack and for the Professional-LawnMower is left to the reader.

If we think about when a person performs a service, which is a sequence of actions, we quickly realize that most of our behaviors have to do with time or elapsed time. For example, we wake up after having slept for x number of hours, go to sleep at y o'clock, and eat at a certain time. Thus, the only external event in this application is time elapsed.

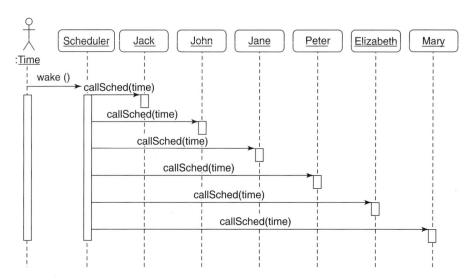

FIGURE 7-8   Scheduler's sequence diagram from lawn-mower example.

A reasonable model of this "real-world" situation is to assume that it only needs to be modeled at 15-minute intervals, so that a person can schedule her/his life at 15-minute intervals and at no finer granularity. Thus, the high-level sequence diagram may look like the one illustrated in Figure 7-8.

The Scheduler is a new object; its sole purpose is to ask an object that uses scheduling to perform a required task based on what the time is now. Each object operates as if it can perform some service (function) every 15 minutes. If one of the objects were scheduled to "mowLawn" at 7 P.M., the schedule will send a message to that object to execute its callSchedJ with the argument of 7 P.M. In each object, the callSchedJ method is the same; it checks its schedule to see what service (function) needs to be performed. In this case, it would be the mowLawn service.

■ ■ SUMMARY

FOLLOWING are the detailed steps of our approach for specifying static behavior and for identifying additional services:

1. List all of the external and internal events to which the application/system needs to respond.
2. From each event, usually a message, determine how and in what sequence messages will be passed between objects necessary to satisfy the request.
3. Define and draw a sequence diagram for each scenario and its variations.
4. If the number of scenarios is large (and you aren't already using use cases), consider creating a use-case model to reduce the number of diagrams.
5. Capture the details of each service associated with the sequence diagram by using one of the documentation techniques given in this chapter.

CHAPTER

8

Dynamic Behavior

This chapter presents techniques for capturing dynamic behavior. For applications that are not control-based, most objects (i.e., classes) will not undergo significant state changes, so that only a few (if any) will require state diagrams. However, in many control-based applications, the state diagrams may be the dominant aspect of the model.

Technically, state diagrams are the formal specifications of the behavior of a class, and thus of an object. Static behavior is really a special case of a modeless state diagram. A modeless state diagram occurs when an object (class) always responds the same way to external and internal events (stimuli). Note that scenarios are not state diagrams; they are examples of execution of the system. They usually involve several objects playing various roles. Thus, they are instances of behavior, and as such they can only illustrate behavior; they cannot define it. Technically, when all state diagrams have been created, all scenarios can be derived from this entire set of state diagrams. In fact, many developers employ scenarios to check the sanity of the model. Similarly, because a scenario is an instance of a use case, a use case is a "slice" of the system behavior across state diagrams from multiple classes.

Introduction

OBJECT-ORIENTED analysis is often described in terms of structure, behavior, and rules. The structural analysis captures the static vision of how the objects are related to each other; it essentially captures the data semantics of the application. A visual, spatial metaphor is used to document these relationships. In all of the earlier chapters, we have focused on capturing the structural aspects of the application. In contrast, behavior analysis captures the time-dependent aspects of the application. For example, it is used to specify how to hire employees, dismiss employees, add diagrams to a document, or delete a word from a document. Thus, whether the behavior is static or dynamic, the method description captures the procedural semantics of the application over time. Rules, which will be discussed in a later chapter, capture the declarative semantics of the application.

If the application has no time-dependent[1] behavior, then capturing the structural aspects of the system and performing static behavioral analysis are sufficient to build the application. This is the situation with our case study so far. However, the world we live in is not static; it changes over time. Dynamic modeling mechanisms provide us a way to capture the behavior of objects, and thus the behavior of the application, over time.

Temporal relationships are difficult to capture. Most applications are best understood by first examining their static structure (data semantics); i.e., the structure of their objects and their relationships (inheritance, association, aggregation) to each other in a moment of time. After capturing this aspect of the application, we want to examine the changes to the objects and their relationships over time. Those aspects (which are parts of the procedural semantics) of an application that are concerned with these changes over time are captured in the *dynamic* model. Thus, this chapter presents mechanisms that help us capture flow of control, interactions, and sequencing of operations in an object-oriented application. The major concepts of dynamic modeling are *events*, which are the stimuli, and *states*, which are object configurations that exist between events. Thus, an application can be described in terms of object behaviors; i.e., an orderly sequence of state changes of objects over time, and the behavior of an object is captured as a chain (or probably a network) of cause (stimuli) and effect (state change) over time.

For example, the chain of cause and effect for an Order object in an order-processing system may be as follows: at placing the order: requisition state; at filling a line item of the order: partially filled state; at shipping of line item: partially shipped state; when all of the line items have been filled and shipped: shipped state. When the order is shipped, an Invoice object is created and the Order object's data is archived and the object is deleted from the system.[2] Figure 8-1 shows a chain diagram depicting this.

---

[1]   The behavior that is being discussed is not truly time-dependent; it is actually dependent on the past history of the system.

[2]   Archiving the data associated with the Order object will allow one to reconstruct the Order object in the event that the customer contests the invoice.

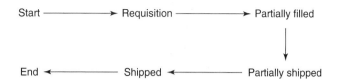

FIGURE 8-1 Chain of cause and effect for an Order object.

Techniques for Identifying Dynamic Behavior

AN object in the real world normally has a lifetime. Often it is created or comes into existence, progresses through certain stages, and then dies or vanishes. For example, a human being is conceived by her/his parents, processes through stages (baby, child, pre-schooler, grammar schooler, teenager, young adult, mid-age, senior citizen), and eventually dies. Some individuals do not visit all stages; and others appear to have reverted back to an earlier stage. However, all humans follow this basic pattern of dynamic behavior throughout their lifetimes.

From our general observations on behavior patterns for different things in the real world, we conclude as follows:

- Most things go through various stages during their lifetimes.
- The order in which a thing progresses through its stages forms a pattern that helps in classifying the kind of thing it is.
- In a pattern, not all progressions between stages are allowed. Some progressions are forbidden by the laws of physics, some by statute, etc.
- There are incidents/events in the real world that cause a thing to progress (or indicate that it has progressed) between stages.

For technical reasons, we also add the following assumptions:

- A thing is in exactly one and only one stage of its behavior pattern at any given time.
- Things progress from one stage to another stage instantaneously.

Note that the granularity of time depends on the degree of abstraction and can vary at different levels of the application. Basically, however, the progression (transition) must be treated as atomic, that is, noninterruptible, at the given level of abstraction. Thus, the incident or event that causes the progression must be treated as atomic, for an incident occurs at a point in time, while a stage (state) is a configuration of objects that exists between incidents.

Let us now test these observations and assumptions on a second example. Figure 8-2 shows the behavior pattern for an airplane. In this example, the airplane goes through numerous stages, which are shown by the bold text. They include parked at the gate, taxiing to runway, and so on. The pattern is simple and is shown in the figure by

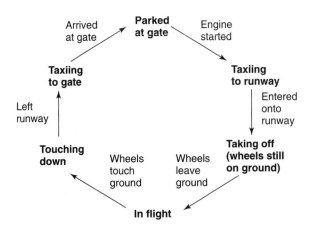

FIGURE 8-2   Behavior pattern for an airplane.

using arrows. The pattern of progressing through stages applies to all instances of airplane. Not all progressions between stages are allowed, as the law of physics prevents an airplane from progressing from parked at the gate to being in flight. There are incidents/events that signal the progression between states. These incidents/events are shown as labels on the arrows. For example, when the airplane is in the "taking-off' stage, "wheels leaving the ground" signals the progression from the "taking-off" stage to the "in flight" stage. The wheels leave the ground instantaneously and at any given instance of time, we can assume that the airplane is in one of these above stages.

It is very important to note that the stages are defined by our perception (model) of reality and that some of the incidents/events are really indicators of the progression (change of state) from one stage to another stage. We will see later that the progressions (changes of state) are used as a vehicle to cause an action (execution of code) to occur during the "instantaneous" progression from one stage to another stage. Thus, stages are defined because the thing may need to take some action when the incident/event occurs. For instance, in the airplane example, when the "wheels leaves the ground," the wheels need to be lifted back into the airplane. Also, when the airplane "touches down," the brakes are applied and usually the engines are reversed.

Common Lifecycle Forms

The pattern that characterizes a *Class* is called its *lifecycle form*. While any pattern/form is possible, two forms appear to dominate the modeling of computer applications at this time. Sally Shlaer and Stephen Mellor (1988) have given names to these patterns. They are:

- Circular lifecycle
  Circular lifecycle generally applies when the object/class has an operational cycle for its behavior.
  Examples include the airplane, a microwave oven, a robotic drill.

■ Born-and-die lifecycle

When an instance gets created and deleted (or rests in a final state) during the life of the system being analyzed, the class is a good candidate for this form. Examples include a human in the history of mankind, an account in a banking system, a logging record, and a bar of candy in the course of a few days.

Models for Capturing Lifecycle

Historically, state models were used with structured methods to show how a system behaves when it receives external events from objects outside of the system. One of the weaknesses of this technique was that we lumped the system into one large object, and the number of states that were needed exploded. Today, we assign a state model (machine) per object (i.e., the state model is part of the class definition of an object). This would reduce the state explosion problem and assign the state to the appropriate objects that exhibit the dynamic behavior for the system. This also makes managing the complexity of dynamic behavior much more maintainable and flexible.

A *state model* establishes relationships among *states* of an object. *Events* establish *transitions* between states as a result of *events*, *actions*, and *activities* performed by the object.

■ *State model*

This is a sequence of states that an object goes through during its lifetime in response to events. It also includes the responses to events.

■ *State*[3]

This represents a stage in the lifecycle of a typical object. A state is technically a period of time during which an object is waiting for an event to occur.

■ *Event*

An event is a condition that can be detected by the object. Events can cause a transition to another state and/or they can cause one or more actions to be triggered. Technically, an event is an occurrence at a point in time where granularity of time depends on the degree of abstraction. Though the granularity of time may vary at different levels of the same application, an event must be atomic (i.e., noninterruptible) at the given level of abstraction. An event is a one-way asynchronous transmission[4] of information from one object to another. It may have parameters with names and types as part of the message sent.

---

[3]   The complete internal state for an object is the combination of the data values of the attributes within the object. This may lead to thousands or millions of states, so the state we choose to describe in a state model usually depends either on a grouping of data values and ranges, or they depend on the group of operations permitted (based on attribute values) on the object during different parts of its lifecycle. Thus, a state is an abstraction of the attribute values of an object.

[4]   Two-way information flow (e.g., call-and-return) can always be modeled as two one-way information flows.

■ *Transition*

A transition is a response by an object to an event received by it. The response produces a change in the object that can constitute a change in state.[5] The mechanism for identifying if a change in state occurs is a *guard condition*.[6] A guard condition is a Boolean expression in terms of event parameters and the state variables and functions of the object to which the state diagram belongs. When an event triggers the transition, the value of the guard condition is evaluated. If the value evaluates to true, the transition occurs; otherwise, the transition does not occur. Not all transitions have an associated guard condition.[7]

■ *Action*

An action is an activity or an operation that is done inside of a state or on a transition. An action is atomic and instantaneous; that is, it is not interruptible at the abstraction level of the associated state. An action might set or modify one of the data members of the object, trigger an event in another object, execute one of the operations on the object, or call one of the public operations of another object. An action can occur during a transition, on entry into a state, during the entire period an object is in a state, on exit from a state, or on arrival of an event that does not cause a state transition.

■ *Activity*

An activity is an operation or set of operations that is executing during the entire period an object is in a state. An activity is not atomic and may be interrupted by an event while it is executing.

Four forms of state models are widely used in analysis: (1) Mealy, (2) Moore, (3) Harel, and (4) modified Harel. The UML state model is based upon the modified Harel. These models differ in terms of where actions are placed in the model. In the Mealy model, an action is performed when the transition is occurring. In the Moore model, an action is performed when an object enters into the state. In the Harel model, an action is performed when the transition is occurring, but it adds substates and other powerful constructs. In the modified Harel, an action can be performed when the transition is occurring, when an object enters a state, and when an object exits a state. UML has also allowed activities that occur while an object is in a state. Thus, UML represents a generalized case and can encompass all of the accepted state models.[8] State models are usually documented graphically using *state transition diagrams*, as shown later in this chapter.

---

[5] Recall that we can choose our states to reflect ranges on attributes rather than individual data values to limit the number of states. Hence, a change in attributes may not be sufficient to cause a change in state.

[6] Guard conditions on transactions is a UML notation. Historically, such conditions in state machine models were called transition rules.

[7] Some guard conditions are simply the Boolean value true. This is a useful approach when a tool requires a guard condition.

[8] This allows individuals familiar with Mealy, Moore, or Harel to capture their state models using UML.

In UML, three additional constructs are added: *history state*, *activity*, and *timing mark*. A *history state* is used to capture the concept that a state must "remember" its substate when it is exited and be able to enter the same substate on subsequent reentry into the state. An *activity* is an operation or set of operations within a state that takes time to complete. Thus, it is not instantaneous and can be interrupted. Some activities continue until they are terminated by an external event (usually a state change) and others terminate on their own accord. A *timing mark* construct is used to capture real-time constraints on transition. The most common use of a timing mark is to capture the maximum limits on the elapsed time between events.

Identifying and Specifying Events

FROM the previous discussion of the lifecycle model, one of the key components that we need to identify is event(s). In this section, we learn techniques to identify and specify events.

Use Case and Scenario

As described in Chapter 4, a *use case* is a generic description of an entire transaction involving several objects. A *scenario* is an instance of a use case. It shows a particular series of interactions among objects in a single execution of the system. This single execution of the system typically constitutes a transaction (from the external object's perspectives) between the external object and the application/system.

Scenarios can be shown in two different ways:

1. *Sequence diagram*

   This shows the interaction among a set of objects in temporal order, which is very useful in understanding timing issues. An alternate form is a text dialog; a form that is widely used by nontechnical requirement writers.

2. *Collaboration diagram*

   This shows the interactions among a set of objects as nodes in a graph, which is helpful in understanding software structure, as all of the interactions that affect an object are localized around it.

Sequence Diagram

Of the two ways to show scenarios, we will only discuss the sequence diagram in this book.[9] The basic elements of a sequence diagram were introduced previously. There is a form of the sequence diagram that captures procedure-calling sequences in situations where there is a single point of control at any given time. In this scheme, a double line is

---

[9] While collaboration diagrams provide greater detail about the relationships among objects, they tend to be more complicated and most novices overlook or misinterpret them.

used to show the period of time in which an object has a thread of control. Thus, a single line indicates that the object is blocked (not in control) and is waiting for an event to give it control.

Example

For better understanding, let us borrow an example from Shlaer and Mellor. Suppose we want to model a scaled-down microwave oven, the One Minute Microwaver. The product requirements are as follows:

1. There is a single control button available for the users of the oven.
2. If the oven door is closed and a user pushes the button, the oven will cook (i.e., energize the tube) for 1 minute.
3. If user pushes the button at any time when the oven is cooking, user gets an additional minute of cooking time. For example, if the user has 31 seconds more cooking time to go and he/she pushes the button twice, the cook time is now for 2 minutes and 31 seconds.
4. Using the button with the door open has no effect.
5. There is a light inside the oven.
6. Any time the oven is cooking, the light must be turned on (so that the user can peer through the window in the oven's door and see if her/his food is boiling over).
7. Any time the door is open, the light must be on (so that the user can see the food or have enough light to clean the oven).
8. User can stop the cooking by opening the door.
9. If user closes the door, the light goes out. This is the normal configuration when someone has just placed food inside the oven but has not yet pushed the control button.
10. If the oven times out (cooks until the desired preset time), it turns off both the power tube and the light. It also then emits a warning beep to tell the user that the food is ready.

From the textual requirements, the following pertinent incidents are identified:

- Opening the door
- Closing the door
- Using the control button
- Completion of the prescribed cooking interval

These incidents are events that may cause the oven to have to perform some operations and also change its state. These incidents are abstracted or captured as events. With those external events, we can create the following set of sequence diagrams for the microwave oven using use cases and scenarios: Scenario 1 is the normal case and is show in Figure 8-3. Please note that all scenarios are developed from an external (user's) perspective. In scenario 2, no additional time was added. This is shown in Figure 8-4. In scenario 3, the user opens the door while food is cooking. This is shown in Figure 8-5.

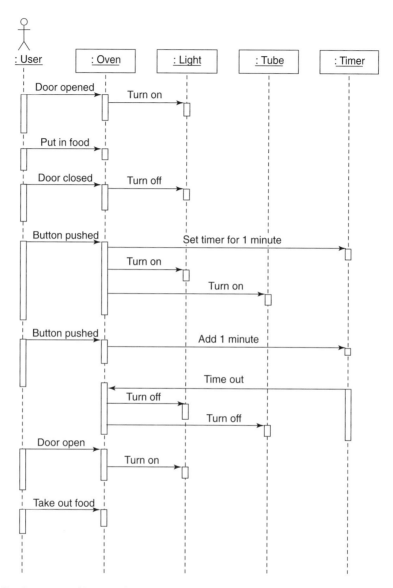

FIGURE 8-3 Sequence diagram for microwave oven in scenario 1.

These scenarios cover all the various sequences that are pertinent to the building of the state model. Technically, the user opens the door and the door notifies the oven that the door is open; similarly for the closing the door. The user also pushes the button and the button notifies the oven that the button has been pushed. However, neither the button nor the door takes any action on its own from these incidents. We modeled it as if the user opening the door is sending a signal to the oven directly; this simplifies the model with no loss of information for our purposes. This is shown in Figure 8-6.

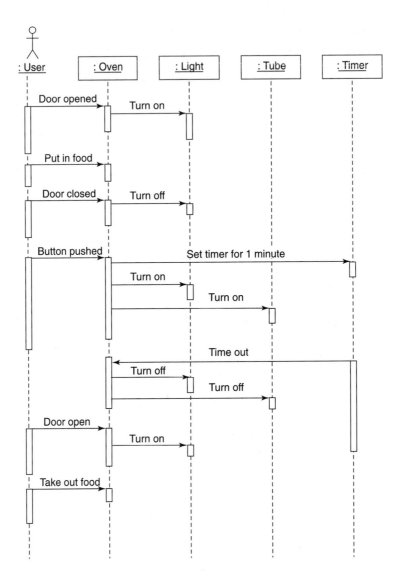

FIGURE 8-4   Sequence diagram for microwave oven in scenario 2.

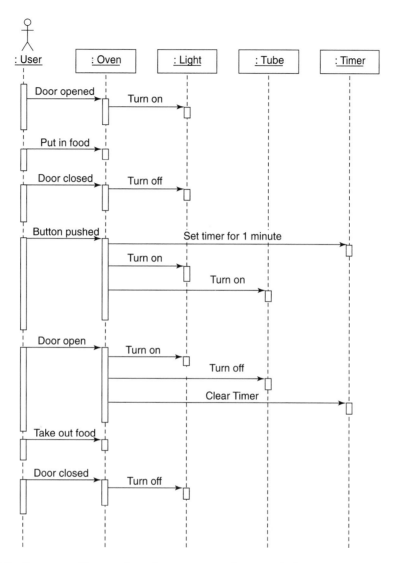

FIGURE 8-5   Sequence diagram for microwave oven in scenario 3.

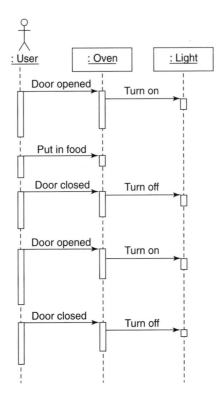

FIGURE 8-6   Sequence diagram for microwave oven in scenario 4. The user is opening and closing the door.

Specifying Dynamic Behavior

USE cases and scenarios are not sufficient documentation for development. We will now look at ways of documenting the events and documenting the dynamic behavior in a form more suited for programming.

Event List

An *event* is the abstraction of an incident or signal in the real world that tells some object of the system that it is (or may be) moving to a new state. In the abstraction process, four aspects of an event should be specified:

1. Meaning

   The meaning of an event is usually captured in a short phrase that tells what is going on in the real world. For example, "wheel leave ground" in the airplane example and "door open" in the microwave example.

2. Destination

   The object[10] that receives the event. By convention, the event is sent only to one receiver.

---

[10] The state model is part of an object. Because lifecycle patterns are by class, we define the state model for the entire class.

3. Label

A unique label must be provided for each event to distinguish different events from each other. This is very important when there are distinct events with similar meanings. Though the label is arbitrary, the suggested format for labeling is to use a letter-number combination. A convenient convention is to use destination-based labeling, in which all events that are received by the same class begin with the class's key letter(s).[11]

4. Event data

An event should be thought of as a service request. Thus, it can and usually will carry data. This data is given to the object as parameters of the service request.

An *event list* is simply a listing of all the events from the scenarios that are applicable to the definition of the state models for the objects within the application/system. The event list for the microwave oven is shown in Table 8-1.

Without the sequence diagram, most of us would consider "putting in the food" and "taking out the food" as important incidents. However, the sequence diagram shows that they do not cause any action to occur and thus are not material to the modeling process. This may seem strange to the novice, as the primary purpose of the microwave is to heat food. In reality, the microwave will work with no food in it, and we can

TABLE 8-1   Event List

Label	Meaning	Source	Destination	Data
V1	Door open	User	Oven	None
V2	Door closed	User	Oven	None
V3	Button pushed	User	Oven	None
V4	Timer timeout	Timer	Oven	None
L1	Turn on light	Oven	Light	None
L2	Turn off light	Oven	Light	None
P1	Turn on tube (energize tube)	Oven	Tube	None
P2	Turn off tube (deenergize tube)	Oven	Tube	None
T1	Set timer for 1 minute	Oven	Timer	None
T2	Add a minute to timer	Oven	Timer	None
T3	Clear timer	Oven	Timer	None

---

[11] The classes's key letter(s) is a developer-defined way to refer to a class with an abbreviation rather than the full class name. For example, a class named Microwave could use mw as the key letters. The use of key letters is an artifact of the C programming roots of C++ in which functions that operated on specific data structures used key letters to allow programmers to remember an association between the function and the data structure upon which it was to operate.

turn on our microwave with nothing in it. So our model does capture accurately how a microwave is actually designed and built. Also the warning beep is an incident, but the processing of that event is handled by the external object (user). Thus, it is not an event that the system will process and thus is not on our event list.

State Transition Table

In dynamic behavior modeling, a *state* is given a number and a name that is unique within the state model. The number is used in the state transition table to depict the next state and does not prescribe the order in which an object would occupy the states. An *action* is a set of operations that must be done when the transition occurs. The following operations are allowed:

- Read and write operations involving their own attributes
- Generate an event to be sent to any other object, including itself
- Generate an event to something outside the scope of analysis (e.g., an operator, a hardware device, or an object in another system/subsystem)
- Create, delete, set, reset, read a timer
- Access services of another object, including objects in its same class

Because the operations allowed are very liberal in an action, it is the responsibility of the analyst/developer to ensure the consistency of the state model as a whole. Thus, analysts should ensure the following:

- Leave the object consistent.
  If an attribute gets updated, any attribute that computationally depends on it must be updated.

- Ensure consistency of relationship.
  If the action creates or deletes an object, it must ensure that any relationships involving those objects are made consistent with the rules stated on the model.

- Leave subtypes and supertypes consistent.
  If action migrates an object from one type to another type, it must ensure that all the proper objects and relationships are managed.

In a *state transition table*, each row represents one of the possible states (stages) of the state model,[12] and each column represents an event that has this state model as its destination. The cells of the table are filled in with the specification of what happens when an instance of class (e.g., your specific microwave oven) in a given state (row in the table) receives a particular event (the column).

---

[12] A state model belongs to an object.

The process of creating the state transition table for each class[13] is as follows:

1. Place all of the events that have the same destination on the columns of the table.

2. Start with one row if you have not identified any stages, or use your stages as possible states.

3. Take each scenario and start filling in the cells in the table, showing the next state above the line and the action below the line.

4. When you run into a conflict (i.e., a cell has to respond to an event differently for two different scenarios), add a new state to the model; this means that there was a change in state (stage) that has not been captured in the original analysis.[14]

5. Keep doing steps 3 and 4 until all of the scenarios are captured in a consistent manner in the table.

6. Now check the empty cells and decide if these are event ignored or can't happen situations.[15]

7. Finally, reduce any identical rows to one row, if you are using the Mealy model.

The state transition tables for the microwave oven are shown in Table 8-2, Table 8-3, Table 8-4, and Table 8-5.

TABLE 8-2

States	L1: Turn On	L2: Turn Off
1. On	Event ignored [4]	2 None
2. Off	1 None	Event ignored [4]

Note 1: When light is on, ignore "on" request; similarly for "off."

---

[13] Because patterns of behavior hold over an entire class, we define a state model for the class. Each object gets its own state model, just like attributes.

[14] This is usually seen as the need to perform different actions when the event is received in the different scenarios.

[15] Steps 6 and 7 are very important to ensure the completeness of the analysis.

TABLE 8-3   Microwave Oven

States	V1: Door Open	V2: Door Closed	V3: Button Pushed	V4: Timer Timeout
1. Idle with door open	Can't happen [1]	___2___ Turn off light	Event ignored	Can't happen [2]
2. Idle with door closed	___1___ Turn on light	Can't happen [3]	___3___ Set timer to 1 minute; turn on light; turn on tube	Can't happen [2]
3. Initial cooking period	___6___ Turn off tube; clear timer	Can't happen [3]	___4___ Add 1 minute to timer	___5___ Turn off tube; turn off light; sound warning beep
4. Extended cooking period	___6___ Turn off tube; clear timer	Can't happen [3]	___4___ Add 1 minute to timer	___5___ Turn off tube; turn off light; sound warning beep
5. Cooking complete	___1___ Turn on light	Can't happen [3]	Event ignored	Can't happen [2]
6. Cooking interrupted	Can't happen [1]	___2___ Turn off light	Event ignored	Can't happen [2]

Note 2: Door is already open.

Note 3: Timer is not running.

Note 4: Door is already closed.

TABLE 8-4   Timer

State	T1: Set Timer	T2: Add Time	T3: Clear Timer	T4: Clock Tick	T5: Fire
1. Idle	2 Set time remaining to 1 minute; set up ticking mechanism	Can't happen [6]	Can't happen [6]	Can't happen [7]	Can't happen [9]
2. Set	Can't happen [8]	5 Add 1 minute to time remaining	1 Clear time remaining: unset tick mechanism	3 Subtract one time tick from remaining time	Can't happen [9]
3. Counting down	Can't happen [8]	5 Add 1 minute to time remaining	1 Clear time remaining: unset tick mechanism	3 Subtract one time tick from remaining time; check if time remaining is <= 0; if so, generate internal T5 signal to cause transition to firing state	4 Generate T3 signal to effect transition from firing to idle
4. Firing	Can't happen [8]	Event ignored [10]	1 Clear time remaining: unset tick mechanism	Event ignored [10]	Can't happen [9]
5. Adding	Can't happen [8]	5 Add 1 minute to time remaining	1 Clear time remaining: unset tick mechanism	3 Subtract one time tick from remaining time	Can't happen [9]

Note 5: Timer is not active.

Note 6: Tick mechanism is not active.

Note 7: Timer is already set.

Note 8: T5 is an internal signal that is generated only when it is in state 3.

Note 9: Too late.

TABLE 8-5   Power Tube

States	P1: Turn On	P2: Turn Off
1. On	Event ignored [5]	2 None
2. Off	1 None	Event ignored [5]

Note 10: When tube is energized, ignore "on" request; similarly for off.

Observe that states 1 and 6 are identical state transitions; states 3 and 4 are also identical. However, in each case, the precondition for entering each state is different. For instance, you can only get into the cooking interrupt state from prior states when the power tube is on and the timer is turned on. A person can be opening and closing the microwave door to cause the state model to move from state 1 to state 2 and back to state 1, which would not require that the timer be cleared and the tube to be deenergized. When we get to diagramming the state models, we will see the impact of these preconditions on the different state models.

We can assume that these objects have methods that really turn on and off the physical devices.

Documenting Dynamic Behavior

WE will look at a graphic form, the state diagram, for documenting the state model in a class.[16]

State Diagrams

A *state diagram* is a graphic form of documenting a state model. It describes in pictorial form all the possible ways in which the objects respond to events sent by other objects.[17] A simple UML state diagram for an object with two states is illustrated in Figure 8-7. The start state is indicated by a transition into it from a solid circle. The solid circle is often interpreted as the initial creation of the object with the transition into the start state a result of completing the initialization of the object.[18] The final state[19] of the object is indicated by a solid circle within a circle.

---

[16] Though each object has its own state model, we define the template for the state model in the class. Remember all objects in the same class have copies of the same state model.

[17] Events may be external or internal.

[18] This perspective allows us to deal with situations in which an object may not be in a consistent state until initialization has been completed. The transition into the initial state is an indication that the object has reached consistency.

[19] The final state is a state that has no exit transition (i.e., you can enter and cannot leave). This does not mean that an object is destroyed.

A state is composed of:

■ Name

A textual string that distinguishes this state from other states. A state may be anonymous (have no name).

■ Entry action (keyword: entry)

Actions executed on entry into the state.

■ Exit action (keyword: exit)

Actions executed on exit from the state.

■ Internal transitions (keyword: on)

Transitions that are handled without causing a change in state.

■ Activity (keyword: do)

An ongoing computation that occurs the entire time the object is in a state.

■ Substates

A nested structure of the state. It may involve disjointed sequentially active substates or concurrently active substates.

■ Deferred events (keyword: defer, NEW)

A list of events that are not handled in that state. These events are postponed and queued for handling by objects in another state.

States are represented in UML by rounded rectangles with a horizontal line that separates the name of the state from the other components of the state. Transitions are directed arrows that link the initial state to the final state. In UML, when an action is listed within a state, it is preceded by a label that indicates when the action is supposed to happen. There are four possible kinds of labels:

■ **Entry**: the action is performed when the state is entered
■ **Exit**: the action is performed just before the transition to the new state
■ **Do**: the action is performed continuously during the entire period that the object is in this state
■ **On** *any event name*: the action is performed when the event occurs and the object stays in the same state.

A transition is composed of:

■ Source state

The state affected by the transition (i.e., the active state). The transition fires when an event is received and a guard condition, if any, is satisfied (obviously the object must also be in the source state at the time).

■ Event

Its reception makes the transition eligible to be fired.

■ Guard condition

A Boolean expression that can be evaluated when a transition is triggered. If the evaluation is true, the transition is fired. If the evaluation is false, the transition may not fire, and if no other transition may be triggered by the event, the event is lost.

■ Action

An executable atomic computation. In this context, it is executed during the transition.

■ Target state

The state that is active after the completion of the transition.

■ Signals

A list of events (signals) that may be generated during the transition.

In UML, a transition is labeled by:

■ The event that causes the transition (mandatory)
■ Any guard condition (optional)
■ Any action that is performed during the transition (optional)
■ Any event that is generated by the transition (optional)

The event associated with the transition is identified by a label followed by the event data enclosed within parentheses. If there isn't any event data, the parentheses will be empty. Any guard condition will appear after the event enclosed within square brackets. Any action performed during a transition appears in the diagram after triggering event and condition separated from them by a "/". An event generated appears after the transition action and is preceded by a carot, "^". The target of the event is separated by a label separated from the event name by a period. The generated event has its associated arguments. It should be noted that a transition must have an associated event, but does not necessarily have an associated guard condition, action, or generated event.

The simple state diagram also illustrates one additional feature: a *transition to self*. A transition to self is a transition from an initial state back to the initial state. There is a distinction between handling an event within a state and as a transition to self. In the case in which an event is handled within the state, the entry and exit actions are not performed. However, on a transition to self, both the entry and exit actions are performed as well as any actions specified in the transition.

The simple state diagram illustrated in Figure 8-7 is sufficient for simple state models. More complex state models will incorporate nested states (i.e., substates). The UML diagram for illustrating a nested state diagram is illustrated in Figure 8-8. The transition from the nested solid circle identifies the entry substate. Actions are associated with the nested states rather than the encompassing state.

UML supports even more complex state models by allowing concurrent substates. Concurrent substates are viewed (for modeling purposes) as having separate threads of

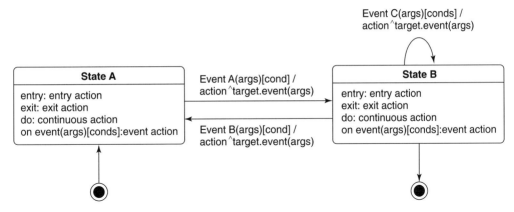

FIGURE 8-7   Simple state diagram.

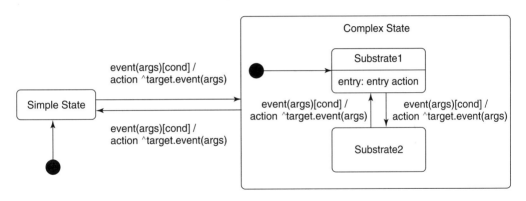

FIGURE 8-8   Nested state diagram.

control. That is, each substate can act independently of the other. An example of concurrent substates for filling out a section of course registration requests is illustrated in Figure 8-9. In this example, a transition to the next state occurs only when all nested concurrent states have reached the exit conditions. This should be contrasted with the situation illustrated in Figure 8-10.

As stated previously, UML supports both Mealy and Moore state diagrams. The choice of how a state model is captured depends upon analyst preference. In the case of our example, either approach is acceptable. Figures 8-11 and 8-12 are the state diagrams (Mealy and Moore) for the state transition diagram of the microwave oven. One of the powerful aspects of UML is that it can support both the Mealy and Moore models. In the Mealy model, states from the transition table were collapsed because the actions are associated with the transition.

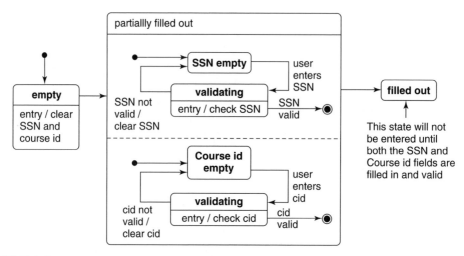

FIGURE 8-9   Nested concurrent substates with exit requiring both concurrent substates to reach exit states prior to exit from the enclosing state.

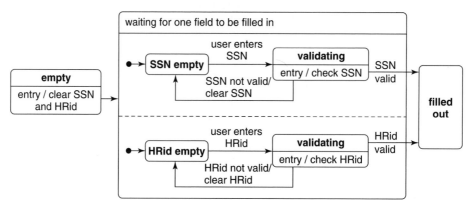

FIGURE 8-10   Nested concurrent substates with exit requiring satisfaction of either of the substates.

In the Moore model, the action is associated with the state. We cannot eliminate identical rows from the model. In our model, the action is associated with the entry into the state. There are models that allow associate action with exit from a state also. UML supports a model that allows action with transition, entry into a state, and exit from a state. However, in practice, we normally associate the action with the transition. The Harel model also associates the action with the transition, but it also allows substates and other powerful capabilities. State models are not the only model that can be used for capturing dynamic behavior. Other models such as Petri Nets exist to handle more sophisticated dynamic behavior. The state model is usually sufficient for most practitioners.

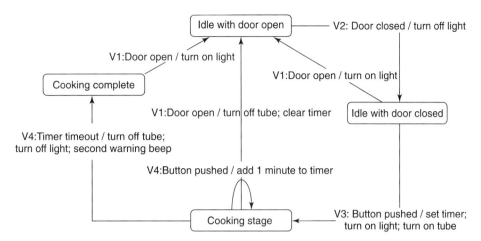

FIGURE 8-11   UML notation for Mealy state diagram for microwave oven.

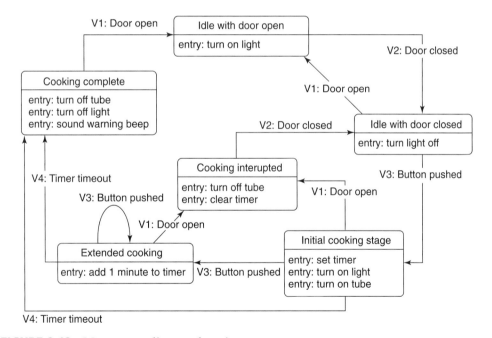

FIGURE 8-12   Moore state diagram for microwave oven.

Recommended Approach

THE steps we recommend for performing behavioral analysis are:

1. Prepare scenarios of all of the typical interaction sequences.
2. Prepare scenarios of all of the accepted business exception cases.

3. If appropriate, prepare scenarios of all of the failures and rare cases. Failures include error conditions, equipment failures, and undesirable and unusual behaviors.[20] In object-oriented methods, the failure conditions that are to be processed by the application/system should be formalized into the analysis model just as normal behaviors.[21]

4. Develop sequence diagrams for all case that will help identify events.

5. Use the sequence diagram to generate an event list. Note that in the example that we assumed that the transition is only dependent on the reception of one event. In some situations, a transition may depend upon the arrival of two or more events from different sources. There are two ways you can handle this situation. First, you can create an intermediate state to hold the reception of one of the events and use it as a holding state for reception of the other event(s). The other choice is to add an attribute or object to hold the data. This would require the programmer to initialize and clean up the attribute or object at the appropriate times.

6. Use the event list and your knowledge of classes to create state transition tables.

7. Use the state transition table to create your state diagrams.

8. Check the state diagrams by testing the scenarios against the diagram.

▪ ▪ SUMMARY

HISTORICALLY, capturing the changes to objects and their relationships over time has been very difficult to manage. In this chapter, we presented a concept and its associated mechanisms to capture this aspect of the application/system. This concept is called dynamic behavior. We learned the following about dynamic behavior:

- ▪ How to identify it by recognizing common lifecycle forms: circular and born-and-die
- ▪ How to identify and to specify events that are the key stimuli to cause objects to change state
- ▪ How to use the events to help us identify and specify the dynamic behaviors using state transition tables
- ▪ How to document this specification in a graphical form by using a state diagram
  - ▪ A couple of types of finite state machines that may be used to implement the dynamic behavior captured using the state transition table.

---

[20] Many of us (real-time process control) know this as failure analysis and understand that proper analysis is highly problem–dependent. The purpose of failure analysis is to take into account the effect of certain kinds of malfunctions and errors and to evaluate strategies for dealing with them. In process control, the goal is to either maintain control, or recover control, or have a graceful and safe shutdown of an industrial or external process. Frequently the failure analysis leads to additional requirements, installation of new sensors, addition of electrical/mechanical safeguards, writing of emergency procedure instruction books, etc.

[21] A word of caution to the meticulous thinker: It is very easy to get carried away and investigate a myriad of possible failures. Economics and time constraints, balanced with safety, should be applied to limit the failure analysis to real and reasonable scenarios. Far-fetched scenarios should not be designed into the system. However, if there is a safety or economic damage concern, it is strongly recommended that a manual procedure be written to handle these situations. Abnormal behaviors are usually extremely complex and can cause the model to grow larger and more complex. This will make the system more difficult to maintain and to modify.

Identifying Relationships

A *poor relation is the most irrelevant thing in nature.*

Charles Lamb

In the third step of our method, we captured how each object provides services. In the process of specifying how it was done, we also demonstrated that some objects need access to services (functions) of other objects to perform the necessary operations to supply the original service. However, in the object-oriented paradigm (unlike the procedural paradigm), an object cannot just call a service (function). The message-passing paradigm requires that a service request be directed to an object. In the fourth step, we address how an object accesses the services of another object.

Accessing Another Object's Services

ONE of the fundamental differences between the object-oriented paradigm and the procedural paradigm is that in the object-oriented paradigm every service request (function call) must be sent to a specific object, while in the procedural paradigm a function can be called directly. For example, in order for object A to send a message[1] to object B, object A must have a "handle"[2] to object B. Thus, in object-oriented technology, the

---

[1]   In C++, call a function.

[2]   In C++, a reference or pointer.

analysts/developers should understand the various vehicles available to give an object access to the handle of another object.

There are three basic ways that one object accesses another object's services:[3]

1. The calling object, which somehow has a handle, passes the handle of the other object as one of the arguments of the function (message) signature.
2. The called object has a relationship (aggregation or link[4]) to the other object. A relationship gives handle(s) to other objects in the relationship.
3. The needed service belongs to an "ancestor" class.[5]

Relationships

IN a world of perfect reuse and portability, each object and/or class would be independent of every other object and/or class. Then, during step 3 (when we captured how each object provides services), we would have been able to specify all the operations of every method with operations that only use data belonging to the object and/or that is passed to the object from the calling object. In this perfect world, all services would be provided using only data associated with the object itself and the calling object. This would make reuse and portability a very easy issue.[6]

Unfortunately, *no object is an island, independent of all others*. Objects typically depend on other objects for services and possibly for error handling, constant data, and exception handling. Some objects are components of other objects, and some objects are used to join other objects. Moreover, objects are, by definition, instances of classes, and classes may inherit attributes and services from other classes. In most applications, the model needs to capture these interdependencies of the various objects.

These interdependencies are called relationships. A relationship is not merely a link that ties one object to another object so that it can access the other object's services. A relationship also carries a semantic meaning. Object-oriented technology gives both

---

[3]   There is a fourth way, the access of static class functions, which may be considered a managed global function.

[4]   Link is a relationship between objects and an association is a relationship between classes.

[5]   The standard object-oriented term for ancestor class is superclass. In brief, the service is inherited from the ancestor.

[6]   There are object-oriented experts who will argue that the use of relationships (association and aggregation) violate the encapsulation and information-hiding principles. This is a correct statement. Unfortunately, all relationships, including generalization (a.k.a. inheritance), violate the encapsulation and information-hiding principles; there are very few experts who would argue against inheritance and polymorphism. We take a more practical approach to object-oriented technology. If a mechanism helps us manage complexity, then we are willing to use it. In practice, one or more groups of collaborating objects are needed to implement a large number of the services. Experience has shown that all the mechanisms/constructs (and then some) that we will be discussing are needed to implement any application/system of any significant capability.

analysts and developers a very rich set of mechanisms or constructs to capture these semantic relationships.

In this chapter, we discuss three very important relationships: generalization, links, and aggregation.[7] These are certainly not new concepts; we work with them everyday. For example, we all learned generalization when we studied taxonomies in biology class. An excellent example of a link is marriage, and an example of aggregation (whole-parts) is a car. Moreover, links in the form of associations have been widely used for years[8] in the database modeling community.

Generalization

GENERALIZATION, as we will use it, has its roots in the knowledge-representation paradigm used in artificial intelligence. Ross Quillian's psychological model of associative memory is one example. In that representation, Quillian introduced the node-link model for representing a semantic knowledge network. The nodes represented classes, and the links represented relationships between objects in the respective classes at the nodes. In a semantic network, both the node and the link had labels. One of the most powerful labels represented the generalization relationship. That link was called the *is_a*. The concept of the is_a relationship is quite simple. If object A has an is_a relationship with object B, then all the attributes and services of object B are the attributes and services of object A. For example, consider the situation in which we have two objects: Person and Employee. Reasonable attributes for Person could be name, age, weight, and height. But an Employee is_a Person. By the definition of the is_a relationship, the attributes of Person are also the attributes of Employee. Note that normally the Employee has additional attributes such as salary, position, organization number, and employee identification number. In this example, the Person object is referred to as the *ancestor* (or parent) node and the Employee object as the *descendent* (or child) node. The ancestor is a generalization of the descendent, and conversely, the descendent is a specialization of the ancestor.

Generalization relationships pose some important properties that differentiate them from other relationships.[9] These properties are the following:

---

[7] Unfortunately, few programming languages explicitly support all these mechanisms.

[8] Some object-oriented authors believe that every piece of information should be attached to a single class; thus, a link violates the encapsulation principle and should not be allowed. However, most of us who have developed large and complex applications/systems believe that some information transcends a single class, and that the failure to treat a link on an equal footing with objects will lead to a model (program) that contains hidden assumptions and dependencies. Thus, during analysis one should model a link to indicate that the information it contains is not subordinate to a single object (class), but is dependent on two or more objects (classes).

[9] In theory, all three aspects (attribute, service, and behavior) can be redefined in the subclass. We have limited the redefinition for a very practical purpose and consistent with the implementation of inheritance in C++. Other languages may give you more flexibility in redefinition and this may seem more powerful. However, there can be too much flexibility. In most languages, the additional flexibility will result in software that is less safe, as we cannot guarantee that the software is well tested.

1. Structural properties

   a. Attributes

     The descendent will have all of the attributes of the ancestor. For instance, Employee will have the age attribute because it is a descendant class of Person.

   b. Nongeneralization relationships

     The descendent will have all of the nongeneralization relationships of the ancestor. For example, if we add a marriage link[10] between two Persons, Employee will also have a marriage link because it is a descendent of Person.

2. Interface properties

   All services provided by the ancestor must also be provided by the descendent.[11] For instance, if the Person object had an addWeight service, then Employee will also have an addWeight service because Employee is a descendent of Person.

3. Behavior properties

   a. Generalization without polymorphism (good child)

     In generalization without polymorphism, all methods supplied by the ancestor for its services are also used by the descendent to provide the corresponding services.

   b. Generalization with polymorphism (bad child)

     In generalization with polymorphism, some methods supplied by the ancestor for its services are also used by the descendent to provide the corresponding services. For the remaining services of the ancestor, the descendent supplies its own customized methods that replace the appropriate corresponding methods.[12]

3. Mathematical properties

   a. Antisymmetry

     If object A is_a descendent of object B, then object B may not have an is_a relationship with object A (object B is not a descendent of object A). For example, Employee is_a Person, but not all persons are employees.

   b. Transitivity

     If object A is_a object B and object B is_a object C, then object A is_a object C.[13] For example, if we add the fact that a SalesPerson is_a Employee to our exam-

---

[10] A *link* is a relationship between two objects. We will learn later that Person is really a class and, as such, the relationship is really an association.

[11] Even if the service of a descendent effectively removes the behavior, it must still provide the interface for that service.

[12] This is perhaps a good time to remind the reader that the "bad" child is often an excellent model in object-oriented analysis and design.

[13] Transitivity makes it possible to organize the objects in a hierarchical manner. Because of this property, generalization is diagrammatically shown as an acyclic directed graph.

ple, then SalesPerson is also a Person. Furthermore, it also has the age attribute because of properties 1a and 4b.

Generalization/specialization is a critical mechanism to the object-oriented paradigm because finding the correct ancestor(s) to assign the services and attributes is crucial to designing a good model. Unfortunately, it is very difficult for novices to realize that most of the objects with which they work are composites of other objects.

To overcome this difficulty, novices should consider every object as a complex object that may be viewed as many different subobjects. Each subobject represents that complex object in a single semantic domain. For example, we are (1) employees in the work domain, (2) taxpayers in the governmental domain, (3) parents and/or children in the family domain, and (4) members in the social club domain.[14] The services we provide and the relationships we have are different for each domain. For example, consider the services *hire*, *promote*, *retire*, and *fire*. All of these services are intimately tied to the fact that each of us is also an employee. When a person is unemployed, these services would not apply. As a taxpayer, a tax audit relationship with a tax auditor may exist. This is a relationship that is very intimately tied to each of us being a taxpayer. It would be improper to use this relationship in the other domains. For instance, taxpayers do not want their auditors known by their employers or by their social clubs.

The proper use of generalization helps us represent composite objects in a manner that manages complexity and thus makes software more maintainable and flexible to change. Although a descendent can be thought of as having all of the attributes, non-generalization relationships, and services of all its ancestors, it is better to consider the descendent as having access to all of these things via the appropriate subobject of which it is a specialization. This will force us to keep the attributes, relationships, and services in the appropriate semantic domain, which reduces coupling and provides higher cohesion. Lower coupling and higher cohesion lead to more maintainable and more flexible software.

Identifying and Specifying Generalization/Specialization

WE recommend using the original list of potential objects minus the objects external to the application as our list of objects that may potentially be used in an is_a relationship. With this list, we apply the following test to each possible pairing of the objects. We ask: Is object A an object B? and Is object B an object A? The allowable answers are *always*, *sometimes*, and *never*. If the answer to both questions is *never*, the two objects are not in an *is_a* relationship with each other. If both answers are *always*, object A and object B are synonymous.[15] If the answer to "Is object A an object B?" is *always* and the answer to "Is object B an object A?" is *sometimes*, then object A has an *is_a* relationship with object B.[16]

---

[14] Although some of these names may also be role names in some applications, we will assume that we want to capture these concepts as objects.

[15] They are either instances in the same class or they are different names for the same class.

[16] The only remaining combination will mean that object B has an is_a relationship with object A.

TABLE 9-1   An is_a Analysis Table

Is A a B?	O	M	S	Ad	E	C	R
Officer	X	a	n	n	n	n	a
Manager	s	X	s	n	n	n	a
Supervisor	n	a	X	n	n	n	a
Advisor	n	n	n	X	n	n	a
Engineer	n	n	n	n	X	s	n
Contractor	n	n	n	n	a	X	n
Representative	s	s	s	s	n	n	X

*A is the row, B is the column, O = Officer, M = Manager, S = Supervisor, Ad = Advisor, E = Engineer, C = Contractor, and R = Representative. In the cells, a = always, s = sometimes, and n = never.

For example, let us look at the following list of objects: Officer, Manager, Supervisor, Advisor, Engineer, Contractor, and Representative. We will apply our test to these objects in a typical corporate environment. The answers are illustrated in Table 9-1.

To use Table 9-1 effectively, we look at the columns with at least one *a* and then start with the columns containing the smallest numbers of *a*'s. In this example, it would be the Engineer column. From the table, a Contractor is_a Engineer. The next column with the least *a*'s is Manager. From the table, Supervisor is_a Manager and Officer is_a Manager. Finally, we are ready for the representative column. If we use the results of the table directly, we have four is_a relationships:

- Officer is_a Representative
- Manager is_a Representative
- Supervisor is_a Representative
- Advisor is_a Representative

However, from earlier is_a relationships, we know that both a Supervisor and an Officer are also Managers. So probably the proper semantics are that the Manager is_a Representative and an Advisor is_a Representative. The Supervisor and the Officer inherit this relationship from Manager.

As an exercise for the reader, consider adding the following three objects to Table 9-1: (1) Jim, who is an Officer, (2) Jack, who is a Supervisor, and (3) Joe, who is an Engineer. When doing this exercise, you should note that the three objects (Jim, Jack, Joe) all satisfy the is_a test.[17]

---

[17] We will learn in a later chapter that generalization/specialization is really applied to classes. Jim, Jack, and Joe are instances. Although a case can be made for an instance being a specialization of a class object, in the object-oriented paradigm, a different mechanism is used to capture this special case—instantiation.

Object Aggregation

To view an object as consisting of subobjects, each of which operates in a single semantic domain,[18] is not the same as viewing an object as consisting of components of objects. To support this second view, another mechanism, *aggregation*, is provided in the object-oriented paradigm. *Aggregation* (or *whole-parts*) is not a new concept to us. Analysts and developers are constantly dealing with aggregate entities consisting of component entities.[19] For example, a purchase order is composed of line items, a weekly timesheet is composed of numerous daily time accounting, and a system is composed of subsystems made from hardware, software, and so on.

Aggregation, like generalization, possesses some important properties:[20]

1. Structural properties

The parts must have some structural or functional relationship to the whole of which they are constituents.

2. Mathematical properties

a. Antisymmetry

If object A is a part of object B, then object B cannot be a part of object A. For example, a purchase order is composed of line items. By antisymmetry, a purchase order is not part of a line item. Note that the line item may be composed of sub-line items. Even in this case, a line item may not be part of a sub-line item.

b. Transitivity

If object A is a part of object B and object B is a part of object C, then object A is a part of object C. For example, a purchase order is composed of line items, which may be composed of sub-line items. By transitivity, a sub-line item is also part of the purchase order.

Attributes, relationships, services, and methods are not inherited in aggregation, in contrast to generalization. Because the properties of an aggregation are very weak, aggregation may be either static or dynamic, and a component of an aggregate may also be conditional. A *static aggregation* has fixed (invariant) components and cannot be changed. A *dynamic aggregation* has components that may vary over time. A *conditional component* either is or is not a component of an aggregate, depending on whether a specific condition holds.[21]

Aggregations are very useful. They reduce complexity by treating many objects as one object. They provide a construct or mechanism that better models specific application domain entities (e.g., purchase order) than does a link. Aggregations also ensure the

---

[18] For example, the generalization/specialization view of an object.

[19] Note: The aggregate is the whole and the component is the parts.

[20] These properties must be satisfied by all instances of an aggregation. Furthermore, when these aggregations are implemented, these properties should be managed. Unfortunately, this is rarely done, as most programming languages do not provide the language mechanisms to support aggregation.

[21] Novices should be very careful with conditional components. They should rarely be used; normally, it is better to capture a variation by specialization (subclassing).

proper visibility (information and service hiding) of the interactions among the components. For example, the individual lights of a traffic signal must be turned on and off in a specific sequence. Thus, the creation of a traffic light object that aggregates the three traffic lights as components will allow modeling the control of the individual components via the aggregate. This is very powerful, as it hides all the complexity from the users of the traffic signal.

Classification of Aggregation

UNFORTUNATELY, because the object-oriented paradigm has not defined the aggregation mechanism very well, most of us have difficulties applying this mechanism properly in practice. The latest literature on this topic argues that this is due to the fact that aggregation, itself, is an "ancestor" concept. It is our belief that we need to use the "descendent" concepts (more specialization) to be able to use this mechanism effectively. These descendent concepts, or different kinds of aggregation, will capture additional properties that will help us better manage complexity.

From a theoretical perspective, linguists, logicians, and psychologists have studied the nature of relationships. One of relationships that has been studied reasonably well is the relationship between the parts of things and the wholes that they make up.[22] In a joint paper, Morton Winston, Roger Chaffin, and Douglas Herrmann discussed this whole-parts relationship. They described several kinds of aggregation (composition or meronymic relationships). In their study, the kind of relationship is determined by the combination of the following basic properties:

- Configuration—whether or not the parts bear a particular functional or structural relationship either to one another or to the whole that they constitute.
- Homeomorphic—whether or not the parts are the same kind of thing as the whole.
- Invariance—whether or not the parts can be separated from the whole.

The paper identified six types of aggregation; we have added a seventh:

1. Assembly-parts (component-integral composition)
2. Material-object composition
3. Portion-object composition
4. Place-area composition
5. Collection-members composition
6. Container-content (member-bunch composition)
7. Member-partnership composition

---

[22] The study of aggregation (particularly whole-parts relationships) is referred to as mereology. The accepted formal theory of whole-parts is typically presented within one of two frameworks: the Calculus of Individuals of Leanard and Goodman and the Mereleogy of Lesniewski.

Assembly-Parts (Component-Integral Composition)

In this assembly-parts aggregation, the whole is comprised of components that maintain their identity even when they are part of the whole. To be an aggregation of this kind, the parts are required to have a specific functional or structural relationship to one another as well as the whole that they constitute. For example, frames are part of a roll of film, bristles are part of a brush, wheels are part of a car, analytical geometry is part of mathematics. In addition, an integral object (whole) is divided into component parts, which are objects in their own right. Furthermore, the components may not be haphazardly arranged, but must bear a particular relationship, either structurally or functionally, with one another and with the whole. Thus, the whole exhibits a patterned structure or organization. Examples include traffic signals, cars, airplanes, toys, machines, and computers.

These items are assembled from parts because, in an assembly-parts aggregation, the assembly does not exist without parts. The whole may be tangible (car, toothbrush, airplane, printer), abstract (mathematics, physics, physiology, accounting, jokes), organizational (NATO, United States, Exxon), or temporal (musical performance, film showing).

However, when a component ceases to support the overall pattern of the object, a different relationship is established. For example, if a memory card is taken out of a computer, the memory card is no longer considered part of the computer. However, the memory card is still considered a computer part or a piece of a computer. Unlike a component, a part or a piece does not participate in the overall pattern of the whole and provides no functional support for the whole. In a component-integral object, a component of the whole can be removed without materially affecting the concept of the whole.

When looking for component-integral object composition in a requirements document, look for the keywords "is part of" and "is assembled from." Examples of this are as follows:

- A keyboard is part of a computer.
- Nuclear physics is part of physics.
- Windows are parts of a house.
- A piano recital is part of the performance.
- Chairs are parts of the office.
- A telephone is assembled from its parts.
- An orchestra is assembled from its various instrument sections.

As these examples show, it is not difficult to identify assembly-part relationships from a requirements document.

Material-Object Composition

In the material-object aggregation, the parts (materials) lose their identity when they are used to make the whole. In fact, the relationship between parts is no longer known once they become part of the whole. Thus, a material-object composition relationship defines an invariant configuration of parts within the whole because no part may be removed from the whole. Examples are "Bread is made from the following ingredients: flour, sugar, yeast," and "A car is made from materials such as iron, plastic, and glass."

Note that while material-object composition defines what the whole is made of, a component-integral object defines the parts of the whole. For example, to describe a component-integral object relationship we would say "A car has the following clearly identifiable parts: wheels, engine, doors, and so on." Thus, components can be physically separated from the whole because the relationship is extrinsic. Note that the relationship in a material-object relationship is not extrinsic, as you cannot separate the flour from the bread once the bread is made.

When looking for material-object composition in a requirements document, look for keywords such as "is partly" and "is made from." Some examples follow:

- Cappuccino is partly milk.
- A chair is partly iron.
- A table is made from wood.
- A high-rise building is partly steel.
- Candy is made partly from sugar.
- Bread is made from flour.

Note that "partly" is not necessary for a material-object relationship. For instance, a mirror may be made of all glass (not "partly" of glass). Furthermore, whether you choose to use the material-object or component integral object to represent a relationship may be domain-dependent. For example, in most situations one would model the ceramics of a sparkplug as material-object composition. However, if in your problem domain you can separate the ceramic from the spark plug, you will need to use the component-integral object composition to capture the relationship.

Portion-Object Composition

In the portion-object aggregation, the relationship defines a homeomorphic (same kind of thing as the whole) configuration of parts as the whole. Usually, portions of the objects can be divided using standard measures such as inches, millimeters, liters, gallons, hours, or minutes. In this manner, the portion-object composition supports the arithmetic operations of subtraction, addition, multiplication, and division.

When looking for portion-object composition in a requirements document, look for such keywords as "portion of," "slice," "helping of," "segment of," "lump of," "drop of," and "spoonful of." Examples of this are as follows:

- A slice of bread is a portion of a loaf of bread.
- A spoon of cereal is a portion of a bowl of cereal.
- A second is part of a day.
- A meter is part of kilometer.
- A cup of coffee is usually part of a pot of coffee.

When the word "piece" is used, however, care must be taken to ensure that the pieces are similar in nature. For example, a piece of candy is candy and a piece of rotten apple is apple, but a piece from an exploded car is not a car.

Note that each slice of bread is considered bread and each cup of coffee is considered coffee. Moreover, both second and day are units of measurement on which you can perform a mix-and-match for the basic arithmetic operations. This observation also holds true for the meter and kilometer units of measurements. However, you may not mix and match seconds with kilometer, as they are different semantic concepts. This similarity between a portion and the whole permits the analyst/designer to allow a portion to selectively inherit properties from the whole. For example, the kinds of ingredients in a loaf of bread are the same as they are in a slice of bread. The component-integral object composition also allows certain properties of the whole to apply to its parts. For example, the velocity of a ball can also be used to imply the velocity of each of its parts.

Place-Area Composition

In the place-area aggregation, the relationship defines a homeomorphic (same kind of thing as the whole) and invariant configuration of parts as the whole. This relationship is commonly used to identify links between places and particular locations within them. Like the portion-object composition, all of the places (pieces, slices) must be similar in nature, but differ in that the places cannot be separated from the area of which they are a part.

When looking for place-area composition in a requirements document, look at the preliminary portion-object composition and ask if this relationship is invariant. If it is, then it is a place-area composition instead of a portion-object composition. Also look at the container-content relationships (see later section) and ask "Are all of the contents homeomorphic and also nonremovable?" If the answer is yes, again it is a place-area composition instead of a container-content relationship. Some examples follow:

- New York City is part of New York State.
- Los Angeles is part of the United States.
- A peak is part of a mountain.
- A room is part of a hotel.
- Yosemite is part of California.

Spend a little extra time to convince yourself that a room as part of a hotel is an example of a place-area composition.

Collection-Members Composition

Collection-members composition is a specialized version of place-area composition. In addition to being a monomeric and invariant configuration of parts within a whole, there is an implied order to its members. One example is an airline reservation with its various flight segments. Here, the order of each flight segment in the itinerary is a very important part of the reservation. Other examples include monthly timesheet—daily timesheets, monthly planner—daily plans; people—organization chart; name—telephone book; name—roledex; and file—file cabinet.

When looking for collection-members composition in a requirements document, look at the preliminary place-area composition and ask if this relationship has an implied order. If it does, then it is a collection-members composition instead of a place-area composition.

Container-Content (Member-Bunch Composition)

The member-bunch composition defines a collection of parts as a whole. The parts (contents) bear neither a functional nor a structural relationship to each other or the whole. Furthermore, the contents are neither homeomorphic nor invariant. The only requirement is that there is a spatial, temporal, or social connection for determining when a member is part of the collection. The container exists and has properties and behaviors of its own. That is, it exists even if there are no contents.

Examples are purchase order—line items; bag—contents of bag; box—contents of box; union—members; company—employees, and so on. In the first example, it is very common for one to place a "blanket" purchase order with no line items. The specific items/works (line items) are added later and there is no implied order in the line items. Furthermore, note that the organization-chart relationship for employee has an implied order and invariant property; while the company-employees relationship is not invariant nor does it capture any implied order.

This type of aggregation should not be confused with inheritance (classification). For example, "Jason is a human" and "airplane is a transport vehicle" are classifications. Jason possesses all the attributes and provides all the services of a human. Similarly, airplane has all the attributes and provides all the services of a transport vehicle.

The container-content relationship is different. It is usually based on spatial or social connections. For example, to say that a shrub is part of a garden implies that it is within the geographical confines of the garden and is probably in close proximity to other plants within the garden. Similarly, an employee's membership in a club implies a social connection. However, for a shrub to be classified as a garden, every shrub would have to be a garden. Similarly, every employee would have to be a club. This relationship has a tendency to be a catch-all for aggregation-type relationships.

Member-Partnership Composition

The member-partnership composition defines an invariant form of the container-content relationship. It defines an invariant collection of parts as a whole.

Examples of this type of relationship include the following:

- Ginger Rogers and Fred Astaire as a dance couple
- Laurel and Hardy as a comedian team
- Jacoby and Myers as attorneys at law
- Lee and Tepfenhart as authors of this book

Members in this relationship may not be removed without destroying the relationship (partnership). For instance, if Laurel leaves Hardy, the comedy team of Laurel and Hardy no longer exists. Hardy can now form a new comedy team with a new partner, but it will be a different partnership.

When looking for member-partnership relationships, review the preliminary list of container-content relationships for invariance. If the relationship is invariant, then make it a member-partnership relationship.

Objects and Aggregation Relationships

Now that we understand aggregation better, we should make two observations about them. In particular, we should recognize the following:

1. An object can be viewed as more than one aggregation. For example, a loaf of bread may be viewed as an aggregate of slices of bread (portion-object composition) and it may be viewed as being made from flour, sugar, yeast, etc. (material-object composition). Both views can be supported simultaneously in the object-oriented paradigm.

2. Transitivity holds only for aggregation of the same kind. For example, the microwave oven is part of a kitchen (component-integral composition) and the kitchen is part of a house (place-area composition). However, the microwave oven is not part of the house. Furthermore, a computer can be an aggregation of a terminal, hardware box, keyboard, and mouse. The hardware box is usually comprised of a CPU, memory, hard disk drive, and floppy disk drive. By transitivity, a CPU is part of the computer. However, a terminal is made of glass, silicon, steel, and plastic. This decomposition of the terminal is not the same as the preceding decomposition[23] of the hardware box. Most of us would not apply the transitivity or antisymmetric properties to the material composition of the terminal in conjunction with the component-integral composition of the computer. At best we would say that the material-composition of the computer is a union of the material composition of the parts.

Links Between Objects

GENERALIZATION and aggregation help us capture relationships between objects when we want to view an object as being a set of other objects. There are relationships between objects that are not generalizations or aggregations, for example, the marriage relationship between a person and his/her spouse. Certainly, this relationship is not viewed as a generalization. If it were, a person will have to inherit all of the in-law relationships of his/her spouse. It is also not an aggregation, in spite of the religious ceremony, as divorces are legal. Thus, we need another mechanism to capture all of these other relationships between objects. In the object-oriented paradigm, this "catch-all" relationship is called a *link*.

From a technical perspective, a *link* is a relationship (physical or conceptual) between objects that lets one object know about another object so that one object may request the services of another object. However, a link should also have a semantic meaning that is consistent with the semantic domain within which the object resides.

---

[23] Both of the earlier aggregations are component-integral compositions.

In object-oriented modeling, all links are considered bidirectional.[24] Thus, once a link is established between two objects, each object may request the services of the other object. A *role name* uniquely identifies one end of a relationship and provides a vehicle for viewing a relationship as a traversal from one object to a set of associated objects.[25]

The role name allows an object at one end of the relationship to traverse the relationship without explicitly using the relationship name. Role names are necessary for a link (association) between two objects of the same class. For example, in a *supervise* relationship between employees in the class **Employee**, the role names Supervisor and Subordinate would help distinguish between two employees participating in the supervise relationship. Role names are also useful to distinguish between multiple links between two objects. For example, consider a manual car wash. The role names from car to employee could be *washer, dryer, waxer, polisher,* and *buffer.* For a specific instance (object) of a car (class), Joe (an instance of **Employee**) is the washer and the buffer because he both washes and buffs the car.

Furthermore, a link can be binary (between two objects), ternary (among three objects), or higher. In practice, it is rare to find links with a semantic meaning that tie together objects of three different object types (classes).[26]

An *association* describes the set of links between two (or more) objects of a single class or of different classes with the same semantic meaning. Thus, a link may be viewed as an instance of an association. Examples of associations between the same class for class **Person** are: married_to and works_for. Today, with the two-income family, two persons may be married to each other, with one of them also being the supervisor of the other in the workplace. We cannot use one link to capture this situation, as the two relationships have different semantic meanings. The couple can get a divorce, but still maintain the same work relationship. An example of an association between two classes is the employment relationship as applied to the classes **Company** and **Person**. That is, "Joe is employed by Exxon" is an instance of a link in this association. Because every link (and thus, the corresponding association) is bidirectional, "Exxon employs Joe" is the link in the reverse direction.

Because an association is an abstraction of a concept, it may also have attributes and services. It may have the same properties and capabilities as a class.[27] Because we normally do not think of a link as an object, novices should be very careful not to assign attributes of the relationship to one of the classes in the relationship. For example, consider a person's salary. It is normally modeled as an attribute in the class **Person**. However, it is actually an attribute of the employment relationship between the classes

---

[24] All links are considered bidirectional during modeling. However, in implementation it is not uncommon practice to drop one direction of a link.

[25] Set means one or more objects. From an object's perspective, traversing a relationship is an operation that yields the related (associated) objects. Thus, in implementation the role name is a derived attribute (attribute that is derived from the assocation rather than being intrinsic in the object) whose value is a set of related objects.

[26] An example of a ternary link would be the relationship among concert, concert tickets, and attendee.

[27] However, in many situations, neither the attributes nor the services of the relationship need to be captured in the model.

Person and **Company**. If you still have doubts, consider the case in which a person has two jobs with two different employers.

The last example raises a pragmatic point: When does one make salary an attribute of **Person** and when does one make it an attribute of the association? Theoretically, the correct answer is that salary is an attribute of the association. From a modeling perspective, we recommend that you use what is appropriate for your business situation. To decide which is appropriate requires good engineering judgement. We recommend that you consider the problem domain, future direction of product, and next release features as factors during the analysis phase.[28]

Identifying and Specifying Links and Aggregations

THE best source for initially identifying some of the links (associations) and aggregations is the requirements document. Reread the requirements document and look for the possibilities of one object being part of another object. These are potential aggregations. Use the suggestions of key phrases and tests described previously.

Also, look for links in the requirements document. Links, like services, are often seen as verbs in a requirements document. Phrases that usually imply a link include "which it gets from," "keeps track of," "changes with," and "depends upon." Furthermore, the detailed description of a service is also a source of identifying links. Most objects that need to collaborate (i.e., use services) with other objects and to access these other objects usually require a link.

Other sources to help find links are the sequence diagrams and the behavior specification documents. Each service request from another object must be supported by some access vehicle. If the "handle" is not passed as an argument, then a relationship must be established between the two objects. Care should be given to naming the relationship, usually a link, in a manner that captures the semantic meaning of the relationship.[29]

When you are studying the behavioral specification document, only put in links that have semantic meaning. If you cannot find a good name for the link, consider whether this handle should have been part of the signature (should have been passed to this object from the calling object).

Remember the following rules to determine whether you have found a link or an object aggregation:

1. An aggregation may not connect an object to itself. This would violate the anti-symmetric property of aggregation. In many circumstances, this rule is extended to the idea that an aggregation should not connect an object of one class to an object of the same class as a mechanism to absolutely prevent an aggregation

---

[28] In design, modifiability, reusability, simplicity, and performance need to be considered.

[29] If CRC cards are used and use cases drove the design of the CRC cards, you have a collection of collaborators. Finding the associations and aggregations are much easier as the collaborators give you a big clue. If the collaborator is transient, then the object probably wants a pointer to the object passed to it from the caller. If the collaborator is persistent, then the object has to have a relationship (either association or aggregation) with the object.

from connecting an object to itself. On the other hand, a link may connect two objects of the same class. For example, supervise is a relation between two employees (instances) of the class **Employee**. The most common example given is marriage between two persons. However, this example is flawed because our society does not legally recognize the union of two persons of any gender as a marriage. Marriage in most societies today is a relationship between an instance of class **Female** and an instance of class **Male**. This example, therefore, captures the constraints on the relationship as defined by present societal standards and shows the importance of capturing the link/association upon the correct object or abstraction. Thus, we see how difficult it is to model properly and capture all the implied constraints.

2. Multiple connections between objects are legal. Each connection should be used to capture a distinct semantic meaning. For example, consider sending a car through a nonautomated car wash. Employees are needed to wash, dry, wax, polish, and, finally, buff the car. Every task may be performed by one employee or each task may be performed by a different employee. If we model these as links to the employees who performed the various tasks, we would have multiple links for an instance (object) of **Employee** (class). For example, Joe could have both washed and buffed the car.

3. Self-associations are possible and common. In this case, role names are essential to capture the relationship accurately.

4. Multiple association does not imply that the same two objects are related twice.

Managing Relationships

ONE of the most difficult tasks in building an object-oriented model is to determine whether a potential relationship is better captured as either an argument in the signature of the service (function), or as a link, aggregation, or generalization/specialization. The following are some guidelines for this task:

■ If the relationship is permanent (static), then it must be captured as a relationship. Now, what does permanent mean? If you consider a scenario as a unit of time, then permanent means that the relationship needs to be known across scenarios. Note that permanent is a relative term. Basically, if it has to be stored in memory for use by some other independent process, then it is permanent.

■ A relationship must capture some concept that applies to the problem domain or some subdomain that is needed for implementation. In other words, there must be a semantic meaning to the relationship. A service should only traverse (use) the relationship when its usage is consistent with that semantic meaning. For example, consider the link for two **Person** objects: married_to. Today, with two-income families, it is possible for one spouse to work for another spouse. It would be improper and poor modeling to use the married_to relationship to get to work domain services of the other spouse. A second link (works_for) needs to be established to capture this different semantic relationship.

- If you think you have an aggregation, make sure that all of the parts are in the same domain and provide the same functional or structural configuration to the whole. Apply transitivity and antisymmetric tests to check for consistency. Note that transitivity is possible only with aggregations of the same kind. It is very common for novices to mix parts of different kinds of aggregation in one aggregation. This will cause the transitivity test to fail. When this happens, you probably need to look at the parts to see if there are different types of aggregates. For example, consider a building that has the following parts: windows, floors, offices, elevators, ceilings, walls, stairs, meeting rooms, cafeteria, atrium, and sundry shop. If you put all of these parts into one aggregation, you have mixed parts from two different semantic aggregations. The offices, floors (meaning one level in a building), meeting rooms, cafeteria, atrium, and sundry shop are defining a functional configuration of the building; while the windows, floors (meaning the physical floor), ceilings, and walls are defining a structural configuration of the building. These parts must be captured in two different aggregations, as they have different semantics.

- An aggregation may not connect two objects of the same kind to each other. This would violate the antisymmetric property of aggregation. For example, a person may not be an aggregate of other persons. However, a link may connect two objects of the same kind. For example, supervise is a relation between two employees (instances) that is valid.

- Aggregation is often confused with topological inclusion. Topological inclusion is a relationship between a container, area, or temporal duration and that which is contained by it. Examples are (1) the customer is in the room, (2) the meeting is in the evening, and (3) Monument Valley is in Arizona and Utah. In each case, the subject is surrounded by the container; however, it is not part of the container in any meaningful semantic domain. For example, a customer is not part of a room, nor is a meeting part of an evening. Furthermore, no part of Monument Valley is Arizona or Utah, because it is part of the Navaho reservation. Topological inclusion is most commonly confused with place-area composition. Note that every part of Dallas is in Texas, while no part of Monument Valley is in Arizona.

- Sometimes, novices confuse attributes with aggregation. Attributes describe the object as a whole (a black box approach); aggregation describes the parts that make the whole (white box approach). Thus, a house may have attributes such as width, length, and height, but it is made from wood, glass, bricks, etc.

- Attachment of one object to another object does not guarantee aggregation. Certainly toes are attached to the feet and they are part of the feet; however, earrings are attached to the ear, but they are not part of the ear. Note that toes provide functional support to the feet, while earrings do not supply any functional or structural support.

- Ownership may also be confused with aggregation. Certainly a car has wheels, and wheels are part of a car. However, the fact that James has a car does not imply that the car is part of James. Thus, ownership is captured by a link.

- Multiple links between objects are legal. Each link should be used to capture a distinct semantic meaning. (See the car wash example for Joe.)

Documenting Relationships

IN the past, nearly every major object-oriented methodologist had his/her own way of documenting classes, objects, relationships, and behaviors. Such is not the case today; the majority of authors employ UML to document relationships. The notation templates for documenting relationships in UML are shown Figure 9-1.

In a generalization diagram, we see that a class is represented by a rectangular icon, and the generalization/specialization is drawn as a solid line from the specialized class to the generalized class with a large triangular arrowhead on the generalized class end. Normally, the specialization classes of the same parent are different alternatives in the same semantic domain and provide for a partitioning of the parent class. However, some applications require that we specialize in several dimensions simultaneously; in these cases, UML allows a discriminator label to be attached to a generalization arc. Arcs with the same label represent specialization in the same dimension. Different dimensions represent orthogonal abstract ways of describing an object of the parent class. Although UML notion doesn't preclude the concepts of multiple classification and dynamic classification, it does not explicitly support these concepts.

Aggregation is a special form of association that deals with the composition of the aggregator class. In an aggregation diagram, a class is represented by a rectangular icon, and the aggregation is drawn as solid lines from the aggregates (parts) to the aggregator (whole) with a diamond arrowhead on the aggregator's end. In UML, two forms of aggregation are recognized. In the first form, the parts may exist independently of the whole; this is represented by the use of the unfilled diamond and is called *aggregation* in

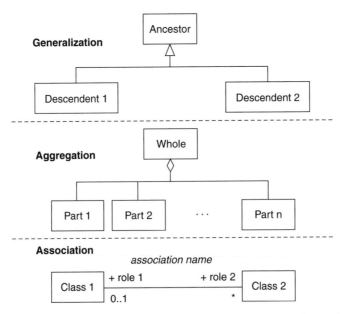

FIGURE 9-1   UML notation for object genralization, aggregation, and association.

UML. In the second form, the parts may only exist as part of the whole; this is represented by the use of a filled diamond and is called *composition* in UML. The multiplicity of the aggregator may be one, many, and optionally one. Multiplicity is captured by using a text expression. The expression is a comma-separated list of integer ranges. A range is indicated by an integer (the lower value), two dots, and an integer (the upper value); a single integer and the symbol '*' are also legal ranges. The symbol '*' indicates any number, including none.

In an association diagram, classes are represented by rectangular icons, and a binary association is represented by a straight, solid line between two rectangular icons.[30] An association may have a name with an optional small "direction arrow" (solid triangle with no tail) showing how to read the association. The name is placed on or adjacent to the association line.[31] The association name may be omitted if role names are used. At each end of the association is a role. Each role may have a name that describes how its class is viewed by the other class(es); this is called the role name. The role names opposite of a class must be unique. The role name also determines the multiplicity of its class; that is, the number of instances of the class that can be associated with one instance of the other class. Multiplicity is captured by using a text expression. The expression is a comma-separated list of integer ranges. A range is indicated by an integer (the lower value), two dots, and an integer (the upper value); a single integer and the symbol '*' are also legal ranges. The symbol '*' indicates any number including none. If the multiplicity is more than one, the keyword {ordered} may be placed on the role, indicating that the instances in the association have an explicit order.

Recommended Approach

OUR steps for finding relationships are as follows:

1. Get a list of potential objects that may be involved in generalization.
2. Create a table of these objects for the "is_a" test.
3. Fill in the cells of the table, using only *always*, *sometimes*, and *never*.
4. Use the table to find all of the generalizations. Remember to eliminate the instantiations.
5. Draw a hierarchical diagram of the generalizations between classes using UML notation.
6. Reread the requirements document and look for aggregations and links (associations). Use the key phrases given earlier as clues to finding these relationships.

---

[30] Ternary relationships are drawn using an additional diamond icon to tie the lines together. This diamond icon is also used for all other higher-order relationships. An association that needs to be a class is captured as a class, and its association with the relation is shown with a dashed line from the class icon for the association to the association (solid line) between the two classes participating in the association.

[31] In theory, an association may have different names in each direction. We do not recommend trying to name associations in both directions.

7. Look for role names, which appear as nouns in most requirements documents. Although many object-oriented authors have stated that role names are optional, we strongly recommend their usage, as it is often easier and less confusing to assign role names instead of, or in addition to, relationship names.

8. Reread the specifications for all of the services and identify the relationships needed to support those services. By rereading each service, the analyst/developer will be able to refine what must be done in each of the object services.

9. If the sequence diagrams, use-case model, and the behavior specifications are documented, read these documents to find additional links.

10. Determine whether each potential relationship is better captured as an argument in the signature of the service (function), or as a link, aggregation, or generalization/specialization.

11. Document the results using UML notation.

Example

Let us return to our lawn-mowing example. Based on the previous analysis, we have the following objects: John, Jane, Peter, Paul, Elizabeth, Mary, Jack, and ProfessionalLawnMower. We will discuss generalization in the next chapter. So now after reviewing the requirements document and the behavior specifications, we realize that capturing the family and its relationships is useful to this application. Figure 9-2 and Figure 9-3 illustrate object aggregations and links that we consider useful in our example. The objects are represented by underlining the name in compliance with the UML specification.[32] The design of the UML association diagram and aggregation diagram is described in the next chapter.

In this example, Jane has access to John's services via the is_married link. John has access to all of the children's services via the father/child links. Mary has access to Jack via the lawn_mowing link. Mary's sibling link, mother/child link, and father/child link are permanent. They are always applicable over time. These are called *static* (and invariant) *relationships*.

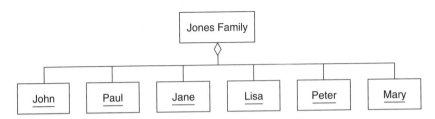

FIGURE 9-2   **Aggregation diagram for the lawn mower example.**

---

[32] It should be noted that many of the tools available on the market do not support construction of such object diagrams.

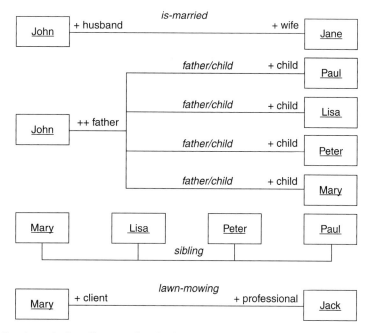

FIGURE 9-3   Association diagram for the lawn mower example.

However, Mary's lawn-mowing link with Jack is less permanent. Mary may choose to change to another professional lawn mower at any time. However, her relationship with a professional lawn mower may be permanent in that there is some professional lawn mower that she uses. In such a case, we consider the link static and variant. In the next chapter, we will use the links to define associations, and we will use the object aggregation to define class aggregation.

■■ SUMMARY

Our steps for finding relationships are as follows:

1. Get a list of potential objects that may be involved in generalization.
2. Create a table of these objects for the "is_a" test.
3. Fill in the cells of the tables, using only *always*, *sometimes*, and *never*.
4. Use the table to find all of the generalizations. Remember to eliminate the instantiations.
5. Draw a hierarchical diagram of these generalizations between classes using UML notation.
6. Reread the requirements document and look for aggregations and links (associations). Use the key phrases given earlier as clues to finding these relationships.

7. Look also for role names, which appear as nouns in most requirements documents. Although many object-oriented authors have stated that role names are optional, we strongly recommend their usage, as it is often easier and less confusing to assign role names instead of, or in addition to, relationship names.

8. Reread the specifications for all of the services and identify the relationships needed to support those services. By rereading each service, the analyst/developer will be able to refine what must be done in each of the object services.

9. If the sequence diagrams, use-case model, and the behavior specifications are documented, read these documents to find additional links.

10. Determine whether each potential relationship is better captured as an argument in the signature of the service (function), or as a link, an aggregation, or a generalization/specialization.

11. Document the results via the UML notation.

Rules

All nature actually is nothing but a nexus of appearances according to rules; and there is nothing at all without rules. When we believe that we have come across an absence of rules, we can only say that the rules are unknown to us.

Emanuel Kant

What has been presented so far is a collection of mechanisms integrated into a consistent paradigm that helps manage the complexity of the procedural aspects of functional modeling.[1] However, there are aspects of an application/system that are nonprocedural (declarative) and are better modeled using other mechanisms. In this chapter, we discuss how the object-oriented paradigm can be extended to include the capability to manage declarative aspects of an application.

Introduction

THE concepts of abstraction, encapsulation, inheritance, relationship, and polymorphism in object-oriented methods support the design and implementation of sophisticated procedural applications. Most object-oriented methods are presently based on the assumption that all aspects of the application/system will be modeled within the procedural paradigm.

---

[1]   Functional modeling has two aspects: procedural and declarative.

However, some applications have many requirements that are given in a declarative manner.[2] When this occurs, the handling of the declarative semantics (rules and facts) is left to the analyst/developer. One of the most difficult tasks for developers is transforming declarative statements into the procedural paradigm. It is very natural for developers to incorporate these declarative statements across the methods of various classes. However, when a declarative statement affects several methods, especially across multiple classes, it must be written in several places. This is not a good practice because (1) there is a transformation of declarative semantics into procedural semantics, and (2) it creates hidden coupling between methods. The first reason makes the model less readily understandable and violates the goal of modeling reality the way the domain experts see it. The second reason makes maintaining and changing the model very difficult.

Applications tend to grow; as they grow, developers encounter more situations in which declarative statements have been distributed across methods. Soon, the model becomes unmaintainable. For example, maintaining an invariant involving two objects may require that similar but not identical tests be inserted into a variety of places within the code. This leads to errors of omission and logic by analysts, designers, and programmers as the application is extended. Because the invariant is not in one place, it is never explicitly stated. Unstated assumptions make modifications of code difficult and error-prone. We need both a method and a mechanism to handle declarative statements.

The needed implementation mechanism is a *data-driven mechanism.* This mechanism simplifies the task of maintaining model integrity in two important ways. First, it enables invariants and constraints to be stated explicitly in a single place, rather than having them scattered in multiple places. This makes the model (and thus code) easier to understand and modify. Second, because it is data-driven, invariants and constraints are reevaluated *automatically* whenever relevant changes are made to an object's attribute. This relieves the analyst/programmer of the burden of explicitly incorporating data integrity rules into their procedural logic. The application's procedural logic is no longer cluttered with code for maintaining model integrity.

The data-driven mechanism is important because many of our declarative requirements are given to us in a data-driven manner. This gives us a way to capture reality as domain experts see it—without the need to transform a declarative requirement (or solution) into a purely procedural model. Declarative statements are usually written at a higher level of abstraction than procedural statements. Implementing declarative statements using this mechanism frees the analyst, designer, and programmer from having to manage flow of control for these statements.

---

[2] We can distinguish between declarative and procedural languages or statements. Most of us have worked with procedural programming languages. They give us the constructs so that we can write a set of instructions that must be executed sequentially. The sequence may vary depending on conditions tested, and a group of instructions may be executed repetitively. However, declarative languages declare a set of facts and rules. They do not specify the sequence of steps for doing the processing.

Rules

RULES capturing declarative semantics are employed for a variety of purposes, such as enforcing invariants in a domain model, auditing complex data structures, monitoring the state of a state machine, or checking constraints while a user inputs data. There are all kinds of rules: some are best captured directly in the classical object-oriented paradigm, while others are better captured via other mechanisms.

One kind of rule that is better captured via another mechanism is the *data-driven rule*. This is due to the property that it requires a mechanism to act as a "monitor" of the model while it observes changes to an object's attributes and reacts when a condition is satisfied. Many applications naturally require this capability. Examples are (1) applications that monitor a physical system, (2) applications that apply business policies or engineering guidelines, and (3) software development tools.

The data-driven mechanism is well-suited to handling rules that monitor things. It supports the situation–action directive without complicating an application's procedural logic. It also satisfies two very important goals of the object-oriented paradigm: (1) the model should be built to reflect the way the domain experts see reality, and (2) whenever possible, the code for the application should be generated from a model that is easy for the domain experts and the end users to understand.

To satisfy these two goals, declarative statements (including rules) need to be rigorous. They must be understandable to the end user so that they can verify that the rules correctly represent business policies and desired application/system behavior. Thus, declarative statements, including rules, should be written in structured English.

Identifying Declarative Statements

DECLARATIVE statements are different from procedural statements. Identifying declarative statements in a requirements document is relatively simple. While procedural statements are always part of a specified sequence (e.g., a procedure, an activity, or a task), a declarative statement stands alone. A declarative statement is independent of any sequence of other statements. It declares a *fact* or a *rule*.

A *fact* statement may be expressed in various ways. The following are all examples of facts:

- A record

Book	Author(s)	Publisher
Object-oriented Analysis	Coad/Yourdon	Yourdon Press
Poor Developer's Guide to Object-oriented Programming in C++	Lee/Tepfenhart	Prentice Hall

- A set of values in a spreadsheet
- A plain statement (e.g., All surgeons are medical doctors.)

- A stand-alone equation:

MIN_MONTHLY_PAYMENT = (PRINCIPAL * INTEREST_RATE)/ 12

Rules usually capture information about how the business should operate. Rules encapsulate business knowledge. Common key words in declarative statements that indicate a rule are:

- It must always hold that ...
- It must always be true that ...
- Under all conditions, when ... then ...
- Under all conditions, if ... then ...
- When ... if... then ...
- ... if only ...
- ... is correct only if ...

A rule may be used as a declarative requirement to:

- enforce *"things that should always be true"* (invariants),
- detect *"things that should never be true"* (constraint violations),
- maintain the integrity of your domain model,
- monitor for and react to important events,
- express domain knowledge (*business policies, engineering rules,* and *situation–action heuristics*),
- specify an operation (function) that would have to be used in many methods, and
- exploit the data-driven or event-driven nature of rules.

Specifying and Documenting Rules

When a requirement is written as a declarative statement, the best practice is to specify it as a rule.[3] A technique that captures rules explicitly and makes them easy to read[4] is structured English. The details of the constructs available in structured English must wait until after the classification of (business) rules.

James Martin and James Odell (1992) has constructed the following classification scheme for rules. Their scheme describes the following types of rules:

- *Integrity rules* state that something must always be true (e.g., a value for an attribute must be in the integer range from 1 to 5).
- *Derivation rules* state how a value (or set of values) is computed (e.g., Tax Withheld = Federal Income Tax + State Income Tax).

---

[3]   Facts can be expressed as rules very easily. They will be derivation rules. Derivation rules are explained later.

[4]   Ideally, we want a technique that captures rules explicitly in a manner that is easy to read and will generate the correct code.

■ *Behavior rules* describe the dynamic aspects of behavior, such as what conditions must be true for an action to performed (e.g., when the door is open, the light in the oven is turned on).

To facilitate mapping these rules into the object-oriented paradigm, we can further refine James Martin's rule categories. Our categories are as follows:

1. *Data integrity rules* state that something must be true about an attribute(s) (e.g., a value for an attribute must be in the integral range from 1 to 5).
2. *Relationship integrity rules* state that something must be true about a relationship (e.g., a manager may not supervise more than ten employees).
3. *Derivation rules*, including facts, state how a value or set of values is computed (PRICE = 1.5 * COST).
4. *Service precondition rules* state that something must be true before a service will be performed (e.g., a cash advance will not be given unless it is past the fifth of the month).
5. *Service postcondition rules* state that something must be true after a service is performed (e.g., order form is stored once it is correctly completed).
6. *Action trigger rules* define the causal relationship between events and actions (e.g., when an order is accepted, send the bill immediately).
7. *Data trigger rules* define the causal relationship between an attribute's condition and an action (e.g., when the stock is below reorder level, then reorder).
8. *Control condition rules* handle situations in which multiple triggers are involved in the rule (e.g., if the product has been sent and the money received or if the purchase order has been canceled and the deposit returned, then the purchase order is closed).

Based on our classification scheme, the constructs in structured English shown in Figure 10-1 capture the rules. In these constructs, a condition is a Boolean expression, an event is a stimulus (signal), and an action is an invocation of a procedural statement.

1. For triggers and control conditions,
   IF condition THEN action
       or
   WHEN event IF condition THEN action
2. For integrity rules,
   IT MUST ALWAYS BE THAT statement of fact
       or
   IT MUST ALWAYS BE THAT IF condition THEN action
3. For service precondition,
   BEFORE service that is to be performed IT MUST BE THAT fact
4. For service postcondition,
   AFTER service that has been performed IT MUST BE THAT fact
5. For derivation rules, fact, usually an equation
       or
   WHEN condition or event THEN action
       or
   IF condition or event THEN action

FIGURE 10-1 Structured English constructs.

Mapping Rules to the Proper OO Concept

IN the 1980s artificial intelligence systems became highly fashionable. The mechanism on which these systems were built was primarily an *inference engine*. An inference engine processes a collection of facts and rules to make deductions using logical inference. The rules an inference engine processes are called *production rules*. Most of us understand declarative semantics from this perspective. However, the rules talked about in this chapter will not be production rules.[5] They are rules linked with the object-oriented model to provide a meaningful and useful model for implementation.

The mapping guidelines for taking a rule into an OO concept are as follows:

1. Service precondition

   A service precondition is mapped onto a service. As suggested by Meyer, the precondition is a requirement that should be guaranteed by the calling object.[6]

2. Service postcondition

   A service postcondition is also mapped onto a service. It is a rule that must be checked by the author of this service. The service must guarantee that the postcondition is satisfied.

3. Control condition

   A control condition is mapped onto a finite state machine. It is usually a condition needed for a change of state.

4. Action trigger

   An action trigger is mapped onto a finite state machine. It is usually an event in a state transition diagram.

5. Relationship integrity

   A relationship integrity is mapped onto a relationship. It normally affects the instantiation, deletion, and addition to a relationship.

---

[5] An inference engine may be used to implement a method in a class; however, we do not recommend this technique.

[6] Meyer: "One of the main sources of complexity in programs is the constant need to check whether data passed to a processing element (method) satisfy the requirements for correct processing. Where should these checks be performed: in the method itself or in its client? Unless class designers formally agree on a precise distribution of responsibilities, the checks end up not being done at all, a very unsafe situation or, out of concern for safety, being done several times. Redundant checking may seem harmless, but it is not. It hampers efficiency, of course; but even more important is the conceptual pollution that it brings to software systems. Complexity is probably the single most important enemy of software quality. The distribution of redundant checks all over a software system destroys the conceptual simplicity of the system, increases the risk of error, and hampers such qualities as extensibility, understandability, and maintainability.

The recommended approach is to systematically use preconditions, and then allow the service author to assume, when writing the method, that the corresponding precondition is satisfied. The aim is to permit a simple style of programming, favoring readability, maintainability, and other associated qualities."

This notion applies to libraries and classes within an applicaton more so than servers in a distributed computing environment. A server that handles multiple clients cannot afford to assume that all clients are well behaved. It must be coded defensively so that a rogue client cannot crash it or corrupt any data stored within it.

6. Data integrity or data trigger

Data integrity and data triggers are mapped onto an attribute. Normally, they are checked every time the attribute changes value.

7. Derivation

A derivation is difficult to map. It is usually used as part of a method. However, there are situations in which it is implemented as a trigger. Care must be taken when you have a derivation rule.

Documenting the Rules Using UML

THE documenting guidelines for the various rules are as follows:

1. Service precondition

A service precondition is mapped onto a service. This needs to be captured as part of the entrance criteria. If there is an operation specification for the service, use the precondition section of the *operational specification* to document this. It not, include this as a comment in the method specification.

2. Service postcondition

A service postcondition is also mapped onto a service. If an operations specification is written for the service, use the postconditions section to document this. The postconditions must also be included in the method description.

3. Control condition

A control condition is mapped onto a finite state machine. It is usually a condition needed for a change of state. This is documented as a guard condition in UML.

4. Action trigger

An action trigger is mapped onto a finite state machine. It is usually an event in a state transition diagram. This is documented as an event in UML.

5. Relationship integrity

A relationship integrity is mapped onto a relationship. It normally affects the instantiation, deletion of, and addition to a relationship. This is documented as a constraint in UML.

6. Data integrity or data trigger

Data integrity and data triggers are mapped onto an attribute. Normally, they are checked every time the attribute changes value. This is best documented by creating a new stereotype, called "data trigger," which is used to capture the actions associated with the rule(s). Then artificial associations are drawn between the classes that need data triggers and the data trigger class.

7. Derivation

A derivation is documented as part of the method.

Implementing Rules

THE mapping guidelines given previously show that service precondition rules, service postcondition rules, control condition rules, action triggers, and derivation rules map very nicely into the classical object-oriented model. However, relationship integrity rules, data integrity rules, and data triggers are not well supported in our model. To handle these rules, a data-driven mechanism is needed. There are two ways to supply a data-driven mechanism:

1. Use the triggers in the database system

   Using triggers in the database system is the classical way of handling data integrity and data trigger rules. Every time the database recognizes a change in data value, it triggers a routine written by the user. The appropriate rules are implemented in that routine. This is reasonably straightforward for simple data-driven rules, but it is a little more tricky for complex rules (such as relationship constraints).

2. Use a language that extends C++ to include rules

   At AT&T Laboratories,[7] researchers and developers have created a new language with constructs that directly support the data-driven mechanisms. This language is R++. R++ is an extension to C++ that bridges the gap between object-oriented procedural semantics and data-driven rules. C++ classes contain two kinds of members: data members and member functions. R++ extends the C++ class construct with a new kind of member, a rule.[8] This enables object-oriented applications to employ data-driven computation. As an extension to C++, R++ fits comfortably with C++ concepts and practices. R++ rules are relatively easy to learn; the syntax is similar and the behavior is much like a "reactive" member function.

   An R++ rule is syntactically defined as follows:

   > rule *class-name* :: *rule-name* {*condition* => *action*}.

   The condition-action pair behaves like an if-then statement:

   > if *condition* then *action*s.

   The action is automatically executed when the condition evaluates to true. The system monitors the data members appearing in the rule's condition, and when a data member changes its data values, it creates a trigger event. The trigger event causes the rule to reevaluate the condition, taking into account new/changed data. If the condition is satisfied, the rule "fires." (When a rule fires, the action is executed.)

---

[7] It should be noted that while the research on R++ is being performed by researchers in AT&T Laboratories, the patent for R++ is held by Lucent.

[8] What R++ calls rules are really only data-driven rules.

Within the condition, part of the rule existential quantifiers (*all* and *exists*) and logical operators (*and* and *or*) are supported. Existential qualifiers and logical operators are used to form compound conditions. In addition, the language supports accessing related objects (thus their associated services) via a concept called *binding*. Service calls (function calls) are also supported in the condition.

Recommended Approach

WHEN declarative statements appear in the requirements document, the following steps are recommended:

1. Separate the declarative statements from the procedural statements.
2. Restate the declarative statements using structured English as rules, taking care that the rules are rigorous and implementable.
3. Map the rules onto the appropriate OO mechanism.
4. If data-driven rules are used, employ a data-driven mechanism to model these rules. We recommend R++ over using database triggers.

■ ■ SUMMARY

DECLARATIVE statements, or rules, are another natural form in which domain experts and end users state their requirements. We, as analysts and developers, should accept declarative statements as a natural part of textual requirements. It follows that declarative statements should be captured within a model. To do this, we must translate the textual declarative requirements into structured English to assure that we have rigorous and implementable requirements. After stating all of the declarative requirements in structured English, we should then map each declarative statement into a rule category. The rule category allows it to be properly assigned to the appropriate object-oriented mechanism in the model.

Because not every rule category could be assigned to a classical object-oriented mechanism, we introduced the data-driven mechanism. This mechanism supports rules triggered by a change in the value of an attribute. As discussed, this is a very valuable extension to the object-oriented paradigm. Historically, triggers in a database system were used to implement this mechanism. However, documenting database trigger functions and getting people to read the documentation were not easily accomplished. An alternative approach was developed at AT&T Labs and Lucent Bell Laboratories. Researchers and developers chose to extend the C++ language to provide a data-driven mechanism as an integral part of the language. This solution is highly desirable because we can see all the code in one place.

As with any tool, data-driven rules are good for some tasks and not as effective for other tasks. We recommend them for:

- Enforcing invariants
- Maintaining data integrity

- Maintaining relationship integrity
- Detecting constraint violations
- Stating business policies and engineering guidelines

A data-driven rule is like a demon that constantly monitors attributes and reacts when appropriate. The action portion of the code sits apart from the routine procedural code and is automatically triggered by relevant changes in the objects that the rule monitors. This relieves the analyst/developer from designing and programming explicit control for the data-driven rule.

The Model

> *The sublime and the ridiculous are often so nearly related, that it is difficult to class them separately. One step above the sublime, makes the ridiculous; and one step above the ridiculous, makes the sublime again.*
>
> Tom Paine

At the end of the fourth step, we actually built an integrated model of the system. If we had executed each step perfectly, we would have our model. Unfortunately, the substeps and guidelines are not adequate to guarantee this result. In fact, the weakness in our method is its inability to help an analyst/developer identify abstract classes.[1] In the fifth step, we will help you find these classes. This is the refinement phase of our method.

Concepts

ALTHOUGH most of us will tell you that the strength of object-oriented technology is that it gives you the mechanism to model reality, in fact it is not an approach that models reality. Anybody who has studied philosophy knows that reality is the state of mind of each individual. So what is object-oriented technology really doing? It models people's

---

[1] This is the inherent weakness in all object-oriented methods. Now, we know why people say objects are hard to find. Because abstract classes capture concepts from our mind, we do not anticipate a technique in the foreseeable future that will help us capture conception.

understanding and processing of reality by capturing the concepts they have acquired. Thus, a vital part of learning this technology is acquiring an understanding of what a concept is and how it is used in object-oriented analysis.

Each concept is a particular idea or understanding that a person has of the world. The person knows he or she possesses a concept when he or she can apply it successfully to surrounding things/objects. For example, a car and a telephone are widely held and understood concepts. We can certainly apply them to things/objects and determine if a thing/object is an instance of a car, a telephone, or neither.

The formation of concepts helps us organize our reality of the world. Psychologists believe that babies start life in a world of confusion and gradually acquire concepts to reduce the confusion. For example, at a very young age a baby learns to differentiate between the sounds of its mother and father.

Humans seem to possess an innate ability to perceive regularities and similarities among the many objects in our world. Every time we recognize these regularities and similarities, we create a concept to organize it. Eventually, we develop concepts (e.g., red and car) and learn to combine concepts to form new concepts (i.e., red car). As we grow older, we construct more elaborate conceptual constructs that lead to increased semantic meaning, precision, and subtleties.

Because we define them, the concepts we form and use are indeed varied. Concepts may be *concrete* (person, car, table, house), *intangible* (time, quality, company), *roles* (mother, programmer, teacher, student), *relational* (marriage, partnership, supervision, ownership), *events* (sale, interrupt, collision, take-off), *displayables* (string, icon, video), *judgments* (high pay, good example, excellent job), and others (signal, atom, gnome, tooth fairy).

These concepts serve as mental lenses with which we try to make sense of and reason about objects in our world. For example, the concept of person helps us reason about several billion objects on this earth. New concepts may (1) help us perceive the same objects in a different way, (2) help us reason about an existing object in a different manner, and (3) add new objects to our awareness. For example, the concept of employee helps us reason in a new way about the several billions of objects. The concept "atomic particle" adds new objects to our awareness, and particle spin as it applies to an atomic particle helps us reason about an existing object in a different manner.

People can possess concepts about things that have existed, do exist, may exist, and probably will not exist. Two concepts, Santa Claus and Fairy Godmother, are objects for some people, yet they are not for others. Concepts like total world peace and solar-powered car do not apply to anything today, but this may not be so in the future. It is highly unlikely that the concept of perpetual motion will apply to anything today or in the future. People also form concepts for which no objects exist. For example, many people have a concept of a perfect mate, yet there is no object that has passed the concept's test.

Concepts and Object-Oriented Model

BY definition, a privately held idea or understanding is called a conception. When that idea or understanding is shared by others, it becomes a concept. To communicate with others, we must share our individually held conceptions and arrive at mutually agreed upon concepts. For example, if your conception of a car is only a 1970 silver

Lamborghini and your spouse's conception of a car is a family station wagon, you may want to come to a common understanding on the concept of a car before the family goes car shopping.

The process of object-oriented analysis is really the process of capturing a set of shared concepts among domain experts, users, managers, and developers. These concepts underly every organizational process, define a shared organizational reality, and form the basis for an organizational language that is used for communication.

To help specify these concepts, the object-oriented paradigm has the following basic mechanisms: class, association, aggregation, generalization/specialization, polymorphism, and instantiation. In later chapters, we will add mechanisms to support concepts that deal with dynamic behavior and to deal with rules. Because this is a living technology, more mechanisms are being developed to provide better support for modeling concepts that are needed to help us better manage complexity. In this section of the book we review these basic mechanisms.

Class

A class describes a group of objects with identical attributes, common behavior, common relationships (link and aggregation), and common semantics. Examples of classes are person, employee, timesheet, company, and department. Each object in a class will have the same attributes and behavior patterns. Most objects get their individuality by having different values for their attributes and having different objects in their relationships. However, objects with identical attribute values and/or identical relational objects are allowed.

The important key to two objects being in the same class is that they share a common semantic purpose in the application domain, beyond the fact that they have the same attributes, common relationships, and common behaviors. For example, consider a grain silo and a cow. If these were objects in a financial application, the only two attributes of importance may be age and cost, and both the silo and the cow may actually be in the same class of farm assets. However, if the application were a farming application, then it is unlikely that the silo and the cow would be in the same class. Thus, interpreting the semantics depends on the application and is the judgment of the domain expert.

Association

An association describes a group of links with common structure and semantics. An association is a way to capture the links between objects in a meaningful way via their classes (object types). An association describes a set of potential links in the same way that a class describes a set of potential objects. In object-oriented modeling, all links, and thus all associations, are considered as bidirectional. Once a link is established between two objects, each object may request the services of the other object. However, the proper usage of the association should require that the association (i.e., the links) be used only to access services consistent with the semantic meaning of the association. In theory, an association can be binary (between two classes), ternary (among three classes), or some higher order. In practice, most associations are binary.

Class Aggregation

A class aggregation describes a group of *object aggregations* with common structure and semantics. Thus, class aggregation is a way to capture the object aggregations between objects in a meaningful way via their classes (object types). Examples of aggregation are purchase order, with its associated line items, and a timesheet with its associated hourly accounting. Although many aggregations are implemented as unidirectional, in analysis these relationships should be considered as bidirectional.

An aggregation may be either static or dynamic, and a component of an aggregate may also be conditional. A *static aggregation* has fixed components that cannot be changed. A *dynamic aggregation* has components that may vary over time. A *conditional component* either is or is not a component of an aggregate, depending on whether a specific condition holds.

Aggregation has become such a useful mechanism for analysis that seven distinct kinds of aggregation have been identified. They are as follows:

- Assembly-parts (component-integral composition)
- Material-object composition
- Portion-object composition
- Place-area composition
- Collection-members composition
- Container-content (member-bunch) composition
- Member-partnership composition

These were described in chapter 9.

Generalization/Specialization

Generalization is an abstraction mechanism for sharing similarities among classes while their differences are preserved.[2] Generalization is the relationship between a class and one or more refined versions of that class. The class being refined is called the *superclass*,[3] and each refined version is called a *subclass*.[4] For example, an aircraft has a manufacturer, identification number, weight, and cost. A helicopter, which also has propellers, and a jet fighter, which also has missiles, are refined versions of an aircraft.

Generalization gives us the capability to define the features of an aircraft once and then just add the additional features for helicopter and jet fighter. In our example, the aircraft is the superclass, and the helicopter and jet fighter are the subclasses.

Attributes, relationships, and services with the same semantic meaning are attached to the superclass and are inherited by the subclasses. Each subclass inherits all the attributes, services, and relationships of the superclass. For example, the jet fighter inherits the attributes, manufacturer, identification number, weight, and cost from the

---

[2]   In most object-oriented languages, including C++, this is implemented using inheritance.

[3]   Called a base class in C++.

[4]   Called a derived class in C++.

aircraft. *It inherited the attributes and not the values.* The jet fighter must determine its own values for these attributes. Generalization is commonly called the "is_a" relationship because each instance of a subclass is also an instance of the superclass.

Generalization is transitive across any number of levels of generalization. The term *ancestors* refers to the generalization of classes across multiple levels. An instance of a subclass is simultaneously an instance of all its ancestor classes. Furthermore, the subclass includes values for every attribute of every ancestor class and relational objects for each relationship in its ancestral classes. In addition, all the services and associated methods of all the ancestral classes may be applied to the subclass.

Each subclass not only inherits all of the aforementioned attributes, but usually adds specific attributes, relationships (associations and maybe aggregations), and services with their associated methods as well. In our example, the jet fighter added missiles as an attribute and probably fireMissile as a service. This attribute and service are not shared by other aircraft.

Polymorphism

One of the goals of OO technology is to reuse code; generalization is one of the most effective vehicles to facilitate code reuse. However, some methods may need to be tailored to meet business needs. When such tailoring is required for a subclass, object-oriented technology has a mechanism, called *polymorphism*, in which the subclass can have a method (behavior) that replaces its superclass's method for a specific service. Thus, when that service is requested from an instance of the subclass, the subclass method is invoked. However, when the service is requested from other instances (assuming no other subclass has also made a replacement for this service), the superclass method is invoked.

For example, consider this simple example. We have a class Employee that has a subclass Executive. From a modeling perspective, an executive is also an employee. One of the services that applies to all employees is payRaise. For all employees, the pay raise is the employee's salary multiplied by the annual inflation. This has been the corporate policy for the last 10 years. With generalization, this has worked very well. Each year at raise time, the payRaise service is invoked for all employees, including the executives. Even though executives are employees, the directors of the corporation decide that executive pay raises should be computed differently than those of the rest of the employees. It is decided that executive pay raises will be five times the annual inflation rate plus a bonus of 15% of the gross revenue.

What mechanism does object-oriented technology have for handling this situation? In this situation, the subclass "executive" can have a method that replaces the employee's payRaise method every time this service is requested for an executive. Although these methods are different, they accomplish the same business purpose (have the same semantics of payRaise). This phenomenon is known as *polymorphism*. The method that gets invoked depends on the class of the object. Thus, the employee and executive example can be captured by making the payRaise service polymorphic.[5]

---

[5] Note that the name and signature of the service are preserved. This differs from C++ function overloading, in which the name of the function or the operator is reused, but the arguments are different. Thus, function overloading is not a vehicle for implementing polymorphism in C++. Polymorphism is implemented in C++ by using virtual functions.

Instantiation

Instantiation is a mechanism in the object-oriented paradigm in which we can create instances of a class. These instances (objects) are the keepers of the data that will make our application/system work. This mechanism is one of the vehicles that we use to make our model dynamic.

Documenting Concepts Using UML

IN earlier chapters, we have informally shown how to document some of the constructs discussed in the preceding section. Now, we will show each of the constructs in a more formal and complete form.

Class Concept

In UML, there are four constructs that can be used for describing the class concept:

- Basic class and object construct
- Parameterized class and bound class constructs
- Interface construct

Basic Class Construct.   In UML, the icon for a class or an object is a solid rectangle containing the name of the *class* (object).[6] The rectangle can be broken into three compartments[7] to identify more than just class name. The top compartment shows the class name. The center compartment shows the attributes. An attribute can be documented to several degrees of completeness: the attribute name; the attribute name and type; and the attribute name, type, and default value. The bottom compartment shows the operations. An operation is documented by stating its signature, covering the name, type, and default value of all parameters, and return type (if it is a function). Because a class may appear in many different diagrams, it is not necessary to show every attribute and operation every time it appears. In some cases, it may make sense to show just a subset of them. An empty compartment does not imply that there are no attributes or operations, just that they haven't been identified in that particular diagram. One can use ellipses, ("...") to denote that there are entries that haven't been shown in this particular diagram. An example of representing class (with and without attributes and operations) is given in Figure 11-1.

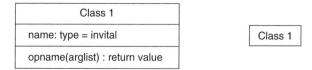

FIGURE 11-1   **Expressing class information in UML.**

---

[6]   In order to distinguish between class and object, objects have their names underlined.

[7]   A seldom-used feature of UML is the presence of a fourth compartment to be used for documenting responsibilities.

FIGURE 11-2   UML templated class and a bound class.

Parameterized Class and Bounded Class Construct.   UML can also deal with *parameterized* (templated) classes and *bound* classes. Parameterized classes are classes that define a basic class in which the data types of one or more of the attributes are a parameter of the class defintion. A bound class is created when the parameters of a parameterized class are bound to a data type. The notation is illustrated in Figure 11-2.

Interface Construct.   UML also supports representing interfaces. Interfaces can be classes that serve as proxies or stubs, or they can be pure abstract classes used to separate interface from implementation. There are two basic representations, one in which the interface is shown as a circle attached to the implementing class and the other in which the interface class is documented using the standard class icon with the <<interface>> prototype specified. The implementing class is shown connected to the interface with a dashed line terminating with an unfilled triangle pointing at the interface. Examples of representing interfaces are illustrated in Figure 11-3.

Association

In UML, an association is documented by a line drawn between the classes participating in it (illustrated in Figure 11-4). Centered and above the line is the name of the association. At the ends of a line, the roles that objects (of the class) hold within the association are identified by role names. The role names may appear above or below the line. The multiplicity of the role is identified by the appropriate marker at the end of the line. Appropriate markers are shown in Figure 11-4. Relation 1 illustrates an association in which Class 1 has a multiplicity of 0 to many and Class 2 has a multiplicity of 1. Relation 2 illustrates an association in which Class 1 has a multiplicity of 1 to many and Class 2 has a multiplicity of 0 or 1. Relation 3 illustrates an association in which Class 1 has a multiplicity of many while the multiplicity of Class 2 is not specified. In this case, one normally assumes that the multiplicity is 1. A qualified association has a box at the end of the line identifying the qualifier. This is illustrated in relation 4 in the figure. Associations are assumed to be bidirectional, meaning that they can be traversed in either direction. In some cases, the association can only be traversed in a single direction. UML denotes this by using a line with an arrowhead that indicates the direction of traversal. This is illustrated in relation 5 in the figure. Relation 6 illustrates a dependency relation. UML also provides a mechanism for associating attributes with an association. This is accomplished by linking an association class with the line for relation with a dashed line. This is illustrated by Relation 7 in the figure.

FIGURE 11-3   UML diagrams for representing interfaces.

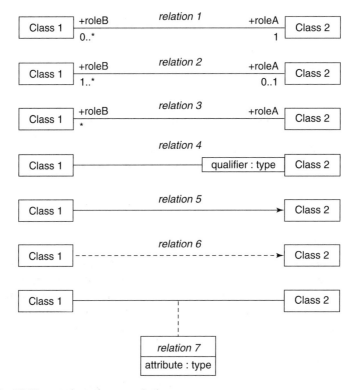

FIGURE 11-4   UML notations for associations.

Class Aggregation

UML distinguishes between two different kinds of aggregations (aggregation and composition), as illustrated in Figure 11-5. The UML concept of aggregation captures the idea of part-whole. UML aggregation is illustrated as an empty diamond on the end that constitutes the whole. The UML concept of composition is that the part-object can only belong to one whole and that the parts are usually expected to live or die with the whole. UML composition is illustrated as a filled diamond on the end that constitutes

FIGURE 11-5 UML notation for aggregation and composition.

FIGURE 11-6 UML notation for generalization/specialization.

FIGURE 11-7 UML notation for an object.

the whole. Multiplicity markers can be employed on the many ends of the aggregation. These markers are the same as those used in associations.

Generalization/Specialization

Class generalization/specialization is documented in UML using a line with an empty triangle that points toward the generalization, as illustrated in Figure 11-6. In the example, Class 1 is superclass for Class 2. It should be noted that UML allows one to document multiple inheritance by establishing multiple generalization/specialization relations from a common subclass or from different classes.

Polymorphism

In UML, polymorphism is documented by showing the service (operation) in both the superclass and the subclass.

Instantiation

UML allows one to document objects as well as classes. An object is denoted using the notation for class with the object name underlined. The object name is denoted by a label separated from the class name by a colon. An example is illustrated in Figure 11-7. If a class creates instances of another class, this can be shown using a dashed arrow illustrating the instantiation dependency between the class and an instance. This is also shown in the figure.

Refining the Model

THE steps for refinement are as follows:

1. Group all objects with the same attributes, similar relationships, and common behavior. If there is a concept within the application domain that defines these objects, use that name for the class. If not, ask the domain expert what concept this may resemble. Use the class that the domain expert provides and regroup your objects.

2. Group the links and object aggregations into associations and class aggregations. Remember that all members of the group must carry the same semantic meaning.

3. Determine whether the classes are specializations of a common superclass. Look for identical attributes, relationships, services, and behaviors across classes and, with them, try to form a class. Again, ask the domain expert if these properties capture a useful domain concept. Remember that these new objects must operate in a useful semantic domain.

4. Look for polymorphism. See if there are services of objects that are the same or similar, but differ in behavior (how the service is provided). If these objects operate in the same semantic domain, make the service polymorphic. Perform all of the preceding steps again until no new superclass is found.

Subsystems

IN building large applications/systems, the analyst/developer has to deal with a number of interesting and different subject matters. For example, in a typical application, we have the following subject matters: the application, interface to external systems, user interface, alarm subsystem and logging subsystem.[8] This is normally too much material for most of us to deal with as a whole. Consequently, we need a strategy for organizing these different matters into more manageable subsystems. The strategy or technique we shall use is based on the work of Shlaer and Mellor. Their strategy relies on the concept of domain.

Domain

A domain is a separate real, hypothetical, or abstract world inhabited by a distinct set of objects that behave according to rules and policies that characterize that domain. For example, an Airline Management domain would be concerned with airplanes, air routes, airports, and gates, as well as with the operating policies and FAA regulations governing their use. However, the User Interface domain is concerned with windows, pulldown menus, dialog boxes, and icons together with a different set of operating policies.

---

[8]   In design, we add the screen subsystem, database subsystem, etc. The operating system, programming languages, software packages, and development environment are all considered part of design.

Each domain forms a separate but cohesive whole. The principle of cohesion helps us keep closely related ideas together and unrelated ideas separate. Because a domain represents a set of closely related objects, rules, and policies, it can be treated as a unit (subsystem) for the purpose of analysis.

To better understand domain, we can look at this concept in terms of objects:

1. An object is defined in one domain.
2. The object in a domain requires the existence of other objects in the same domain.
3. The objects in one domain do not require the existence of objects in a different domain.

For example, consider an airline management application. (1) The air route should be only in the Airline Management domain. (2) Air route by itself is not much use to us without airplanes and airports. (3) Air routes and airplanes can exist without windows or dialog boxes. Conversely, windows and icons can exist without air routes and airplanes.

Although an object in one domain does not require the existence of an object in another domain, it is very common for an object in one domain to have a counterpart instance in another domain. For example, an airplane in the Airline Management domain may have a counterpart airplane icon in the User Interface domain.

To help us recognize domains, Shlaer and Mellor have given us a classification scheme:[9]

1. *Application domain*. This is the subject matter from the customer/user perspective. This is what we normally call business requirements analysis.
2. *Service domain*. This domain provides generic mechanisms and utility functions to support the application domain. These are the domains that are hard for us to identify.
3. *Architectural domain*. This domain provides the generic mechanisms and structures for managing data and control for the system as a whole.
4. *Implementation domain*. This domain includes the programming language, operating systems, networks, and common class libraries.

Bridge

According to Shlaer and Mellor, a bridge exists between two domains when one domain needs to use the mechanisms and/or capabilities provided by the other domain. The domain that requires the capabilities is known as the *client*, while the domain that provides them is called the *server*. For example, the Airline Management domain (client) may use the User Interface domain to display the air routes to the user. During analysis, the bridge defines a set of external services (from the client's perspective) and a set

---

[9] In analysis, we are concerned only with Application Domains and Service Domains. In design, Architectural Domains and Implementation Domains are considered.

of requirements (from the server's perspective). For instance, in our airplane example, the airplane icon must be able to derive its position from the position of the airplane object in the Airline Management domain.

Organizing Subsystems

ACCORDING to Rumbaugh et al. (1991), the decomposition of a system into subsystems may be done both horizontally and vertically. Although most of us have numerous ways to decompose a system, any decomposition reduces to one or the other or a combination of these two kinds.

Horizontal Layers

A layer system is a set of semantic domains (virtual reality), each built in terms of the ones below it and providing the basis of implementation for the ones above it. Examples of this approach are the protocol layers of OSI and the TNM layers for telecommunication operating support systems. For the nontelecommunication technologist, an interactive graphic system is another example. Here, windows are made from screens that are made from pixels driving some I/O device. The layers are the application domain, window domain, screen domain, pixel domain, and hardware domain.

The goal is to make each layer as independent as possible. Although there is usually some correspondence between objects in different layers, the communication between layers is basically one-way. A subsystem knows about the layers below it,[10] but has no knowledge of the layers above it. Thus, a client-server relationship exists between the layers.[11]

Usually, only the top layer, which is the application domain, and the bottom layer, which is the hardware domain, are specified in the requirements document. One of the purposes of analysis is to find all the intermediate layers. It is good practice to have at least one layer (service domain) between the application layer and the hardware layer, as this will facilitate porting to other hardware/software platforms.

Vertical Partitions

Vertical partitions divide a system into several weakly-coupled subsystems,[12] each of which provides one kind of service. For example, consider a computerized work management system for maintenance personnel. There may be a separate subsystem for rou-

---

[10] In some paradigms, the communication may only be to the layer immediately below it. This restriction will preserve the information-hiding and encapsulation principles between layers and will make software more maintainable, as a designer only needs to check the layer below it. However, in practice this is too restrictive. During design, performance considerations usually force us to allow the upper layer to access all the services in any lower layer.

[11] The upper layers are the clients for the lower layers.

[12] If the subsystems are independent of each other, then it is more effective to consider them as separate systems.

tine work, troubleshooting, time reporting, and salary administration. There is only a very weak coupling between these subsystems. Routine work is only coupled to time reporting as to the hours worked. Salary administration uses time reporting to determine how much to pay; however, it has neither coupling to routine work nor troubleshooting.

Combination

A system can be successively decomposed into subsystems using both vertical partitions and horizontal layers in various combinations. Horizontal layers may be partitioned and vertical partitions may be layered. Most large systems require this kind of mixture.

Identifying Subsystems

TO identify subsystems, we are going to use the fact that there should be coupling between objects in the same domain and low coupling across domains. If we draw a model that captures only the associations and class aggregations, we would find a clustering of classes. We will use each cluster as a potential subsystem. To help us determine if the cluster is a subsystem, Shlaer and Mellor have the following suggestions:

1. Give the domain a name and prepare a mission statement for it.
2. Find the bridges (services to other subsystems) for the domain.
3. See if these services are consistent with the mission statement.
4. Determine if you can replace this set of objects with a different set of objects with the same mission.

If all these are true, the cluster is a subsystem. If you find a number of intersubsystem relationships defined between the same two subsystems, a cluster may have been split improperly. Look again at your class definitions to see if you can redefine the classes to make the clusters better behaved.

Documenting Subsystems

SUBSYSTEMS can be documented in UML utilizing packages. A package diagram identifies a grouping of software elements, typically a collection of classes. UML uses a stylized folder to represent a package. A package diagram is illustrated in Figure 11-8. In this diagram, the accounting and customer subsystems communicate with each other as indicated by the double-arrowed line between them. The Bank package exists in a layer above the Accounting and Customer packages. The Bank package communicates with the packages below it, but they can not make requests to it, as evidenced by the single-direction arrows.

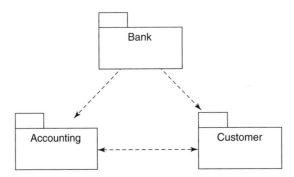

FIGURE 11-8   Package diagram illustrating subsystem interactions.

Recommended Approach

OUR recommended approach consists OF the following steps:

1. Group all objects with the same attributes, similar relationships, and common behavior. If there is a concept within the application domain that defines these objects, use that name for the class. If not, ask the domain expert what concept this may resemble. Use the class that the domain expert provides and regroup your objects.

2. Group the links and object aggregations into associations and class aggregations. Remember that all members of the group must carry the same semantic meaning.

3. Determine whether the classes are the specialization of a common superclass. Look for identical attributes, relationships, services, and behaviors across classes and try to form a class. Again, ask the domain expert if these properties capture a useful domain concept. Remember that these new objects must operate in a useful semantic domain.

4. Look for polymorphism. See if there are services of objects that are the same or similar, but differ in behavior (how the service is provided). If these objects operate in the same semantic domain, make the service polymorphic. Perform all of the preceding steps again until no new superclasses are found.

5. Draw a model that captures only the associations and class aggregations.

6. Identify the cluster of classes and assume they are potential subsystems.

7. Give this custer a name and a mission statement.

8. Use the bridge and replacement test to determine if it is a subsystem (separate domain).

Example

Let us return to our lawn-mowing example.

Refinement

In this section, we will refine our model in the one semantic domain: home care.[13] Based on the analysis, we have the following objects: John, Jane, Peter, Paul, Elizabeth, Mary, Jack, FamilyLawn, and ProfessionalLawnMower.

We will start by trying to group objects together. First, Paul, Elizabeth, and Mary are objects that have the same attributes, common relationships, and common behavior. Jack and ProfessionalLawnMower also appear to be in the same class. In fact, ProfessionalLawnMower is a class and Jack is an instance of that class.

Although we have identified ProfessionalLawnLower as an object, it is also a class. This is one of the difficulties in reading a requirements document. In one usage, a name of a class is used to refer to itself as an object and in another usage, the name is used to refer to itself as a collection of instances of an object type. Now you understand the problem with step 1; when you list objects, you are also listing classes.[14] Our first cut at listing objects is shown in Figure 11-9.

If we review all of the classes listed in Figure 11-8, we notice that class **ChildA** and class **ChildB** are almost identical. The difference is that the two classes have different methods for the "mow the lawn" service. Because the semantic meaning and signature for the service are the same, this situation is best captured using polymorphism. Thus, we can create a superclass **Child** for subclasses **ChildA** and **ChildB**. This model is adequate if we presume that we deal only with one generation of a family and ignore the fact that a professional lawn mower can also be in a family. This more flexible and more accurate model is left as an exercise for the reader. The model shown in Figures 11-10 through 11-12 is adequate for our limited application. The class descriptions are illustrated in Figures 11-13 through 11-17.

Class	Instance(s)
Family	Jones
ProfessionalLawnMower	Jack
ChildA	Mary, Elizabeth, Paul
ChildB	Peter
Father	John
Mother	Jane
Lawn	Family lawn

FIGURE 11-9   List of initial classes instances for the lawn-mowing example.

---

[13] The subsystem identification steps are shown in the case study.

[14] This cannot be wrong, for every class is also an object. However, the reverse is not true (i.e., there are objects that are not classes).

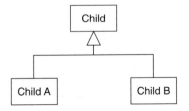

FIGURE 11-10   Class generalization diagram for lawn-mowing example.

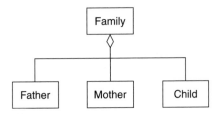

FIGURE 11-11   Class aggregation diagram for lawn-mowing example.

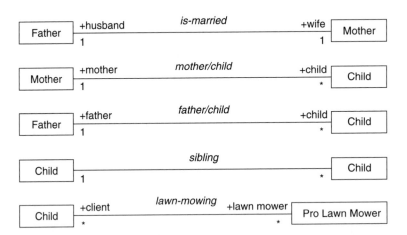

FIGURE 11-12   Class association diagram for lawn-mowing example.

CLASS NAME	Father

ATTRIBUTES
schedule, mycondition

SERVICES
prototype: mow_the_lawn (no arguments)
{
get SCHEDULE for evening (7pm-9pm)
Next, if SCHEDULE has open slot,
then:
place mowFamilyLawn in slot.
return "Yes, I will mow the lawn this evening"
else:
return "No, I cannot mow the lawn"
endif
}
prototype: mowFamilyLawn (no arguments)
{
If MYCONDITION is equal to "tired",
then: // get children via father/child association
for each child in selected Children
ask each child to "mow the lawn" for 5 dollars.
if answer is "yes",
then:
remove "mowFamilylawn" from SCHEDULE.
return;
else:
endif:
endfor:
perform mowing the lawn.
else:
perform mowing the lawn.
endif:
}

FIGURE 11-13   Example of a class CRC card from the lawn-mower.

CLASS NAME	Family

ATTRIBUTES
none

SERVICES
constructor will create the family (see later chapter)

FIGURE 11-14   Example of a class CRC card from the lawn-mower.

CLASS NAME	Child
SUBCLASSES	ChildA, ChildB

ATTRIBUTES
schedule

SERVICES

prototype: mow_the_lawn (address_of_lawn, dollar_amount)
   // there is no method specified, we will require that each
   // subclass specify a method for providing this service.

FIGURE 11-15   Example of a class CRC card from the lawn-mower example.

In this example, we introduced a second form of polymorphism. In the earlier example, the superclass **Employee** had a method specified for the service payRaise; the subclass **Executive** then specified its own method for payRaise. However, we could have added another subclass, **Supervisors**, that does not specify its own method for payRaise. In that event, instances of **Supervisors** will use the method specified in the superclass **Employee**. Here, the superclass **Child** defines the prototype for the service mow_the_lawn, but did not specify a method for performing the service. When this is done, every subclass must specify its own method for handling the service. There is no default specification in the superclass. Both subclasses **ChildA** and **ChildB** must have methods for the service mowTheLawn.

You should also recognize that the differences between **ChildA** and **ChildB** are that they have different methods for implementing the service mowTheLawn, and that only **ChildA** has an association with **ProfessionalLawnMower**. The rest of the class descriptions are left as an exercise for the reader.

CLASS NAME	ChildB
SUPERCLASS	Child

ATTRIBUTES
no additional attributes; remember, it will inherit schedule from child

SERVICES
prototype: mow_the_lawn (address_of_lawn, dollar_amount)
{
get SCHEDULE for evening (7pm-9pm)
Next, if SCHEDULE has open slot,
then:
place mowLawn in slot.
associate ADDRESS_OF_LAWN with mowLawn.
return "Yes, I will mow the lawn this evening."
else:
return "No, I cannot mow the lawn."
endif:
}

FIGURE 11-16 Example of a class CRC card from the lawn-mower example.

Subsystems

Since Chapter 4 and including our work on refinement, our emphasis has been on modeling the semantic domain: home care. Thus, we been focused on the objects that support the system in performing the Look For Work Conditions and the Run Simulation Forward One Time Unit use cases. These use cases are driven by the Asynchronus Event Daemon and the Simulation Clock, respectively. The result is a subsystem, The Lawn-Mowing Model, which is a specialized version of Home Care.

However, our model is not complete. First, we have not incorporated into our model the generation of events for the observer watching the simulation as dictated by the Run Simulation Forward One Time Unit use case. Furthermore, there are two other use cases, Subscribe To Simulation Information and Set Simulation Parameters, that are driven by the observer and director actors respectively, which we have not addressed at all.

Developing the model for these two use cases is not instructional and there are standard GUI libraries (e.g., Microsoft's MFC). Thus, we are not going to develop

SUPERCLASS	Child
CLASS NAME	ChildA

ATTRIBUTES
no additional attributes; remember, it will inherit schedule from child

SERVICES
prototype: mow_the_lawn (address_of_lawn, dollar_amount)
{
if DOLLAR_AMOUNT is less than $5,
then:
get SCHEDULE for evening (7pm-9pm)
Next, if SCHEDULE has open slot,
then:
place mowLawn in slot.
associate ADDRESS_OF_LAWN with mowLawn.
return "Yes, I will mow the lawn this evening."
else:
return "No, I cannot mow the lawn."
endif
else:
use lawn-mowing association to get
a professional lawn mower: plm
ask plm to "mow the lawn (ADDRESS_OF_LAWN, self, ADDRESS)".
if plm's response is "yes"
then:
return "Yes, I will mow the lawn this evening."
else
return "No, I cannot mow the lawn."
endif:
endif:
}

FIGURE 11-17 Example of a class CRC card from the lawn-mower example.

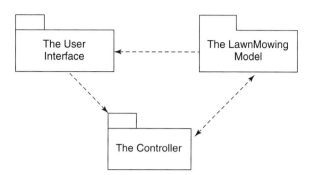

FIGURE 11-18 The three subsystems comprising our Home Care Simulation System.

the model necessary to support these other two use cases. However, these two use cases introduce two additional subsystems: the user interface and the controller. The user interface is the subsystem by which the observer and the director interact with the system. The user interface model will consist of classes and objects associated with windows, buttons, menus, and other interface classes. The controller is the subsystem that handles subscriptions and setting simulation parameters. The controller will consist of classes and objects associated with keeping time, subscriptions, and events.

With these two subsytems, our design is complete. Figure 11-18 illustrates how the three subsystems interact. In this figure the controller subsystem drives the LawnMowing Model through the time simulation and establishes subscriptions to LawnMowing Model elements. The user interface subsystem does not communication directly with the LawnMowing Model subsystem. It sends the subscription requests to the controller, which then forwards them to the LawnMowing Model subsystem. During the simulation, the LawnMowing Model subsystem will generate events. These events will be forwarded to the appropriate subsystem based on subscriptions. This will include the user interface and the controller subsystems.

■ ■ SUMMARY

THE substeps of model refinement and subsystem identification are as follows:

1. Group all objects with the same attributes, similar relationships, and common behavior. If there is a concept within the application domain that defines these objects, use that name for the class. If not, ask the domain expert what concept this may resemble. Use the class that the domain expert provides and regroup your objects.

2. Group the links and object aggregations into associations and class aggregations. Remember that all the members of the group must carry the same semantic meaning.

3. Determine whether the classes are specializations of a common superclass. Look for identical attributes, relationships, services, and behaviors across classes. With these common attributes, relationships, services, and behaviors, try to form a class. Again, ask the domain expert if these properties capture a useful domain concept. Remember these new objects must operate in a useful semantic domain.

4. Look for polymorphism. See if there are services of objects that are the same or similar, but differ in behavior (how the service is provided). If these objects operate in the same semantic domain, make the service polymorphic. Perform all of the preceding steps again until no new superclasses are found.

5. Draw a model that captures only the associations and class aggregations.

6. Identify the cluster of classes and assume they are potential subsystems.

7. Give this cluster a name and a mission statement.

8. Use the bridge and replacement test to determine if it is a subsystem (separate domain).

12

Design

M *any things difficult to design prove easy to performance.*

Samuel Johnson

A t the end of the fifth step, we completed the application model. Now we are ready to consider the technology necessary to implement the model. In this chapter, we add to the model all the technology-dependent objects (classes) to make the application implementable.

We do not discuss or describe object design patterns in this book, despite the large degree of interest this topic area has generated. We justify this by our observation that the use of design patterns by people without significant experience in object-oriented methods has led to considerable problems. Design patterns, although simple and easy to understand in themselves, can be very difficult for inexperienced people to apply correctly. We have observed that novices tend to warp their object models into the patterns that they understand best. Instead we have chosen to give a few general rules on how to map an object model into a good and usable design that can be easily implemented. We are leaving design patterns to an advanced book on design.

Introduction

AFTER you have modeled a business solution to your application/system, you must decide on an approach to implement the business solution using available technology. *System design* is the high-level strategy for implementing the business solution, and *detailed design* is the low-level strategy of the implementation of the application/system.

In system design, the developer must do the following:

- Organize the system into subsystems.
- Identify concurrency inherent in the model.
- Allocate the subsystems to processors and tasks.
- Choose a vehicle and an approach for data storage.
- Determine a control strategy for accessing global resources.
- Choose an implement of control for the software.
- Consider start-up, shut-down, and failure strategies.

In detailed design, the developer must do the following:

- Add the objects/classes from the architectural and implementation domains.
- Design efficient algorithms for complex services.
- Optimize the design of the application/system.
- Maximize the use of inheritance.
- Redesign the associations for efficiency.
- Determine the best representation of classes.
- Package the classes and associations into reusable units.

Obviously, detailed design will follow system design.

System Design

ALTHOUGH all of the issues and decisions a developer must make in system design are critical to the success of the project, we will only discuss dividing the system into a small number of components and the control strategy for the software.

Subsystems

Each major component of the system is called a *subsystem*.[1] Each subsystem should deal with a separate subject matter called a domain. Each domain can be independent of the rest of the system.[2] A good clue to a domain is that it has its own terminology with a different semantic meaning; it is a separate real, hypothetical, or abstract world that is inhabited by a distinct set of objects that behave according to the rules and

---

[1] This is the same concept as discussed in the previous chapter. In analysis, we use subsystems to manage complexity in the application domain. Now, in design, we use subsystems to manage the complexity in the architectural and implementation domains.

[2] It is our opinion that effective reuse is not at the object/class level as proclaimed by most experts, but at the domain level. An example of successful domain reuse is seen with the many application service domain packages available.

policies of the domain. A subsystem is neither an object nor a function, but a package of classes, associations, operations, events, and constraints that are interrelated and that has reasonably well-defined and, hopefully, a small number of interfaces with the rest of the system.

A subsystem is usually defined by the services it provides, just like an object or class is. The relationship between the rest of the system and the subsystem can be peer-to-peer or client/server.

In a peer-to-peer relationship, either side may have access to the other's services. Communication is not necessarily done by a request followed by an immediate response, so there can be communication cycles that can lead to subtle design errors.

The client/server relationship, however, is much simpler; the client calls on the server, which performs some service and replies with the results. The client needs to know the interface of the supplier, but the supplier does not need to know the interface of the client. All of the interactions are done through the supplier's interface.

There are all kinds of suggestions on how to decompose a system. The decomposed system can be organized in two ways: by horizontal layers or by vertical partitions.

A layered system is an ordered set of subsystems in which each of the subsystems is built in terms of the ones below it and provides the basis for building the subsystem above it. The objects in each layer can be independent, although there is some correspondence between the objects of various layers. However, knowledge is only one way; a subsystem knows about the layers below, but it does not know about the subsystems above it. Thus, a client/server relationship exists between layers. An example of a layered system is a windowing system for a computer user interface.

A vertically partitioned system divides a system into several independent or weakly coupled subsystems, each providing one kind of service. For example, an operating system includes a file subsystem, device controller, virtual management subsystem, and an event interrupt handler. In a vertical partition system, a peer-to-peer relationship exists between subsystems.

A real system may be successfully decomposed into subsystems using both layers and partitions in various combinations; a layer can be partitioned and a partition can be layered. Most large systems require a combination of layers and partitions.

Architectural Frameworks

In reality, because many of the decisions that should be made at the system design stage are given to the developers, much of the design process is figuring out how to integrate these givens into a working system. One of the major improvements in software development is that software vendors have given developers a subsystem that performs specific services very well for applications. Thus, developers should take advantage of written and tested subsystems when possible. Moreover, most developers have built certain architectural frameworks that are well suited for certain kinds of applications. If you have applications with similar characteristics, you should use these corresponding architectures as a starting point for your design.

The kinds of systems are as follows:

- **Batch**. A data transformation is done on an entire set of inputs.
- **Continuous**. As input changes in real-time, a data transformation is performed in real-time.
- **Interactive**. External interactions dominate the application.
- **Transaction**. The application is concerned with storing and updating data, often including concurrent access by many users and from many different locations.
- **Rule-based**. The application is dominated by concern about enforcing rules.
- **Simulation**. The application simulates evolving real-world objects.
- **Real-time**. The application is dominated by strict timing constraints.

The steps for performing an object-oriented system design for the first four architectural frameworks are as follows:

Batch Architectural Framework

1. Break the transformation into subtransformations, so that each subtransformation performs one part of the transformation.
2. Define temporary objects for the data flows between subtransformations. Then each subtransformation only needs to know about the objects on each side of itself (i.e., its inputs and outputs).
3. Expand each subtransformation into other subtransformations until the operations are straightforward to implement.
4. Restructure the pipeline for optimization.
5. Use the new set of objects to form classes that loosely couple to the original object model.

Continuous Architectural Framework

1. Identify all of the objects that need continuous updates.
2. Draw a sequence diagram for the continuous transformation.
3. Make the inputs and outputs of the services temporary objects that contain the values that change continuously.
4. Refine or define methods for each object/class that will process the incremental changes for the object.
5. Add any additional objects needed for optimization.
6. Use the new set of objects to form classes that loosely couple to the original object model.

Interactive Architectural Framework

1. Separate the objects that form the interface from the objects that define the semantics of the application; they are in two different domains.

2. Use predefined (library) objects to interface with external agents. For example, most windowing systems have libraries that give developers the windows, menus, and buttons for usage.

3. Use an event-driven (callback) approach to decomposition.

4. Separate physical events from logical events and assign them to the correct objects. Logical events are part of the application and physical events are probably part of the interface domain. Be careful; many times a logical event corresponds to multiple physical events.

Transaction Architectural Framework

1. Map the object model into a database.

2. Determine the resources that cannot be shared.

3. Determine the unit of a transaction (the objects that must be accessed together during a transaction) using a sequence diagram.

4. Design the concurrency control for the transactions. Most database systems support this.

Software Control Within a Framework.   There are two kinds of control flows within a software system: external and internal. External control is the flow of externally visible events among the objects in the system, while internal control is the flow of control within a method.

There are three ways to control external flows: procedural-driven sequential, event-driven sequential, and concurrent. Similarly, the three ways to control internal flows are: procedure calls, quasi-concurrent intertask calls, and concurrent intertask calls. Both the internal and external control strategies chosen are highly dependent on the resources (language, operating system, etc.) available and the pattern of interactions in the application.

Because all of the major object-oriented languages, such as Smalltalk, C++, and Objective C, are procedural languages, procedural-driven sequential is the most common way to control external flow. In this style, the control resides within the application code. The application code issues requests for external inputs and waits for them to arrive. When they arrive, control is resumed within the procedure that made the call. Although this style is easy for most developers to implement, the developer must convert the events in a sequential flow of operations (methods) between objects. This is done using a sequence diagram.[3] This style of control is useful when there is a regularity of external events. However, this style is not very good for handling asynchronous events, error conditions, flexible user interfaces, and process control systems.

In the event-driven sequential style, the control resides within a dispatcher or monitor provided by the language, subsystem, or operating system. Application procedures are attached to events and are called by the dispatcher when the corresponding events occur (callback). The application makes procedure calls to the dispatcher for

---

[3]   Sequence diagrams are discussed in Chapter 7 on behavior.

input/output, but does not wait for it in-line. Events are handled by the dispatcher, and all application procedures return control to the dispatcher instead of retaining control until input arrives.

Event-control style is more difficult to implement with standard programming languages (Smalltalk, C++, or Objective C). This style permits a more flexible pattern of control than the procedural style. Because it simulates cooperating processes within a single multithreaded task, a single errant method can block an entire application. However, event-control style produces more modular design and can better handle error conditions.

In the concurrent style, control resides in several independent objects, where each is a separate task. A task can wait for input, but other tasks continue to execute. There is a queuing mechanism for events, and the operating system resolves scheduling conflicts among tasks. JAVA is an object-oriented language that directly supports tasking and concurrency.

Documenting System Design

Diagrammatically, a system architecture, the system design, is documented in UML utilizing three different diagrams: a package diagram, a component diagram, and a realization diagram. A package diagram shows software partitioning. A component diagram describes relationships among the software components of the system. A realization diagram places the components on hardware platforms. These diagrams are typically accompanied by textual descriptions of the components, connections, and hardware.

As was introduced in the previous chapter, a package diagram identifies a grouping of software elements, typically a collection of software classes. A simple package diagram is illustrated in Figure 12-1. One can explicitly include in the package icon all of the classes that are members.

The component diagram identifies the components that form the system, along with the connections among individual components, as illustrated in Figure 12-2. The UML specification identifies five prototypes for components, namely (1) application, (2) library, (3) table, (4) file, and (5) document. According to the UML specification, a component is drawn as a rectangle with two smaller rectangles overlaid upon one side of it. However, the UML specification does suggest alternative representations for the later four prototypes. Dependencies are illustrated as dotted arrows. One can include within the component diagram explicit identification of the classes that a component realizes (implements). This is illustrated by a dotted arrow to the UML representation for a class.

The deployment diagram captures relationships between components and the hardware on which they are hosted. Components are captured in the deployment diagram using the same graphical mechanism as in the component diagram. However, components are placed inside graphical boxes that represent hardware devices (nodes) in the system. A node does not have to be a generalized processing computer, but can include sensors, RAID disk arrays, and other devices that are an integral part of a system. Solid lines are used to indicate hardware connectivity between nodes. A simple deployment diagram is illustrated in Figure 12-3.

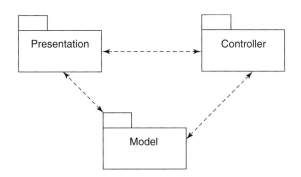

FIGURE 12-1 Simple package diagram for a model-controller-view system.

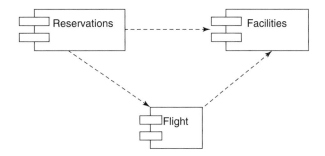

FIGURE 12-2 Component diagram for an airline reservation and flight scheduling system.

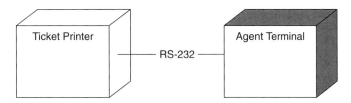

FIGURE 12-3 Deployment diagram illustrating an agent terminal connected to a specialized printer for printing tickets.

Detailed Design

DURING analysis, we determined the objects/classes, their associations, and their structure from an application perspective. During design, we have to add the implementation objects and optimize data structures and algorithms for coding.

There is a shift in emphasis from application domain concepts to computer concepts. Given the classes from the application, the designer must choose among different ways to implement them. Factors that may be important include execution time, memory usage, and disk I/O access. However, optimization of design should not be carried to excess, as there must be a practical trade-off between optimization and ease of implementation, maintainability, and extensibility of the final product.

Usually, the simplest and best approach is to take the classes found in analysis into design. Design then becomes the process of adding implementation objects, adding implementation details, and making implementation decisions. Occasionally, an analysis object/class does not appear in the design, but is distributed among other objects/classes for computational efficiency. Some redundant attributes or an object/class may be added for efficiency.

Thus, detailed design is primarily a process of refinement and adding implementation objects that are technology-dependent. These new objects and additional details should help better organize the application and augment the analysis model.

Class Design

During analysis, we focused on the logical structure of the information that is needed to build a business solution. During design, we need to look at the best way to implement the logical structure that helps optimize the application performance. Many of the effective implementation structures that we need are instances of container classes; examples are arrays, lists, queues, stacks, sets, bags, dictionaries, associations, and trees. Most object-oriented languages already have libraries that provide such classes.[4]

Although we have defined business algorithms for building a business solution during analysis, we may need to optimize the algorithms for implementation. During optimization, we may add new classes to hold intermediate results and new low-level methods. These new classes are usually implementation classes that are not mentioned directly in the client's requirements document. They are usually service domain classes that support the building of the application classes. When new methods are added, some have obvious target objects as their owner. However, some methods may have several target objects for their owner. Assigning responsibility for the latter kind of service can be very frustrating.[5] This is the fundamental problem when we invent implementation objects; they are somewhat arbitrary and their boundaries are more a matter of convenience than of logical necessity.[6]

If we need to avoid recomputation to improve performance, we should define new objects/classes to hold these derived attributes (data). Remember that derived attributes must be updated when base values change. This can be done by:

1. **Explicit code**. Because each derived attribute is defined in terms of one or more attributes of base objects, one way to update the derived attribute is to insert code

---

[4] The Standard Template Library (STL) is the C++ library that provides container classes. This will be covered in a later chapter.

[5] These "implementation" services can also be easily overlooked as they are not inherently services of only one class.

[6] This becomes more difficult when we need to assign a service in an inheritance hierarchy. For implementation classes, the definitions of subclasses may be quite arbitrary and fluid. It is quite common to see services move up and down the hierarchy during the design step.

in the update attribute method of the base object(s). This additional code would explicitly update the derived attribute that is dependent on the attribute of the base object. This is synchronizing by *explicit code*.

2. **Periodic recomputation**. When base values are changed in a bunch, it may be possible to recompute all the derived attributes periodically after all the base values are changed. This is called *periodic recomputation*.

3. **Triggers**. An active attribute has dependent attributes. Each dependent attribute must register itself with the active attribute. When the active attribute is being updated, a trigger will be fired that will inform all the objects containing the dependent attributes that the active attribute has a changed value. Then it is the responsibility of the derived object to update its derived attribute. This is called updating by *triggers*.

Sometimes the same service is defined across several classes and can be easily inherited from a common superclass. However, often the services in different classes are similar but not identical. By slightly modifying the prototype of the service, the services can be made to match so that they can be handled by a single inherited service. When this is done, not only must the name and the signature of the service match, but they should all have the same semantic meaning. The following adjustments are commonly made to increase inheritance:

1. When some services have fewer arguments than other services, the missing arguments are added, but ignored in the method.

2. When a service has few arguments because it is a special case of a more general service, you can implement the special service by calling the general services with all of the arguments.

3. When attributes in different classes have the same semantic meaning, choose one name for the attribute and move it to a common superclass.

4. When services in different classes have the same semantic meaning, choose one name for the service and apply 1 or 2 to take advantage of polymorphism.

5. When a service is defined on several different classes, but not in other classes that semantically should be in one group, define the service in the superclass and declare it as a no-op method in the class that does not care about providing this service.

6. When common behavior has been recognized, a common superclass can be created to implement the shared behavior, leaving the specialized behavior in the subclasses. Usually, this new superclass is an abstract class.[7]

It is strongly recommended that you do not use inheritance as purely an implementation technique. This happens when developers find an existing class that has implemented a large number of the services needed by a newly-defined class, even

---

[7] Sometimes it is worthwhile to abstract out a superclass even if there is only one subclass in your application that inherits from it. If it has useful semantics, it will probably be needed in future extensions of the application or in other applications.

though the two classes are different semantically. The developer may then want to use inheritance to achieve partial implementation of the new class. This can lead to side effects because some of the inherited methods may provide unwanted behaviors. It can also lead to brittle inheritence hierarchies that are difficult to change as the analysis model evolves to reflect changing requirements. A better technique is to use delegation,[8] which allows the newly formed class to delegate only the appropriate services.[9]

Association Design

In implementing associations, the designer must consider the access pattern and the relative frequencies of the different kinds of access. If the number of hits from a query are low because only a fraction of the objects satisfy the criteria, an index should be used to improve the access to objects that are frequently retrieved. However, this will be at a price, as this will use more memory and updates will be slower. Sometimes adding a new association that is derived from the base association will provide direct access to the appropriate data.

If the association is only traversed in one direction, an association can be implemented as an attribute that contains an object reference. If the multiplicity is 1, it is simply a pointer to the other object. If the multiplicity is >1, then it is a pointer to a set of pointers to objects. If the many end is ordered, a list is used in place of a set. A qualified association can be implemented using a dictionary object.

A two-way association can be implemented as follows:

1. Add an attribute to the class on one side of the association and perform a search when a reverse traversal is required.
2. Add an attribute to both sides of the association. Use the same multiplicity techniques as for an association that is traversed in one direction.
3. Create an associate class, independent of either class. An associate class is a set of pairs of related objects stored in a single-variable size object. For efficiency, it is common to implement an associative object as two map objects.[10]

If the association has no services, but has attributes, attributes of an association can be implemented as follows:

1. If the association is one-to-one, the association attributes can be stored as attributes on either class.
2. If the association is many-to-one, the association attributes may be stored in the class on the many side.

---

[8] In delegation, you create an association between the class and the newly formed class. Then the newly formed class can delegate the service from itself to the corresponding service of the existing class.

[9] Languages such as C++ let a subclass selectively make service public. When used properly, inheritance can do the equivalent of delegation for such languages.

[10] Map objects are explained in Chapter 15.

3. If the association is many-to-many, it is best to create an associative class and assign the association attributes to the associative class.[11]

Generalization and Inheritance

Most object-oriented languages incorporate generalization into the language via class inheritance. Typically, a child class can inherit the attributes, services, behaviors, and relationships of the parent class(es).[12] By using this mechanism, the object-oriented paradigm gives analysts/developers a very powerful mechanism that not only helps organizes complex objects, but also facilitates code sharing and code reuse in implementation. The properties of class inheritance are as follows:[13]

1. Structural

   a. Attributes

      Objects (instances) of the descendent class, which is a subclass of the parent class, will have values for all of the attributes of the ancestor class.

   b. Nongeneralization relationships

      Objects (instances) of the descendent class, which is a subclass of the parent class, will have all the nongeneralization relationships of the ancestor class.

2. Interface

   All of the services that are provided by the ancestor class must also be provided by the descendent class. For an object that is an instance of the descendent class is simultaneously an instance of its ancestor class.

3. Behavioral

   a. Inheritance without polymorphism (good child)

      In inheritance without polymorphism, *all* of the methods that are supplied by the ancestor class for its services are also used by the descendent class to provide the corresponding services. This is code reuse and code sharing.

   b. Inheritance with polymorphism (bad child)

      In inheritance with polymorphism, some of the methods that are supplied by the ancestor class for its services are also used by the descendent class to provide the corresponding services. For the remaining services of the ancestor class, the descendent class supplies its own customized methods that replace the appropriate corresponding methods for use by instances of the descendent class.[14]

---

[11] This approach can also be used for many-to-one assocations because they can often evolve into many-to-many.

[12] The parent classes are called superclasses; we have also used ancestor class in this book.

[13] This is not as simple a topic as we may lead you to believe. The assumptions made on these properties are quite varied among the object-oriented languages. We have given you the properties that are consistent with C++ that will implement generalization/specialization as defined in analysis.

[14] The ancestor class decides which services may be redefined using the keyword virtual. This must be planned for when defining the ancestor class.

4. Mathematical

   a. Antisymmetry

      If class A is a subclass of class B, then class B may not be a subclass of class A. In other words, if object A is a descendent of object B, then object B cannot also be a descendent of object A.

   b. Transitivity[15]

      If class A is a subclass of class B and class B is a subclass of class **C,** then class A is a subclass of class B. An instance of class A is also an instance of class C and class B.

Delegation

The object-oriented model that we have built is based on the notion of class and not on the notion of an object. However, there are object-oriented computational models that are based on the object. These systems are usually called prototype systems. In a prototype system, there is no such mechanism as a class. Only objects exist, and an object may have a delegation relationship with any other object. When a service is requested from an object, it does the following:

1. If it has a method for the service, it will execute its own method.

2. If it has no method, it will delegate the execution of that service to an object that has a delegation relationship with it.

3. The delegation relationship is transitive. So if the delegated object does not have a method for the service, it will attempt to delegate the execution of the service to other objects with which it has a delegation relationship.

The reader should note that relationship is between objects, and that the delegation relationship is more generic than the is_a relationship because it can be used between any two objects.[16] Moreover, delegation can be established dynamically (at run-time), while class inheritance is fixed at creation time.

For a prototype system, analysis is done by thinking about a particular object and then drawing similarities and/or differences for other objects based on the particular object(s). Any object may be a prototype object during the analysis. The idea is to start with individual objects and then to specialize and generalize them as more complex cases are considered.[17] Lieberman has described this approach as compared to the object-oriented approach:

> Prototype systems allow creating concepts first, then generalizing them by saying what aspects of the concept are allowed to vary. Set-oriented (object-oriented) systems require creating the abstraction description of the set (class) before individual instances can be installed as members.

---

[15] Transitivity makes it possible to organize the objects (classes) in a hierarchical manner. Because of this property, generalization is diagrammatically shown as an ancestral tree.

[16] Furthermore, in some languages not only the execution of services may be delegated, but also the attributes can also be inherited or shared.

[17] Our method is a modified prototype approach to building an object-oriented system.

In a sense, this method of analysis is much closer to the way humans learn. We learn by either generalizing or specializing on instances. From this, one may be led to conclude that delegation is a better mechanism for implementing generalization/ specialization. However, we will see in the next section that it is not quite that simple.

Orlando Treaty

Historically, there has been much debate over which mechanism (inheritance or delegation) is a more powerful concept for implementing generalization/specialization. Since 1987, we have seen that delegation can model inheritance, and conversely inheritance can model delegation. During OOPSLA 1987, which took place in Orlando, Florida, Lynn Stein, Henry Lieberman, and David Unger discussed their differences about delegation and inheritance and came up with a statement that reflected a need for both mechanisms. That resolution became known as the Orlando Treaty. In essence, the treaty recognizes two modes of code sharing: anticipatory sharing and unanticipatory sharing. Class inheritance-based systems are best for anticipatory code sharing and delegation-based systems are more suited for unanticipated code sharing.

The treaty characterized three dimensions for code sharing:

1. **Static versus dynamic**. Is the sharing determined when the object is created or can it be determined dynamically (at run-time)?
2. **Implicit versus explicit**. Are there explicit operations to indicate the code sharing?
3. **Per object versus per group**. Is sharing defined for whole groups of objects or could it be supported by individual objects?

Traditional object-oriented languages (i.e., C++, Smalltalk, and Simula) use static, implicit, per-group strategies in the design of their languages. By contrast, delegation-based languages use dynamic, explicit, and per-object strategies in the design of their languages.

The Orlando Treaty further acknowledges that:

> no definite answer as to what set of these choices is best can be reached. Rather, that different programming situations call for different combinations of these features: for exploratory, experimental programming environments, it may be desirable to allow the flexibility of dynamic, explicit, per-object sharing; while for large relatively routine software production, restricting to the complementary set choices—strictly static, implicit, and group-oriented—may be more appropriate.

There is a trade-off here between the two strategies. Delegation requires less space, but execution time is slower because of run-time binding. In contrast, class inheritance has faster execution but requires more space. If the class system is strongly typed,[18] there is an additional trade-off between safety versus flexibility. From the

---

[18] C++ is a strongly typed language. One of the main features requested from development was this feature so that more testable and more reliable software can be delivered.

previous discussion, one can conclude that delegation is great for building prototype systems; however, high-performance and production-quality systems will be better if they use a strong-typed, class-based language, like C++.

Multiple Inheritance

We have intentionally given examples that use only single inheritance (each subclass has one and only one immediate superclass). However, there are real situations that are very effectively modeled by letting a subclass inherit from more than one immediate superclass. For instance, in our Person example, we assumed that all students are not employees. However, a better model may be that a person is both a student and an employee. With single inheritance, we would not be able to directly represent this multiple parent relationship. Other examples are German car manufacturer, BorderedText-Window, and transformer toy. A German car manufacturer has properties that are due to it being a German company and also properties that are due to it being a car manufacturer. BorderedTextWindow has properties of a bordered window and properties of a text window. Finally, a transformer toy can act as a robot, car, plane, and boat. The mechanism that allows us to model these situations is called *multiple inheritance*.

With multiple inheritance, we can combine several existing (parent) classes to form a new subclass of all the parent classes. It can access all of the methods and contain all of the attributes and relationships of all of the parent classes. For example, let us use the inheritance tree from our original example that includes the Platypus. In this inheritance tree, the class **Platypus** inherits from both **Mammal** and **Endangered**. This is an example of multiple inheritance and is shown in Figure 12-4.

A more comprehensive example may be as follows. Let Carol, Frank, Mary, Susan, and Karen be employees of a company. Carol is in administration and her manager is

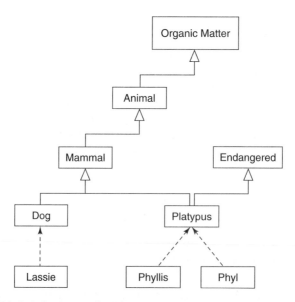

FIGURE 12-4   Multiple inheritance for platypus.

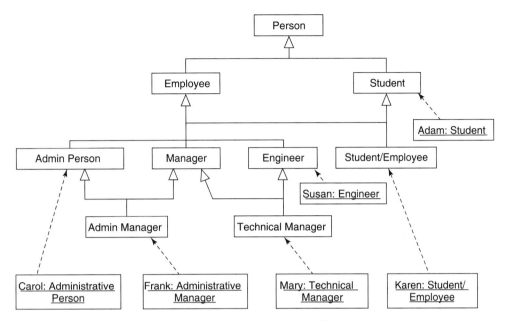

FIGURE 12-5 Multiple inheritance for student employee Karen.

Frank. Susan is in engineering and her manager is Mary. Karen works part-time and is also a student. Adam is also a student, but he does not work for the company. The inheritance tree for this example is shown in Figure 12-5.

Documenting Detailed Design

A detailed design is documented using many of the same diagrams that appear in the documentation of an analysis model. In particular, the detailed design will employ a generalization/specialization class diagram, state diagrams, and collaboration diagrams. Diagrams that illustrate associations and aggregations will not appear in a design because those elements of the analysis model will have been incorporated as new classes and/or as attributes of previously identified classes. In addition, a detailed design will incorporate component diagrams. These component diagrams will explicitly identify the classes realized by the components.

■ ■ SUMMARY

IN this chapter, we briefly discussed design. Despite the brevity on this topic, we have a few recommendations:

1. In system design, we believe that a subsystem must be a collection of objects (classes) in a single semantic domain.

2. In system design, we believe in using the client-server paradigm for establishing communication relationships between subsystems. We believe this will produce more robust and more maintainable software.

3. For software control, we believe that both procedural-driven and event-driven are applicable, depending on the application/system to be built. In fact, we have used both simultaneously in one system.

4. We recommend using UML's deployment diagram to capture the physical topology upon which the software application/system will reside.

5. We recommend using the Utilities class of UML to capture underlying support functions of the operating system and non-OO libraries.[19]

6. In detailed design of classes, it is best to take classes as found in analysis and keep them in the design. Then we should add implementation classes.[20]

7. In detailed design of association, we recommend implementing all associations with their attribute(s) as classes unless there are performance issues. A class implementation of association with attribute(s) accurately models the application/system, and thus will help make the software more maintainable and flexible for future features.

8. In detailed design, use delegation instead of inheritance if you expect to have the subclass and the superclass implemented on different processors.

9. In detailed design, multiple inheritance should be used only if all of the parent classes will reside on the same processor. If the parent class(es) resides on different processors, use delegation to implement multiple inheritance.

10. Consult with an OO expert to find opportunities to use (1) templates, (2) patterns, (3) stereotypes, and (4) composite capabilities of UML. Also have the expert review all of your diagrams. Ensure that the expert reviews closely (1) multiple inheritance, (2) aggregation, (3) nonbinary associations, (4) category classes, (5) mapping of rules to constraints, and (6) exception handling. Adjust your diagrams to reflect the opportunities recommended by the expert.

11. We recommend using the component diagram of UML to capture your detailed physical design of components.

---

[19] A utilities class in UML is a class that is used to capture global variables and procedures. This is a modeling artifact rather than an implementation artifact. The global variables and procedures are not made accessible via an instance of this class.

[20] Adding implementation classes follows the same method as we described in the book, except now the domain is the appropriate technology.

CHAPTER

13

C++ Fundamentals

> *The idea is that to be useful, a language feature must not only be elegant, it must also be affordable in the context of a real program.*
>
> Bjarne Stroustup (The C++ Programming Language)

After completion of the design steps, we have built a model that is now ready for implementation in C++. However, before we show how the model maps easily into C++, we need to cover the fundamentals for C++. Readers who know C++ may skip this chapter.

The purpose of this chapter and the next five chapters is not to teach the reader how to program in C++. The intent is to show how a design created by following the methods in this book translates into C++ code. This is consistent with our goal of providing a practical guide for the development of object-oriented applications using C++. We recommend that readers who are unfamiliar with C++ purchase a good book on the C++ language and one on programming in C++ for their development environment.

History

THE C programming language was developed by Kernighan and Ritchie at Bell Laboratories in 1978. Their goal was to develop a portable, small, simple, and fast programming language that did not prevent the programmer from doing what needed to be

211

done. It basically put *full trust* in the programmer.[1] In 1988 an ANSI Standard for the language was approved by the ANSI committee X3J11.

C++ development started in 1983 and was inspired by SIMULA67. Bjarne Stroustrup, also of Bell Laboratories, developed it as an evolution of C. Within 6 months of its first release in 1985, there were commercial ports of C++ available on more than 24 platforms, ranging from PCs to mainframes. In 1989, the ANSI X3J16 committee[2] for the standardization of C++ was created. The International Standards Organization (ISO) later joined in the standardization effort. In 1997, the Final Draft International Standard (FDIS) was unanimously approved by the ANSI committee. In 1998, with a few minor changes, the FDIS was approved by ISO and became an international standard.[3]

C++ is the most widely used programming language for object-oriented programming. Because most of its enhancements to the C language support creating classes with the same richness as the built-in data types, C++ supports the object-oriented concepts and mechanisms discussed in this book. In addition, C++ added stronger type checking than most languages to prevent many conversion errors and illegal initialization of data structures. These and other capabilities make it the ideal language for object-oriented development of large software systems. However, it neither requires nor enforces object-oriented paradigm usage in writing programs. C++ is first and foremost a multi-paradigm language; it allows you to write code in the classical procedural paradigm of structured methods as well as the object-oriented paradigm of object-oriented methods.

Programming Elements

A program is composed of elements called *tokens*, which are a collection of characters (alphabetic, numeric, and special) that constitute the basic vocabulary recognized by the compiler. The compiler translates these tokens into instructions that the computer understands. Tokens are separated by white space and/or comment text inserted for readability and documentation.

In C, a comment is written as follows:

```
/* possibly many lines   */
```

C++ added a rest-of-the line comment written as follows:

```
// this is a new C++ comment
```

---

[1] This means that the language allows programmers access to very low-level operations and direct access to memory. It trusts the programmer to do the right thing.

[2] The official name of the ANSI X3J16 committee was later changed to J16.

[3] The ANSI/ISO Standard for C++ is available for download from the ANSI Website: http://www.ansi.org.

This comment extends only until the end of the line, while the C comment may contain the C++ comments. For example:

```
/*   begin of C comment

     x = x+y;           // this is the new C++ comment

     end of C comment     */
```

There are five kinds of tokens:

- Keywords
- Identifiers
- Literals
- Operators
- Punctuators

Each of these is discussed in the paragraphs that follow.

Keywords

Keywords are explicitly reserved words that have a predefined meaning in C++. They include words for data type declaration, statement formulation, access control, and alternative representations of operators and punctuators. Table 13-1 lists the keywords.[4] The underlined entries are part of the ANSI C standard. The bold entries are necessary for supporting object-oriented programming. The italic keywords are interesting for implementation reasons. Words that are associated with logical operators are also included in this table.

Identifiers

An identifier is a sequence of alphanumeric characters along with the underscore character. The identifier must not start with a digit. Although legal, it is not advisable to use an underscore as the first character because the compilers and hidden library code use the underscore as the first character. Uppercase letters and lowercase letters are treated as distinct characters. In theory, an identifier can be arbitrarily long, but due to limitations in some compilers, 31 characters is a good limit.

According to the ANSI C Standard Library naming convention, all uppercase letters should be used for constants, macros, and structures. Mixed uppercase and lowercase are used for functions and variable names.

---

[4] For details on each reserved word, consult an introduction to C++ programming book.

TABLE 13-1   C++ Reserved Words

and	and_eq	asm	<u>auto</u>	bitand
bitor	bool	<u>break</u>	<u>case</u>	catch
<u>char</u>	**class**	compl	<u>const</u>	*const_cast*
<u>continue</u>	<u>default</u>	**delete**	<u>do</u>	<u>double</u>
dynamic_cast	<u>else</u>	<u>enum</u>	explicit	export
<u>extern</u>	false	<u>float</u>	<u>for</u>	**friend**
<u>goto</u>	<u>if</u>	inline	<u>int</u>	<u>long</u>
mutable	*namespace*	**new**	not	not_eq
operator	or	or_eq	**private**	**protected**
public	<u>register</u>	*reinterpret_cast*	<u>return</u>	<u>short</u>
<u>signed</u>	<u>sizeof</u>	<u>static</u>	*static_cast*	<u>struct</u>
<u>switch</u>	template	**this**	throw	true
try	<u>typedef</u>	typeid	*typename*	<u>union</u>
<u>unsigned</u>	*using*	**virtual**	<u>void</u>	<u>volatile</u>
wchar_t	<u>while</u>	xor	xor_eq	

TABLE 13-2   C++ Arithmetic Operators

Mathematical Operator	Function Description	Assignment Operator
%	Modulus	%=
+	Addition	+=
++	Increment	
−	Subtraction	-=
--	Decrement	
*	Multiplication	*=
/	Division	/=
	Assignment	=

Literals

Literals are constant values (e.g., 1 and 3.14159). All native C++ data types (see "Native Data Types") may have literals.

Operators

Operators are characters and/or character sequences with a special meaning. Most of the operators are used to perform arithmetic or logical operations. Table 13-2 lists the

TABLE 13-3

Operator	Reserved Word	Function Description	Assignment Operator	Reserved Word
!	not	Logical NOT		
<		Less than		
<=		Less than or equal		
>		Greater than		
>=		Greater than or equal		
==		Equal		
!=		Inequality (not equal)		
&&	and	Logical AND	&=	and_eq
| |	or	Logical OR	| =	or_eq
&	bitand	Bitwise AND	&=	
|		Bitwise inclusive OR		
^	xor	Bitwise exclusive OR	^=	xor_eq
?		Conditional operator		
~	compl	Compliment		

arithmetic operators and their associated assignment operators.[5] The equality, relational, and logical operators are given in Table 13-3, along with their associated assignment operators and reserved keyword equivalents.

Punctuators

Punctuators include parentheses, braces, commas, and colons. They are used to give structure to other tokens of the language.[6]

Native Data Types

C++ provides a predefined set of data types and the operators to manipulate these data types.[7] The following data types are predefined:

- Basic data types
- Constant values

---

[5] An assignment operator associated with an operator is a short-hand notation for performing the operation and then assigning the result to the variable on the left-hand side of the operator. For example, x+=3 is the same as x = x + 3.

[6] Please consult an introduction to C++ book for more details.

[7] C++ may define a number of data types, but it does not specify their size. The size will depend upon the operating system and platform. This is one thing that does make C++ difficult to port from machine to machine.

- ■ Symbolic variables
- ■ Pointer types
- ■ Constant types
- ■ Reference types
- ■ Enumeration types
- ■ Array types
- ■ Typedef names

Each of these is described in the paragraphs that follow.

Basic Data Types

The following basic data types[8] are predefined:

- ■ Integer (int, short, long)
  (e.g., 1, 111, 1050)

- ■ Floating point decimal (float, double, long double)
  (e.g., 1.1, 123.3456)

- ■ Character (char)
  (e.g., 'a,' 'd,' '2')

- ■ Character string[9] (char*)
  (e.g., "the big black cat," "license plate x123")

- ■ Boolean (bool)
  (e.g., true, false)

The integral types[10] are char, short, int, and long. They may be signed or unsigned. The single and double quotes are necessary in the character and string examples, respectively.

Constant Values

Every literal constant has an associated basic data type and is nonaddressable. The different kinds are:

1. Literal integer constant (decimal, octal, hex)
   (e.g., 1, 024, 0x1A, 0X1B2)

---

[8] The name is followed with the keywords in parentheses. The keywords are used in the language to identify them.

[9] In the chapter dealing with the Standard Template Library (STL), a string class is introduced to replace explicit use of character strings.

[10] Integral means that all of these types may be treated as integers.

    2. Signed/unsigned and long[11]

        (e.g., 1L, 8LU, 27lu

    3. Literal floating-point constant (scientific, decimal)

        (e.g., 1.23e–3, 2.14E3, 3.14159)

    4. Single precision (F/f) and double precision (L/l)

        (e.g., 1.23e-3F, 3.14159L)

    5. Literal character constant

        (e.g., 'a,' 'd,' '2,' ")

    6. Nonprintable characters plus ' and " use a backslash

        (e.g., \n, \', \", \?, \\, \7 (bell))

    7. Literal string constant[12]

        (e.g., " ", "a," "\a string?{}[]")

Symbolic Variables

In ANSI C (and thus in C++), a symbolic variable is identified by a user-supplied name. Each variable is comprised of a specific data type and is addressable. Two values are associated with a symbolic variable:

- rvalue: its data value
- lvalue: its location value (memory location)

    For example,

```
char c;
c = c - '0';
```

    The first line is a definition as storage is allocated; we could have made it a declaration by using the keyword extern. The second line will subtract the rvalue of the constant '0' from the rvalue of the symbolic variable c. The lvalue of '0' is determined by the compiler and is not directly accessible to the programmer.

    The following example also includes initializing the rvalue of the symbolic variables:

```
int y = 40;
char c ('d');
```

In the first line, the symbolic variable y is defined and its rvalue is initialized to 40. In the second line, the symbolic variable c is defined and is initialized to the character d.

---

[11] 27lu is legal, but a long unsigned number is not good practice.

[12] The compiler adds a null character at the end of the string.

Pointer Types

In ANSI C (and thus in C++), a pointer variable holds an address as its value in memory. This provides for indirect reference, and because C++ is a strong-typed language, each pointer has an associated data type. Examples are:

```
int* ptr1;                      /* legal, but bad practice */
unsigned char *ptr2;
int *ptr3, num;                  // preferred style
int xx, *ptr4;
```

In lines 1 and 2, we showed that the '*' may be placed next to the data type or next to the variable. In lines 3 and 4, we see that placing the '*' next to the variable is better practice. It makes code more readable.

A pointer may be initialized with an lvalue of the data element of the same type. For example:

```
int j;
int *ptr = &j;
```

In line 2, the pointer variable ptr will be initialized with the lvalue of j.[13]

In C++, all character string manipulations are done using character pointers (char*). Every character string constant is of type char*, and the *n* variable of type char* may be initialized to a character string. For example:

```
char *strptr = "This is it\n";
```

This line will make the rvalue of strptr equal to 'This is it' with a new line control character and a null character following that literal string.

Constant Types

The const modifier to a symbolic variable transforms the variable into a symbolic constant. It is a read-only variable, so it must be initialized. For example:

```
const  int  bufSize = 1024;
```

Its address may not be assigned to a pointer, but a pointer to a const data is allowed. For example:[14]

```
const int *ptr_to_const;
```

---

[13] In this context, the & is the address operator rather than the logical and operator.

[14] Assignment of either a const variable or a non-const variable to a constant pointer is allowed. However, in both cases, the data cannot be changed using the constant pointer.

A const pointer is also allowed. For example:

```
int *const const_ptr;
const int *const const_ptr_to_const;
```

In the latter line, both the pointer and what the pointer points to must be specified when instantiated and may never change.

Reference Types

A reference type is defined by following the type specifier with the address operator (&). This variable, which we also call the reference type, must be initialized. It is an alias and cannot be made to alias another variable, so it is a const reference. All operations on the reference or the variable act on the variable (object) to which it refers. For example:

```
int& y;
```

In the example, *int* is the type specifier, & is the address operator, and *y* is the reference or the variable.

A second example is:

```
double y = 11.12345;
double &refY = y;
refY += 2.54321;              // y = 13.66666
```

It is commonly used in arguments and as the return type of a function.

Enumeration Types

An enumeration is declared with the enum keyword and a list of enumerators that are separated by commas and enclosed in braces. For example:

```
enum {yes,  no, maybe };
```

It declares a set of symbolic integral constants, and there is no addressable storage associated with each enumerator. A value may be explicitly assigned to an enumerator, and a tag name may be assigned and used as a type specifier. For example:

```
enum Opinion2 {yes,  no = 30, maybe };
Opinion2  reply = no;               // legal
Opinion2  reply = 1;                // illegal
```

Line 3 is not legal because reply is an instance of data type 'Opinion2' and can only be assigned a value from the set of symbolic integral constants. The only symbolic integral constants defined for 'Opinion2' are yes, no, and maybe.

Array Types

An array definition consists of a type specifier, an identifier, and a dimension. For example:

```
float float_array[100];
```

The dimension value is computed at compile time and must be a constant expression.[15]
An array is a collection of data of a single data type. Access and assignment are by position in the array. For example:

```
float   yy = float_array[10];
```

Elements of the array are numbered beginning with 0. The language provides no compile or run-time range checking on indexes.
Multidimensional arrays are declared by specifying additional dimensions. For example:

```
float yy[5][10];
```

This declares a static two-dimensional array, with rank 5x10. Strictly speaking, yy is an array of five items, which are arrays of ten items. Any of the following expressions, yy, yy[i], yy[i][j], may appear in an expression.

Typedef Names

A typedef definition begins with the typedef keyword followed by the data type and the identifier (typedef name). For example:

```
typedef int Length;
```

In this example, Length may be used anywhere int is allowed in the language. It provides mnemonic synonyms for existing predefined, derived, and user-defined data types. The identifier is not a new data type, but a synonym for the existing data type. Furthermore, the identifier may be used anywhere a type name may appear. Typedef is used to make programs more readable and to encapsulate machine-dependent aspects of the program.

What Is a Statement?

A statement is the smallest executable unit within a C++ program. There is a large variety of statement types, but they are all terminated by a semicolon. The simplest statement is the empty or *null statement*, which takes the following form:

```
    ;    // null statement is like a no-op
```

---

[15] The chapter dealing with the Standard Template Library introduces the vector class that can be used to replace an array.

A null statement is useful when the syntax of the language requires a statement, but the logic of the application does not.

One of the most commonly seen statements is the *assignment statement*. For example:

```
x =  y + 1;
```

The right-hand side of this statement is evaluated and converted to a value compatible with the left-hand side variable (y +1 is assigned to x). C++ provides assignment operators that combine an assignment and some other operator (these were identified in Table 6-2). For example:

```
x +=  y ;     // this is same as  x = x + y;
x *=  y ;     // this is same as  x = x * y;
```

C++ provides auto increment and auto decrement operators in both prefix and postfix form. For example:

```
++k;                   // this is same as   k = k + 1;
l = --k ;              // this is same as   k = k - 1; l = k;
m = k++ ;                  // this is same as   m = k; k = k + 1;
```

Expressions

An expression is composed of one or more operations. Operations are captured in C++ by operators. For example, the addition operation is captured by the operator +. The arguments of the operation are referred to as operands. For example, the addition operation requires two operands.

Nearly all operations are unary (requiring only one operand) or binary (requiring two operands). Binary operators have a left and a right operand. Care must be taken because some operators represent both unary and binary operations. For example, the operator * is used to capture the dereference operation when it is used as a unary operator. However, as a binary operator, it is used to capture the multiplication operation.

An expression evaluation performs all of the operations captured in the expression and yields a result. Usually, the result is an rvalue of a data type that is determined by the data types of the operand(s). The order of the operator evaluation is determined by the precedence and associativity of the operators. Although ordering is very natural, the reader should consult an introductory C++ book for the actual ordering.

Compound Statements

A compound statement is a series of statements surrounded by the braces '{' and '}' and is used principally to group statements into an executable unit. For example, a C++ function is a compound statement. A compound statement is also used when the language syntax permits only a single statement to be specified and the application logic requires two or more statements to be executed.[16]

Statement Flow Control

THE default flow of control is sequential in C++, so every C++ program begins with the first statement of main(). Each statement is executed in turn. When the final statement is executed, the program ends. However, sequential execution of statements is typically inadequate except for the simplest programs. In the following sections, we look at some of the control statements available in C++.[17]

If Statement

An if statement tests a particular condition. The form of an if statement is as follows:

```
if ( expression )  statement;
```

Whenever the expression evaluates to true (nonzero), a statement (or a compound statement) is executed. Otherwise, the statement is skipped. In either event, the following statement is executed after the if statement has completed.

Closely related to the if statement is the if-else statement. It has the following form:

```
if ( expression ) statement-1;
else              statement-2;
```

If the expression is nonzero, then statement-1 is executed and statement-2 is skipped. However, if the expression is zero, then statement-1 is skipped and statement-2 is executed. As with the if statement, after the if-else statement has completed, the following statement is executed.

Here is an example of using the if-else statement to get the minimum of two numbers:

```
if (y < x)
    min  = y;
else
    min  = x;
              /* Below is the "following statement"  */
cout << "minimum is " << min;
```

If y < x evaluates to true, then the min is assigned the value of y; if y < x evaluates to false, then min is assigned the value of x. In either case, min is printed.

---

[16] Although it is possible to place a compound statement where you can place a statement, a compound statement is not terminated by a semicolon.

[17] Please consult an introduction to C++ book for details and for a complete set of control statements.

For Statement

The for statement is an iterative statement typically used with a variable that is incremented or decremented. It is most commonly used to step through a fixed-length data structure, such as an array. The syntactic form of a for statement is:

```
for ( init-statement; expression-1; expression-2)
execution-statement;
```

The init-statement can either be a declaration or an expression. It is usually used to initialize a variable; however, it may be null. Expression-1 serves as the loop control. Iterations are performed as long as expression-1 evaluates to true. In each iteration, the statement is executed. The execution-statement may either be a single statement or a compound statement. If the first evaluation of expression-1 is false, the execution-statement is never executed. Expression-2 is evaluated after each iteration of the loop. It is usually used to modify the variable initialized in the init-statement. If the first evaluation of expression-1 is false, expression-2 is never evaluated.

The following is a simple example of using a for statement for initializing an array:

```
const int Max = 50;
float  float_array[Max];
for (int i =0; i <Max; i++)
{
    float_array[i]  = i;
}
```

In this example, each member of the array is initialized to its own index value as a floating-point number. For instance, float_array[0] = 0.0, and float_array[15] = 15.0.

What Is a Function?

WHETHER we are using structured methods or object-oriented methods, there is a stepwise refinement process that involves decomposing a process (a service in object-oriented technology) into smaller subprocesses. Function constructs are used to capture the processes and subprocesses. The "main" program in C++ is a sequence of function calls that may call other functions.

C++ provides the function mechanisms to perform some tasks, and the C++ libraries provide additional function mechanisms. The next chapter introduces the most significant of these libraries. For now, an important example of additional function mechanisms supplied by libraries is the input/output mechanisms that experienced C++ programmers take for granted. In fact, input/output is not directly part of the language. The reader should be aware that there are several standard libraries for input/output in use with C++. There are the ANSI C standard library, stdio.h; the early C++ stream library, stream.h; and the newest C++ stream library, iostream.h. In this book, we will use iostream and present only the basics.[18]

---

[18] Please consult an introduction to C++ programming book for details.

TABLE 13-4   **Standard C++ Input and Output Objects**

Stream	Description
cout	Standard out, normally the screen
cin	Standard in, normally the keyboard
cerr	Standard error, normally also the screen

TABLE 13-5   **Isostream Operator**

Operator	Description
<<	"Put to" output stream
>>	"Get from" input stream

The iostream.h library defines and declares three standard streams for the programmer. These are illustrated in Table 13-4. The iostream.h library overloads the two bit-shift operators for get inputs and to send outputs as described in Table 13-5. In addition to all of the library functions, user-defined services for a class of objects are also functions.

Function Invocation

A C++ program is made up of one or more functions, one of which is main(). Every program execution begins with main(). When a C++ program is executing and encounters a function name, the function is called[19] and control is passed to that function. After the function does its work, control is passed back to the calling environment, which can then continue its processing. A simple example of a program is as follows:

```
#include <iostream.h>
#include <string.h>

main()
{
    char *  s;
    cout << "\nHello, all" << endl;
    cout<< "\nPlease enter your name" << endl;
    cin >> s;
    if ( strlen(s)  > 20 )
        cerr << "Error, name is" <<  strlen(s) -20 <<
                "characters too many" << endl;
}
```

---

[19] In many textbooks, this is called invocation (i.e., the function is invoked).

This program uses both the string and the iostream libraries. The first output statement puts a string "Hello, all" on the screen. The "\n" ensures a new line, and the endl is a special identifier that flushes the stream and adds a new line. The second output statement is similar to the first input statement, which expects a string of characters followed by the Enter (Return) key. The following statement uses the strlen function to get the length of the input string. If the input string is greater than 20 characters, it informs the user that the string is x characters too long.

Function Definition

The C++ code that describes what a function does is called the *function definition*. It takes the following form:

```
function-header
{
    statements
}
```

Everything before the left brace is part of the function-header of the function definition, and everything between the braces is the body of the function definition. The function-header takes the following form:

```
return-type function-name ( signature )
```

The return-type that precedes the function-name determines the data type of the value that the function returns. The return mechanism will be explained later. The function-name is self-explanatory, and the signature is a list of parameters (arguments) that the function expects the caller of the function to provide. C++ allows multiple functions to have the same name, but does require that the function-name combined with the signature be unique.

Parameters are syntactically identifiers, and as such they can be used in the body of the function. Technically, these are formal parameters because they are placeholders for actual values that are passed to the function when it is called. Upon function invocation, the values of the argument corresponding to the formal parameter are used in the body of the function when it is executed. Following is a function definition for the minimum function:

```
int min( const int x, const int y)
{
    if ( y < x  )
        return ( y );
    else
        return ( x );
}
```

The return statement has two purposes. First, when a return statement is executed, control is passed immediately back to the caller. Second, if an expression follows the keyword return, the value of the expression is returned to the caller. When an expression exists, it must be assignment-convertible to the return-type of the function definition header. Note that when there is no expression, the return-type of the function must be void. This is used when the caller does not expect a value to be returned.

Function Prototype

In C++, a function can be declared before it is defined. This capability is used in object-oriented programming to preserve encapsulation. Such a declaration is called a function prototype and has the following form:

```
type  name ( argument-declaration list );
```

Here, type is the return type of the function that may be either a user-defined data type or void. The name is the function name, and the argument-declaration list is a comma-separated list of data types. This list defines the data types of the values that the caller must provide to the function. It is also very common to have argument identifiers in the list; thus, the prototype can be identical to the function header.

Inlining

In C++, when the keyword *inline* prefaces a function declaration, the compiler will attempt to replace the function call with code. The compiler will parse the function and provide the semantic equivalent of a non-inline version of the function. The compiler will not allow complex functions to be inlined. This keyword basically replaces the Macro expansion.[20]

Storage Class

EVERY variable and function in the C++ kernel language has two attributes: type and storage class. We have discussed native data types; now we need to discuss the storage classes. There are five storage classes: automatic, external, register, static, and volatile. Their corresponding keywords are: *auto, extern, register, static,* and *volatile.*

Auto

Variables declared within a function body are, by default, automatic, which is usually the most commonly used storage class. If a compound statement contains variable declarations, then the variables can only be acted upon with the scope of the enclosing compound statement. Declarations of variables within blocks are implicitly of storage class automatic. The keyword *auto* is used only to explicitly specify the automatic storage class.

When a block is entered, the system allocates memory (usually from the stack space) for the automatic variables. Within the block, these variables are defined and are

---

[20] Most style guides recommend that one avoid use of function-like macros and macro constants because they are type-unsafe, hard to debug, and can easily bloat the size of the executable file. C++ provides much better alternatives.

considered local to the block. When the block is exited, the system releases the memory reserved for the automatic variables. The values for these variables are no longer available. If the block is reentered, the system will once again allocate memory for the automatic variables, but the previous values are lost.

Extern

When a variable is declared outside a function, storage is permanently assigned to it and its storage class is *extern*. Such a variable is considered global to all of the functions declared after it. Furthermore, upon block or function exits, the extern variable remains in existence. External variables never disappear; they exist throughout the life of the program. They are used to transmit values across functions. However, this can be dangerous because the variable can be hidden if the identifier is redefined. The keyword *extern* is used to tell the compiler to look elsewhere for the definition of this variable. The variable may be in this file or some other file.

Because functions can also get information via the parameter-passing mechanism, most object-oriented experts would recommend infrequent use of external variables because they violate the encapsulation principle.

Register

The register storage class tells the compiler that the associated variables should be stored in high-speed memory registers if it is physically and semantically possible. Because resource and semantic constraints may not make this request possible, the variables will default to automatic when they cannot be made register.

This should be used only when the programmer is concerned with speed. Then choose a few variables that are most frequently accessed and declare them to be of the storage class register. However, be aware that contemporary optimizing compilers are frequently more astute than the programmer. Most of us consider this storage class of limited usefulness.

Static

Static declarations allow a local variable to retain its previous value when the block or function is reentered. This is in contrast to an automatic variable, which loses its value upon exit and must be reinitialized upon reentry. An example of this value-retention use of static is shown by adding codes to the min function to maintain a count of the number of times it is called:

```
int min( const int  x, const int y)
{
    static int called_count = 0;
    called_count++;
    if ( y < x  )
        return ( y );
    else
        return ( x );
}
```

A depreciated use of static in external declarations was to provide a privacy mechanism for maintaining the modularity of programs.[21] The term *privacy* refers to the visibility or scope restrictions on the accessibility of variables and functions. Static external declarations are visible only within the file in which they are defined. Thus, unlike external variables that can be accessed by other files, a static declaration is available only throughout its own file.

In C++, external variables and static variables are initialized to zero if they are not explicitly initialized by the programmer. In contrast, automatic and register variables are not initialized by the system and can start with "garbage" values. For object-oriented programming, static should be used only as a privacy mechanism.

Volatile

Volatile is a storage class that instructs the compiler to read the value of the variable from its source every time it is accessed, instead of storing it in a faster processor register. This storage class allows a program to use values that can change due to circumstances outside of explicit control of the program or within multi-threaded applications. For example, a program can read the value of the current bit rate of a modem directly from a port. However, the value can change during the execution of the program due to changing line conditions. The compiler might mistakenly assume that the value is unchanging and store the value in a register missing a change in value.

Type Conversion

C++ is a strongly typed programming language. This is good or bad, depending upon your perspective. It is good in the sense that it enforces one to clearly identify type, prevents incorrect access to data, and assures that operations over values are semantically valid. On the other hand, strong typing makes it difficult to transition from treating a value at one level of abstraction (for example, as a shape object) in one part of the program and treating it at a different level of abstraction (for example, as a rectangle, circle, or line object) elsewhere.

To provide the programmer with the ability to change type and storage class, C++ provides a number of type conversion operators. These are: static_cast, const_cast, dynamic_cast, and reinterpret_cast. The use of type conversion operators allows the programmer to use values in a fashion appropriate for the domain while allowing the compiler to enforce type restrictions.

static_cast

C++ provides the static_cast operator to convert between types with type checking performed at compile time. This operator is used for most conversions between fundamental data types such as int, double, float, and so on. An example of using static cast follows:

```
float t=3.14;
int x = static_cast<int> (t);     // x has a value of 3
```

---

[21] Instead of using static to provide privacy, one should use an *unnamed namespace* for that purpose.

The first line declares a float variable t and assigns it the value of 3.14. The second line declares an integer variable, x, and assigns it the result of converting 3.14 to an integer value.

const_cast

The const_cast is provided to cast away const or volatile values. The const cast does not change type. It only affects the const-ness of a value. It is typically used inside of a class method that has been declared const to violate that declaration.[22] Use of const_cast is a very advanced C++ topic and should only be performed under very specific circumstances. It is recommended that the reader who feels a strong desire to change the constness of some attribute should refer to an advanced book on C++.

dynamic_cast

The dynamic_cast is incorporated in C++ to give the kind of cast operation that was provided by C.[23] The dynamic_cast is normally used for *downcasting*. Downcasting is casting from a base-class pointer to a derived-class pointer. This can be dangerous, but dynamic_cast uses run-time information to assure that the cast is allowed. If the cast is not allowed, the result is 0. An example of using dynamic_cast follows:

```
Shape *s = static_cast<Shape *> (new Square());
// Square is a type of Shape
Square *mySquare = dynamic_cast<Square *> (s); // mySquare points to s
Circle *oops = dynamic_case<Circle *> (s);   //oops points to 0
```

The first line in this example declares a variable, s, which is a pointer to an instance of the class **Shape**. **Shape** is a virtual class. An instance of type **Square** is created using the default constructor Square() and is cast to type **Shape** for assignment to the pointer s.[24] The second line uses the dynamic_cast operator to allow the pointer to a **Shape** to downcast it to a pointer to a **Square**. The third line uses dynamic_cast in an attempt to downcast the pointer to a **Shape** to a pointer to a **Circle**. The attempt fails because the **Shape** is not actually a **Circle**, but a **Square**.

reinterpret_cast

The reinterpret_cast is primarily provided to allow nonstandard casts, but can be used for standard casts. An example of using the reinterpret_cast is:

---

[22] It is not a good practice to violate promises made in the declaration of a method. One of the worst is to promise that values won't be changed and then force them to change.

[23] C++ supported the cast mechanism of C, but the standard introduced four different cast operators that are the preferred cast mechanism.

[24] Default constructors are discussed later. All that is important for now is that we have created an instance of a square.

```
main()
{
    int i = 1, *intPtr;
    void *voidPtr = &i;
    intPtr = reinterprete_cast<int *> (voidPtr);
}
```

This example shows how a void pointer can be cast into an int pointer. It should be noted that using reinterpret_cast can lead to serious execution time errors. In addition, this cast can exhibit different behaviors on different computers.

Namespace

THIS section discusses a feature that C++ provides that is of high value for very large systems and is of little value for small programs. This feature is namespace. Namespace is a mechanism that promotes understandability, eases maintenance, and supports development of very large systems. Namespaces provides a means to resolve names used in programs. It allows several development teams to use the same names for classes, variables, and functions without running into naming conflicts at the source code level.

A namespace provides a scope where global identifiers and global variables are placed. To define a namespace, one uses the namespace keyword, a name for the namespace, and places all of the code elements that are to be associated with the namespace within curly braces. The following program illustrates defining a namespace containing a set of global variables:

```
namespace myConstants {
    const int i=34;
    const float pi=3.1415;
}
namespace yourConstants {
    const int i=29;
}
```

These namespaces will be used in the following program examples.

To use a namespace member, one can identify a scope with the **using** statement before the name is used or the member's name must be qualified with the namespace name and the scope operator, ::. This is demonstrated in the following code segment:

```
using namespace yourConstants;
int j = i;
int k = myConstants::i
```

In this code fragment, j will be assigned a value of 29 because it will use the value of i defined in namespace named yourConstants. The variable k will be assigned a value of 34 because the scope operator identifies the i used here as belonging to the namespace named myConstants.

The using keyword can also be used to identify only special elements within a namespace. This is accomplished by identifying the namespace member that is to be used. An example is:

```
using namespace myConstants::pi;
```

This lets the compiler know that where every pi appears, it should use the member in myConstants.

Recommended Approach

THIS chapter has covered some of the basic concepts of C++. Readers who are unfamiliar with C++ should:

1. Purchase a programming book on C++
2. Purchase a reference book on the C++ Standard

■ ■ SUMMARY

IN this chapter, we learned about:

1. Tokens
2. Important keywords
3. Native data types
4. Statements
5. Two-flow of control statements (if and for)
6. Functions
7. Invoking a function
8. Storage classes
9. Cast operators
10. Namespace

Implementing Class

*T*o *know what we think, to be masters of our own meaning, will make a solid foundation for great and weighty thought.*

C. S. Peirce, *How to Make Our Ideas Clear*

The class mechanism in C++ allows developers to define their own data types in addition to the ones native to the language. At the initial implementation of the application/system, developers use this mechanism to implement the classes found in the model. Then in future releases of the application, developers will find class useful when (1) they need to add functionality to an existing data type (either native or user-defined), and (2) they need to introduce a new abstraction that cannot map onto one of the defined data types or be derived from it.

Components of a Class

A C++ class is composed of four major parts:

1. **Collection of data members**. In object-oriented technology, this is the collection of attributes. There may be zero or more data members of any data type in this collection.

2. **Collection of member functions declaration**. This is the set of function prototypes that can be applied to the objects of that class. In object-oriented technology,

this corresponds to the services. There may be zero or more function prototypes in the collection.

3. **Level of visibility.** Each member (data or function) may be specified as having the following level of access (visibility): *private*, *protected*, or *public*. In object-oriented technology, all the data members should be private and all the services should be public.[1]

4. **Associated tag name.** This name serves as a type specifier for the user-defined class. Thus, the name may be used in the program where the native data type may appear.

The public member functions are referred to as the *class interface*. A class with private data members and public member functions is called an *abstract data type*.[2] A class in C++ supports the principle of information hiding and encapsulation. It also binds a collection of data members to a set of functions, and defines the characteristics of all instances created by that class. In brief, it provides the basic unit of reusability.

Class Definition

A class definition is composed of two parts: class header and class body. The class header is composed of the keyword class followed by the class tag name. The class body is enclosed by a pair of curly braces; the closing brace must be followed by either a semicolon or a declaration list. For example:

```
class Person
{
private:
     char name[40];
     char sex;
     int age;
};
class Dog
{
private:
     char name[40];
     int age;
} myDog, Lassie;
```

Note that in the Person example there is no declaration list. However, in the Dog example, two objects, myDog and Lassie, are declared.

---

[1]   This is implementation of the information-hiding and encapsulation principles.

[2]   Now you know why some people call object-oriented analysis the discovery of abstract data types.

Class Body

WITHIN the class body, data members, member functions, and their associated levels of visibility are specified.

Visibility

Each member of the class has a level of visibility. There are three levels of visibility (public, private, protected) that a member may have. If a level of visibility is not explicitly stated for a member, the default visibility of private is used. The rules for using levels of visibility within the class body are:

- All member declarations following a *public*: keywords are accessible by other classes (objects).
- All member declarations following a *private*: keywords are accessible only by the class itself.
- All member declarations following a *protected*: keywords are accessible only by the class and its subclasses.
- A subsequent use of *public*:, *protected*:, or *private*: will override earlier definitions only for the members that follow the keywords *public*:, *protected*:, or *private*:.

The preferred order for organizing the member of the class is public, protected, and private. When an object is instantiated, all members (data and functions) are accessible to its member functions. The level of visibility applies only to functions of another object, whether it is in the same class or in a different class. When a function has access to the private data of all objects of its class, it has *class scope*. Most member functions have access only to the private data of the object against which it was invoked; this is the *object scope*.

Data Members

The declaration of data members is the same as variable declarations in the language, with the exception that an explicit initializer is not allowed. For example, the following code will not work:

```
class Person
{
    int height =0; int weight; char * name;    /* Illegal Example   */
}
```

Initialization is done in the constructor for the class (see later chapter). As with variable declarations, it is legal to combine the int declaration of multiple data members into one declaration. For example:

```
class Person
{
    int height, weight; char * name;
}
```

When possible, declare data members in increasing size of storage to optimize the alignment of storage on all machines. However, data members can also be of user-defined types. A class object can be declared as a data member only if the class definition has already been seen by the compiler before its use as a data member. However, when a declaration of a data member is a pointer or a reference to a class, a forward declaration of the class may be used. For example, the following is a definition of Woman using a forward declaration to Man:

```
class Man;                          //  forward declaration
class Woman
{
private:
    char name[40];
    Man * husband;                  //  pointer to Man object that is husband
}
```

A class is not considered defined until the closing brace of the class body is seen by the compiler; however, the class is considered to be declared after the opening brace. This allows a class to define pointers and references to itself as data members. Consider a link list of persons:

```
class LinkPerson
{
private:
    Person me;
    LinkPerson *next;
    LinkPerson * prev;
}
```

Member Functions

Member functions of a class are declared inside the class body. A declaration consists of the function prototype. The function prototype is composed of a return type and a name, followed by a signature enclosed in parentheses. The signature consists of a comma-separated list of argument types. An argument type is any native type, derived type, or user-defined type. An argument name may follow each type specifier. For example:

```
class Person
{
public:                                    // member functions
    char*     getName();
    char      getSex();
    int       getAge();
    void      setName(char *)
    void      setSex(char s);
```

```
        void        setAge(int a);
    private:                                    // data members
        char name[40];
        char sex;
        int age, height, weight;
    }
```

The argument list is referred to as the signature of a function because it distinguishes between two functions with the same name. The name alone does not necessarily uniquely identify a function. However, the name and its signature *will* uniquely identify a function. For example:

```
    class Person
    {
    public:                                     // member functions
        char        getSex();
        void        setSex(char );
        void        setSex(int );
        ...
    private:                                     // data members
        char name[40];
        char sex;
        int age, height, weight;
    }
```

We can use the setSex() function by using an integer as an argument as well as using char as an argument. This may be needed because in one application the gender may be captured as an integer (e.g., 1 for female, 0 for male), while in another application gender is captured as a character (e.g., f for female, m for male).

Member functions are distinguished from other functions by the following characteristics:

■ Member functions have full access privileges to the private, protected, and public members of the class, whereas other functions have access only to the public member of the class.

■ Member functions of one class do not have access privileges to members of another class. However, when one class has a relationship with another class, it has access to the other class's public members.

■ Member functions are defined only within the scope of the class, whereas ordinary functions are defined at file scope. This means that member function names are not visible outside the scope of the class. This requires that other classes have access to an instance of the class before they can use the class's services.

■ Member functions can overload only other member functions of its class.

Generalization Using Inheritance

IN addition to capturing the attributes and the service prototypes, the generalization/specialization relationship must also be captured in the header file. We will look at the code necessary to represent the multiple inheritance for Platypus. Following are the abbreviated class definitions:

```
class Endangered
{  // class definition for Endangered  }
class OrganicMatter
{  // class definition for Organic Matter  }
class Animal: public OrganicMatter
{  // class definition for Animal  }
class Mammal: public Animal
{  // class definition for Mammal  }
class Platypus: public Animal, public Endangered
{  // class definition for Platypus  }
```

In this example, "class Animal: public OrganicMatter" tells the compiler that OrganicMatter is the superclass of Animal. The public keyword means that the public members of OrganicMatter will also be public members of Animal, the protected members of OrganicMatter will also be protected members of Animal, and the private members of OrganicMatter will also be private members of Animal. The line "class Platypus: public Animal, public Endangered" tells the compiler that the platypus has two superclasses as parents, both with public inheritance. In a later chapter on implementing generalization/specialization, we will discuss other keywords associated with inheritance. The syntax for implementing generalization/specialization using inheritance is:

```
class class-tag-name: public parent's class-tag-name
```

Recommended Approach

THE fundamental building block of object-oriented technology is the class. One of the first things we have to do in coding is to translate the classes given in the model into class definitions.

To help with this, the following guidelines are given:

1. Variables (attributes) are declared as **private** members. This is necessary for information hiding.
2. Methods (services) are declared as **public** members. This is necessary for other objects to have access to the public services of an object of this class.
3. Services that are only used by methods within the class are declared as **private** members.

4. Variables (attributes) and methods are declared as **protected** members if they need to be accessible to subclasses (derived classes) and not to the client classes of the derived classes.

5. Data members must be defined in the class declaration.

6. In order to separate the function declaration (interface definition) from the function definition (implementation definition), place the code for the member functions outside the class declaration, either in the same or a different file.

7. Do not make a data member public unless (a) you make it read-only
   or (b) changing the data member has no impact on the behavior of the object.

8. Do not make implementation-related member functions public.

9. Each member function of a class should either modify or provide access to data members of that class (strong cohesion).

10. A class should depend on as few other classes as possible (weak coupling).

11. Classes should not communicate via global variables.

12. Minimize information exchanged between classes. Call by pointer or reference can help.

13. All application generalization relationships are implemented as public inheritance.

14. Use abstract base classes as appropriate.

Example

In C++, the class definition is placed in the header (.h) file. Following is an example of a class definition for Window class:

```
// include files are normally first
#include <iostream.h>
#include <string.h>
#include <stdlib.h>
    // we put typedef here for ease of understanding
typedef float Length;
    // forward declarations are placed here for compiler
class Shape;
class  LinkScreen;
    // start class definition
class Window
{
public:
                    // public services (instance methods)
    void add_box (Length x, Length y, Length width, Length height);
    void add_circle (Length x, Length y, Length radius);
    void move (Length deltax, Length deltay);
    int group_selection ();
    void ungroup_selection ();
```

```
private:
                    //private attributes (variables)
        Length xmin; Length ymin;
        Length xmax; Length ymax;
        LinkScreen  *next;
                /private method(s)
        void add_to_selection (Shape* shape);
    };
```

Here we see a typical class definition; the keywords are in bold only for ease of understanding. The include files are given here for tutorial purposes. The iostream.h gives the developer access to cout, cin, and cerr as well as all standard operators and manipulators associated with stream input/output. The string.h gives the developer access to the standard functions that help manipulate char * like a string. The stdlib.h gives access to the mathematical functions.

Normally, the services in string.h and iostream.h are needed to define operations used in the methods. Thus, they usually only need to be put in the .C files. In general, the only include files that should be in the .h file are the superclass(es) of the class being defined. Normally, all usage of classes in the .h file is by reference or pointer, so only a forward declaration of the other class is needed. However, the exception is when another class is embedded in the class being defined. In this case, the programmer must use an include file because a forward declaration will not suffice.

■ ■ SUMMARY

THE components of a class definition in a header (.h) file are as follows:

1. All of the "include" files
2. All of the typedefs
3. All of the forward declarations
4. Header (keyword **class** and tag-name) plus inheritance
5. Opening brace; i.e. {
6. Keyword **public:**
7. All of the public service prototypes
8. Keyword **private:**
9. Attributes (as variables) and private service prototypes
10. Close brace
11. Optional instance declarations
12. Semicolon; i.e. ;

CHAPTER
15

C++ Libraries

M^y *library Was dukedom large enough.*

William Shakespeare

A knowledge of C++ fundamentals is sufficient to write code that works, but many of the common functions that programmers have come to expect are missing from the language directly. C++ provides the function mechanisms to perform some tasks, and the C++ libraries provide additional function mechanisms. The draft standard C++ library is comprised of three separate sets of libraries: the C standard libraries, the C++ libraries, and the Standard Template Libraries (STLs). In this chapter, all of the libraries are introduced in terms of what functionality they provide, but only those that are actually used in the remainder of this book are addressed in greater detail.[1] The libraries used in this book are: <cstdlib>, <iostream>, <string>, <iterator>, <map>, and <set>.[2] Readers who are already familiar with the C++ libraries may skip this chapter.

---

[1] It should be noted that many C++ programmers can work for years using only a handful of the C++ libraries. This book gives a very cursory introduction to the C++ libraries. One of the books covering the C++ libraries is easily 800 pages. It is recommended that the reader get a book on the C++ libraries. The goal in this chapter is to identify the libraries and explain why they are used and to provide sufficient detail about the libraries that are used so that the examples in the remaining chapters of the book are understandable.

[2] The tables appearing in the descriptions of these libraries are taken from *The C++ Standard Library: A Tutorial and Reference* by Nicolai M. Josuttis.

For many years, there were several different standard ways of referring to a header file. Of those, two extensions were most common: .h and .hpp. In the draft standard for C++ libraries, it was decided not to specify the file extension. As a result, most implementations do not incorporate a file extension. Use of these libraries in a file is invoked as:

```
#include <iostream>
```

This lets the compiler know that the file to be included comes from a standard library with a name iostream.

C Standard Libraries

C++ was originally viewed as C with objects added to it. As a result, the original libraries of C++ were the C libraries. This allowed C++ programs to incorporate C code without major revision. Much of the functionality provided by the C libraries has been replaced in the C++ libraries. However, in terms of maintaining legacy C++ code, odds are great that the code relies upon these libraries. The header filenames for the C libraries are given in Table 15-1. Because none of these libraries is used in this book, we will only identify when each library is used or if it should be avoided.

<cassert>

This library defines a function, assert(cond), which can be used to test a condition and force a program to exit should the condition resolve to 0. This function is often used to establish if memory allocation was successful.

<cctype>

This library provides functionality to assess character type. This allows one to determine if the character is a digit, graph, lowercase, uppercase, or space, and to convert characters from lower- to uppercase and vice versa.

<cerrno>

This library defines a variable that can be used to pass error conditions from within a function to the calling routine.

TABLE 15-1   C Headers

<cassert>	<climits>	<cstdarg>	<ctime>
<cctype>	<clocale>	<cstddef>	<cwchar>
<cerrno>	<cmath>	<cstdio>	<cwctype>
<cfloat>	<csetjmp>	<cstdlib>	
<ciso646>	<csignal>	<cstring>	

<cfloat>

This library provides numerical limits for floating-point types.

<ciso646>

The iso646.h library was added to C as part of ISO standardization to provide macros for operators that are difficult to type on international keyboards. This library introduces the tokens and, and_eq, bitand, bitor, comp, not_eq, or, or_eq, xor, and xor_eq. C++ already provides these keywords, so use of this library is unnecessary.

<climits>

This library identifies the numeric limits for integer types.

<clocale>

This library provides the functionality to tailor a program to various locales. This allows money, date, and numbers to be displayed according to the local convention.

<cmath>

The <cmath> library provides commonly used mathematical functions. In fact, it provides 22 different mathematical functions.

<csetjmp>

This library allows the programmer to specify an immediate jump out of a deeply nested function callback to an error handler. This functionality has been superseded by the exception mechanisms of C++ and should not be used.

<csignal>

This library provides functionality to raise and handle signals. Signals are a mechanism that allows one to jump out of the normal flow of processing as a result of an error condition, exception (e.g., divide by zero), or interrupt (e.g., cntrl-c).

<cstdarg>

This library provides functions for handling arguments passed into the main routine when the program is started. Unfortunately, this library has been pushed to its limits with respect to C++. It has been suggested that any typical implementation of C++ will almost certainly fail if the macros are pushed too hard.

<cstddef>

This library defines the NULL pointer (a pointer defined as (void *) 0), an unsized type for size units, ptrdiff_t, which is a signed type for the difference between two pointers, and the function offsetof(), which is a function that returns the offset of a member in a structure or union.

<cstdio>

The <cstdio> library provides all of the input/output functionality of C in the form of functions. The C++ class library <iostream> provides the functionality one needs for input and output using objects. The only time a C++ program will require this library is when maintaining legacy code that combines C and C++.

<cstdlib>

For some odd historical reason, the <cstdlib> library provides some mathematical functions that are commonly used. In addition to providing some mathematical functions, cstdlib also provides three functions and two defined constants. These functions are still commonly used in programs,[3] and are shown in Table 15-2 and Table 15-3.

<cstring>

Historically, one of the most important libraries for non-C programmers to understand was the <cstring> package of functions. The C community, and thus the C++ community, agreed to treat the type char* as a form of string type. The understanding is that strings will be terminated by the character value of zero and that programmers will use the functions provided in <cstring> to manipulate the abstraction. Fortunately, the functionality provided in this library is now provided in the <string> C++ class library.

<ctime>

This library contains the functions for manipulating and formatting time. A commonly used function in this library is time(), which returns the current time.

TABLE 15-2   Exit Functions in <cstdlib>

Function	Effect
exit()	Exits program, cleaning up the static objects
abort()	Forcefully exits the program
atexit()	Takes a function as an argument and calls it on program exit

TABLE 15-3   Constants defined in <cstdlib>

Constant	Interpretation
EXIT_SUCCESS	Program has completed normally
EXIT_FAILURE	Program has ended abnormally

---

[3]   Many people, the authors included, believe that the exit functions should not be used in properly constructed C++ programs. One should throw an exception to the main and allow the main the exit normally.

<cwchar>

This library provides the same kind of functionality as <cchar> except it deals with wide characters.

<cwctype>

This library provides the same functionality as <cctype> except it deals with wide characters.

C++ Class Libraries

ONE of the problems of relying on C libraries was that they didn't fit the object-oriented paradigm. This was a direct result of the C emphasis on structures, functions, and procedures. C++ added a number of class-oriented libraries. These libraries contained classes that provided key functionality for the programmer in an object-oriented form. The original C libraries were retained to provide backward compatibility and because in some cases, the appropriate representation for a given programming need was a function (e.g., mathematical operations). The headers for these libraries are identified in Table 15-4. The C++ standard libraries extend or replace many of the functions that are defined in the C libraries.

<bits>

This library provides the ability to define and use bit flags and bit masks. An instance of the **bit** class provides a fixed length sequence of bits.

<bitstream>

This library defines the class **bitstring** and supporting functions. This is similar to the class **string**, except rather than a variable length sequence of characters, this is a variable sequence of bits.

<complex>

This library provides representations for complex numbers and arithmetic over complex numbers. It provides three separate classes, **float_complex**, **double_complex**, and

TABLE 15-4   C++ Class Library Headers

<bits>	<exceptions>	<istream>	<streambuf>
<bitstring>	<fstream>	<new>	<string>
<complex>	<iomanip>	<ostream>	<strstream>
<defines>	<ios>	<ptrdynarray>	<typeinfo>
<dynarray>	<iostream>	<sstream>	<wstring>

long_double_complex, which support complex numbers of size float, double, and long_double, respectively. It provides overloaded functions and operators for manipulating complex numbers.

<defines>

This library defines a constant and some basic types that are widely used in the C++ Standard library. It provides what is commonly called "language support." This captures implementation-dependant type information (machine and compiler).

<dynarray>

This library provides a template class that defines dynamic arrays of type T. The type T must have a default constructor, a copy constructor, an assignment operator, and a destructor. This template class lets you represent and manipulate in-memory sequences that vary dynamically in length.

<exceptions>

This library is used to extend the C++ exceptions capability. This library constitutes an advance C++ programming practice that is not addressed in this book.

<fstream>

This library provides definitions of classes for use in reading and writing to files.

<iomanip>

This library provides several templates and manipulators that exploit them. This is a basic library that provides three template classes for performing insertions and deletions.

<ios>

This library provides the virtual base class that is used in the definition of other input/output stream classes. One does not typically use this library directly.

<iostream>

Input/output is not directly part of the C++ language. The newest C++ stream library, <iostream>, provides C++ programmers with an extremely powerful mechanism to perform input and output. This library bundles together the libraries <ios>, <streambuf>, <istream>, and <ostream>. The <iostream> library defines and declares four standard streams for the programmer. These are illustrated in Table 15-5. The <iostream> library overloads the two bit-shift operators for get inputs and to send outputs as described in Table 15-6. In addition to all of the library functions, user-defined services for a class of objects are also functions.

TABLE 15-5   Standard C++ Input and Output Objects

Stream	Description
cout	Standard out, normally the screen
cin	Standard in, normally the keyboard
cerr	Standard error, normally also the screen
clog	Standard log, normally the same stream as standard error

TABLE 15-6   Iostream Operators

Operator	Description
<<	"Put to" output stream
>>	"Get from" input stream

An example of using iostream operators follows:

```
#include <iostream>
using namespace std;
main()
{
    string a("Hello");
    int b=0, c=3;
    float d=3.14;
    cout << a << endl;
    cout << b << ',' << c << endl;
    cout << "PI = " << d << endl;
}
```

This program works because C++ provides default iostream operators for the basic data types. The library defines 'endl' as a constant for a newline.

One can also define the operators for user-defined classes. The definition of these operators is performed using overloaded operators, as illustrated in the following example. This example can be simplified using friend functions that will be described in a later chapter.

```
#include <iostream>
using namespace std;
```

```
class simple {
    private:
        int value;
    public:
        simple(int i) { value = i;}
        void setValue(int i) { value = i;}
        int getValue() { return value; }
}

istream &operator>>(istream &input, simple &s) {
    int i;
    input >> i;
    s.setValue(i);
    return input;
}

ostream &operator<<(ostream &output, simple &s) {
    output << s.getValue();
    return output;
}

main () {
    simple very_simple(1);
    // creates an instance of s with the value set to 1
    cout << very_simple << endl;    // prints out 1
}
```

The iostream operators return the stream they are reading or writing. This allows multiple reads or writes to appear on the same line.

<istream>

The istream library provides the istream class, which derives from the ios class. This class provides you with the ability to extract characters from a stream. The best known object of this class is **cin**, which is defined in library <iostream>. For more information about using cin, see the <iostream> library description.

<new>

This library provides the ability to extend the new operator in C++ and represents a very advanced C++ topic. This library should only be used if you want to take extraordinary control over storage allocation.

<ostream>

This library is the natural complement to the istream library—providing the ability to write to a stream. The best known object is **cout**, which is defined in the <iostream>

library. We typically include <iostream> in programs to achieve input and output, rather than <ostream>.

<ptrdynarry>

This library provides a template for managing dynamic arrays of pointers to instances of type T.

<sstream>

This library is a variation of the <strstream> library that is designed to work with the <string> library.

<streambuf>

This library provides the class streambuf, which is the principal engine for all iostream operations. Like the library, <ios>, we rarely have occasion to include this library directly in a program because the other stream libraries already include it.

<string>

The C++ <string> library does more than just replace the basic functionality of the C <cstring> library. It provides an object-oriented way of dealing with strings. This means that one can create strings using standard C++ mechanisms, use overloaded operators tailored for strings, and employ additional functions.

An example of using <string> is given in the following program:

```
#include <string>        // include the C++ string library
using namespace std;     // declare that we are using the std namespace
int main (int argc, char** argv)
{
    string a("abc");     // declare and initialize string a to contain "abc"
    string b("def");     // declare and initialize string b to contain "def"
    string c("abcdef"); // declare and initialize string c to contain
                         // "abcdef"
    string d;            // declare string d (default initialization to the
                         // empty string)
    d = a + b;           // join strings a and b and assign the result to
                         // string d
    if (d == c) {        // compare the two strings
        cout << "Strings are equal" << endl;
    }
}
```

This simple program will print out that the strings are equal.

<strstream>

This library defines three classes that allow you to read and write character sequences stored in memory.

<typeinfo>

This library supports runtime type identification (RTTI). It provides definitions for two classes, **typeinfo** and **badtype_id**. You will need to include this file only if you use the operator typeid.

<wstring>

This library provides string functionality utilizing wide characters.

Standard Template Library

THE standard template library is one of the most significant improvements in object-oriented programming since the founding of the C++ programming language. The STL is based upon the generic programming paradigm. It enables a higher level of reusability than that achieved using basic classes. Instead of data hiding, it is based on *data independence*. Data independence is characterized by two key features: adaptability and efficiency. It relies upon templates and operator overloading to provide a common abstraction over multiple data types.

STL is actually a collection of libraries that provide templates. The templates are used to define the major container classes necessary for implementing associations and aggregations. STL provides templates for general containers, iterators, numeric containers and algorithms over them, and general utilities. The headers are listed in Table 15-7; libraries that define container classes are in bold; numerical containers are in italics; and iterators, algorithms, and general utilities are in plain text.[4]

One of the difficulties most people new to the STL face is understanding generic programming. The majority of material dealing with STL focuses on generic programming and the internals of the template classes. This book, consistent with its intent to serve as a practical guide, emphasizes how to use the template classes.

TABLE 15-7   STL Headers

<algorithm>	<functional>	<memory>	<stack>
<bitset>	<iterator>	*<numerics>*	<utility>
<complex>	**<list>**	**<queue>**	*<valarray>*
<deque>	**<map>**	**<set>**	**<vector>**

---

[4] It should be noted that there are two major branches of the library: the ANSI draft version and the original HP version. Both branches provide the same containers, algorithms, and features. The major difference between the two branches is the header files in which they are defined. As a result, if one is using the HP version, minor modifications must be made to take into account '#include' difference.

<algorithm>

This library provides all of the generic algorithms of STL with the exception of the generalized numeric algorithms. These algorithms include functions to manipulate containers: for_each() counting elements, establishing the minimum and maximum, searching for elements, comparing ranges, copying elements, transforming elements, swapping elements, assigning new values, replacing elements, removing specific values, removing duplicates, reversing the order of elements, rotating elements, permuting elements, shuffling elements, moving elements to the front, sorting elements, partial sorts, sorting, searching elements, and merging elements. These are useful functions.

<bitset>

This library provides fixed-sized arrays of bits or Boolean values.

<complex>

This library handles complex numbers.

<deque>

This library provides the deque template, which is one of the three sequence containers provided by STL. It provides random access to a sequence of varying length, with constant time insertions and deletions at both the beginning and the end of the sequence.

<functional>

The functional library contains all of the STL function objects and function adaptors.

<iterator>

The iterator library defines templates that create iterators for navigating sequences. Iterators come in several different categories, based on the capability provided and the kind of sequence. These categories appear in Table 15-8.

TABLE 15-8 Categories of Iterators

Category	Providers	Ability
Bidirectional	list, set, multiset, map, multimap	Reads and writes forward and backwards
Forward		Reads and writes forward
Input	istream	Reads forward
Output	ostream, inserter	Writes forward
Random Access	vector, string, array, deque	Reads and writes with random access

An iterator is declared for a sequence using the sequence type and the word itera-tor separated by the scope operator. An example is:

```
vector<int>::iterator pos;
```

This declares an iterator variable, pos, which operates on a vector of integers. An iterator designed to traverse sequences in the reverse order can be declared as:

```
list<int>::reverse_iterator pos;
```

A reverse iterator functions in the same manner as a forward iterator, with the exception that the increment and decrement operators have been reversed. Hence, incrementing a reverse iterator moves one backwards through the list while incrementing a normal iter-ator moves one forward through the list.

All sequences support two methods for getting iterators for a specific instance of the sequence: These two methods are begin() and end(), which return iterators pointing to the first and last elements of the sequence, respectively. These are often used in loops to visit each element in turn. Examples of using end() appear in the examples for <set> and <map>.

<list>

The <list> template class provides a generic doubly linked list capability that can be used to make lists of integers, floats, user-defined classes, and any other data type for which the <, >, <=, >=, != and == operators have been defined. In addition, a copy mech-anism must exist for the data type.

<map>

The <map> library provides map and multimap containers. Maps and mulitmaps pro-vide random access to data values via key values. The distinction is that a map contains elements, each of which is accessed by a unique key. A multimap can contain multiple elements, any number of which are accessed by the same key. The data value and key value must both possess the following properties:

1. The key/value pair must be assignable and copyable.
2. The key must be comparable with the sorting criteria.

In this section, only map is described with the understanding that multimaps have equiv-alent operations. A map has a sort operator associated with it to facilitate rapid retrieval of values based on the key. Table 15-9 identifies the various ways in which a map can be cre-ated. The italicized map in the table is meant to represent one of the following two forms:

1. map<Key, Elem>
2. map<Key,Elem,Op>

The first form defaults to sorts based on the less than operator (< operator). In systems without support for default template parameters, the second form must always be used.

TABLE 15-9 **Creating and Destroying a Map**

Operation	Effect
map c	Creates an empty map
*map c*1(op)	Creates an empty map that uses op as the sorting criteria
*map c*1(c2)	Creates a copy of another map of the same type
map c(beg,end)	Creates a map initialized by the element of the range [beg,end]
map c(beg, end,op)	Creates a map with the sorting criterion op initialized by the elements of the range [beg,end]
c.~*map*()	Destroys all elements and frees the memory

An element is actually a key/value pair that is captured as a templated type in the std namespace. In the tables that follow, the notation elem means such a pair. There are three methods for constructing a pair.

1. Use pair<>

   One can create a pair directly. For example:

   ```
   std::pair<std::string,int> ("John",32)        // uses implicit conversion
   std::pair<const std::string,int> ("John",32) // uses explicit conversion
   ```

   These lines would be the argument in the insert() member function.

2. Use value_type

   The correct type can be passed explicitly by using value_type, which is provided as a type definition by the container type. For example:

   ```
   std::map<std::string,int> a;
   a.insert(std::map<std::string,int>::value_type("John",32));
   ```

3. Use make_pair()

   The make_pair function produces a pair object that contains the two values passed as arguments.The appropriate type conversions are provided by the insert() member function. For example:

   ```
   std::map<std::sring,int> a;
   a.insert(std::make_pair("John",32));
   ```

An example of the first type appears in the code example following the tables.

The nonmodifying operations that apply over maps are identified in Table 15-10. The map assignment operations are identified in Table 15-11. A map provides some specialized search operations to locate elements based on the key. These operations are identified in Table 15-12. The operations to return an iterator are given in Table 15-13, and the operations to insert and remove elements in the map are identified in Table 15-14.

TABLE 15-10   Nonmodifying Map Operations

Operation	Effect
c.size()	Returns the actual number of elements
c.empty()	Returns whether the map is empty
c.max_size()	Returns the maximum number of elements possible
c1 == c2	Returns whether c1 is equal to c2
c1 != c2	Returns whether c1 is not equal to c2
c1 < c2	Returns whether c1 is less than c2
c1 > c2	Returns whether c1 is greater than c2
c1 <= c2	Returns whether c1 is less than or equal to c2
c1 >= c2	Returns whether c1 is greater than or equal to c2

TABLE 15-11   Map Assignment Operations

Operation	Effect
c1 = c2	Assigns all elements of c2 to c1
c1.swap(c2)	Swaps the data of c1 and c2
swap(c1,c2)	Global function to swap the data of c1 and c2

TABLE 15-12   Special Search Operations

Operation	Effect
c.count(key)	Returns the number of elements with the key
c.find()	Returns the position of the first element with the key or end()
c.lower_bound(key)	Returns the first position where an element with the key would get inserted
c.upper_bound(key)	Returns the last position where an element with a specific key would get inserted
c.equal_range(key)	Returns the first and last positions where elements with a given key would get inserted

TABLE 15-13   Iterator Functions

Operation	Effect
c.begin()	Returns a bidirectional iterator for the first element
c.end()	Returns a bidirectional iterator for the position after the last element
c.rbegin	Returns a reverse iterator for the first element of a reverse iteration
c.rend()	Returns a reverse iterator for the position after the last element of a reverse iteration

TABLE 15-14   Operations to Insert and Remove Map Elements

Operation	Effect
c.insert(elem)	Inserts a copy of elem and returns the position of the new element
c.insert(pos,elem)	Inserts a copy of elem and returns the position of the new element. pos is used as a hint, pointing where the search to insert should begin
c.insert(beg,end)	Inserts a copy of all elements of the range [beg,end]
c.erase(elem)	Removes all elements with the value elem and returns the number of removed elements
c.erase(pos)	Removes the element at iterator position pos
c.erase(beg,end)	Removes the elements of the range [beg,end]
c.clear()	Removes all elements, but does not destroy the map
c[key]	Returns a reference to the value of the element with key; inserts an element with key if it does not yet exist

Following is an example of using the map template in a program:

```
#include <map>
#include <string>
using namespace std;
main()
{
    map<string,int> NameAgeMap;
    map<string,int>::iterator pos;
    NameAgeMap["Bill"] = 43;
    NameAgeMap.insert(pair<const string,float> ("John", 18));
    NameAgeMap.insert(make_pair("Sue",35));
    cout << NameAgeMap["Bill"] << endl;          // prints 43
    cout << NameAgeMap["John"] << endl;          // prints 18
    pos = NameAgeMap.find("Sue");
    if (pos != NameAgeMap.end()){
        cout << pos->second << endl; // prints 35
    }
    cout << NameAgeMap["Fred"] << endl;          // prints 0

}
```

This program illustrates several important points about using the map template. The first three lines tell the compiler to include the map and string libraries and inform it that we are using the std namespace. This allows us to use string, make_pair, and map without explicitly identifying the package each time they appear in the program.

The main declares a map that has a string key and an integer value in the stored map element (key/value pair). The map declared in this fashion is empty; that is, it contains no entries. An iterator for traversing the map is declared as well.[5]

The next few lines insert key/value pairs into the map. The first line inserts Bill as a key and a value of 43 using one mechanism for adding an element. The second line inserts an element with an explicit cast of a pair containing the string "John" and value 18. The third entry inserts an element to the map using the make_pair approach. Here a pair is created and the elements cast into the appropriate type by the insert operation.

The next two lines access the value using the map as though it was an associative array with the key serving as an index.

The following three lines access the value using the find method. This returns an iterator, which is set to the position in the map where it encountered the key. If it didn't encounter the key, then it points to the end of the map. The if statement checks to assure that the value returned was not the end of the map (which is actually beyond the last pair in the map). Access to the value is through an attribute of the iterator, namely pos->second. There is another attribute, pos->first, which gives access to the key. While we can modify the value of pos->second directly, we cannot modify the value of pos->first because it is declaring a const value in the key/value pair.

---

[5]   More information about iterators will be provided later in this chapter.

The last line has an interesting side effect. This side effect arises because an element doesn't exist in the map with the key "Fred." As a result, the part of the statement that reads, NameAgeMap["Fred"], performs three actions: it inserts a new pair into the map with the key "Fred," it defaults the value to 0, and then it prints out the value of 0. If this is the effect that was desired, then great. However, if it is the result of user-input, this could be bad. Because of this possible side effect, the approach immediately preceding this one is preferred.

\<memory\>

This library provides the template class, auto_prt, which is used for *any* types in namespace std. This is employed within other STL libraries. It is unusual to have to include this library explicitly.

\<numerics\>

The numerics library provides four categories of algorithms for generic numeric processing over sequences. These categories are accumulate, inner product, partial sum, and adjacent difference. Within each category, the developer can change the operator to provide different behaviors. It is not necessary that the elements in the sequence be numeric as long as appropriate operators exist.

\<queue\>

The queue library provides the queue container adaptor and the priority queue container adapter. A queue is a data structure in which elements are inserted at one end and removed from the opposite end. The order of removal is identical with the order of insertion. A priority queue is a queue in which the largest element in the queue is removed first. Largest, in this class, is the element that has a maximum value according to some sort function. A priority queue has some comparison operator associated with it.

\<set\>

The set library provides set and multiset capabilities. A set provides a container in which the contents are not explicitly sequenced like a list, but are sorted to enable rapid access to elements within the container. Sets and multisets use keys to access elements. We use sets and multisets to implement many-to-one and many-to-many associations and aggregations. To use a set or multiset, you must include the header file \<set\>:

```
#include <set>
```

This includes the code that defines both sets and multisets.

A set can be created as shown in Table 15-15, where the entry *set* may be one of the forms given in Table 15-16. Sets and multisets provide nonmodifying operations (identified in Table 15-17) for establishing the size and for performing comparisons. These operations require that elements and the sorting criteria must have the same types. Sets and multisets provide fast search operations (identified in Table 15-18) to locate entries. Iterators are required to access data because sets and multisets do not provide direct element access. The operations to get iterators are identified in Table 15-19.

TABLE 15-15   Create, Copy, and Destory Operations

Operation	Effect
set c	Creates an empty set/multiset
set c(op)	Creates an empty set/multiset with op as the sorting criterion
set c1(c2)	Creates a copy of another set/multiset of the same type
set c(beg,end)	Creates a set/multiset that is initialized with the elements of range [beg,end)
set c(beg, end, op)	Creates a set/multiset with the sorting criterion op initialized by the elements of the range [beg,end)

TABLE 15-16   Declarations of Set/Multiset

set	Effect
set<elem>	A set that sorts with less< (operator <)
set<Elem, Op>	A set that sorts with op
multiset<Elem>	A multiset that sorts with less< (operators <)
multiset<Elem, Op>	A multiset that sorts with op

TABLE 15-17   Nonmodifying Operations

Operation	Effect
c.size()	Returns the actual number of elements
c.empty()	Returns whether the container is empty
c.max_size()	Returns the maximum number of elements possible
c1 == c2	Returns whether c1 is equal to c2
c1 != c2	Returns whether c1 is not equal to c2
c1 < c2	Returns whether c1 is less than c2
c1> c2	Returns whether c1 is greater than c2
c1 <= c2	Returns whether c1 is less than or equal to c2
c1 >= c2	Returns whether c1 is greater than or equal to c2

TABLE 15-18   Search Operations

Operation	Effect
count(elem)	Returns the number of elements with value elem
find(elem)	Returns the position of the first element with value elem
lower_bound(elem)	Returns the first position where elem would get inserted
upper_bound(elem)	Returns the last position where elem would get inserted
equal_range(elem)	Returns the first and last positions where elem would get inserted

TABLE 15-19   Iterator Functions

Operation	Effect
c.begin()	Returns a bidirectional iterator for the first element
c.end()	Returns a bidirectional iterator for the position after the last element
c.rbegin()	Returns a reverse iterator for the first element of a reverse iteration
c.rend()	Returns a reverse iterator for the position after the last element of a reverse iteration

TABLE 15-20   Inserting and Removing Elements

Operation	Effect
c.insert(elem)	Inserts a copy of elem and returns the position of the new element and, for sets, whether it succeeded
c.insert(pos,elem)	Inserts a copy of elem and returns the position of the new element (pos is used as a hint point to where the insert should start the search)
c.insert(beg,end)	Inserts a copy of all elements of the range [beg,end) (returns nothing)
c.erase(elem)	Removes all elements with value elem and returns the number of removed elements
c.erase(pos)	Removes the element at iterator position pos
c.erase(beg,end)	Removes all elements of the range [beg,end)
c.clear()	Removes all elements

Sets and multisets provide operations to insert and remove elements. One must be careful because the return types of the insert operations differ between sets and multisets. This is a consequence of the fact that sets may contain only a single element with a particular value while a multiset allows duplicates.

<stack>

The stack library provides the stack container adapter. A stack is a container that allows the user to insert an element at one end, remove an element from the same end, retrieve the value at the same end (without changing the stack), and test the stack for emptiness.

<utility>

The utility library defines the template class, **pair**, and provides templated comparison operations !=, >, <=, and >=. This library is used within other STL libraries such as <map>.

<valarray>

This library provides the class **valarray** for processing arrays of numeric values.

<vector>

This library provides a vector template, which is one of the three kinds of sequence containers provided by SQL. A vector provides random access to a sequence of varying length; with constant time insertions and deletions at the end of the sequence.

Recommended Approach

READERS who are unfamiliar with C++ or have not kept up with recent changes in the C++ standards should purchase a good book covering the current C++ standard libraries.

■ ■ SUMMARY

THIS chapter has introduced the C++ libraries. It has covered:

1. The C libraries
2. The C++ class libraries
3. The Standard Template libraries

CHAPTER

16

Implementing Static Behavior

> *O*f things which hold together by nature there are two kinds: those that are unborn, imperishable, and eternal, and those that are subject to generation and decay.
>
> Aristotle, in *Zoology*

One of the major goals in our analysis was specifying the behavior of all the services associated with a class. In the previous chapter, we learned how to declare a service identification using a function prototype. In this chapter, we will see how to turn a service specification into executable code. In the previous chapter, we declared the functions by specifying their prototype in the .h file and within the body of the class definition. Capturing the definitions of the functions (i.e., to capture the behaviors of the services) is discussed in this chapter.

Function Definition

THE form of a function definition is:

```
return-type function-name (list of arguments)
{
    statements
}
```

For example, the function definition of a function that returns the greatest common denominator is:

```
int  greatest_common_denominator( int arg1, int arg2 )
{     // return the greatest common denominator
    int temp;
    while ( arg2 )
    {
        temp = arg2;
        arg2 = arg1 % arg2;
        arg1 = temp;
    }
    return ( arg1 );
}
```

A function that does not return a value has a return type of *void*. The actions performed when a function is called are specified between the braces. The collection of statements or actions is sometimes called the *body* of the function and is also a block from a programming perspective. A function may cause another function to be executed by calling the other function within the body of itself.

A function call can cause one of the following to occur:

■ If the called function has been declared inline, the body of the function is expanded at the point of its call during compilation. This is used to optimize small and frequently called functions and still support the information-hiding principle of object-oriented technology.[1]

■ If the function is not declared inline, the function is invoked at run time. A function invocation transfers control to the function being called and suspends execution of the calling function. When the called function has completed, the suspended calling function resumes execution at the point immediately following the call.

Return Type

The return type plus the argument list define the public interface of the function. The calling function needs to know only the public interface to call the function. As shown in previous chapter, the prototype, which includes the public interface, is declared in the .h file of the class.[2]

---

[1] However, there is a compilation cost to this. Every time a change occurs in the .h file that contains the inline function, all of the other files that use the inline function will recompile even if the change in the .h file has nothing to do with the inline function.

[2] Because a function can only be defined once, the function definition is typically specified in its own file with other related functions. Normally, all of the function definitions of the functions in a single class are contained in one file. This file is called the .C for the class.

The return type of a function may be a native data type, a derived type, a user-defined type, or void. For example, consider the following lines of code:

```
    // forward declaration and enum definition
class Dog;
enum Gender { male, female };
    // function declarations
int  getAge();
char * getName();
Gender getSex();
void setAge( int newAge );
Dog*  getDog();
```

The getAge() function has a native return type, the getName() function has a derived return type, the getSex() function has a user-defined return type, and the setAge() function has a void return type. The getDog() function has a derived, user-defined return type and returns a pointer to an instance of the class Dog.

Neither an array nor a function may be specified as a return type. However, a pointer to an array or a function can be specified as a return type. For example:

```
int[100] get100randomNumbers();   // this is not legal
int *     get 100randomNumers();  // this is legal
```

However, when you return a pointer or a reference to an object, there are some pitfalls of which you need to be aware (see "Passing Arguments"). A function without an explicit return value is assumed to have a return type of int; thus a function that does not return a value must declare a return type of void.

Return Statement

The return statement is used to terminate a function that is currently executing and return control to the calling function. There are two forms for the return statement, *return* and *return expression*.

The first return statement is used when the return type is void and the second is used for the nonvoid return types. The expression may be arbitrarily complex and may involve a function. However, for ease of maintenance, it is recommended that the expression be only a variable of return type. An implicit conversion will be applied, if possible, in instances when the variable is not of the return type. A function can return only one value. If the application logic requires that multiple values be returned, the developer might do any of the following:

■ Return an aggregate data type that contains multiple values. In this case, the developer will create a class to represent the aggregate and usually will return a pointer or a reference to that class.

- Formal arguments may be defined as either pointer or reference types. This will allow the function to have access to the lvalue of these arguments. Then the lvalue may be used to change the rvalue of these variables.
- A global or static variable may be defined outside the function. Because a global variable is accessible from within any function when properly declared, the function can return a second "return" value via the global variable.

Only the first method is recommended for object-oriented technology when multiple values need to be returned. The second method is used when the function must access the member functions of that variable (object). The third method should rarely be used for the following reasons:

1. The functions that utilize the global variable(s) now depend upon the existence and type of the global variable. This makes reuse more difficult.
2. There is a loss of encapsulation. Global dependencies increase the likelihood of introducing bugs when programs are modified.
3. If a global variable has an incorrect value, the entire program must be searched to find the error; there is no information hiding.
4. Global variables violate the information-hiding and encapsulation principles of object-oriented technology.
5. Recursion is more difficult to get correct.

Function Argument List

The argument list of a function may not be omitted. A function that does not take any arguments can be represented either with an empty argument list or the single keyword *void*. For example, the following two declarations of getAge are equivalent:

```
int     getAge()     { return age; }
int     getAge(void) { return age; }
```

The signature consists of a comma-separated list of argument types. An argument type is any native type, derived type, or user-defined type. An argument name usually follows each type specifier. The argument name is used in the body of the function to access the argument as a variable of the defined type given in the signature.

Because it is used in the body as a variable, each argument name appearing in a signature must be different from the others and different from the local variable names used in the body. The shorthand, comma-separated type-declaration syntax may not be used in the list of arguments.

If argument names are specified in both the declaration and definition of a function, different names may be used in each. However, the type specifier must be the same. Omitting an argument or using an argument of the wrong type would be caught at compile time because C++ is a strongly typed language. Both the return type and the argument list of every function call are type-checked during compilation. If there is a mismatch between an actual type and a type declared in the function prototype, an implicit conversion will be applied where possible. However, if an implicit conversion is not possible or if the number of arguments is incorrect, a compile time error is given.

We suggest that the argument list to any function be small. Some developers limit the number of arguments to seven; thus less than seven. If one wants to adhere to this guideline, what does one do with functions that require a long argument list? There are two ways to handle this:

1. The function may be trying to do too much; you may want to divide the function into two or more smaller specialized functions.
2. Define a class type to do the validity checking. The validity checking can then be performed inside the class member function instead of the using function. This provides better encapsulation and reduces the size of the code of the function.

It is sometimes impossible to list the type and number of all the arguments that might be passed to a function. In this case, you can suspend type-checking by using ellipses (...) within the function signature. Ellipses tell the compiler that zero or more arguments may follow and that the types of the arguments are unknown. The printf() function is an example of the necessary use of ellipses. The printf() function is declared in C++ as follows:

```
printf( const char *,  ... )
```

This requires that every call to printf() be given a first argument of type char *, and after that there can be zero or more arguments. For example:

```
printf( "Good Day, you all\n" )
```

uses only one argument, while

```
printf( "Good Day %s\n",  userName )
```

uses two arguments. The % indicates the presence of another argument, while the **s** indicates the type of the argument.

Note that the following two functions are not equivalent:

```
char func();
char func( ... );
```

Func() is declared a function that takes no arguments, while func(...) is declared a function that takes zero or more arguments.

Passing Arguments

WHEN a function is called, storage on a structure (referred to as the program's run-time stack) is allocated to the function. Furthermore, each formal argument is provided with storage space within the structure. The storage size is determined by the type specifier for the argument. That storage remains on the stack until the function is terminated. At that point, the storage is freed and is no longer accessible to the program.

The arguments found between the parentheses of the function call are referred to as the *actual arguments* of the call. Argument passing is the process of actual arguments initializing the storage of the formal arguments. We shall discuss argument-passing mechanisms: pass-by-value, reference, or pointer, and passing an array.

Pass-By-Value

The default process of argument passing in C++ is to copy the rvalue of the actual argument into the storage allocated in the structure of the run-time stack for the formal argument. This is called *pass-by-value*.

In the process of pass-by-value, the contents of the actual arguments are not changed because the function access manipulates its local copies, which are on the run-time stack. In general, changes made to these local copies are not reflected in the values of the actual arguments. Once the function terminates, these local values are not accessible to the program. This means that a programmer of the calling function does not need to save and restore argument values when making a function call.

Without a pass-by-value mechanism, each argument would have to be saved before a function call and restored after the function call by the programmer because they may be altered. The only exception is when arguments corresponding to formal arguments are declared const. Passing-by-value has the least potential for side effects and requires the least work by the programmer of the calling function. Unfortunately, as well-behaved as pass-by-value is, it is not suitable for every function. Examples of these situations include:

- Passing a large object as an argument.[3]
- When the value(s) of the argument(s) must be modified by the function.

In such a situation, either of the following alternatives is available to the programmer:

- Make the formal argument declaration as a pointer to the type specifier.
- Make the formal argument declaration as a reference to the type specifier.

---

[3] The time and space required to allocate and copy the class object onto the run-time stack are too high for a real-world application.

Reference or Pointer Argument

The declaration of the formal argument as a reference or pointer overrides the default pass-by-value mechanism. The function receives the lvalue of the actual argument rather than a copy of the argument itself. This now gives the function access to the public data of the object. This is very useful when the function needs to change the values of the actual argument. Remember that the pass-by-value mechanism only allows the function to manipulate local copies of the argument.

Examples.   Examples of the three "passing arguments" mechanisms are as follows:

```
void Collision::calv(Ball ball1,  Length deltay)
{
        // this is pass-by-value; a copy of Ball is made
        // if we would have had Rectangle Ball, a copy of ball as a
        // rectangle
        // is made.
        // In addition, a copy of deltay as a Length is given.
}


void Collision::calp (Ball* ball2, Side* top)

{
        // this is pass by pointer; pointers to instance of Ball and
        // to instance
        // of Side are sent to the routine. We will assume that deltay is
        // a data member of Side.
        // The routine can call the services of Ball and Side.
}

void Collision::cala(Ball& ball3, Side& lside)
{
        // this pass by reference; addresses to Ball and lside are send to
        // the
        // routine. The routine can call the services of Ball and Side.
}
```

In C++, the argument access syntax is different for each mechanism:

```
void Collision::calv(Ball ball,  Length deltay)
{
        ball.rect();
        ymin = ymin + deltay;
                    //  here you use the copies of the values directly.
}
```

```
void Collision::calp (Ball* ball, Side* top)
{
    // here we use the operator "->" to access the  methods of a
    // class in object-oriented C++.
    ball->setYmin ( ball->getYmin() + top->getDeltay() );
    // assuming there are member functions called setYmin
    // getYmin for class Ball and getDeltay for class Side.
}

void Collision::cala(Ball& ball, Side* lside)
{
    // here we use the operator "." to access the  methods of a
    // class in object-oriented C++.
    ball.setYmin ( ball.getYmin() + top->getDeltay() );
    // assuming there are member functions called setYmin
    // getYmin for class Ball and getDeltay for class Side.
}
```

Array Argument.   Arrays in C++ do not use the pass-by-value mechanism. Rather, an array is passed as a pointer to its zeroth element. For example, the statement

```
int& getValue( int[10], int);
```

is treated by the compiler as

```
int& getValue( int *, int);
```

The array size of 10 is ignored by the compiler in the declaration of formal arguments. The following declarations are equivalent:

```
        //  all of the declarations below are equivalent
int& getValue( int *, int);
int& getValue( int [ ], int);
int& getValue( int [ 10 ], int);
int& getValue( int [ 40 ], int);
```

This has the following implications for the programmer:

- The changes to an array argument within the called function (i.e., getValue) are made to the actual array of the call and not to a local copy. In cases in which the array being passed as an argument must remain unchanged, programmers need to simulate a pass-by-value mechanism. The most straightforward way to do this is to pass a copy of the array to the function.

■ The size of the array is not part of the type specification. Neither the function nor the compiler knows the actual size of an array when it is being passed. Array size checking is not done at compile time.

For example:

```
int& getValue( int [ 40 ], int); // compiler sees it as getValue( int*, int)
main()
{
    int   i, *pointer, intArray[20];
    pointer = getValue(  &i, 21 )  // will compile, run-time error
    pointerf = getValue( intArray, 30 ); // will compile, run-time error
}
```

Return-type as Reference or Pointer

THE default mechanism for return-type is pass-by-value. For object-oriented programming, returning a pointer or reference to an object may be more desirable and more efficient. When a function is returning a pointer or a reference, the programmer should be aware of three pitfalls:

1. Returning a reference to a local object. The local object goes out of scope with the termination of the function. The reference is left aliased to undefined memory. For example:

```
// this code will not work
Person * createPerson( char *  name)
{         // the declaration below declares p as a pointer to Person
          // and the function Person() creates a Person object
      Person *p = Person( name );
      return p;
          // note: p is also undefined when the function is terminated
}
```

2. The value returned is the actual lvalue of the object. Any modification performed by the calling function will change the object being returned. For example:

```
int&  getValue( int * intArray, int j)
{    // this function returns the reference to the j-th element of the
     // intArray
     return  intArray[j];
}

     // let there be an array of digits
```

```
int dArray[] = {9, 8, 7, 6, 5, 4, 3, 2, 1}
    // here is a short program that will change the value of dArray
main()
{
    getValue( dArray, 0 ) ++;
    // this will change the value for dArray[0] from 9 to 10.
    // does* the programmer intend to do this?
}
```

3. Returning a reference to a dynamic object. The calling program is responsible for deleting the object when it is no longer needed. For example:

```
// Method associated with a class People
Person *People::createperson(char *name)
{
    Person *p = new Person(name) // creates a person in dynamic storage
    return p;                    // returns a pointer to the person
}
```

```
// In the main program (or in another object) we make a local instance
// of people and call the
// createPerson function
main()
{
    People *pp=People();            //create a local instance of people
    Person *aPerson == pp->createPerson("Michael"); // create a person
    ... // Use the person here
    delete aPerson;  // needed to prevent a memory leak
}
```

Casting

IN C++, many of the library functions specify the argument type as a reference. However, in object-oriented programming, programmers deal mostly with pointers. Usually, the function deals with a collection of objects, and collections are easier to handle as an array of pointers. For example, relationships usually return a collection (i.e., array) of pointers to objects. The operator *, used as a unary operator, will cast a pointer to a reference. For example, let us assume we have the following two methods that belong to different objects:

```
Collision::detect_collision (GO_formation* f, Ball* b)
```

and

```
Lib_Collider::collide ( GO_formation& form)
```

If we need the service of collide in the detect_collision method, how do we do it?

```
Collision::detect_collision (GO_formation* f, Ball* b)
{
    Lib_Collider collider;
    collider.collide(*f)
        // here f is dereferenced into an address
}
```

Const and Defaults

Const

The proper use of the const keyword will improve the robustness of C++ code. Const controls side effects in the language and is used to replace macro definitions in the language. This is very important if you plan to use a symbolic debugger because #define is processed by the preprocessor and its name is not available to the debugger. For example:

```
main()
{
    #define Min 1              // this makes Min a constant
                               // Min is not defined for the debugger
    const int Max=10;          // this makes Max a constant
                               // Max is defined for the debugger

}
```

Min is not available to a symbolic debugger because this is translated by the preprocessor to a 1. Hence, use of #define for constants is not recommended.

Const is also used to guarantee that the function will not alter an argument passed to it by a reference or pointer. For example:

```
void function1( Window& win1 )
{
    //   C++ will allow you to modify data members
    //   of the instance win1.
}

void function2( const Window& win2 )
{
    //   C++ will not allow you to modify data members
    //   of the instance win2.
}
```

Another use of const is to declare a function that will not alter the data within the object. This is important because when a function that accepts a const pointer to a class as a formal argument, it means that the function may only access a const function of that class. For example:

```
class Point
{
public:
    int  X( )    { return  x_value;    }
    void  X( int new_x )  { x_value = new_x }
private:
    int  x_value;
    int  y_value;
}

void function1( const Point& p )
{
    Point  local_pt;  int  local_num;
    local_pt = p;           // Legal
    local_num =  p.X();     // Illegal because X() does not promise to
                            // not change p
    p.X( 14 );              // Illegal because X() changes p

}
```

However, when the get value function is declared const (must be done in the function prototype in the .h file):

```
class Point
{
public:
    int  X( )  const { return  x_value;    }
    void  X( int new_x )  { x_value = new_x }
private:
    int  x_value;
    int  y_value;
}

void function1( const Point& p )
{
    Point  local_pt;  int  local_num
    local_pt = p;               // Legal
    local_num =  p.X();         // Legal
    p.X( 14 );                  // Illegal
}
```

The keyword const may be used in two positions in a pointer declaration, as follows:

```
char* const  pointer1="Constant Pointer";
const char* pointer2="Constant Data";
const char* const pointer3="Constant Data and Constant Pointer";
char*   pointer4;
```

In the preceding examples, const to the left of the * means constant data, while const to the right of the * means a constant pointer.

Default Initializers

A function may provide default argument initalizers for one or more of its arguments by using the initialization syntax within a signature. In object-oriented programming, default initializers are usually used only in constructors.

Identifiers Scope

RECALL that an identifier is a name for a data item or object. The identifier must be unique when used, because the program usually uses the identifier to access the data (rvalue). This does not mean, however, that a name can be used only once in a program. A name can be reused if there is some context to distinguish between different instances of the name. A good example of using context is overloading a function name, as in the following:

```
void     setSex(char );
void     setSex(int );
```

This example shows the signature of a function being used as a context. The two functions have the same name (setSex), so the name is overloaded. However, each function has a unique signature.

A second and more general context is *scope*. C++ supports three kinds of scope: *file scope, local scope,* and *class scope.* A name may be reused in a distinct scope; each variable has an associated scope that, together with the name, uniquely identifies that variable. A variable is visible (accessible) only to the code within its scope. For example, a local variable declared within a compound statement is accessible only by the statements within the compound statement.

Local scope is that portion of the program contained within the definition of a function. Each function represents a distinct local scope. Furthermore, within a function, each compound statement (or block) containing one or more declaration statements represents an associated local scope. Local block scopes may be nested. The argument list is treated as being within the local scope of the function.

Class scope occurs when every class maintains its own associated scope. Within class scope are the names of all its class members.[4]

---

[4]   Both data members and member functions are within the class scope.

File scope is the outermost scope of a program; it encloses both local and class scope. It is that portion of the program that is not contained within a class or a function definition.

A variable defined at the file scope that is accessible to the entire program is referred to as a *global variable*. Global variables should not be used in object-oriented programming because they violate both the encapsulation and information-hiding principles. In spite of all this, there may be situations where it makes sense to access variables or functions not within the scope of the code. What mechanism in C++ supports this? The *scope operator* ("::") supports the ability of a line of code to access public functions or variables in another scope. An example of an object-oriented use of the scope operator is provided in a later chapter when static members are discussed.

Recommended Approach

IN writing the code for the class definition in the header file, the data members are defined, but the functions are only declared. We must now define the functions. A function can be defined in either the .h file[5] or the .C file.

Definition in .h file

The definition of an inline function[6] within the header file may be either placed within the class body or defined outside the class body. When the definition of a member function is placed inside the class body, the function is automatically handled as an inline function. For example:

```
class Person
{
 public:    // member functions
     char*      getName();
     char       getSex();
     int        getAge() { return age }
     void       setSex(char s)
     void       setAge(int a) { age = a; }
private:    // data members
     char name[40];
     char sex;
     int  age, height, weight;
}
```

---

[5] All functions defined in the class declaration in a .h file are inline functions. In this case, code will be generated in line to replace the function call written by the programmer. This will cause the program to run faster, but it will take more storage and execution space.

[6] Inline functions should be only a few lines of code. In fact, inline is only a suggestion to the compiler, who will actually decide if inline will be enforced.

In this example, the getAge function returns the age of the person as an integer. The setAge function changes the age of the person to the first and only argument passed as part of the signature; it does not return anything. Furthermore, both functions are inline.

If the function definition contains more than two statements, it is advised that the function be defined outside of the class body. However, to do this requires using the scope operator to identify the function as a member of the correct class. Furthermore, if the function is to be inline, it must explicitly declare itself to be inline. For example:

```
inline void Person::setSex(char s)
{          // sex can only be m or f
    if ( s == 'm' || s == 'f' )
          { sex = s; return; }
    else
          {  // error in input, ignore request
             return;
          }
}
```

The preceding code defines setSex as an inline function that is defined outside of the class body. Normally, when this is done, the code follows the class definition.[7]

Note that an inline function has some of the properties of a function in that:

- It is a class member.
- Type-checking is done at compile time.
- Overloading is permitted on the function by value.

An inline function also has some of the properties of a macro in that:

- Code is expanded in the calling object.
- Code is linked at compile or link time and not at run time.
- More code space is used.
- Execution time is faster.
- There is no recursion.

The most common functions to inline are the get and set functions because the overhead of a function call far exceeds inlining the couple of instructions for these functions. However, the reader should be aware that inlining violates the encapsulation principle. If you change the .h file of a class, all the other classes may recompile because they are tied to the .h file via the inline function of that class.

---

[7] The extra code validates the input; nowadays, it is usually done in the user interface. The business application may assume that what they are getting is a legal value.

Definition in .C file

In practice, most application functions will be defined in the .C file[8]. Following is an example of placing the definition of setAge in the .C file.[9]

```
void  Person::setAge(int  a)
{
     age = a;
}
```

To help us code the function body, the following coding rules for instance member functions are given:

1. A member function has access to:
   - All members (data and functions) of the object
   - All arguments passed to it via the calling object
   - All local variables within its (method) scope
   - Global variables within its class scope
   - *this*, which is a pseudo-data member of any object (contains the address of the object)
2. When you need to declare local variables, keep variables at the smallest possible scope.
3. When you need to access a function of a superclass, place the superclass name and scope operator before the function name.
4. To increase robustness of code, use the const keyword appropriately. Const should be used to:
   - Replace macro definitions
   - Guarantee that functions will not alter an object passed by reference or pointer
   - Declare a function that will not alter the object

To close this section, we will apply the coding rules to our example as follows:

```
class Person
{
 public:    // member functions
     char*       getName()  const { return name; }
     char        getSex()   const { return sex; }
     int         getAge()   const { return age; }
     void        setSex( const char s) { sex = s; }
     void        setAge(const int a) { age = a; }
```

---

[8] .C is an UNIX convention, .cpp is a MicroSoft convention, and .pp is a Turbo C++ convention.

[9] Neither function is inline; inline functions must be defined in the .h file.

```
private:     // data members
    char name[40];
    char sex;
    int   age, height, weight;
}
```

■ ■ SUMMARY

TO implement the service specification, we can place the code in either the .h file or the .C file.[10] The .h file is appropriate when we have a few lines of code and having this code inlined would be better than a separate subroutine call. However, most application functions should be in the .C file, as they are usually more than a few lines of code and subroutine calls are the most effective way of implementing these functions.

Coding the service specification is more restrictive than coding a procedural function. The rules for coding a function[11] are:

1. A member function has access to:
   - All members (data and functions) of the object
   - All arguments passed to it via the calling object
   - All local variables within its (method) scope
   - Class global (static) variables within its class scope
   - *this*, which is a pseudo-data member of any object (contains the address of the object)
2. When you need to declare local variables, keep variables at the smallest possible scope.
3. When you need to access a function of a superclass, place the superclass name and scope operator before the function name.
4. Const should be used to:[12]
   - Replace macro definitions
   - Guarantee that the function will not alter an object passed by reference or pointer
   - Declare a function that will not alter the object

---

[10] If the code is going to be part of a library, putting code in the .h file allows a client of that library to change the code; if it is in the .C file, then the client cannot change it.

[11] These are the guidelines for coding an instance member function; not all the rules apply to a static function. The rules for a static function are left to the reader.

[12] To increase robustness of code, use the const keyword appropriately.

CHAPTER

17

Implementing Dynamic Behavior

*W*ho controls the past controls the future. Who controls the present controls the past.

George Orwell

One of the major goals in our analysis was specifying the behavior of all the services associated with a class. In the previous chapter, we learned how to turn a static behavioral specification into executable code. We captured the definition of static functions. In this chapter, we will see how to turn a dynamic behavioral specification into executable code. We will discuss capturing the definitions of the functions (i.e., to capture the dynamic behaviors of the services that are best modeled with a state machine).

In writing the code for a dynamic class, it is best to use a state machine that is part of a library supplied by a third party. If such a library is available, use it. This book does not cover the implementation of dynamic behavior using such libraries, as the exact mechanism will depend upon the particular product used. Instead, we will show you a simplified way of writing code for a state model for instructional purposes. In the code, we do not address the issue of atomic action that may not be interrupted; this is beyond the scope of this book.

Elements of Dynamic Behavior

IN this chapter, we capture dynamic behavior in the form of code. This is perhaps one of the most complicated aspects of object-oriented programming because we are talking about coding functions that implement multiple kinds of behavior. Our task is straightforward:

1. We must capture information about states.
   - Code identifying all of the allowed states
   - Track the current state
2. We must implement the actions performed.
   - The actions themselves are state-independent
3. We must implement the transition semantics.
   - Transition guard conditions
   - Exit action
   - Transition actions
   - Entry actions
   - Do actions

We begin by examining the transformation of a simple state model into code. We then extend that to include nested substates.

Simple State Diagrams

To help illustrate implementing dynamic behavior, we use the microwave oven example[1] developed in Chapter 8 and illustrated in Figure 17-1. The approach taken here will consist of the following activities:

1. Implement the actions performed by the object.
2. Introduce an enumerated data type for capturing state.
3. Add a state variable to the class.
4. Introduce helper functions for managing state entry and exit actions.
5. Implement the event handlers (method functions) for responding to events.

Not covered here is the establishment of the initial state as part of initialization (covered in the next chapter).

Implementing dynamic behavior is a matter of selecting the appropriate set of static behaviors to execute. As a result, we must first implement the actions identified in

---

[1] For instructional purposes on state model coding, we will assume that the microwave oven is the object; i.e., there is no refinement of the oven class. If you want to see a refined solution to the microwave oven-example, please see Chapter 23.

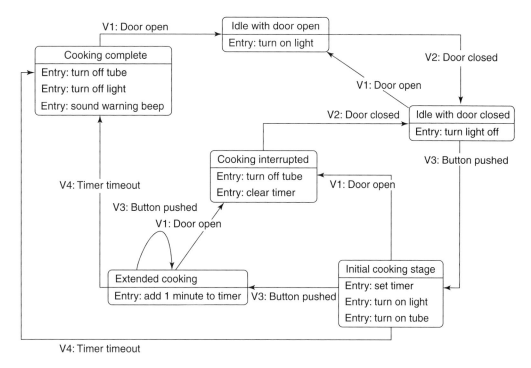

FIGURE 17-1 State diagram for microwave oven from chapter 8.

the state diagram. These actions are state-independent and are implemented using the methods described in the previous chapter. There will be one method for each action that an object can perform.

From the diagram we can see that we will have methods for turning on and off the light, turning on and off the tube, adding a minute to the timer, clearing the timer, setting the timer, and sounding a beep. These methods are declared as follows:

```
class Microwave {
    protected:
      void turnOnLight();
      void turnOffLight();
      void turnOnTube();
      void turnOffTube();
      void addMinuteToTimer();
      void clearTimer();
      void setTimer();
      void soundBeep();
    ...
    }
```

The methods are declared protected because they are associated with state actions performed within the object, and other objects should not be able to invoke them directly. This is one aspect of information hiding—we keep the basic primitive actions localized to the object and require others to request more abstract services of the object.

We capture the various states accessible to the object by defining an enumerated data type that possesses a value for each distinct state. An object will use a data member to track the current state. Some guidelines to follow are:

1. Create a state variable.
   - The number of theoretical states are too large.
   - When you add attributes that are state-independent, it has no effect.
   - States are easier to create than repartitioning of the variables.
2. Name the state to capture accurately the condition of the class.
   - People will make assumptions based on the name.

Future designers/programmers will make extensions based on their interpretation of the name. Example code for the microwave oven follows:

```
class Microwave {
    enum state { InitialCooking, Complete, IdleDoorOpen, IdleDoor-
    Closed, Interrupted, Extended }; protected:
     state myState;
  ...
  }
```

The second line defines the enumeration as a new data type, state, with six allowed values: InitialCooking, Complete, IdleDoorOpen, IdleDoorClosed, Interrupted, and Extended. The data type has scope only within the class. The fourth line defines a data member of type state. This data member is the mechanism by which the state is captured. The only allowed data values are those defined within the enumeration.

Two additional helper methods are defined to capture the behaviors associated with entering and exiting states. These methods are declared as protected. All actions to be performed on state entry (or exit) are now localized to one method.[2] This frees us

---

[2] Capturing all of the entry or exit behaviors for all of our states in one method might be viewed by some as increasing coupling, but we are actually decreasing coupling by introducing a new abstraction. Code for capturing entry into a particular state is localized in this one method as opposed to coding a duplicate within every method that produces a transition. The alternative, for objects with complex behaviors, would be to introduce a single method entry or exit for every state. This has the effect of significantly increasing the overall complexity of our object. In this example, it is the difference between adding one method and six methods.

from having to repeat the same set of code in multiple places within our program. The code for this follows:

```
void Microwave::onEntry() {
    switch (myState) {
    case InitialCooking:
        setTimer();
        turnOnLight();
        turnOnTube();
        break;
    case Complete:
        turnOffTube();
        turnOffLight();
        soundBeep();
        break;
    case IdleDoorOpen:
        turnOnLight();
        break;
    case IdleDoorClosed:
        turnOffLight();
        break;
    case Interrupted:
        turnOffLight();
        clearTimer();
        break;
    case Extended:
        addMinuteToTimer();
        break;
    default:
        // should signal an error here
    };
}
```

This code utilizes the switch statement of C++ to select the appropriate actions to perform based on the current data value of the myState data member. Some guidelines follow:

1. Use switch statements over if-then or if-then-else statements.
   - If-then clauses will not scale.
   - If-then-else clauses are not easy to read and can lead to subtle bugs.
2. Always provide a default case.
3. Do not let one case clause run into another.

Two key points should be made: Every case should end with a break statement and there should always be a default condition in the switch statement. Even though some states will not have actions to perform on entry and on exit, it is reasonable to include those states in the helper methods because it will make maintenance of the code easier. Similar code can be written for an onExit() method and onTransition() method.[3]

The class definition will be modified to declare these helper methods:

```
class Microwave {
        enum state { InitialCooking, Complete, IdleDoorOpen,
        IdleDoorClosed, Interrupted, Extended };
        protected:
                void turnOnLight();
                void turnOffLight();
                void turnOnTube();
                void turnOffTube();
                void addMinuteToTimer();
                void clearTimer();
                void setTimer();
                void soundBeep();
                state myState;            // state data member
                void onEntry();           // helper method for managing state
    ...
        }
```

This has implemented the logic to invoke the entry and exit actions to the various states.

It is now necessary to introduce a method for each event to which the object must respond. There are four messages to which the microwave oven must respond: door open, door close, push button, and timer time-out. Capturing these messages will introduce four new methods, doorOpen(), doorClose(), buttonPush(), and timerTimeout().[4] There are no arguments in the methods because the corresponding messages do not have any arguments. In the case in which arguments had been present in a message, the method implementing it would include arguments. The resulting header for the Microwave class is as follows:

```
class Microwave {
        enum state { InitialCooking, Complete, IdleDoorOpen,
        IdleDoorClosed, Interrupted, Extended }; protected:
                void turnOnLight();
                void turnOffLight();
                void turnOnTube();
                void turnOffTube();
                void addMinuteToTimer();
```

---

[3]   In this example, both onExit() method and onTransition() are not required because we do not have any states that require processing on exit, nor do we have any transition actions.

[4]   We assume that these events are external to the "Oven" object.

```
            void clearTimer();
            void setTimer();
            void soundBeep();
            state myState;              // state data member
            void onEntry();            // helper method for managing state
        public:
            void doorOpen();
            void doorClose();
            void buttonPush();
            void timerTimeout();
    ...
    }
```

These methods are declared as public because they are the interfaces by which other objects invoke dynamic behavior.

The state-specific code for handling an event can be rather complex. It must perform the checks for the guard conditions, and if the guard conditions are met, it will then perform the sequence of actions required for the transition. In the case of the microwave oven, our task is simplified by the fact that we don't have guard conditions on the transitions. In this case, we implement the switch condition to select the appropriate code for the current state. This is similar to what was done for the helper methods. The cases will key off the current state to select the state-specific handler for the event. The logic is captured in code in the following fashion:

```
    void Microwave::doorOpen() {
        switch (myState) {
        case InitialCooking:
            myState = Interrupted;
            onEntry();
            break;
        case Complete:
            myState = idle;
            onEntry();
            break;
        case IdleDoorOpen:
            // Shouldn't get here, the door is already opened!
            break;
        case IdleDoorClosed:
            myState = IdleDoorOpen;
            onEntry();
            break;
        case Interrupted:
            // Shouldn't get here, the door is already opened!
            break;
        case Extended:
            myState = Interrupted;
```

```
                onEntry();
        default:
            // signal an error condition here!
        };
    }
```

All states should be represented in this case statement because state is an internal property of an object, and event generators will send the event to the object without knowing the internal state. As a result, every state should handle the event in some fashion, even if it just means that the object ignores the event.

In some cases, an event can result in any one of several transitions based on the guard condition. To capture the logic of guarded transitions, we construct an if-else condition statement inside the case statement for each particular state. The if-else set of conditionals is structured from the most restrictive condition to the least restrictive condition. This assures that the appropriate transitions are performed for a given set of circumstance. An example follows:

```
if (cond1) {          // most restrictive condition
    onExit();         // must do the exit action
    action1();        // must do the transition action
    state = state2;   // set the new state
    onEntry();        // perform the entry action for new state
}
else if (cond2) {     // less restrictive condition
    onExit();         // must do the exit action
    action2();        // must do the transition action
    state = state3;   // set the new state
    onEntry();        // perform the entry action
}
else                  // least restrictive condition
{
    // must handle the default case
}
```

This code performs the exit action for the past state, the action associated with the transition, and the entry action for the new state for each possible transition out of the past state for a given event. The final else condition handles the case where the state has a default action that it performs for that event. The "do action" needs to be handled differently because it is not part of the atomic action and is a long, continuous action that can be interrupted. Internal transitions are also not handled. Both are beyond the scope of this book.

Nested State Diagrams

Implementing nested state diagrams is only slightly more sophisticated than implementing simple state diagrams. The basic principles are identical. In the same way that

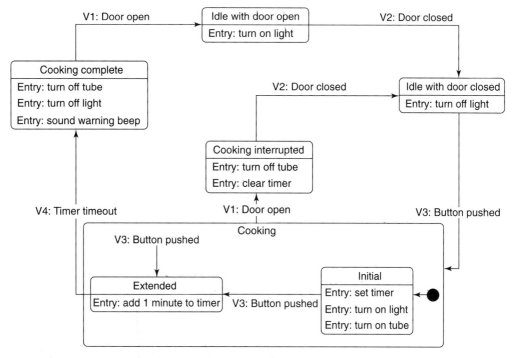

FIGURE 17-2   **Microwave example utilizing nested state diagrams.**

we implemented state as a state variable, we will use a substate data member with an enumeration for identifying the substates.[5]   In this section, we will use a modified version of the microwave oven that incorporates nested states within a cooking state, as illustrated in Figure 17-2.

   In exactly the same manner as was done for the simple state diagram, we first code all actions that can be performed by our microwave oven. The results are:

```
class Microwave {
    protected:
        void turnOnLight();
        void turnOffLight();
        void turnOnTube();
        void turnOffTube();
        void addMinuteToTimer();
        void clearTimer();
        void setTimer();
        void soundBeep();
    ...
    }
```

---

[5]   There are other ways to implement substates that are beyond the scope of this book.

The code for this case is identical with the previous example.

In this example, we now have five primary states, with one of them having two substates. We shall introduce two enumerated data types to capture this information. One enumerated data type will capture the primary states while the other will capture the substates associated with cooking:

```
class Microwave {
    enum state {Cooking, Complete, IdleDoorOpen, IdleDoorClosed,
               Extended };
    enum cookingState { NotInState, Initial, Extended};
    protected:
        state myState;
        cookingState myCookingState;
...
}
```

As this example illustrates, the cooking state has a third state that is not illustrated in the diagram. The intent is to capture an implied semantics concerning the situation in which the microwave oven is not in the cooking state.

As was done previously, we declare the same set of helper functions—onEntry() and onExit(). However, there are differences in their implementation to account for the substates for the cooking state. In addition, we add helper methods for the cooking substates:

```
class Microwave {
    enum state { InitialCooking, Complete, IdleDoorOpen,
        IdleDoorClosed, Interrupted, Extended };
    protected:
        void turnOnLight();
        void turnOffLight();
        void turnOnTube();
        void turnOffTube();
        void addMinuteToTimer();
        void clearTimer();
        void setTimer();
        void soundBeep();
        state myState;              // state data member
        void onEntry();             // helper method for managing state
        void onExit();              // must have this now
        void onCookingEntry();      // new helper method
        void onCookingExit();       // new helper method
...
}
```

The revised code for the onEntry() method follows:

```
void Microwave::onEntry() {
    switch (myState) {
    case Cooking:
        onCookingEntry(); // This now lets us take care of managing /
                          // entry into cooking separately.
        break;
    case Complete:
        turnOffTube();    // this is the onEntry code
        turnOffLight();   // this is the onEntry code
        soundBeep();      // this is the onEntry code
        break;
    case IdleDoorOpen:
        turnOnLight();    // this is the onEntry code
        break;
    case IdleDoorClosed:
        turnOffLight();   // this is the onEntry code
        break;
    case Interrupted:
        turnOffLight();   // this is the onEntry code
        clearTimer();     // this is the onEntry code
        break;
    default:
        // should signal an error here
    };
}
```

The major difference from the previous example is that we now call a helper method for entry into the cooking state.[6] The code for the onCookingEntry() is responsible for setting the substate information and performing the entry actions required for the specific substate. In our case, this is simple because there is only a single entry point and no history:

```
void Microwave::onCookingEntry() {
    switch (myCookingState) {
    case NotInState:
        myCookingState = Initial;
        onCookingEntry();
        break;
```

---

6   This example is rather trivial in the sense that cooking only has two substates. However, when a state has multiple substates and re-entry conditions based on past history, these methods can become quite complex. The separation of managing substates into separate methods allows us to manage that complexity by focusing on smaller portions of the problem at any given time.

```
case Initial:
    setTimer();       // this is the onEntry code
    TurnOnLight();    // this is the onEntry code
    TurnOnTube();     // this is the onEntry code
    break;
case Extended:
    addMinuteToTimer();  // this is the onEntry code
    break;
default:
    // shouldn't get here!
    break;
};
}
```

If our microwave oven had more complex behavior while cooking, we might have to establish the appropriate entry substate and then use a switch statement to handle the variety of behaviors expected based on the specific entry substate.

We modify the onExit() method so that it calls the onCookingExit() method, which will capture the exit conditions for substates:[7]

```
void Microwave::onExit() {
switch (myState) {
case Cooking:
    onCookingExit();
    break;
case Complete:
    break;
case IdleDoorOpen:
    break;
case IdleDoorClosed:
    break;
case Interrupted:
    break;
default:
    // should signal an error here
};
}
```

This allows us to capture more complex behaviors in the cooking state should they exist (or get added in the future). The implementation for this microwave oven sets the myCookingState data member to the NotInState value.

---

[7] The onExit() method was unnecessary in the simple state diagram because none of the states incorporated exit conditions. The version of the microwave presented here does not have explicit onExit actions, but has an implicit one associated with substate management.

Finally, we have to implement the handler code for the events. This is similar to what was done before, but we now have to take into account the substates. This can be done in one of two manners:

1. Incorporate an additional switch statement within the primary event handler code
2. Provide a helper method that captures handling events within a state

If there are not many substates, the first approach may be preferable. In general, however, the second approach is the better approach. We will demonstrate the second approach here for the button pushed event. First we declare the appropriate substate handler methods:

```
class Microwave {
    enum state { InitialCooking, Complete, IdleDoorOpen,
        IdleDoorClosed, Interrupted, Extended };
    protected:
        void turnOnLight();
        void turnOffLight();
        void turnOnTube();
        void turnOffTube();
        void addMinuteToTimer();
        void clearTimer();
        void setTimer();
        void soundBeep();
        state myState;          // state data member
        void onEntry();         // helper method for managing state
        void onExit();          // must have this now
        void onCookingEntry();  // new helper method
        void onCookingExit();   // new helper method
        void buttonPushed();
        void doorOpen();
        void doorClose();
        void timerTimeout();
        void buttonDownInCooking();
        void doorOpenInCooking();
        void timerTimeoutInCooking();
    ...
}
```

The button Pushed() method will call invoke the appropriate state-specific behavior. In the case of the cooking state, it will invoke the buttonPushedInCooking() method. This is demonstrated in the following code fragment:

```
void Microwave::buttonPushed() {
    switch (myState) {
    case Cooking:
```

```
            buttonPushedInCooking();
            break;
        case Complete:
    ...
        };
    }
```

The buttonPushedInCooking() method implements the handling associated with the substates. This is shown in the following code:

```
void Microwave::buttonPushedInCooking() {
    switch (myCookingState) {
    case NotInState:
        // This should not happen
        break;
    case Initial:
        onCookingExit(); // In case we have exit condition
        myCookingState = Extended;
        onCookingEnter();
        break;
    case Extended:
        onCookingExit(); // transition to same state.
        onCookingEnter();
        break;
    default:
        break;
    };
}
```

The case for the Extended substate illustrates how transitions to self are implemented. First we execute the exit method for leaving the state and then execute the entry method for returning to the state.

Concurrent State Diagrams

Implementing concurrent state diagrams is only slightly more sophisticated than implementing simple state diagrams. The basic principles are identical. In the same way that we implemented state as a state variable, we will use concurrent threads to capture each of the concurrent state models. However, threaded programming in C++ is outside the scope of this book.

Recommended Approach

IN writing the code for a dynamic class, it is best to use a state machine that is part of a library supplied by a third party. However, if this is not available, you can use the previous sample code as a reference model for building a state machine of your own.

To help us code the state machine, the following coding rules are given:

1. Create a state variable.
   - The number of theoretical states are too large.
   - When you add attributes that are state-independent, it has no effect.
   - States are easier to create than repartioning of the variables.
2. Name the state to capture accurately the condition of the class.
   - People will make assumptions based on the name.
   - Future designers/programmers will make extensions based on their interpretation of the name.
3. Use switch statements over if-then or if-then-else statements.
   - If-then clauses will not scale.
   - If-then-else clauses are not easy to read and can lead to subtle bugs.
4. Always provide a default case.
5. Do not let one case clause run into another.
   - Use a break at the end of a clause.
   - Create private functions (subroutines) for common logic shared across clauses.

■ ■ SUMMARY

TO implement the state model for a class, we can use a third-party state machine template or we can write our own state machine using the reference model discussed previously.

Coding the state machine is more restrictive than coding a procedural function. The rules for coding a state model are:

1. Create a state variable.
2. Name the state to capture accurately the condition of the class.
3. Use switch statements over if-then or if-then-else statements.
4. Always provide a default case.
5. Use a break at the end of a clause.
6. Create private functions (subroutines) for common logic shared across clauses.

Instantiating and Deleting Objects

> *Had I been present at the Creation, I would have given some useful hints for the better ordering of the universe.*
>
> Alfonso the Wise, *King of Castile*

In the previous implementation chapters, we learned how to implement classes and their associated methods. However, actions and tasks that we expect an application/ system to perform are usually on specific objects. In fact, we explained the object-oriented communication and control mechanisms as a message-passing paradigm between objects. We should expect that the execution of the program does not operate on classes, but on a specific object(s). For a program to be able to operate on a specific object, it must be able to create and destroy it. In this chapter, we will learn how objects are created and destroyed by the program.

Introduction

AN object needs memory and some initial values when it is used by the program and/ or function. For most of the native and derived data types supplied by the language, the language provides for this through declarations that are also definitions. For example:

```
void Compute::funx()
{
    int n = 300;
    short z[100];
    struct  noClass { int i1, int i2 }  inG2 = { 5, 70 };
      . . .
}
```

All of the objects (i.e., n, z[100], and inG2) are created at function (block) entry when the function funx() is called. Typically, memory space is taken from a run-time system stack. Assuming that we are on a system that defines integers to be 4 bytes and short to be 2 bytes, the int object n would be allocated 4 bytes off the stack, the array of short object z would be allocated 200 bytes off the stack, and the noClass object inG2 would be allocated 8 bytes off the stack. In each case, the compiler will generate the code for the construction and initialization of these objects. Furthermore, because these are local variables, the compiler will generate the code to deallocate these objects upon exit from the function.

In creating user-defined data types (classes), the user of these data types (classes) can expect similar management of the class-defined objects. A class needs a mechanism to specify object creation and object destruction behavior, so that other functions can use objects of this class in a manner similar to the native data types.

Constructors

A constructor is a special member function with the same name as the class. It allows the client programmer to initialize data values of data members of the object, change values of static variables of a class, and create aggregate objects.[1] It will also involve allocating free store when the keyword *new* is used with the constructor. A constructor is called or invoked when its associated type is used in a definition. It is also invoked when pass-by-value is used to pass an argument of this type to a function.

A constructor may be overloaded and can take on arguments; however, it may neither specify a return type nor explicitly return a value. Overloading is commonly used as a vehicle to provide a set of alternative initializations. For example, let us declare three constructors for the class Person. The first constructor will initialize the private data member sex, the second constructor will initialize the private data member age, and the third constructor will initialize the private data member name. Consider the following example:

---

[1]   A constructor is called only at instantiation (i.e., when an object is created).

```
class Person
{
    public:
        Person( const char inputSex );
        Person( const int inputAge );
        Person( const char * const input_name );
            . . .
}
```

In this example, there are three constructors. The first one takes one argument, a single character. The second one takes one argument, an integer, and the third one takes one argument, a pointer to a character array. The definitions of the three constructors are as follows:

```
Person::Person( const char inputSex )
{       // note:  the other data members (name, age) are undefined.
    sex = inputSex;
}

Person::Person( const int inputAge )
{       // note:  the other data members (name, sex) are undefined.
    age = inputAge;
}

Person::Person(  const char * const input_name )
{       // note:  the other data members (sex, age) are undefined.
    name = new char[strlen(n) + 1];
    strcpy(name, n);
}
```

Note that the constructor has no return type and cannot use a return-expression statement. Because initialization is usually linear code, the return statement is usually not written. Moreover, there is usually nothing complicated about the constructor code.

The constructor's power lies in the mechanism that invokes it implicitly for each object of the class. It is invoked when its class type is used in a definition and when pass-by-value is used for an argument of this type in a function call. When the function is invoked, the mechanism will allocate the storage necessary to contain the nonstatic data members defined in the class. It will allocate storage either from the stack or the heap based on whether the keyword new is used.

If no constructor is declared with a class, the compiler provides a default constructor. This constructor requires no arguments and will only allocate the space; it will not initialize any data members. One should take care when relying on the default constructor. Data members of built-in types are not guaranteed to be initialized. It is wise to initialize all data members in the constructor. For example, a more practical constructor for the Person class is:

```
Person( const char *    const input_name
                        const char inputSex
                        const int inputAge
                        const int inputWeight
                        const int inputHeight )
```

The preceding constructor will initialize all of the data members. However, classes with a large number of data members that use a constructor to define an object require programmers to attend to every small detail of the class. It would be nice to be able to provide default values that are, although not universally applicable, appropriate in a majority of the cases. This would free programmers to enter only the applicable values that apply to their function.

A constructor (and any function) may specify a default value for one or more of its arguments using the initialization syntax within the signature. For example, consider the following signature for constructor of Person that initializes only the name, sex, and age of a Person object:

```
Person(char* n, char s='U',
            int a= -1);
```

This constructor provides default argument initializers that can be invoked with or without a corresponding actual argument. If an argument is provided, it overrides the default value; otherwise, the default value is used. For example:

```
main()
{
    Person Baby1("Undecided"); // This is a baby in infancy
    Person Baby2("Susan", 'F'); //  This is a baby girl in infancy
    Person Bill("Bill Gates", 'M', 35); // This is Bill Gates in middle age
    Person Rich("Rich", , 50); // This is an illegal use of default values
    Person p50(, , 50); // This is an illegal use of default values
};
```

Note that the arguments to the call are resolved positionally. A programmer must then do the following:

■ Specify the default initializer for all or only a subset of its arguments.
■ Supply the rightmost uninitalized argument with default initializer before any arguments to its left may be supplied.
■ Specify the default initializer(s) in the function declaration contained in the .h file, and not in the function definition in the .C file.
■ Arrange the arguments so that those most likely to take user-specified values occur first.[2]

---

[2] This is done because once a default is used for an argument, all arguments to the right of it must also be defaulted.

Destructors

A destructor is a member function whose name is the class name preceded by the tilde (~). This function is the complement of the constructor and is used to "deinitialize" and "destruct" an object of the class. It performs any necessary cleanup before the object is destroyed. Typically, it is used to destroy complex or aggregate objects, or change values of the static variables of a class. Like a constructor, a destructor may neither specify a return type nor explicitly return a value. Destructors are implicitly invoked when objects of their class must be destroyed. This happens upon block exit and function exit when an object of the class has been declared a local variable.

A destructor may not take any arguments and, therefore, may not be overloaded. For example:

```
class Person
{
    public:
        Person (int AnAge, char SomeSex)  {Age = AnAge; Sex = SomeSex;}
        Person () {Age = 0; Sex = 'b';}
        ~Person ();      // this is the destructor
    private:
        int Age; char Sex;
};
```

Note that in the preceding example there are two constructors (both inline functions) and one destructor.

The destructor has no return type and cannot return a value. For example:

```
class String
{
    public:
        String (const char * s, int len) { //this is the constructor
            length = len;
            ptrtostr = new char[ len + 1 ]; //this allocates space
            strcpy( str, s );               //this copies the string
        }
        ~String () {     // this is the destructor
                    delete str; }
    private:
        int length; char * ptrtostr;
};
```

A destructor mechanism is automatically invoked whenever an object of its class goes out of scope or the delete operator is applied to the class pointer. First, the mechanism calls the destructor function. After it has executed, the mechanism deallocates the storage associated with that object. However, an object created by using the new operator is always within scope; it needs to be explicitly deleted. Because the "str" memory is allocated via the new operator, the String destructor must explicitly delete it. However, the storage for length does not have to be deleted as it is a native data type.

The delete operator comes in two forms:

```
delete expression
delete [ ] expression
```

The expression is usually a pointer variable used in the assignment statement from a new operation. The brackets are used when the new operator involves an array of objects. The bracketed delete ensures that the destructor mechanism is invoked on each object in the array. For example, consider the following:

```
String *ptr = new String( "new string",10);
```

You must then use the following delete statement—delete [ ] ptr;—before the array created by the String constructor goes out of scope to reclaim storage, or there will be memory leaks.

There are no constraints on what can be done within the destructor. In fact, a common programming technique is to put print statements within both the constructors and destructors. A programmer may cause it to execute any actions and any functions subsequent to the last use of the object.

When either a reference or a pointer to a class goes out of scope, the destructor mechanism is not invoked. In the case of pointers, the programmer must explicitly apply the delete operator to the pointer to delete the object. For example:

```
class Pers
{
    public:
        Pers (int AnAge, char SomeSex) {Age = AnAge; Sex = SomeSex;}
            // this is inline definition of method
        Pers () {Age = 0; Sex = 'b';}
        ~Pers ();
    private:
        int Age; char Sex;
};

    //code in a calling method
void f()
{
    Pers *joe = new Pers(32, 'm');
    Pers mary(21, 'f');
    Pers *kate = new Pers(50, 'f');
    Pers jim;
```

```
jim = Pers(19, 'm');
Pers *baby = new Pers();
delete joe, kate, baby;  //all pointers to objects
        // mary and jim are local variables and
        // will be deleted when the function goes out of scope
}
```

If the pointer to which a delete is applied does not address a class object (i.e., the pointer has a value of zero), the destructor mechanism is not invoked. It is unnecessary to write the following statement:

```
if ( pointer != 0) delete pointer;
```

If no destructor is declared with a class, the compiler provides a default destructor. One should take care when relying on the default destructor because it will not free up memory allocated by member functions during the life of the object.

We advise making all destructors of base classes virtual. If this is not done, there may be memory leaks, as illustrated in the following example:

```
Class A
{
    public:
            A();
            ~A();
};
Class B: public A
{
    public:
            B();
            ~B();
};
void funct()
{
    A* p = static_cast<A *>  new B();
    delete p;
}
```

In this example, the destructor that will be invoked on p will be the ~A().[3] However, making the destructors of A and B virtual will assure that the destructor for B will be invoked.

---

[3]   Note the use of static_cast in this example. This is a proper use of the static_cast operator—casting an object from its actual class to its superclass.

Using Constructors and Destructors Properly

NOW, let us look at how to use the constructor and destructor. There are two ways to create an instance (object) of a class:

1. On the stack as a local variable (instance), as in the following:

```
void    F1()
{
    Person p; // local to this function
    ....
};
```

2. On the heap, returning a pointer to the instance, as in the following:

```
void   F2()
{
    Person*  p = new Person; //outlives this function
        ....
};
```

Similarly, each of the two ways of constructing an instance has a corresponding way of destroying that instance:

1. On the stack as a local variable (instance), as in the following:

```
void    F1()
{
    Person p; // local to this function
        ....    // p is destroyed when it is out of scope
};
```

2. On the heap, returning a pointer to the instance, as in the following:

```
void    F2()
{
    Person*  p = new Person; //outlives this function
        ....
    delete p; //p is explicitly destroyed
};
```

The delete function does not have to be in the same function. However, when you leave it to another function and it does not remember to delete the object, there will be memory leaks (i.e., the object lives forever).

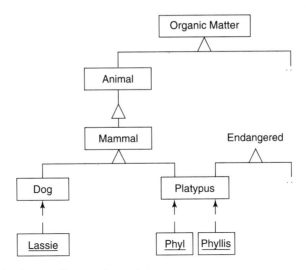

FIGURE 18-1 Inheritance diagram for a platypus.

Generalization and Constructors

LET us go back to the ancestor tree for Platypus, as shown in Figure 18-1. The ancestor tree has been modified to make Platypus inherit from both the Mammal and Endangered classes. Now, let us create an instance of Platypus and see how the constructors for the following classes are involved: Platypus, Mammal, Animal, OrganicMatter, and Endangered. Following are the class constructors:

```
Endangered::Endangered( )
        {           //initialization code for Endangered }


OrganicMatter::OrganicMatter( )
        {           //initialization code for OrganicMatter }

    Animal::Animal( ): OrganicMatter( )
            {           //initialization code for Animal  }
        Mammal::Mammal( ): Animal( )
        {   //initialization code for Mammal }
            Platypus::Platypus1( ): Mammal( ), Endangered( )
            {   //initialization code for Platypus  }
```

The appropriate superclass constructor(s) is specified in the constructor. Generalization/specialization using inheritance for implementation will be discussed in depth in a later chapter.

Recommended Approach

Creating an Object

An instance of a Class can be created in two ways:

1. On the stack as a local variable (instance), as in the following:

```
void    F1()
{
    Person p; // local to this function
    ....
};
```

2. On the heap, returning a pointer to the instance, as in the following:

```
void    F2()
{
    Person*  p = new Person; //outlives this function
    ....
};
```

We can use the array notation (" []") to create more than one instance:

```
void    F1()
{
    Person*  parray = new Person[10]        // 10 instances
    parray[0].getAge();                     // access first instance
}
```

This can only be used when you have a constructor that takes no arguments for the class Person.

Destroying an Object

When does an object get destroyed?

1. For objects that are allocated on the stack, the object is destroyed (the space on the stack for the object is released) when the object goes out-of-scope. A commonly used idiom to force the destruction of local instances is to wrap them with a scope. This can be useful with transaction-based applications. For example:

```
Create_win::multitran(cal)
{
    {
        Transaction t1;
```

```
                        /* some database code  */
    }    //    t1 destructor is called, which forces the commit of the
              // transaction

    {

         Transaction t2;
              /* some database code */
    }    //    t2 destructor is called, which forces the commit of the
              // transaction

}
```

2. For objects that are allocated on the heap, the object must be explicitly destroyed using the delete operator. Examples for the appropriate mechanism for destroying an object are:

   a. For a local variable (instance), when it goes out of scope:

```
void    F1()
{
     Person p; // local to this function
     ....      // p is destroyed when it is out of scope
};
```

   b. On the heap, using the delete operator:

```
void    F2()
{
     Person*  p = new Person; //outlives this function
         ....
     delete p; //p is explicitly destroyed
};
```

   c. Deleting all instances in an array using [ ]:

```
void    F1()
     {
     Person*  parray = new Person[10] //10 instances
     parray[0].getAge();  // access first instance
};

void    F2()
{
     ....
     delete [] parray; //all 10 instances are deleted
};
```

The delete operation may be performed from any function that has access to the object. In the last example, the parray of the Person objects was created in the first function, but deleted in the second function. Take care to ensure that other objects having access to this object are not left in a state in which they have an invalid pointer.

Coding Guidelines

THIS section summarizes coding guidelines on constructors and destructors:

Constructor Coding Guidelines

- Constructors create instances from a class definition.
- The instance space is allocated before any user-defined constructor is called.
- Constructors can be defined with values to initialize data members or to be passed to setup functions.
- Constructors implicitly return an instance of a class (local variable) or a pointer to an instance (when new is used).
- In coding the constructor, do not define a return type or make an explicit return.
- A class can have many constructors, each of which accepts different arguments.
- Array creating may only be used when there is a constructor with no arguments.
- Each class should define a default constructor (no args), a copy constructor (arg = a reference to the same class), and an assignment operator (if the class contains pointers).
- Constructors should be used for data member initialization.

Destructor Coding Guidelines

- There is only one destructor per class.
- If you do not write one, the compiler will provide a standard one, but it may not be what is needed.
- It deletes instance(s) of a class.
- The instance space is freed after any user-defined destructors are called. Do not free the instance space in your code.
- Destructors do not take any arguments.
- A destructor method should perform any necessary cleanup before an object is destroyed.
- Any type of operation can be performed within a destructor. Usually, destructors are used to destroy complex or aggregate objects, or change the values of the static variables of a class.
- It is to declare base class destructors as virtual functions.

■ ■ SUMMARY

WE use constructors and destructors to create and delete objects in our application. Following is a review of the earlier sections:

- To create an instance of a class, a special constructor operation should be used.
- Multiple constructors for a single class can be defined, distinguished by the number and types of their arguments.
- A constructor is executed whenever a new instance of a class is requested.
- Each class has one destructor.
- Destructors do not take any arguments.
- A destructor method should perform any necessary cleanup before an object is destroyed.
- Any type of operation can be performed within a constructor or destructor.

19

Implementing Generalization/Specialization

> N*o man is an island.*
>
> John Donne

In the previous chapter, we saw how an object is created (instantiated). To create objects properly, however, we also need to establish the proper relationships between objects. Now we will begin to look at implementing relationships. This chapter is devoted to the generalization/specialization relationship.

Inheritance

FROM a maintenance and development perspective, inheritance is the one mechanism that helps manage code sharing, code reuse, and code extensions. Through inheritance, developers can build new classes on top of an existing hierarchy of classes. This avoids redesigning and recoding every time from scratch. The new classes will inherit both the functions and attributes from existing classes. Inheriting functions enables code sharing and thus reuse, while inheriting attributes enables structure sharing among objects. The combination of these two aspects of inheritance provides a very powerful software modeling and coding mechanism.

In object-oriented analysis and design, generalization/specialization is the mechanism of deriving a new class from an old one. That is, an existing class can be added to and the addition altered to create a specialized class. Because a class becomes a user-defined type in object-oriented programming, generalization/specialization in C++ is implemented through inheritance via the mechanism of class derivation. In C++, generalization/specialization is implemented as a hierarchy of related types that share code and external interfaces (function prototypes).

In C++, a derived class is used to define a subclass of a *base class* (superclass). A base class is any predefined class definition. A derived class inherits the services (function members) and the attributes (data members) of the *base class* (superclass). It then can be altered by adding both data members and function members, modifying existing member functions, and modifying the access privileges. To modify an existing member function, C++ provides a *virtual* function mechanism. By declaring a function virtual in its base class, a derived class may redefine the function.[1] When a class hierarchy is translated into a set of related derived classes, a base class pointer may be used to address any object of the derived classes. When a virtual function is accessed via a base class pointer, C++ will provide the mechanism to execute the appropriate function definition at run time.

Specifying a Derived Class

A class **Derived** can be derived from another class **Base** using the following form in the header file for **Derived**:

```
#include "Base.h"
class Derived: public Base
{
     // member declarations
};
```

The keyword *public* defines the visibility of its inherited members. There is a choice of three keywords: *public, protected,* and *private.* Each keyword specifies different accessibility of the derived class to the base-class members. This will be discussed later in this chapter. An example of a standard class definition and a derived definition is:

```
class Person
{
    public:
          Person(char* n, char s, int a);
          char*     getName();
          char      getSex();
          int       getAge();
          void       setName(char* n);
```

---

[1]   For example, each derived class may have its own customized method for the virtual function. That customized method is used by objects of the derived class for the virtual function.

```
            void        setAge(int a);
            ~Person() {}
        private:
            char        name[40];
            char        sex;
            int         age, height, weight;
};

class Employee: public Person
{
        public:
            Employee(char* n, char s, int a, int n = 0): Person(n,s,a){
                    salary=n;}
            int         getSalary() {return salary;}
            void        setSalary(int a) {salary = a; }
            ~Employee() {}
        private:
            int         salary;
};
```

In this example, **Employee** is a derived class and **Person** is the base class. Using the keyword *public* following the colon in the derived class header means that the protected and public members of the class **Person** are to be inherited as protected and public members of the class **Employee**. Private members of **Person** are not accessible to the class **Employee**. For example, the class **Employee** has no way of accessing the weight data member, but it can access the age via the two functions getAge() and setAge(). "Class Employee" is a subtype of the type "class Person." An instance of **Employee** is also an instance of **Person**, but an instance of **Person** may not necessarily be an instance of **Employee**.

Frequently a derived class extends the base class by adding new members. In this example, **Employee** has added one new data member (salary) and four new functions (constructor, destructor, getSalary(), setSalary()). The results may be summarized as in Table 19-1.

TABLE 19-1 Relationships Along Lines of Inheritance for Services and Attributes

Class	Employee Services	Employee Attributes
Person	getName	char name[40];
	getSex	char sex;
	getAge	int age;
	setName	int height;
	setAge	int weight;
Employee	getSalary	int salary;
	setSalary	

This table shows that every instance of **Employee** has its own data fields for name, sex, age, height, weight, and salary, and only the salary attribute is truly an "employee" semantic domain attribute. The other attributes of employee are in the "person" semantic domain. Similar reasoning should be applied to the services. For good cohesion and low coupling, applications dealing with an instance of **Employee** as an "employee" should never need to access the services associated with an employee being a person.[2] However, the services (functions) are shared and available to all of the instances. In fact, the common services of **Person** are shared with other instances who are either instances of **Person** or from another derived class of **Person**.

Inheriting from a Derived Class and Implementing Association

A class can be derived from another derived class. For example, let us add **Manager** to the hierarchy of **Person** and **Employee** as follows:

```
const int Max = 20;
class Manager: public Employee
{
    public:
        Manager(char* n, char s, int a, int n = 0): Employee(n,s,a,n)
    {
            for (int i=0; i<Max; i++) group[i] = 0;}
        Employee   *getEmployee(int n) {return group[n];}
        void setEmployee(Employee *e, int a) {group[a] = e;}
        ~Manager() {delete [] group;
    private:
        Employee    *group[Max];
};
```

In this example, **Manager** is the derived class and **Employee** is the base class. The use of the keyword *public* following the colon in the derived class header means that the protected and public members of the class **Employee** are to be inherited respectively as protected and public members of the class **Manager**. Private members of **Person** and **Employee** are not accessible to the class **Manager**. For example, the class **Manager** has no way of accessing the weight data member, nor can it access the salary data member directly.

"Class Manager" is a subtype of the type "class Employee," which is a subtype of "class Person." An instance of **Manager** is also an instance of both **Person** and **Employee**. But an instance of **Person** may not necessarily be an instance of **Manager**, nor an instance of **Employee**.

Manager has added one new data member (*group) and four new services (constructor, destructor, getEmployee(), setEmployee()). The group variable is an array of

---

[2]   The object-oriented paradigm and language allow an application access only to the services of Person when an instance of Employee is viewed as a Person object.

TABLE 19-2   **Manager Inheritance**

Class	Manager Services	Manager Attributes
Person	getName getSex getAge setName setAge	char name[40]; char sex; int age; int height; int weight;
Employee	getSalary setSalary	int salary;
Manager	getEmployee setEmployee	*group[Max];
	by class	by instance

the pointer to the instances of **Employee**. This is a very common way of capturing an association. Notice that because arrays are not initialized by the language, there is an array initialization code in the constructor. Also notice the use of the braces in the delete statement of the destructor. The results may be summarized as in Table 19-2.

Every instance of **Manager** has its own data fields for name, sex, age, height, weight, salary, and group. Once again, the only attribute that is uniquely "managerial" is the group that the manager supervises. The attribute of salary is still tied to the concept of employee, while the rest of the attributes are tied to the concept of person. Conceptually, a manager is an employee and a person. We realize that many developers may not agree with the preceding statement; however, this is what the model says.

Following is a program that uses the three previous classes:

```
main()
{       //   created as an instance of Employee
    Employee Ed("Edward", m, 21, 20000);
        //     Edward gets a raise!!
    ed.setSalary(25000);
        //   Time for a boss
    Manager Jane("Jane", f, 25);
        //     Managers get paid a lot!!
    jane.setSalary(100000);
        //      Put Ed in Jane's group
    jane.setEmployee( &ed, 0)
        //          Lower Edward's salary
    Ed.setSalary(15000);
    };
```

Adding Polymorphism

A function defined in the base class may be overridden when the keyword *virtual* is specified in the prototype declaration of the function in the base-class header file. A virtual function must be defined in the base class, normally in the .C file. If a derived class wants to override this function, it must declare and define a derived function that matches the original function in name, signature, and return type. The selection of which function definition is invoked is dynamic. For example, it is very common in object-oriented programming to have a collection of pointers to base objects. These pointers normally point to objects of the base class and objects in a derived class(es).

Because the virtual function is defined in both classes, there must be a rule by which one of the functions is invoked. The rule is that the function selected is based on the class of the object being pointed to, and not on the pointer type.

If the object being pointed to is an object of the derived class, the function invoked would be the function of the derived class. If a derived class does not have this function declared in its class definition, then the default is to try and find its base class. If it cannot find it in its base class, it would search the "base class" of the base class, ad infinitum, until it is found. Remember, the function must be defined in the original base class.

It should be noted that there is a difference between selection of an appropriate overridden virtual function and the selection of an overloaded member function. Overloaded member functions can be determined at compile time because they must have a unique signature. They can also have different return types, although we have not seen an example of this. An overridden virtual function has an identical signature and return-type. It cannot be resolved at compile time. Once declared virtual, this property is carried to all redeclarations and redefinitions in its derived classes. It is unnecessary in the derived class to use the function modifier virtual. In the following example, polymorphism is added to setSalary() for **Employee** so that the company can give bonuses to the managers.

In this example, the **Employee** class code is:

```
class Employee : public Person
  {
    public
        Employee(char* n, char s, int a,int n=0) : Person(n, s, a)
                        {salary= n;}
        int      getSalary() { return salary; }
        virtual void   setSalary(int a) { salary = a; }
        ~Employee() {}
    private:
        int      salary;
  };
```

Note that the only change to **Employee** is to declare setSalary() virtual. This gives permission to the derived class to override this function. Based on the preceding code for **Employee**, the **Manager** class code is:

```
const int Max = 20;
int bonus () { return 25000; } // big bonuses here
```

```
class Manager: public Employee
{
    public:
        Manager(char* n, char s, int a, int n = 0): Employee(n, s, a, n){
            for (int i=0; i<Max; i++) group[i] = 0; }
        Employee   *getEmployee(int n)   { return group[n]; }
        void setEmployee(Employee *e, int a) { group[a] = e; }
        void setSalary( int s) {Employee::setSalary( s + bonus() ); }
        ~Manager() { delete [] group; }
    private:
        Employee   *group[Max];
};
```

Note that in class **Manager**, setSalary() is both redeclared and redefined. This means that the implementation of setSalary() is different from that of **Employee**. When all of the new salaries are set, all managers will increase their salary by an additional bonus of $25,000, while the salaries of the nonmanagement employees will increase only by the set amount. The results are shown in Table 19-3.

TABLE 19-3   Manager Salary Example

Class	Manager Services	Manager Attributes
Person	getName getSex getAge setName setAge	char name[40]; char sex; int age; int height; int weight;
Employee	getSalary ~~setSalary~~	int salary;
Manager	getEmployee setEmployee setSalary	*group[Max];
	by class	by instance

The strikethru on the setSalary() function in **Employee** means that an object of type **Manager** will not use the function definition given in the class **Employee**. Instead, it will use the setSalary() function definition given in its own class.

The use of polymorphism hides behavior from the user of the services. For example, because of the way we have defined setSalary(), the following program using the latest definition of setSalary() will yield the same results as the earlier main program that used only the employee's setSalary() function.

```
main()
{
    Employee Ed("Edward", m, 21, 20000);
        // Edward gets a raise!!
```

```
Ed.setSalary(25000);
    // Time for a boss
Manager Jane("Jane", f, 25);
    //Manager gets paid a lot!!; less obvious
Jane.setSalary(75000);
    // Put Ed in Jane's group
 Jane.setEmployee( &ed, 0)
    // Lower Edward's salary
Ed.setSalary(5000);
};
```

In the previous program in which the manager inherited without polymorphism, Jane's salary was exactly $100,000, as shown in the main program code where the coder of the main program knows her salary. In this program, however, the coder would have assumed that her salary was $75,000, but, in fact, it is still $100,000 because when her salary is set, a bonus is added to the base salary. Now, we understand the real reason why managers are so excited about object-oriented technology!

Abstract Class

The base class (also called a root class) of a type hierarchy may contain a number of virtual functions. These virtual functions are often dummy functions, which have an empty body in the root class and are given a specific meaning in the derived classes. In C++, the pure virtual mechanism is used to handle this situation. In a pure virtual function, the function definition is given in its derived classes. As a result, the body of the function is undefined in the base class. Notationally, it is declared in the base class as follows:

```
class BaseClass
{
    public:
        virtual   int      foo() = 0;
};
```

A class with at least one pure virtual function is an *abstract* class. For example, consider the following:

```
class Item
{
    public:
        virtual void       cut() =0;
        virtual void       move(Length dx, Length dy) =0;
        virtual Boolean     pick(Length px, Length py) =0;
        virtual void       ungroup() =0;
};
class Shape: public Item
{
    public:
```

```
                void cut() =0;
                void draw() { write(Color_Foreground);}
                void erase() { write(Color_Background);}
                void move(Length dx, Length dy) =0;
                virtual Boolean    pick(Length px, Length py) =0;
                void ungroup() {}
                virtual void write(Color color) =0;
        protected:
                Length x; Length y;
    };
    class Box: public Shape
    {
        public:
                Box (Length x0, Length y0, Length w, Length h);
                ~Box ();
                Boolean pick(Length px, Length py);
                void move(Length dx, Length dy);
                void cut();
        protected:
                Length width; Length height;
    };
    class Circle: public Shape
    {
        public:
                Circle (Length x0, Length radius);
                ~Circle ();
                Boolean       pick(Length px, Length py);
                void          move(Length dx, Length dy);
                void          write(Color color);
                void          cut();
        protected:
                Length radius;
    };
```

Here, there are two abstract base classes: **Item** and **Shape**. All of the functions of **Item** are pure virtual. **Shape** defines only one of these functions, ungroup(). In addition, it added a new virtual function, write(). **Box** and **Circle** do not have any pure virtual functions, so they are sometimes called *concrete classes*. The reason is that the program can instantiate an instance of a concrete class, but it may not instantiate an instance of an abstract class. From the previous discussion this must be so, because an abstract class has undefined methods. However, we can still use a pointer of the abstract class to refer to instances of the derived classes.[3]

---

[3]   C++ uses a virtual function table to manage access to virtual functions. The table provides the capability for an instance to know the correct member function to use even when the function is referenced in the context of a superclass.

Multiple Inheritance

MULTIPLE inheritance allows a derived class to be derived from more than one base class. The syntax of the class declaration for the derived class is extended to allow for a list of base classes. The template for the header file of a derived class with multiple inheritance from base classes bc1, bc2, bc3, bc4 is:

```
#include "bc1.h"
#include "bc2.h"
#include "bc3.h"
#include "bc4.h"

class Derived: public bc1, public bc2, public bc3, public bc4
{
    member declarations
};
```

For example, consider the following two base classes:

```
class Font
{
    public:
        Font ( Length w, Length h);
        ~Font ();
        void         write(Color color);
private:
        Length width; Length height;
};
class String
{
    public:
        String( char *c);
        ~String ();
        char *getString();  //  return the string
        void print();  //  to stdout
};
```

A class Text, in order to be created, needs to inherit the font capabilities from **Font** and the character capabilities from **String**. Following is the class definition of **Text** that uses multiple inheritance:

```
#include "Font.h"
#include "String.h"
class Text : public Font, public String
{
    public:
```

```
Text ( Length width, Length height, char *pointer) :
    Font( width, height), String ( pointer)
            { other initialization code      }
~Text ();
        ...     //  new member functions
private:
        ...     //  new data members
};
```

Once again, we see how multiple inheritance works, as illustrated in Table 19-4. Note that in this chart the services and attributes are not indented. This is to show that **String** is not a derived class of **Font**. When an instance of **Text** is being created, it will first create an instance of **Font** and then create an instance of **String**. Both of these instances will then become part of the new instance of **Text**. Specifically, the instance of **Text** inherits the print service from **String** and the write service from **Font**.

TABLE 19-4   **Multiple Inheritance**

Class	Text Services	Text Attributes
Font	write()	Length width Length height
String	*getString() print()	
Text		

In deriving from multiple base classes, it is possible to have identically named members from different classes. This may result in ambiguities. For example, consider the following, where class **Font** has added a print function to its definition:

```
class  Font
{
    public:
        Font ( Length w, Length h);
        ~Font ();
        void write(Color color);
        void print(); // to stderr
    private:
        Length width; Length height;
};

class String
{
    public:
        String( char *c);
```

```
        ~String ();
        char *getString();  //  return the string
        void print();  //  to stdout
};
```

Now suppose we want to add a display function to **Text** that prints the string in the correct font. We want to reuse code, and we write the following code:

```
class Text : public Font, public String
{
    public:
        Text ( Length width, Length height, char *pointer) :
            Font( width, height), String ( pointer)
            { other initialization code      }
        ~Text ();
        void  display()  { print( ); }
            ...    //  new member functions
    private:
        ...    //  new data members
};
```

This will result in a compile-time error because the compiler does not know which print() function it should use. This ambiguity is shown in Table 19-5.

TABLE 19-5   Ambiguity of Print Due to Inheritance

Class	Text Services	Text Attributes
Font	write() print()	Length width Length height
String	*getString() print()	
Text	display()	

Text has two print functions defined. Determining which one to use is normally solved by using the scope operator. For example, if **Text** intended to use the print() function of **String**, the following code would apply:

```
void  display()  { String::print( ); }
```

Another source of ambiguity is when a derived class inherits from classes that are derived from a common base class. For example, consider an employee who is also a customer.[4] We want to create a new class **Employee/Customer** that inherits from both

---

[4]   For example, an instance of Employee that is also an instance of Customer.

TABLE 19-6   Class C/E

Class	C/E Services	C/E Attributes
Person (superclass of Employee)	getName getSex getAge setName setAge	char name[40]; char sex; int age; int height; int weight;
Employee	getSalary setSalary	int salary;
Person (superclass of Customer)		char name[40]; char sex; int age; int height; int weight;
Customer	getSaving setSaving	int saving;
CustomerEmployee		

Employee and **Customer**. However, **Customer** is also a derived class of **Person**. To represent this situation, this instance (Person) would have classes (**Employee** and **Customer**) that are both derived classes of **Person**. Following is the code used to add the two new classes. Table 19-6 shows the results of the inheritances.

```
class Customer : public Person
{
    public:
        Customer(char* n, char s, int a, int n = 0) : Person( n, s, a)
            { saving = n; }
        int      getSaving() { return saving; }
        virtual void    setSaving(int a) { saving = a; }
        ~Customer() {}
    private:
        int   saving;
};
class CustomerEmployee : public Customer, public Employee
{
    public:
        ...    // new member functions
    private:
        ...   // new data members
};
```

There are two sets of values for the attributes of **Person**. The functions are not duplicated because they are the same for instances of **Person**. If the functions are all public functions and the programmer wants to maintain two sets of data, then he/she must access the appropriate data by scoping the public functions. For example, to access the age, which is stored as part of **Customer**, the following code needs to be written:

```
int custAge = Customer::getAge( );
```

To change the age of **Employee** to 20, use the following code:

```
Employee::setAge( 20 );
```

This will change only the age data member associated with **Employee**; the age data member associated with **Customer** is unchanged.

How can we use multiple inheritance and still have only one copy of Person? In C++, there is a mechanism called *virtual inheritance* that allows a derived class to inherit from other classes with the same base class. Only one copy of the base class is inherited. In the following example, we modify the inheritance of **Employee** and **Customer** to use virtual inheritance:

```
class Employee : virtual public Person
{
    public:
        Employee(char* n, char s, int a, int n = 0) : Person( n, s, a)
            { salary = n; }
        int      getSalary() { return salary; }
        virtual void    setSalary(int a) { salary = a; }
        ~Employee() {}
    private:
        int    salary;
};
class Customer : public virtual Person
{
    public:
        Customer(char* n, char s int a, int n = 0) : Person( n, s, a)
            { saving = n; }
        int      getSaving() { return saving; }
        virtual void    setSaving(int a) { saving = a; }
        ~Customer() {}
    private:
        int    saving;
};
```

The keyword *virtual* has been added. The order of public and virtual does not matter (they can be reversed). Now, the **CustomerEmployee** class can be defined using the revised **Customer** and **Employee** classes as follows:

```
class CustomerEmployee : public Customer, public Employee
{
    public:
        CustomerEmployee( char* n, char s,int a, int n = 0, int sav = 1000 ) :
        Person( n, s, a), Employee( n, s, a, n),Customer( n, s, a, sav)
            {  ...          }
        ...      //  new member functions
    private:
        ...      //  new data members
};
```

In **CustomerEmployee**, the base class **Person** is explicitly initialized. The results of this new code are shown in Table 19-7. Now there is only one set of values for **Person**.

TABLE 19-7   Class C/E

Class	C/E Services	C/E Attributes
Person	getName getSex getAge setName setAge	char name[40]; char sex; int age; int height; int weight;
Employee	getSalary setSalary	int salary;
Customer		int saving;
	getSaving setSaving	
C/E		

Virtual Destructors

HOW does the model and the language handle a **Person** object who is deceased? Ideally, you would like to delete that person as a **Person** object as well as delete all of its derived classes. Unfortunately, when you delete a specific person who is also an employee, only the destructor of **Person** is called. It is necessary to call the destructor of **Employee**. This becomes more complex in the case where the person is a manager.

Without another mechanism, one would have to know all the derived classes of the deceased person. However, there is a mechanism that will support the destruction of a **Person** object without knowing all of its derived classes. This mechanism is a *virtual destructor*. Specifying the destructors in a derivation hierarchy as virtual guarantees that the appropriate destructors are invoked whenever delete is applied to a base class pointer. The destructor of a class that is derived from a class that declares its destructor virtual is also virtual. In the following example, virtual destructors are added:

```
class Person
{
    public:
        Person(char* n, char s, int a);
        char*    getName();
        char     getSex();
        int      getAge();
        void     setName(char* n);
        void     setAge(int a);
        virtual  ~Person() {}
    private:
        char name[40];
        char sex;
        int  age;
};
class Employee : public Person
{
    public:
        Employee(char* n, char s, int a, int n = 0) : Person( n, s, a)
{ salary = n; }
        int      getSalary() { return salary; }
        virtual void    setSalary(int a) { salary = a; }
        virtual  ~Employee() {}
    private:
        int  salary;
};
const int Max = 20;
class Manager: public Employee
{
    public:
        Manager(char* n, char s,  int a, int n = 0) :
                Employee( n, s, a, n)
           { for (int i=0; i<Max; i++)  group[i] = 0; }
        Employee   *getEmployee(int n) { return group[n]; }
        void setEmployee(Employee *e, int a) { group[a] = e; }
        virtual    ~Manager() { delete [] group;}
    private:
        Employee    *group[Max];
};
```

Derived Class Visibility

ONE of the difficulties for novices when programming functions of derived classes is knowing what data members they may access. Figure 19-1 is a visual aid to help you

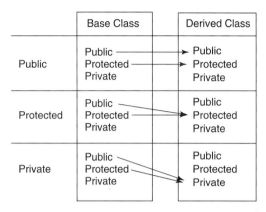

FIGURE 19-1 Derived class visibility.

TABLE 19-8 Derived Class Visibility

Defined in Class X	Private	Protected	Public
Used in Class X	Yes	Yes	Yes
Used in Class Y	NO	Yes	Yes
Used in Class Z	NO	Yes	Yes
Used in Class F	Yes	Yes	Yes
Other code	NO	NO	Yes

while you are programming. Let **X** be the base class and let **Y** be its derived class via public inheritance. Let **Z** be the derived class of **Y** and finally let **F** be a friend of **X**. Table 19-8 shows how the privacy specification of inheritance affects the accessibility of the derived class to the various data members in the base class.

■ ■ ■ SUMMARY

IN object-oriented programming the derived class capabilities and its supporting mechanisms, including virtual functions and virtual destructors, are used to implement the generalization/specialization hierarchy of the object-oriented model. Key points to remember follow:

■ Superclasses are base classes in C++.

■ Subclasses are derived classes in C++.

■ Polymorphic functions are implemented as virtual functions.

- Virtual destructors are used to support deleting instances of derived classes from base-level functions.
- Multiple inheritance may be used to capture behavior and attributes that are part of separate semantic domains.
- Abstract classes are used to capture concepts that help organize the domain.

Here is a summary of inheritance and some C++ coding reminders:

- Variables (attributes) declared in the base class are inherited by its derived classes and need not be repeated in the derived classes.
- However, the derived classes can only directly access variables that are *public* or *protected*.
- Furthermore, if the base class is *privately* inherited, then the inherited public members of the base class become private members of the derived class. Clients of the derived class then have no access to the inherited methods or variables.
- Functions declared in a base class are also inherited in the derived classes.
- Constructors, destructors, and friends are not inherited.
- If a function can be overridden by a derived class, then it must be declared *virtual* in its first appearance in a base class.
- Virtual functions are called using the same syntax as nonvirtual functions.
- Functions that override inherited functions must be declared in the derived class.
- *Virtual* as a keyword prefix to a member function declaration in a class header allows the function to be replaced by any derived class.
- The *virtual* keyword is required only at the first definition of a member function within the hierarchy; that is, at the base class where it is first defined.
- All usage of virtual in subsequent derived classes is optional. However, it is usually considered good documentation practice to include it in the derived classes.
- A virtual function and its overridden versions must have the same name, signature, and return type.
- All member functions except constructors and overloaded **new** can be virtual.
- In a pure virtual function, the function prototype is provided by the base class. In other words, implementation must be provided by a derived class.
- Specifying the destructors in a derivation hierarchy as virtual guarantees that the appropriate destructors are invoked whenever delete is applied to a base-class pointer.
- When a base class needs constructors or destructors to allocate, initialize, or deallocate base-class objects, the derived class must call the constructor or destructor of the base class.
- In multiple inheritance, construction of a derived class, by default, is done by constructing the base classes in the same order as their declaration.

CHAPTER

20

Implementing More Relationships

. . . until death do you part.

Marriage Vows

In the previous chapter, we discussed the implementation of generalization/ specialization. However, as we built the analysis model, we used two additional types of relationships, aggregation and association. Although aggregation and association are not explicitly supported in many object-oriented languages including C++, we believe that they should be implemented in a standard way. In this chapter, we look at some accepted mechanisms for implementing these two relationships.

Introduction

SOME of the issues involved in implementing association and aggregation were presented in the design chapter. They are repeated here for reference, as these issues are usually revisited during implementation.

Implementing Association

There are two approaches to implementing associations: buried pointers and distinct association objects. Because C++ (like most languages) does not support association objects directly, the most common approach uses buried pointers.

A binary (one-to-one) association is usually implemented as an attribute in each of the classes participating in the association. You can also implement a binary association as two Map objects, with each Map object giving access in one direction across the relation.

A many-to-one association requires either a set of objects or an array of objects (if the association is ordered). In this case, a collection class object from the STL library is the best implementation.

In implementing associations, the implementor must consider the access pattern and the relative frequencies of the different kinds of access. If the number of hits from a query is low because only a fraction of the objects satisfy the criteria, an index should be used to improve the access to objects that are frequently retrieved. However, this is at a price, as it will use more memory and updates will be slower. Sometimes, adding a new association that is derived from the base association will provide for direct access to the appropriate data.

The simplest association to implement is one that is only traversed in one direction. In this case, it can be implemented as an attribute that contains an object reference. If the multiplicity is 1, it is simply a pointer to the other object. If the multiplicity is more than 1, it is a pointer to a collection. In most cases, an appropriate collection is a STL set or STL list containing pointers to objects. If the many end is ordered, a STL list is used in place of a set. A qualified association can be implemented using a map object.

There are three ways to implement a two-way association:

1. Add an attribute to the class on one side of the association and perform a search when a reverse traversal is required.
2. Add an attribute to both sides of the association. Use the same multiplicity techniques as for an association that is traversed in one direction.
3. Create an associate class, independent of either class. An associate class is a set of pairs of related objects stored in a single-variable-sized object. For efficiency, it is common to implement an associative object as two map objects.

If most of the traversal is from the "many" side to the "one" side and new members are added frequently to the links, then number 1 is recommended. When updates are infrequent and speed of access in both directions is critical to your application, number 2 is recommended. An associative class is recommended when maximum flexibility is needed for future enhancements and performance is not an issue.

Implementing Attributes of an Association

If the association has attributes but no services, then the attributes of an association can be implemented as follows:

1. If the association is one-to-one, the association attributes can be stored as attributes of either class.
2. If the association is many-to-one, the association attributes may be stored in the class on the "many" side.
3. If the association is many-to-many, it is best to create an associative class and assign the association attributes to the associative class.

Implementing Aggregation

Because aggregation is also not supported in most object-oriented languages, including C++, it is implemented using rules similar to those used for association. There are two approaches: buried array of pointers and embedded objects.

1. An aggregation can be implemented as an array of pointers to objects. This is done when we have either replaceable components or directly accessible components in the aggregate.

2. An aggregation can also be implemented as a distinct contained object. This is done when we want the components of the aggregation to be changed only through methods of the container object.

Pointers

BECAUSE the foundation of implementing association and aggregation is a pointer to an instance of a class and a container of pointers to instances of a class, pointer variables will now be discussed in depth.

In C++, pointers are used to reference variables or machine memory addresses. As we have shown, pointers are intimately tied to array and string processing. Both the string and the array may be thought as special forms of pointers, where the pointer is associated with a contiguous piece of memory for storing an indexible sequence of values.

Pointers are used in programs to access variables. If x is a variable, then &x is the address (lvalue) in memory of its stored value (rvalue). The variable that contains the address as its stored value (rvalue) is called a pointer variable; pointer variables can be declared in a program and then used to take addresses as values. The form for declaring a pointer is as follows:

```
type  * variable ;
```

The type may be a native type, a derived type, or a user-defined type, and the variable is an identifier. For example, the declaration

```
Person  *p;
```

declares p to be a pointer type that points to an instance of **Person**. The legal range of values for p (and any pointer) includes the special address 0 (zero) and a set of positive integers that are interpreted as addresses on a computer.

Here are some examples of assignment statements using p:

```
Person  Jim("Jim",m,30)
p = &Jim;                    // the address of Jim is the rvalue
p = 0;                       // rvalue = 0
p = (Person * ) 1234;        // allowed, but not good practice
```

In the first assignment statement, we can think of p as referring to Jim, pointing to Jim, or containing the address of Jim. All are correct. Note that the compiler decides the actual address to assign the variable Jim. This can vary from computer to computer, and may be different for different executions on the same computer. The second assignment statement is the special value 0. This value is typically used to indicate an exception condition. For instance, the operator *new* returns a pointer value of 0 when free storage is exhausted. This value is also used to indicate that the object requested was not found in function calls. The third assignment statement assigns an actual memory address. The cast is necessary to avoid a type error. However, assigning a memory address is not recommended for any application.[1]

In using pointers for programming, one of the difficulties is that earlier C++ libraries use pass-by-reference as an argument type to pass objects instead of pass-by-pointer. To use the libraries, the programmer must use the dereferencing or indirection operator '*'. If p is a pointer to a variable v, then '*p' is the rvalue of v. [2] The indirect value of p is the rvalue (stored value) of v. In a sense, the dereference operator '*' is the inverse operator for the address operator '&'. The following code may help better explain this:

```
Person Jim("Jim",m,20), unknown;    // unknown is uninitialized
Employee *Donna("Donna",f, 21, 40000);
Dog    *d = new Dog( );   // create an instance of Dog
Person *p ;               // p is uninitialized
p = &jim;                 // p has an address of Jim
unknown = p;              // illegal assignment
unknown = *p;             // legal, assuming the assignment operator has
                          // been defined for Person class
p = &unknown;             // legal; p now points to unknown
p = d;                    // legal in K&R C; illegal in C++
p = <reinterpret_cast> (Person *) d;// legal, but should not be done
p = Donna;                // legal; Employee is a derived class of Person
                          // note: if inheritance was private, then this is
                          // illegal private inheritance is treated as an
                          // unrelated class.
Donna = p;                // illegal
```

The following rules will help you deal with pointers:

- Pointers to different classes (types) may not be equated without casting.
- The exception is that a public inherited subclass (derived class) pointer can be assigned to a superclass (base class) pointer.
- A base-class pointer must always be cast to a legal derived-class pointer.
- An object pointer may always be assigned the void pointer. However, a void pointer must be cast to a legal object pointer.

---

[1]   This may need to be done in hard real-time systems for performance.

[2]   In other words, the direct value of p is the lvalue (address) of v.

Arrays

AN array is used to capture a large number of values of the same data type. The elements (values) of the array are accessible using subscripts. Arrays of all types are possible, including arrays of arrays. An array declaration allocates memory starting from a base address. In C++, an array name is a pointer constant to the base address of the array.

An array can be initialized by a comma-separated list of expressions enclosed in braces, as in the following:

```
int array[5] { 23, 11, 107, 706, 1 };
```

When the list of initializers is shorter than the size of the array, then the remaining elements are initialized to zero. An array declared with an explicit initializer and no size expression is given the size of the number of initializers. Therefore, the statement

```
char jane[ ] = { 'j', 'a', 'n', 'e' };
```

is the same as

```
char jane[ 4 ] = { 'j', 'a', 'n', 'e' };
```

If external and static arrays are not explicitly intialized, the compiler will automatically create code to initialize all elements of these arrays to zero. However, this is not true for automatic arrays; their elements will hold undefined values.

To illustrate these ideas, a program to sum the values of an array follows:

```
#include <iostream.h>
const int SIZE = 7
main( )
{
    int v[SIZE]  { 7, 6, 5, 4, 3, 2, 1 };
        // initialize the sum to zero
    int  sum = 0;
    for( int i = 0; i < SIZE; i++ )
    {
        cout << "v[" << i << "] =  " << v[i] << '\t'l;
        sum += v[i];
    }
    cout << "\nsum = " << sum << end;
}
```

The array v requires memory to store seven integer values. The zeroth element is always the first element of the array. If we assume that a system needs 4 bytes to store a value of type int and that v[0] is stored at location 100, then the remaining array elements are stored at 104, 108, 112, 116, 120, and 124.

It is recommended that C++ programmers use symbolic constants for the size of any array, because the code will need to use this value. This makes it possible to change a single value when the size of the array needs to be resized. Notice that the *for* statement is neatly tailored to provide a terse notation for dealing with array computations. Also note that the subscript must lie in the range of 0 to SIZE-1. An array subscript value outside this range will usually cause a run-time error because the subscript cannot be checked at compile time. An "out-of-bound" subscript can cause system-dependent errors at run time, and thus be very confusing. It is the responsibility of the programmer to ensure that all subscripts stay within bounds.

Pointer arithmetic provides an alternative to array indexing. Following is a program that does the same computation using pointer arithmetic:

```
#include <iostream.h>
const int SIZE = 7
main( )
{
    int v[SIZE]   { 7, 6, 5, 4, 3, 2, 1 };
         //  initialize the sum to zero
    int   sum = 0, * p;
    for(p = &v[0]; p < &v[SIZE]; p++ )
    {
         sum += *p;
    }
    cout << "\nsum = " << sum << end;
}
```

In this example, the pointer variable p is initialized to the base address of the array v. The successive values of p are equivalent to &v[0], &v[1], ... &v[SIZE-11]. The basic rule for pointer arithmetic is:

If j is a variable of type int, then p + j is the jth offset from the address p. The value of p + j is computed as follows:

```
pointer value + sizeof(type of pointer) * j
```

Assume that we have the following program on a system where long double is 8 bytes:

```
#include<iostream.h>
main()
{
    long double v =0, *p = &v, *newp;
    newp = p + 1;
    cout << "next location is" << newp << endl;
}
```

The output of newp is the address in memory 8 bytes after the address of v.

Friends

IN some instances, we need to give nonmembers of a class access to the nonpublic members of the class. When this is the case, C++ has a mechanism called *friend* to provide this capability in a controlled manner that preserves some of the information hiding necessary for encapsulation. The friend mechanism has been shown to be needed for overloading the stream input ("<<") and output (">>") operators and iterators.

Friends are functions or classes that have direct access to all the members (private, protected, and public) of another class. A friend function can itself be a member function of another class declaration. Friend breaks the encapsulation and information-hiding principles and should rarely be used. However, using a friend is better than making a data member public.

Static Members

IT is sometimes necessary that all objects of a particular class access the same variable. This may be some condition flag or counter related to the class that changes dynamically in program execution. Examples are averages and running totals. Sometimes it is more efficient to provide one variable for all objects in one class than to have each object maintain its own copy. Examples of this are error-handling routines common to the class, and pointers to free storage for the class. For these situations, a static class member is an effective mechanism to use.

A static data member acts as a global variable for its class. For object-oriented programming, there are three advantages to using a static data member over a global variable:

1. Information hiding can still be enforced. A static member can be made nonpublic; a global variable cannot.
2. A static member is not entered into the program's global name space. This reduces the possibility of an accidental conflict of names.
3. Even if the static member is public, a weak form of encapsulation is preserved. Nonmembers require the use of a scope operator (e.g., X::PublicStaticMember) to access the static member, while a function can access a global variable (e.g., PublicStaticMember) directly.

There is only one instance of a static data member of a class—a single shared variable that is accessible to all objects in the class. Static members obey the public/private/protected access rules in the same manner as nonstatic members. Static data members may also be constant, class objects, or pointers to class objects.

A static member function is used to access static data members of the class. It is not allowed to access any nonstatic data member. A static member function does not contain a *this* pointer; therefore, any explicit or implicit reference to a *this* pointer will result in a compile-time error. Note that an attempt to access a nonstatic class member is an implicit reference to a *this* pointer and will result in a compile-time error.

The definition of a static function is the same as a nonstatic member function; however, a static member function may not be declared *const* or *volatile*. A static member function may be invoked through a class object or a pointer to a class object in the same manner that a nonstatic member function is invoked. However, a static member function can be invoked directly even if no class object is ever declared.[3]

Implementing Association

Binary Association

The most direct mechanism is to implement a binary association as an attribute of each class.[4] Following is an example of using buried pointers to capture the spousal relationship between two people:

```
class Person
{
    public:
        Person(char* n, char s, int a);
        Person* getSpouse() { return spouse; }
        void setSpouse(Person* p) ;
            . . .
        ~Person() {}
    private:
        char name[40];
        char sex;
        int age;  . . .
        Person*  spouse;
}
```

In this example, we have added the spousal relationship that is a "from-Person-to-Person" relationship. By adding an attribute that is a pointer to the Person class, this relationship is captured. The setSpouse() function establishes one side of the relationship, while the getSpouse() function navigates the relationship.

The reader should note that it is the programmer's responsibility to establish and update both sides of the relationship. This is often rather tricky. For example, managing the spouse relationship can be accomplished within the setSpouse method as follows:

```
void Person::setSpouse(Person *p)
{
    if (spouse != p)     // if this is not the current spouse
    {
```

---

[3] This is done by use the class scope operator.

[4] This allows traversal in both directions.

```
        if (spouse == 0) // not currently married (p isn't nil because of
                         // first if)
        {
            spouse = p;// set the spouse
            spouse->setSpouse(this); // let the new spouse know about
                                     // the marriage
            return;   // nothing else to do
        }
        if (spouse->getSpouse() == this) // the old spouse doesn't know about
                                         // the divorce
        {
            Person *old = spouse;// use a local variable to hold old spouse
            spouse = 0;// handle the divorce on this side of relation
            old->setSpouse(0); // inform the other person of the divorce
        }
        spouse = p;     // now set the new spouse even if it is no spouse (nil)
        if (spouse != 0)// if this wasn't a divorce
        {
            spouse->setSpouse(this); // let the new spouse know about the
                                     // marriage
        }
    }
    return;
}
```

This implementation of setSpouse() first checks to make sure that the spouse is a change in value and must be handled. There are two basic cases that it must handle: (1) this is a new marriage and (2) it is already married. In the first case, it sets the spouse attribute and informs the other spouse of the marriage. This gives the spouse a chance to establish its side of the association. In the second case, it must first allow the previous spouse to update its role in the marriage. If the previous spouse believes the marriage still exists, then it must first be divorced. In order to divorce the spouse, it sets its spouse attribute to nil and informs the other person of the divorce by invoking the setSpouse() method with a nil argument. It then sets the spouse attribute to the new spouse specified in the argument of the method. If the new value for the spouse attribute is an actual instance of **Person** (not nil), then it informs the new spouse of the association. Otherwise, this was a divorce and the spouse attribute holds a nil value.

If there are attributes of the association, each attribute should be added to only one of the classes. The frequency of accessing the attribute within the functions of each class should be used as the criteria for assigning the attribute.

Many-to-One Association

One way to implement a many-to-one association is to have buried pointers to the singleton object as an attribute of the objects on the "many" side. Then the program can navigate the relationship from the "many" side to the "one" side. The program can navigate the relationship directly from the "many" side to the "one" side. However, navigating from the "one" side to the "many" side requires a search of all of the objects on the "many" side using the association attribute. The following is an example of how to implement a many-to-one association using buried pointers:

```
class Person
{
    public:
        Person(char* n, char s, int a);
        Person* getFather() { return father; }
        Person* getMother() { return mother; }
        Person   getChildren( );
        void addChild(Person *p) { children.insert(p); }
        void setFather(Person* p) { father = p; if (p)
                    p->addChild (this); return; }
        void setMother(Person* p) { mother = p; if (p)
                    p->addChild (this); return; }
        ~Person() {}
    private:
        char name[40];
        char sex;
        int   age;  . . .
        Person*  father;
        Person*  mother;

}
```

In this example, two many-to-one relationships have been implemented: children-to-father and children-to-mother. The data member "Person * father" is the implementation of the buried pointer on the "many" side for the children-to-father relationship. The setFather() function is used to establish the relationship from the child to the father; setFather() is declared as a private function because it should be restricted to creation time. In fact, the best way to implement this is to have a father and a mother as required arguments in the constructor of the Person class. Then, a Person object may not be created without a father or a mother. If this is done, the two private functions, setFather() and setMother(), would not be needed. The getFather() function is used by the child to get to the father.

The getChildren() function is the function on the "one" side of the relationship and allows a father or mother to navigate either the children-to-father or the children-to-mother relationship to get all of its children. The code for this is not given. If this is implemented in a relational database, an SQL call that searches the appropriate column for a match is appropriate; while in an object-oriented database, a set may need to be traversed. In either case, a collection of pointers to the Person objects is returned.

The reader should note that if the relationship is between two classes, this function would be in the class on the "one" side and all the other functions and attributes are in the class on the "many" side. It should also be noted that there is no set function on the "one" side because there is no attribute added to the class on the "one" side. The traversal from the "one" side to the "many" side can be very expensive.

Rumbaugh suggests that if fast traversal is critical, then it would be better to add attributes to both sides of the association. In this case, the attribute added to the class on the "one" side is not a buried pointer, but a set of pointers to a class object on the other side. This has the disadvantage of making updates of the relationship fairly complex. In the following example, father is on the "one" side of the association, while child is on the "many" side of the association.

```
class Person
{
    public:
        Person(char* n, char s, int a, Person *mom, Person *dad);
        Person* getFather() { return father; }
        Person* getMother() { return mother; }
        Person  getChildren( );
        void addChild(Person *p) { children.insert(p); }
        void setFather(Person* p) { father = p; if (p)
                        p->addChild(this); return; }
        void setMother(Person* p) { mother = p; if (p)
                        p->addChild(this); return; }
        ~Person() {}
    private:
        char name[40];
        char sex;
        int    age;
        Person*  father;
        Person*  mother;
}
```

The implementation of the setFather(), setMother(), addChild(), and removeChild() will be complex if we incorporate into the model the ability to adopt children. In addition, the destructor for Person will become more complex. These methods must manage the integrity of the relationship. If there are attributes of the association (such as the date of birth), then they should be kept in the class on the "one" side of the relationship (the child).

Many-to-Many Association

A many-to-many association can be implemented in either of the following ways:

1. Add an attribute to both sides as a set of pointers to class objects of the other side. This is good for traversal, but has update complexity.
2. Implement a distinct association object that is independent of either class in the association. An association object is a set of pairs stored in a single-variable-size object. The set would consist of two pointers, one to each of the classes in the association.

The first technique is similar to the approach used in implementing a many-to-one association using buried pointers on both sides.

To better understand the second technique, let us add the class Company and the relationship "works-for" between Person and Company. Initially, you might decide that

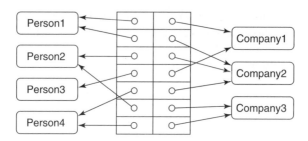

FIGURE 20-1   Association object: works-for.

this is a many-to-one relationship. However, an individual may work for more than one company, and a company usually has more than one employee. This is a many-to-many relationship. Using the association object, we can create an object that has a set of pairs of pointers. In each pair, the first pointer points to a Person object and the second pointer points to a Company object. This is illustrated in Figure 20-1.

The first pair captures that person1 works for company1, and the second pair captures that person1 works for company2. The rest of the pairs should be self-explanatory. A very maintainable way of implementing an association object is to use multimap objects.

Implementing Friends

FRIENDS are methods or classes that have direct access to all of the members (private, protected, and public) of another class. A friend breaks the encapsulation and information-hiding principles and should rarely be used. However, using a friend is better than making a data member public. A friend method can itself be a member method of another class declaration. A good use of a friend is for iterators for a collection of classes.

Class as a Friend

Here is an example that makes a class GoodGuy a friend to the class Text:

```
class Text : public Font, public String
{
        friend class GoodGuy;
    public:
        Text ( Length width, Length height, char *pointer) :
        Font( width, height), String ( pointer)
        { other initialization code      }
        ~Text ();
        ...     //  new member functions
    private:
        ...     //  new data members
}
```

The friend statement declares that the class GoodGuy, and all of its functions may have direct access to all the members of class Text.

Function as a Friend

Here is an example of making a function GoodMethod a friend:

```
class Text : public Font, public String
{
friend int Goodguy::GoodMethod(char *);
public:
Text ( Length width, Length height, char *pointer) :
      Font( width, height), String ( pointer)
      { other initialization code      }
~Text ();
...     //  new member functions
private:
...     //  new data members
}
```

This is more restrictive than the previous example, as only the function GoodMethod may access all of the members of the class Text.

The following example shows a function f1() that can access the members of two classes:

```
class X
{
    public:
        friend void     f1(X* x, Y* y);
    private:
        int x1; int x2;
}

class Y
{
    public:
        friend void     f1(X* x, Y* y);
    private:
        int y1, y2;
}

void f1(X* x, Y* y)
{
    y->y1 = x->x1;
    y->y2 = x->x2;
}
```

The function f1() has access to the private members of both class X and class Y. Both classes are declared with a friend function for f1. Obviously, if every class declared f1 as a friend function, f1 becomes a function that can access any data.

Implementing a One-Many Association Using a Friend

The following is an example that uses Friend to implement adding and removing an item from a group. The group may be used to capture the many sides of an association. What follows are the two class definitions:

```
class Item
{
    friend Group:addItem(Item*);
    friend  Group:removeItem(Item*);
    public:
           // some public stuff
        Group* getGroup () {return group}
    private:
        // some private variables, etc.
        Group* group;
}

class Group : public Item
{
    public:
        Group (); //create an empty set
        ~Group (); //destroy a set
        void addItem (Item*); //add an item
        void removeItem (Item*); //delete an item
        Boolean includes (Item*); // test for an item
        int size (); //get number of items in set
    private:
        void add (Item*); //add an item to the set
        void remove (Item*); //delete an item
                            //from the set
    }
```

In the previous example, the friend declarations for services addItem and removeItem allow these services of Group to access the private data of Item, namely the attribute Group*. This means that Group can maintain the integrity of the instances of Item by ensuring that they have a valid pointer as a data item for the attribute Group*. If it is necessary to add a member to the group (add a link), both pointers must be updated. Similarly, to remove (or delete) a member also requires that both pointers be updated. The code for the addItem and removeItem functions is:

```
void Group::addItem (Item *item );
{
    // make referential variable = "this" group
    item->group = this;
    // add an item to the set of "this" group
    this->add (item);
}

void Group::removeItem (Item *item );
{
    // make an item member of "null" group
    item->group = 0;
    // remove item from "this" set
    this->remove (item);
}
```

In the addItem service, the line "item->group = this" directly accesses the group variable of Item. Technically, this violates the encapsulation principle of object-oriented technology. However, remember that a relationship is not truly an attribute,[5] and a relationship implemented as an attribute violates the encapsulation principle. For us to manage the integrity of the relationship, we need to access the relationship attribute that is stored within Item. A friend then becomes a very valuable ally because we want the relationship updated simultaneously on both sides.

Implementing Aggregation

IN UML, there are two forms of the "aggregation" concept that are captured in its notation: aggregation (unfilled diamond) and composition (filled diamond). The decision to choose these two forms was driven much more by implementation than by the formal analysis concepts discussed in Chapter 9. Thus, corresponding, in implementation there are two ways to implement an aggregation: buried pointers and embedded objects.

Buried Pointers

Buried pointers are implemented in a similar manner to what was done in implementing an association. To understand this, let us add two more classes to our Person example. The two classes are Hand and Body. Because a person should have a body and two hands, we will use this example to show how to implement composition (aggregation).

---

[5] It is implemented as an attribute, so we have lost some information that needs to be managed.

The following code is for the buried pointers implementation:

```
class Person
{
    public:
        Person(char* n, char s, int a);
        ...
        ~Person() {}
    private:
        char    name[40];
        ...
        Person*  spouse;  //binary relationship
        Body*    body;   //ptr to body
        Hand*    l_hand; //ptr to left hand
        Hand*    r_hand; //ptr to right hand
}
```

The constructors for initializing the pointers are the same as for an association. Similarly, because each object (body, l_hand, and r_hand) of the composition exists by itself, other functions may access the other objects directly. This is also true with the spouse object in the association.

Embedded Objects

Using the same example, here is the implementation using embedded objects for composition:

```
class Person
{
    public:
        Person(char* n, char s, int a);
        ...
        ~Person() {}
    private:
        char    name[40];
        ...
        Person*  spouse;             //binary relationship
        Body    body;               //object within object
        Hand    l_hand;             //object within object
        Hand    r_hand;             //object within object
}
```

In this implementation, the objects body, l_hand, and r_hand, are not accessible directly by any other class and any nonmember function of this class. The objects are embedded within an instance of Person. Only that object has access to these objects. Furthermore, embedded objects must be initialized in a manner similar to inheritance. Following is a sample constructor:

```
Person::Person(char* n, char s, int a): l_hand(5), r_hand(5)
    // body is implicitly constructed
    // l_hand and r_hand are
    // explicitly constructed
{
            ....
}
```

The disadvantage of this method is that the arguments of the constructor call for l_hand and r_hand are hard-coded. A more flexible constructor is:

```
Person::Person(char* n, char s, int a, int lh_f, int rh_f)
          : l_hand(lh_f), r_hand(rh_f)
{
            ....
}
```

Implementing Static Members

IT is the unique property of a static data member that its variable (a single instance) exists independently of any objects in the class. This allows it to be used in ways that are illegal for nonstatic data members. For example, static members are accessible anywhere the class is in scope, and static data members act as global variables for the class. Normally, a static data member holds data that needs to be shared among all instances of the class. It is declared with the keyword *static* and is accessible in the form "className::identifier," when the variable has public visibility. For example:

```
class Person
{
 public:
    static int    pubdata;
private:
    static int    pridata;
}

main()
{
    int tmp1 = Person::pubdata; // legal
    int tmp2 = Person::pridata;  // illegal
}
```

Pridata does not have public visibility, so it is not accessible to any function, including the Main() function. However, pubdata has public visibility and is accessible to all functions that use the proper form for accessing it.

The initialization of static data members is different from that of nonstatic data members. Static data members must be initialized once in a single source file. The source file is not within a function, and initialization must be done before main is called. Within the source file, static members are initialized in their sequence in the source file. All static data members (public and private) must be initialized. The syntax for initialization is similar to variable initialization with scoping. An example is:

```
int Person::pubdata = 15;
```

This would initialize pubdata to 15.

Static member functions are services that are provided by the class, and do not require an instance of the class in order to be accessed. A static member function can be called without an instance prefix, and is accessible by the form "className::functionName" (signature). For example:

```
class Person
{
 public:
      static int getTotal(); // get the number of person instances
        ...
 private:
      static int no_of_people; // this is incremented by the constructor
                              // and decremented by the destructor
}

main()
{
   int total = 0;
   total = Person::getTotal()
   Person* p;
   int ptotal = 0;
   ptotal = p->getTotal();
}
```

The static function getTotal() is accessed directly by using its class name and the scoping operator in the second statement of Main(). In the fifth statement of Main(), it is accessed as a function (service) of an object of the class Person. Both means of access are legal.

However, a static member function may only use static variables and arguments of its signature in its function definition. Following is an example that illustrates what is legal and illegal in a static member function:

```
class Person
{
 public:
        static    int    pubdata;
        static    int    clsfcn1();
                  int    instdata1;
                  int    instfcn1();
 private:
        static    int    pridata;
        static    int    clsfcn2();
                  int    instdata2;
                  int    instfcn2();
}

Person::clsfcn1()
{
int tmp1 = Person::pubdata; // legal
int tmp2 = Person::pridata;  // legal
int tmp3 = Person::instdata1;  // illegal
int tmp4 = Person::instdata2;  // illegal
int tmp5 = Person::instfcn1();  // illegal
int tmp6 = Person::instfcn2();  // illegal
int tmp7 = Person::clsfcn2();  // legal
}
```

Thus, a static function may access any static data members or any other static functions of the class within its function definition. However, it has no access to the nonstatic members.

Recommended Approach

BECAUSE a lot of database-layer software for object-oriented systems uses pointers and collections of pointers, we will recommend using the buried pointer approach to implement both association and aggregation. Static functions will be used as a mechanism to access shared data among objects of the same class.

■ ■ SUMMARY

IN this chapter, we learned about pointers, arrays, friends, and static members. We also learned how to use these mechanisms to support the implementation of association and aggregation. Furthermore, we learned how to use static data and static functions to handle the "global data" shared by objects in the same class.

The following summarizes the key points of this chapter:

- Pointers are used to implement association and aggregation.
- The following are some rules regarding pointers that you should keep in mind:
  a. Pointers to different classes (types) may not be equated without casting. The exception is that a public inherited subclass (derived class) pointer can be assigned to a superclass (base-class) pointer.
  b. A base-class pointer must always be cast to a legal derived-class pointer.
  c. An object pointer may always be assigned the void pointer. However, a void pointer must be cast to a legal object pointer.
- An array is used to implement the "many" side of a relationship.
- Friends give a nonmember object access to the nonpublic members of the class. This violates the encapsulation and information-hiding principles so it should rarely be used.
- Aggregation may be implemented either by buried pointers or by embedded objects.

CHAPTER

21

Introduction to the Case Studies

This book has presented many different alternatives that can be taken in developing an object-oriented system. The following chapters present two case studies demonstrating that the different approaches to developing an object oriented model lead to the same end—working systems. This chapter introduces the two case studies. The first case study presents a breakout game that is developed utlizing expert knowledge. The second case study presents a microwave oven that is developed utilizing use cases as the means for bounding the domain.

Case Study 1: Breakout

WHEN you started to play tennis, one of the most tedious exercises for improving your return was hitting the ball against a backboard or a brick wall. Wouldn't it have been more interesting if you received points for hitting a specific spot or a specific brick? This would help focus your returns on specific spots and thereby increase your accuracy (critical in playing against an opponent). However, if a spot or a brick was always worth the same value, the tendency would be to focus on the brick with the highest value. If you did this, it would not help your game because you would return the ball to a specific spot. To lead you to return to a variety of spots, the point value of each spot or brick would have to vary periodically. You could then be motivated to learn to return the ball accurately to a multitude of spots by attempting to make the highest score. This would help your game.

Our case studies are based on a game very similar to "solitaire tennis." The game is Breakout. Most readers may already be familiar with this game because it was one of the first interactive computer video games. The game is very simple and yet requires the use of all of the major concepts and mechanisms of object-oriented technology. We have used this game to teach object-oriented technology for many years and have found it extremely effective. The requirements for the game follow.

Requirements

Breakout is an interactive video game. The playing field consists of three sides and a wall of bricks. The player is given a paddle that can be moved horizontally. It is used to hit a ball against the wall of bricks. The goal of the game is to score points by removing bricks from the wall. A diagram of the game is shown in Figure 21-1.

There are two types of bricks in our game: regular and speed bricks.[1] When a ball hits a brick:

- The ball bounces off
- Regular bricks disappear and score 10 points
- Speed bricks speed up the ball by a factor of 2 and score 20 points

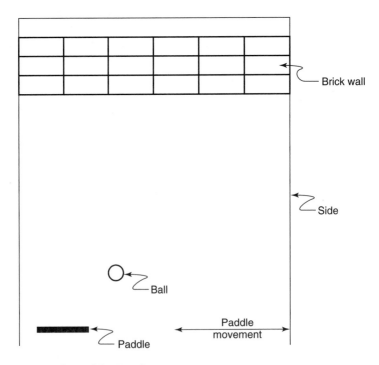

FIGURE 21-1   User view of the Breakout game.

---

[1] Though the present requirement is for two types of bricks, we are considering adding other types of bricks to the system later.

When the last brick is removed from the wall, a new wall is displayed (put into play) and the game resumes with the new wall. Whether the new wall is the same as the original wall in design is left to the developers.

Obviously, the ball will also bounce off the paddle and the three sides. However, the "bottom side" (below the paddle) is missing; thus when the ball passes behind the paddle, it is basically lost.

Play begins with the ball taking off from the paddle and moving in a random, upward direction. The ball maintains a constant speed and direction until it hits something or is lost. When it hits something, it bounces off and changes direction. It does not change its speed unless it hits a speed brick. The ball continues to move if it is in the field of play. When a ball is lost, the next ball comes into play after a 1-second delay. The game is over when the last ball is lost (no balls are left to be put into play). In the design of this game, we will allow each player three balls.

Acquiring Domain Expertise

The previous section is a typical requirements document. Like most requirements documents, it is incomplete and lacking the specific domain details needed to accurately model the application. One of the most common questions asked is "how do we get the missing domain information?" The simple answer is to get academic or on-the-job training. Because the world changes so rapidly, we must find other more immediate ways of acquiring this expertise. Some ways are:

- Observe first-hand. That is, go to the field and see what is happening.
- Listen to a domain expert. This usually means a one-to-one discussion in which you ask a lot of questions.
- Check against previous model(s). This is especially useful in an industry like communications, in which many of the CCITT standards already use the object-oriented paradigm to describe their needs.
- Check against the competition, because they have probably published their model in some conference proceeding
- "Read, read, read." There is written literature on everything.
- For a novice, the *Encyclopedia Britannica* is an excellent source to learn the foundations as well as the terminology of the field. Once you have done your homework, a domain expert is usually more receptive to helping you acquire the additional knowledge necessary to do your job. Try textbooks and professional journals in the field.
- If you are pioneering a new domain, prototyping may be the best and only means.

In any event, we have chosen the Breakout game as the case study because most of us are at least quasi-domain experts. To further help you in following the case study, we describe additional information that analysts/developers acquired from experts. This is needed in the third step of our method for specifying the behaviors of the objects in the game.

Expert's Knowledge

Mechanics of Breakout.   When a ball hits another object, there are two issues—what happens to the ball and what happens to the other object. First, we will apply some basic physics. The ball will reflect at the same angle as the ball's entry angle when it hits a flat surface. It is safe to assume that the ball hits a flat surface because in nearly all computer games, objects are modeled as rectangles. We can even assume that the ball is a square and all of the other objects are rectangles. For instance, a side is a very narrow rectangle. The ball's reaction is a new direction based on the norm of the flat surface of the obstacle (object) that it hits. This is shown diagrammatically in Figure 21-2.

A ball can hit multiple objects simultaneously. Examples are (1) a side and a brick and (2) two bricks simultaneously. The angle of reflection in those situations is the net effect of the individual reflections of each collision without considering other collisions.

A library subsystem is provided to handle certain details of the game. This would be expected if we are members of a video game-producing software company.

Time Sequencing in Simulations.   In the early 1960s, there were two schools of computer engineers: analog and digital. The analog school felt that the future of the computer was in analog because the real world is continuous and not discrete, like a digital computer. As we know today, the digital school won. There are two reasons why the digital school won. First, many of the applications that needed automation were already being modeled using a discrete model. Second, it was always possible to model any continuous action as a sequence of discrete actions.[2]

The decision to use digital computers also fit very nicely in the information technology world because nearly all the applications/systems that are built fit into the digital school. Unfortunately, engineering (especially process control) applications largely do not fit nicely into the digital school. In engineering applications, we have always had to find the right granularity of time necessary to make a digital model effective.

There is a similar problem with the Breakout game. The ball and paddle both move continuously in an idealized environment. To simulate continuous movement, we must determine a time slice that is small enough. In engineering, the control frequency

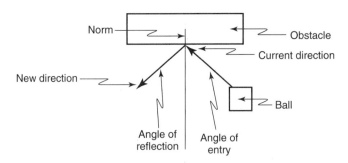

FIGURE 21-2   Collision mechanics for the Breakout game.

---

[2]   The trick here is to find a granularity small enough so that no key event is lost.

necessary to maintain a stable process is usually the driving factor for the granularity of the time slice. Similarly, the frequency needed to update the display device is the driving factor determining the granularity of the time slice.

It is a known fact among video game developers that you must refresh the screen every 66.7 milliseconds to give the illusion of continuous motion. To build an optimal game, it is necessary to display a new location for both the ball and the paddle every 66.7 milliseconds. This is implemented as an external event that is generated every 66.7 milliseconds. From a modeling perspective, we can consider the external event as telling the application that another 66.7 milliseconds has elapsed. When this occurs, both the ball and the paddle must provide a "move" service that will move themselves based on elapsed time.

There is a second external event (i.e., start button) that puts the game into play. This event causes the objects to be created and placed in the proper positions so that the game can be played. However, during analysis, we normally do not worry about how to create the objects. Later, usually during design, we will use the "start button" event to sequence the creation of the appropriate objects. For now, we will assume that the wall of bricks is in place, the paddle is displayed in the middle of the screen, and the ball is on the paddle with a velocity in an upward (toward the wall of bricks) direction.

Provided Technology Services

After modeling a business solution for your problem, you must decide on an approach to implement the business solution using available technology. This is usually called the design. We advocate that a design should involve the addition of implementation objects to the domain objects to help realize the domain model on the computer. In this section, we describe three subsystems. We describe them and their associated classes to help you implement the Breakout game. The three subsystems are:

1. Geometric subsystem
2. Display subsystem
3. Collision subsystem

Each of these subsystems is described in greater detail in the sections that follow.

Geometric Subsystem.   This geographic subsystem provides the rectangle class and all of the geometric services that we associate with a rectangle. It provides a Cartesian coordinate system for the rectangles to reside in (using Point class) and services to tell whether two rectangles intersect. It also provides services to move the rectangle in the Cartesian coordinate. The UML diagram for the geometric subsystem is illustrated in Figure 21-3.

Display Subsystem.   This subsystem provides services that superimpose bitmaps onto displayable rectangles, such that the extent of the bitmap is considered a rectangle (Displayable class). It provides the following bitmaps: ball, paddle, scoreboard, top, side, slow brick, speed brick, and digits (0–9). The bitmaps are in the Bitmap class and the PicTable class is used to link the Bitmap objects to Displayable objects. It also provides support for getting input signals (events) from the "human player" by supporting

Geometric Subsystem

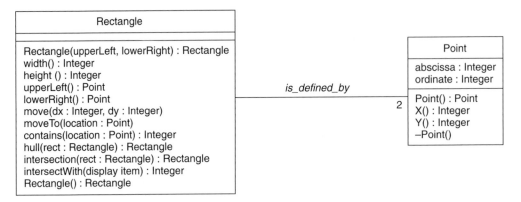

FIGURE 21-3   UML diagram for the geographic subsystem.

FIGURE 21-4   Bitmap of ball.

a Mouse class. Finally, it provides window initialization (Gfx-Env class) to deal with all the details of creating an x-window. Figure 21-4 shows the ball bitmap. Image sizes are shown in Table 21-1.

The Display subsystem is composed of classes associated with displaying the elements of our model. The Display subsystem is shown in Figure 21-5. You may use the images via an instance of the class PicTable. The height and width are given in pixels. The name is the name that you would use with getPic. For example, to get a ball image, which is pictorially a square, you would use the method as follows:

```
PicTable* pre_defined_icons = new PicTable();
char *pointer_ball = "Image_ball"
Picture *pic_ball;
    . . .
pic_ball = pre_defined_icons->getPic(pointer_ball);
    . . .
```

Collision Subsystem.   This subsystem provides a generic representation of stationary objects (Gr_obj class). More importantly, it provides a mechanism for forming a collection of stationary objects (GO_formation class) and handling collisions between a moving rectangle and any stationary object that is in the collection. Given an initial position of a rectangle in motion and a collection of stationary objects (GO_formation), it can determine when a collision occurs and compute the rebound position of the rectangle. The collision subsystem is shown in Figure 21-6.

TABLE 21-1 Image Sizes

Name	Height	Width
Image_ball	16	16
Image_paddle	5	30
Image_scoreboard	100	200
Image_top	15	500
Image_side	800	15
Image_brick	16	32
Image_slow_brick	16	32
Image_speed_brick	16	32
Image_hello_world	64	64
Image_zero	18	18
Image_one	18	18
Image_two	18	18
Image_three	18	18
Image_four	18	18
Image_five	18	18
Image_six	18	18
Image_seven	18	18
Image_eight	18	18
Image_nine	18	18

Case Study 2: Microwave Oven

IN several chapters of this book, the microwave oven was introduced to help explain state diagrams. These chapters were based on modeling the microwave oven as a single object so that we can have a simple and readily understandable example for teaching these concepts. In this case study, the microwave oven is studied as a system. This case study will demonstrate some important design considerations that we could not cover in the rest of the book.

Problem Definition

Problem Charter.   The system to be built is a simple microwave oven.

The system will have one kind of user: a person who wants to microwave food. However, though we plan to enter the market with a simple, low-cost microwave oven, the application should be designed so that we can add features and capabilities to the application very easily.

Display Subsystem

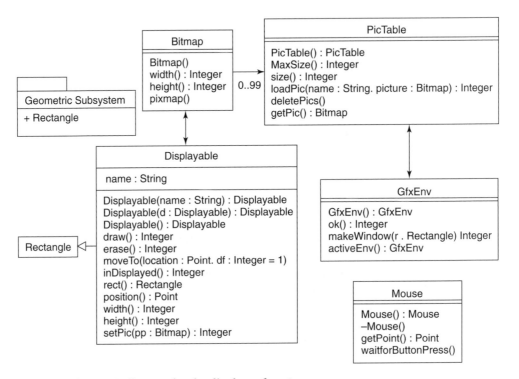

FIGURE 21-5   UML diagram for the display subsystem.

Collision Subsystem

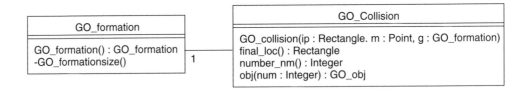

FIGURE 21-6   UML diagram for the collision subsystem.

General Description

The system to be built is a simple microwave oven. The microwave oven has two buttons: a cook button and a cancel button. When the cook button is pressed once, the oven will cook for 1 minute. If the cook button is pressed while the oven is cooking, the cook time will be extended by 1 minute. Cooking can be terminated at any time by pressing the cancel button.

Some specific requirements for the initial system:

1. Whenever the oven is cooking, the light inside the oven must be on to allow the cook to see the food. The light should also go on when the oven door is opened. At all other times, the light must be off.

2. Cooking can only be initiated when the door is closed.

3. Cooking is initiated by pressing the cook button. Pressing it once results in the oven cooking (by energizing the power tube) for 1 minute.

4. Pressing the cook button while the oven is cooking extends the cooking time by 1 minute. One can then press the cook button any number of times during cooking to add as many minutes as desired.

5. When the oven completes cooking, the power tube and the light are turned off. The oven will then alert the cook by beeping three times.

6. While the oven is cooking, opening the door will interrupt cooking. Any remaining cooking time is cleared and the oven will not beep.

7. Pressing the cancel button while the oven is cooking will cancel cooking. The light is turned off and any remaining cooking time is cleared. The oven does not beep three times for this cooking interruption.

8. Each time the cancel button or the cook button is pushed, a single beep is issued so that the cook knows that the oven has acknowledged the pushing of the button.

9. If the cook button is pressed while the oven door is open, nothing happens except a single beep.

10. If the cancel button is pressed when the oven is not cooking, nothing happens except a single beep.

11. The microwave oven has no requirement to display the cooking time.

CHAPTER

22

Case Study:
The Breakout Game

This case study follows the efforts of a team as it develops the common game—Breakout. In this chapter, we follow the individual steps taken and trace the reasoning that leads the team to its final product.

Step 1: Finding the Objects

THE team enhanced Abbott/Booch by using categories (as suggested by the leading authors in object-oriented) as an aid, and knowledge of the game to identify objects. The results are shown in Table 22-1.

The team members decided to do two things. First, they had wisely added the highest score and the list of highest scorers to the requirements. "Real developers" know they are never given all of the requirements. Second, they added a keyboard and a monitor.[1] However, no hardware objects should be included at this time, because they are design objects. Remember that the idea now is to capture the game model of the domain experts.

With the model, we should be able to play the game mentally without any hardware. Taking this into account, the team removed the design objects from the list. Note that it is common to have both the domain objects and the design objects intertwined in a requirements document. The ability to separate these objects into their proper domain is critical to a high-quality object-oriented model. Thus, domain expertise is a critical factor in building a high-quality business model.

---

[1] Another team may even want to know the raster size, scan rate, etc. of the monitor. However, no hardware objects should be included at this time because they are design objects. The idea now is to capture the game model of the domain experts.

TABLE 22-1   **List of Potential Objects**

Breakout Game	Goal	Points
Brick	Ball	PointsAdded
Paddle	BallxIsLost	Ball1
Ball2	Ball3	Side1
Side2	Side3	Paddle
BallxMoving	SpeedBrick	RegularBrick
BallHit_RegularBrick	BallHitSpeedBrick	BallHitSide
LastBrick	LastBall	Keyboard/Joystick
HighestScore	InteractiveVideoGame	Score
RemovingBrick	Wall	BrickDisappearing
Player	BallPassesBehindPaddle	GameOver
PlayingField	Brick1,..,n	PaddleMove
BallBounce	NewWall	GameEnd
Monitor	ListOfHighestScores	

Step 2: Identifying Responsibilities

REMEMBER that the goal of step 2 is to find *business* attributes and services that will be useful to solving your business problem. This step is the beginning of our abstraction process as we start to identify the relevant attributes and services, thus narrowing our problem/application space.

Looking at Adjectives

The suggested process is to first look at the adjectives in the requirements document. From the requirements document, the four potential adjectives/nouns that may be useful are: regular brick, speed brick, last ball, and last brick. Here is where the advice of just using adjectives is a little tricky.

In the case of the last brick, the "last" is not a property of any specific brick; a brick becomes the last brick only when all of the other bricks are gone. This is different from another attribute of brick, namely point value. As stated in the requirements, each brick has a point value, and that point value is applicable to all of the bricks. Thus, point value is an attribute of brick, while the last is not an attribute.[2]

For ball, however, "last" ball could be preset and unchangeable. We may also want to make "last" an attribute of the "last ball." As tempting as this is, the team recognized that this is not a very flexible model.

For "speed brick," the team argued that because the requirements said that the speed factor presently is 2, the speed-up factor can be hard-coded into the code for the

---

[2] For an attribute to be in a class, it must be applicable to every instance (object) in the class.

method. A rejected alternative was to add additional attribute called "speed" to every speed brick. This was suggested to capture the speed-up factor that the brick possesses. Again, this is possible, but the team has programmers who want to write code. The team has modeled the requirement in a manner that leads to software that is inflexible and hard to maintain. The second alternative of adding a speed attribute is better. Different speeds can be individually assigned to each brick.

Asking Question 1

The team then asked Question 1, "How is this object described in general?" The results are shown in the CRC cards that follow (Figure 22-1 through Figure 22-33). Figure 22-8 is a description of a paddle for tennis or ping-pong; the team will later discover that these may not be the best choices.

In Figure 22-7, Playing Field is defined as the area within which the game is played. The boundary of this rectangular playing field is defined by its four sides.

In Figure 22-10, the team has assumed that the Sides define the boundary of the Playing Field. It can be argued that a Side is like a line with no width. This may be conceptually correct, but in practice all lines have some thickness.

OBJECT NAME	**Breakout Game**
ATTRIBUTES	
highest score, list of highest scorers	

FIGURE 22-1   CRC card for Breakout game.

OBJECT NAME	**Points**
ATTRIBUTES	
none	

FIGURE 22-2   CRC card for Points.

OBJECT NAME	**Brick**
ATTRIBUTES	
length, width, depth, color, position, density, weight	

FIGURE 22-3   CRC card for Brick.

OBJECT NAME	Wall
ATTRIBUTES	
length, width, depth, color, position, weight	

FIGURE 22-4   CRC card for Wall.

OBJECT NAME	Ball
ATTRIBUTES	
diameter, color, position, weight	

FIGURE 22-5   CRC card for Ball.

OBJECT NAME	Player
ATTRIBUTES	
name, height, weight, skill-level, etc.	

FIGURE 22-6   CRC card for Player.

OBJECT NAME	Playing Field
ATTRIBUTES	
length, width	

FIGURE 22-7   CRC card for Playing Field.

OBJECT NAME	Paddle
ATTRIBUTES	
length, width, ~~handle size, weight, hitting surface material, etc.~~, <u>depth</u>.	

FIGURE 22-8   CRC card for Paddle.

OBJECT NAME	Score
ATTRIBUTES	
points_accumulated	

FIGURE 22-9   CRC card for Score.

OBJECT NAME	Side
ATTRIBUTES	
length, width/depth(?), position	

FIGURE 22-10   CRC card for Side.

OBJECT NAME	Interactive Video Game
ATTRIBUTES	
none	

FIGURE 22-11   CRC card for Interactive Video Game.

OBJECT NAME	Goal
ATTRIBUTES	
none	

FIGURE 22-12   CRC card for Goal.

OBJECT NAME	Removing Brick
ATTRIBUTES	
none	

FIGURE 22-13   CRC card for Removing Brick.

OBJECT NAME	Brick Disappearing
ATTRIBUTES	
none	

FIGURE 22-14   CRC card for Brick Disappearing.

OBJECT NAME	Points Added
ATTRIBUTES	
none	

FIGURE 22-15   CRC card for Points Added.

OBJECT NAME	"Game over"
ATTRIBUTES	
none	

FIGURE 22-16   CRC card for Game Over.

OBJECT NAMES	ball1, ball2, ball3
ATTRIBUTES	
same as Ball plus ball_number	

FIGURE 22-17   CRC card for Ball1, Ball2, and Ball3.

OBJECT NAMES	brick1, brick2, ..., brickn
ATTRIBUTES	
same as Brick	

FIGURE 22-18   CRC card for Brick1, Brick2, through Brickn.

OBJECT NAMES	side1, side2, side3
ATTRIBUTES	
same as Side	

FIGURE 22-19 CRC card for Side1, Side2, and Side3.

OBJECT NAME	"Ball x is Lost"
ATTRIBUTES	
none	

FIGURE 22-20 CRC card for Ball x is Lost.

OBJECT NAME	"Ball x moving" or "Ball move"
ATTRIBUTES	
none	

FIGURE 22-21 CRC card for Ball x Moves.

OBJECT NAME	regular brick
ATTRIBUTES	
same as Brick plus point_value	

FIGURE 22-22 CRC card for Regular Brick.

OBJECT NAME	speed brick
ATTRIBUTES	
same as regular brick plus speed_factor	

FIGURE 22-23 CRC card for Speed Brick.

OBJECT NAME	"Ball passes behind Paddle"
ATTRIBUTES	
none	

FIGURE 22-24 CRC card for Ball Passes Behind Paddle.

OBJECT NAME	new wall
ATTRIBUTES	
new pattern, etc.	

FIGURE 22-25 CRC card for New Wall.

OBJECT NAME	ball hit x
ATTRIBUTES	
none	

FIGURE 22-26 CRC card for Ball Hit x.

OBJECT NAME	last ball
ATTRIBUTES	
when there is no other ball	

FIGURE 22-27 CRC card for Last Ball.

OBJECT NAME	game end
ATTRIBUTES	
when all balls are lost	

FIGURE 22-28 CRC card for Game End.

OBJECT NAME	list of highest scorers
ATTRIBUTES	
array of names and the person's score	

FIGURE 22-29 CRC card for List of Highest Scorers.

OBJECT NAME	last brick
ATTRIBUTES	
when brick_count is 1	

FIGURE 22-30 CRC card for Last Brick.

OBJECT NAME	"paddle move"
ATTRIBUTES	
none	

FIGURE 22-31 CRC card for Paddle Move.

OBJECT NAME	highest score
ATTRIBUTES	
point-value	

FIGURE 22-32 CRC card for Highest Score.

OBJECT NAME	ball bounce
ATTRIBUTES	
none	

FIGURE 22-33 CRC card for Ball Bounce.

Asking Question 2

The most difficult question that needs answering is "What is our problem domain?" This will have an impact on the reusability of the classes (templates for instantiating an object) that are designed. Question 2 is really the process of abstraction (the object keeps only the attributes applicable to the problem domain). The attributes that are considered germaine are determined by the scope of the problem domain. The team defines the problem domain as the world of interactive video games. The team revisited its objects and attributes within this bounded domain. The results are shown in Figure 22-34 through Figure 22-45. A deleted attribute is shown with a strikethrough and a new attribute is shown with an underline. Their rationale is given in the following paragraphs.

OBJECT NAME	Breakout Game
ATTRIBUTES	
highest score, list of highest scorers	

FIGURE 22-34   CRC card for Breakout game.

OBJECT NAME	Brick
ATTRIBUTES	
both teams: length, width, depth, color, position, ~~density~~, ~~weight~~	

FIGURE 22-35   CRC card for Brick.

OBJECT NAME	Wall
ATTRIBUTES	
length, width, depth, ~~color~~, position, ~~weight~~	

FIGURE 22-36   CRC card for Wall.

OBJECT NAME	Ball
ATTRIBUTES	
diameter, color, position, ~~weight~~	

FIGURE 22-37   CRC card for Ball.

OBJECT NAME	Player
ATTRIBUTES	
name, ~~height, weight~~, skill-level, ~~etc.~~	

FIGURE 22-38   CRC card for Player.

OBJECT NAME	Playing Field
ATTRIBUTES	
length, width, <u>depth</u>	

FIGURE 22-39   CRC card for Playing Field.

OBJECT NAME	Side
ATTRIBUTES	
length, ~~width/depth(?)~~, position, <u>width, depth</u>	

FIGURE 22-40   CRC card for Side.

OBJECT NAME	"Ball x is Lost"
ATTRIBUTES	
none	

FIGURE 22-41   CRC card for Ball x is Lost.

OBJECT NAMES	side1, side2, side3, <u>side4</u>
ATTRIBUTES	
same as Side	

FIGURE 22-42   CRC card for Side1, Side2, Side3, and Side4.

OBJECT NAMES	brick1, brick2, ..., brickn
ATTRIBUTES	
same as Brick plus point_value and sometimes speed_factor	

FIGURE 22-43   CRC card for Brick1, Brick2, through Brickn.

OBJECT NAME	regular brick
ATTRIBUTES	
same as Brick plus point_value	

FIGURE 22-44   CRC card for Regular Brick.

OBJECT NAME	speed brick
ATTRIBUTES	
same as regular brick plus speed_factor	

FIGURE 22-45   CRC card for Speed Brick.

In current interactive video games, the density and weight of a brick are not attributes that are captured in the abstraction because it is not used.[3] Depth can be debated, as there are three-dimensional interactive video games. This is shown in Figure 22-35.

Because Wall is a collection of Bricks, it is reasonable to assume that the color will be defined for each brick and that the "color" of the wall is determined by the brick. In a sense, the "color" of the Wall is derivable. Again, the weight is not captured in the abstraction for this problem domain.

Skill-level was left as an attribute. The team wants to entice players at different levels to compete with each other, thus increasing our revenue. Name was kept as a way to identify players who makes the highest score list. This is shown in Figure 22-38.

As you can see in the requirements documentation, the paddle is abstracted into a rectangle. Thus, many of the attributes of a "real paddle" are not applicable to this abstraction. The team eliminated all attributes except for length and width, and added depth for consistency. This is shown in Figure 22-8.

---

[3]   If the team believed that weight and density are used in determining the angle of reflection in a collision, then it would have left the weight and density in the list.

Playing Field is defined as the area within which the game is played. The team has decided that the concept of a playing area is useful for determining when a ball is still in play. Remember that the idea here is to capture the objects (concepts) that are meaningful to the domain experts. Does a domain expert of video games use the concept of a playing area that determines if the ball is in play? If it helps, isn't the playing area written into most rule books about games?

Depth is added to the team list of attributes to handle three-dimensional video concepts. This is shown in Figure 22-39. In order to be consistent with the three-dimensional concept, and the fact that even a conceptual rectangular boundary must have some depth, we have added the attributes width and depth. The team's concept of a side also includes a nonvisible side for the playing area to be bounded. This is sometimes called an open side of the playing field. This is shown in Figure 22-40 and Figure 22-42.

Figure 22-41 is a consequence of the "Ball passes behind Paddle." The original thinking based on the written requirements is that this is due to the fact that the ball passes "behind the Paddle." Observing other video games, however, we realize that the requirements writer assumed that once the ball goes behind the paddle, there will be no way for the ball to stay in the field of play. But the real requirement is that the "ball is lost" when the ball leaves the playing field.

Thus, knowing or capturing the playing field as a concept is fundamental to the video game. This kind of unintentional misstatement of requirements is very common in documents. One of the most difficult tasks of the analyst/system engineer is to capture the intent, not just the statements, of the user/customer.

From the game definition, we recognize that each of the bricks that will be part of the "wall of bricks" needs to have a point value so that the player can score points when the ball hits a brick. However, some bricks, specifically speed bricks, will also speed up the ball by some speed factor.

The team recognized, however, that not all the bricks in the wall will be speed bricks. This leads to a very interesting discussion: whether speed factor is an attribute of all the bricks in the wall.

One team member brings up the fact that for the regular brick, we just make the speed factor equal to 1. This would make all the bricks alike. However, another team member argues that this is not proper, as one of the rules for being an attribute is that value is always needed and is used.[4]

Though there are some situations where having one attribute that is not used by some objects may be acceptable in design—usually for performance reasons, the team takes the purist approach and creates two classes: regular bricks and speed bricks. Some of the bricks have a speed factor and other bricks do not have a speed factor. Thus, the wall is composed of two different types (speed bricks and regular bricks) of objects. This is shown in Figure 22-43 through Figure 22-45.

---

[4]   If you do not enforce the rule, in theory everything can be instantiated from one class construct where most of the attributes are not used.

Asking Question 3

Now that the team has bounded attributes, it now applies the Western school of thinking to object-oriented analysis. They looked at the minimal specification of attributes necessary to satisfy this application. From the requirements document, it is clear that the writer/buyer is specifying a two-dimensional game. They revisited the objects and attributes within this bounded domain. The results are shown in Figure 22-46 through Figure 22-57. Again, the rationale is given in the following paragraphs.

OBJECT NAME	Breakout Game
ATTRIBUTES	
highest score, list of highest scorers	

FIGURE 22-46   CRC card for Breakout game.

OBJECT NAME	Brick
ATTRIBUTES	
length, width, ~~depth~~, ~~color~~, position, ~~density~~, ~~weight~~	

FIGURE 22-47   CRC card for Brick.

OBJECT NAME	Wall
ATTRIBUTES	
length, width, ~~depth~~, ~~color~~, position, ~~weight~~	

FIGURE 22-48   CRC card for Wall.

OBJECT NAME	Ball
ATTRIBUTES	
diameter, ~~color~~, position, ~~weight~~	

FIGURE 22-49   CRC card for Ball.

OBJECT NAME	Player
ATTRIBUTES	
name, ~~height~~, ~~weight~~, skill-level, ~~etc.~~	

FIGURE 22-50   CRC card for Player.

OBJECT NAME	Paddle
ATTRIBUTES	
length, width, ~~handle size~~, ~~weight~~, ~~hitting surface material~~, ~~etc.~~, <u>depth</u>.	

FIGURE 22-51   CRC card for Paddle.

OBJECT NAME	Playing Field
ATTRIBUTES	
length, width, <u>depth</u>	

FIGURE 22-52   CRC card for Playing Field.

OBJECT NAME	Side
ATTRIBUTES	
length, ~~width/depth(?)~~, position, <u>width, depth</u>	

FIGURE 22-53   CRC card for Side.

OBJECT NAMES	side1, side2, side3, <u>side4</u>
ATTRIBUTES	
same as Side	

FIGURE 22-54   CRC card for Side1, Side2, Side3, and Side4.

OBJECT NAMES	brick1, brick2, ..., brickn
ATTRIBUTES	
same as Brick plus point_value and sometimes speed_factor	

FIGURE 22-55   CRC card For Brick1, Brick2, through Brickn.

OBJECT NAME	regular brick
ATTRIBUTES	
same as Brick plus point_value	

FIGURE 22-56   CRC card for Regular Brick.

OBJECT NAME	speed brick
ATTRIBUTES	
same as regular brick plus speed_factor	

FIGURE 22-57   CRC card for Speed Brick.

In the application, the world is two-dimensional; thus, the depth of the brick is not applicable to the abstraction. This is also true of the wall. This is true for all objects with depth as an attribute. The result of assuming a two-dimensional world is shown in Figure 22-47 and Figure 22-48.

In answering Question 2, the team added depth as an attribute. In Question 3, however, the team deleted the same attribute. Adding an attribute to the list and then deleting the attribute is a symptom of an unclear problem domain/application scope. There is usually much frustration when each individual has his or her own definition of the domain/application that is inconsistent with the rest of the team. (It is more than frustration; the team must have a common vision!)

Based on the preceding analysis, a new list of potential objects has been constructed. This list is shown in Table 22-2. The team eliminated Goal and Points because these objects did not have any attributes and were not used as independent objects. All of the events (i.e., Removing Bricks, Ball Hit Paddle) were eliminated because they found no attributes. This is very common with events; in the attribute step, the analysis discovers no attribute.

TABLE 22-2 List of Potential Objects After Step 2

Breakout Game	~~Goal~~	~~Points~~
Brick	Ball	~~PointsAdded~~
Paddle	~~BallxIsLost~~	Ball1
Ball2	Ball3	Side1
Side2	Side3	Paddle
~~BallxMoving~~	SpeedBrick	RegularBrick
BallHit_RegularBrick	~~BallHitSpeedBrick~~	~~BallHitSide~~
~~LastBrick~~	~~LastBall~~	~~Keyboard/Joystick~~
HighestScore	~~InteractiveVideoGame~~	~~Score~~
~~RemovingBrick~~	Wall	~~BrickDisappearing~~
Player	~~BallPassesBehindPaddle~~	~~GameOver~~
PlayingField	Brick1,..,n	~~PaddleMove~~
~~BallBounce~~	~~NewWall~~	~~GameEnd~~
~~Monitor~~	ListOfHighestScores	

Looking at Services

The team applies the Abbott/Booch technique of looking at verbs in the requirements document. Then team members analyze the method for providing those services. In rereading the requirements, they found the following verb phrases:

1. "Ball hits a brick." The grammatical object of that sentence is Brick. So Brick needs to provide a hit service.
2. "Points are added to the player's score." This implies that an add service needs to be added either to player, score, or both. The easy way is to add the service to both.[5]
3. "Paddle can be moved horizontally." This implies a move service for Paddle.
4. "Ball bounces off." This implies a bounce service for Ball.
5. "Speed bricks speed up the ball." This implies a speed increase service for Ball.
6. "Ball hits the paddle." This implies a hit service for Paddle.
7. "Ball hits the side." This implies a hit service for Side.
8. "Brick removed from the wall." This implies a removal service for Wall.

---

[5] The reader is encouraged to perform an analysis of which approach would be best.

Figures 22-58 through 22-64 show the CRC cards the team has after adding the services to the objects. We did not show the CRC cards for objects in which no services were found using verbs.

OBJECT NAME	Brick
ATTRIBUTES	
length, width, depth, color, position, ~~density~~, ~~weight~~	
SERVICES	
been_hit	

FIGURE 22-58   CRC card for Brick after adding services.

OBJECT NAME	Ball
ATTRIBUTES	
diameter, ~~color~~, position, ~~weight~~, speed	
SERVICES	
bounce, speed_increase	

FIGURE 22-59   CRC card for Ball after adding services.

OBJECT NAME	Player
ATTRIBUTES	
name, ~~height~~, ~~weight~~, skill-level, ~~etc.~~	
SERVICES	
add_points	

FIGURE 22-60   CRC card for Player after adding services.

OBJECT NAME	Score
ATTRIBUTES	
points_accumulated	
SERVICES	
increment_score	

FIGURE 22-61 CRC card for Score after adding services.

OBJECT NAME	Side
ATTRIBUTES	
length, ~~width/depth(?)~~, position, <u>width</u>, <u>depth</u>	
SERVICES	
been_hit	

FIGURE 22-62 CRC card for Side after adding services.

OBJECT NAME	Wall
ATTRIBUTES	
length, width, ~~depth~~, ~~color~~, position, ~~weight~~	
SERVICES	
brick_removed	

FIGURE 22-63 CRC card for Wall.

OBJECT NAME	Paddle
ATTRIBUTES	
length, width, ~~handle size, weight, hitting surface material, etc.,~~ <u>depth</u>.	
SERVICES	
been_hit	

FIGURE 22-64   CRC card for Paddle.

Step 3: Specifying Behaviors

THE team was then ready to analyze the scenarios to identify and specify additional services that each of the objects must provide to make this game work.

The paddle scenarios were identified as follows:

1. Paddle may be moved because there is no obstruction.
2. Paddle movement requested puts the paddle outside of the playing field.
3. Paddle strikes the ball in moving.

The ball scenarios were identified as follows:

1. Ball may be moved because there is no obstruction.
2. Ball movement requested will take a ball into a side.
3. Ball hits the paddle.
4. Ball hits a brick.
5. Ball hits a brick and a side.
6. Ball hits two bricks.
7. Ball hits three obstacles (not very likely, but theoretically possible).

First, the team observes that paddle movement is not determined by time. Paddle movement is determined by the person in control of the joystick/mouse/keyboard. What is needed to change position of the paddle of a joystick/mouse/keyboard is another object, call it mouse, that provides the service. Following are the adjustments made by the team to handle the paddle scenarios.

The team discussed whether this object should just return delta x, as the y value needs to be fixed as per our requirements. The proper placing of requirements to the correct object affects the reuse issue. If it returns delta x, it makes it easier for the paddle object to do its work. However, this is less flexible. What will happen when you want to use the mouse object in another application where you want to get delta y also? This is a very subtle issue regarding "to which object does a constraint apply?" The mouse is actually allowed to move in any direction that makes sense. In fact, what is being requested is that the paddle object interpret the deltas from the mouse in a manner where only the x values are changed. This would keep the issue in the proper semantic domain, because the mouse is really a technology object and is not part of the problem domain.

Position is added to the attribute list. This is needed to compute the hull. In computer graphics, every displayable object is really a rectangle. This is because nearly all pixel maps are rectangles. Thus, the position of a displayable object is by convention the upper left corner of the rectangle.

In specifying the service for Paddle, the team identified three new services for side: getUL getLR, and InPath. The "getUL" service will get the position (x, y) of the upper left corner of the side. The "getLR" will get the position (x,y) of the lower right corner of the side. The side has some width, so the x value for the upper left corner is different from the x value for the lower right corner. The "inPath" service is very simple; conceptually, it accepts a geometric object with a position as an argument and determines if the side is occupying any of that space.

From physics, the path or the area that an object will travel in a given period of time is called a hull. One of the things that needs to be determined is whether the hull of the paddle occupies the same space as one of the sides. If it does, the paddle must not be allowed to move beyond that edge.

For the second scenario, the team decided to add range limits (maximum x value and minimum x value) as attributes of Paddle. For the third scenario, the team first considered having Paddle invoke a service of Ball to change direction, but decided that the move algorithm handles this situation. The team's adjustments to the paddle object and the addition of the mouse object are given in Figure 22-65 and Figure 22-66.

The team decided that speed bricks and regular bricks did not behave the same, so they specified the method for each object. Brick and brick1, brick2 and so on, are all now either a speed brick or a regular brick. Finally, the team decided that scoring is done by informing the player that the score needed to be incremented.[6] The objects for the team appear in Figures 22-67 through 22-75.

OBJECT NAME	**Paddle**
ATTRIBUTES	
length, width, <u>position, min-x, max-x</u>	
SERVICES	
prototype: move()	
{ // structured english definition	

---

[6]   In fact, many other teams have decided that score or points accumulated is not an object, but just an attribute of the player.

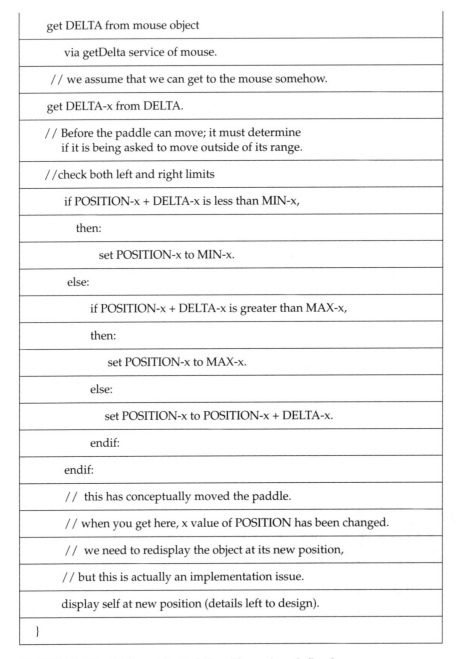

| get DELTA from mouse object |
| via getDelta service of mouse. |
| // we assume that we can get to the mouse somehow. |
| get DELTA-x from DELTA. |
| // Before the paddle can move; it must determine
if it is being asked to move outside of its range. |
| //check both left and right limits |
| if POSITION-x + DELTA-x is less than MIN-x, |
| then: |
| set POSITION-x to MIN-x. |
| else: |
| if POSITION-x + DELTA-x is greater than MAX-x, |
| then: |
| set POSITION-x to MAX-x. |
| else: |
| set POSITION-x to POSITION-x + DELTA-x. |
| endif: |
| endif: |
| // this has conceptually moved the paddle. |
| // when you get here, x value of POSITION has been changed. |
| // we need to redisplay the object at its new position, |
| // but this is actually an implementation issue. |
| display self at new position (details left to design). |
| } |

FIGURE 22-65   **CRC card for Paddle with services defined.**

OBJECT NAME	Mouse
ATTRIBUTES	
previous location	
SERVICES	
prototype: getDelta() // same as team 1	

FIGURE 22-66   CRC card for Mouse.

OBJECT NAME	Score
ATTRIBUTES	
points_accumulated	
SERVICES	
prototype: increment_score(points)	
{	
add POINTS to POINTS_ACCUMULATED.	
}	

FIGURE 22-67   CRC card for Score with services defined.

OBJECT NAME	Regular Brick
ATTRIBUTES	
position, length, width, pointValue	
SERVICES	
prototype: inPath(hull) //same as Side	
prototype: getNorm() //same as Side	

prototype: been_hit()
{   // This is now simple
ask Player to increment its value by pointValue
via add_points service of Player.
tell Wall that this brick has been removed
via brick_removed service
disappear.
}

FIGURE 22-68   CRC card for Regular Brick with services defined.

OBJECT NAME	**Speed Brick**
ATTRIBUTES	
position, length, width, <u>pointValue, SpeedFactor</u>	
SERVICES	
prototype: inPath(hull) //same as Side	
prototype: getNorm() //same as Side	
prototype: been_hit()	
{ // This is now simple	
ask Player to increment its value by pointValue	
via add_points service of Player.	
ask Ball to increase speed by SPEEDFACTOR	
via speed_increase service.	
tell Wall that this brick has been removed	
via brick_removed service	
disappear.	
}	

FIGURE 22-69   CRC card for Speed Brick with services defined.

OBJECT NAMES	Ball, ball1, ball2, ball3

ATTRIBUTES
position, width/length, velocity

SERVICES
prototype: move(elapsed_time)
{ // this is based on only ball hitting one obstacle.
compute DELTA as
VELOCITY*ELAPSED_TIME.
compute hull as
if DELTA-y is positive,
then:
set hull's start POSITION to ball's POSITION.
else:
set hull's start POSITION to ball's POSITION + WIDTH.
endif.
set hull's end POSITION to   hull's start POSITION + DELTA.
ask collision to move me
via the moveBall service.
return
}
prototype: changeDirection (new_direction)
{
set DIRECTION to NEW_DIRECTION.
}
prototype: changePosition (new_position)
{

set POSITION to NEW_POSITION.
}
prototype: speed_increase(speedFactor)
{
set VELOCITY to VELOCITY*SPEEDFACTOR.
}

FIGURE 22-70   CRC card for Ball with services defined.

OBJECT NAME	Collision
ATTRIBUTES	
????	

SERVICES
SERVICES
prototype: moveBall(hull)
{ // this handles simultaneous hits.
For each obstacle that can be in the way:
// ask each obstacle whether it is in the way.
if obstacle->inPath(hull),
then:
hit_object is obstacle.
endif:
endFor:
If hit_object(s) is not found,
then: // it can move unobstructed
ask ball to set its POSITION to POSITION + VELOCITY*ELAPSED_TIME via setPosition service.

else: // it has hit an obstacle(s).
compute NEW_DIRECTION as   net effect of all the angles of reflection.   (Details are left to design.)
ask ball to set its DIRECTION to NEW_DIRECTION   via setDirection service.
For each obstacle that is hit:
ask the object to respond   via its been_hit service.
endfor:
endif:
return
}

FIGURE 22-71 CRC card for Collision with services defined.

OBJECT NAMES	Side, side1, side2, side3
ATTRIBUTES	
length, width, position	
SERVICES	
prototype: getUL() // same as Team 1	
prototype: getLR() // same as Team 1	
prototype: inPath(hull) // same as Team 1	
prototype: been_hit()	
{ // this service was found earlier	
// does nothing	
}	

FIGURE 22-72 CRC card for Side with services defined.

OBJECT NAME	Player
ATTRIBUTES	
name, skill_level	
SERVICES	
prototype: add_points(points)	
{	
ask score to add POINTS via increment_score service.	
}	

FIGURE 22-73   CRC card for Player with services defined.

OBJECT NAME	Wall
ATTRIBUTES	
length, width, position, <u>brickCount</u>	
SERVICES	
prototype: brick_removed()	
{ // Assume that brick count keeps track of the number of bricks	
subtract 1 from brickCount	
}	

FIGURE 22-74   CRC card for Wall with services defined.

OBJECT NAME	Breakout Game
ATTRIBUTES	
ball_array[3], active_ball, lost_flag	

SERVICES
prototype: start() // this is called at beginning of game
{ // structured english definition
set ball_array[1] to ball1.
set ball_array[2] to ball2.
set ball_array[3] to ball3.
set active_ball to 1.
set lost_flag to false.
}
prototype: awake() // this is called by system every 66.7 milliseconds
{ // structured english definition
ask paddle to update its position
via move service of paddle.
ask ball_array[active_ball] to update position, direction, and speed
via move service of ball.
if lost_flag is true,
then:
reset lost_flag to false.
// take active ball out of play
set active_ball to active_ball + 1.
if active_ball > 3,
then: //all three balls are played
end game.
else:
// initialize new ball to starting position.
endif:
endif:
}
prototype: ball_lost() // this is called by side4
{ // structured english definition
set lost_flag to true.
}

FIGURE 22-75 CRC card for Breakout game.

The team has not done a complete analysis. The cases when a ball gets out of play, or the creation of a new wall have not been addressed. This is a very common practice, as practitioners really perform the first few steps in an interactive manner. So, as for earlier steps, we will not be very concerned about completeness at this time. However, notice that each of the objects assumed that it can access any object it wants. This is not correct. In the next section, the team will address the various vehicles for objects to access services of other objects.

Step 4: Specifying Relationships

THE team members reread the requirements document and used their specification of services to help define aggregations and links for them. They started by using the *is a* test to find generalizations/specializations. The results are shown in Table 22-3. The generalizations/specializations found from that table are shown graphically in Figure 22-76.

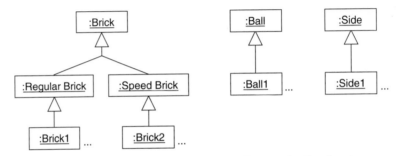

FIGURE 22-76   Object generalization/specialization diagram for Breakout game.

TABLE 22-3   Use of IS_A Table

Is A a B	Ba	ba	S	s	PF	Br	RB	SB	b1	b2
Ball	X	s	n	n	n	n	n	n	n	n
ball?	a	X	n	n	n	n	n	n	n	n
Side	n	n	X	s	n	n	n	n	n	n
side?	n	n	a	X	n	n	n	n	n	n
Playing field	n	n	n	n	X	n	n	n	n	n
Brick	n	n	n	n	n	X	s	s	s	s
Regular brick	n	n	n	n	n	a	X	n	s	n
Speed brick	n	n	n	n	n	a	n	X	n	s
brick1	n	n	n	n	n	a	a	n	X	n
brick2	n	n	n	n	n	a	n	a	n	X

Consistent with UML, objects that are underlined are actually instances. They will be removed from the model in the refinement step.

For the team, the following potential aggregations and links were identified by rereading the requirements document: Following are the results:

1. **Aggregations:**
   Wall of bricks
   Playing field consist of four sides

2. **Links:**
   Brick and score
   Player and paddle

The following potential aggregations and links were identified by reviewing the methods:

1. **Aggregations:**
   Breakout with everything

2. **Links**
   Mouse and paddle
   Ball and collision
   Collision and obstacle
   Hit_object and obstacle
   Brick and score
   Brick and wall
   Player and regular brick
   Wall and regular brick
   Player and speed brick
   Ball and speed brick
   Wall and speed brick
   Player and score

The team members discussed the results of their findings before drawing their model. They knew that they have found (just like with identifying objects) a list of relationships that are potential aggregations and links. The relationships that need to be modeled by aggregations and links are the relatively permanent relationships. The temporary relationships are better modeled by requiring the calling object pass them as part of the message (an argument of the function call).

They required a criterion to determine which of the vehicles to use when capturing these potential relationships. The criterion is as follows:

If the relationship's existence spans beyond the present method (i.e., kept beyond at least one method), then the analyst/developer should consider modeling this as a relationship. Though not clearly stated in most object-oriented books, aggregations and links (i.e., associations) are used to capture the static relationships between objects. Here, static does not mean that it cannot be altered, but that it is applicable over time. This is not the standard definition of persistence. It is usually kept for the life of a transaction and not a method. The problem is that transient relationships can also be kept using pointers. But a static relationship really was intended to map back to persistence.

This guideline must be balanced against the fact that the primary purpose of the model is to capture the domain expert's model of reality. Some judgments still must be made as to which potential relationships should be modeled as an aggregation or link.

With this guideline, team members came to the conclusion that (from a domain perspective) the wall is made from bricks and it ceases to exist when there are no more bricks. They decided it is an assembly-parts type aggregation, with the understanding that it is also a dynamic aggregation because the number of bricks may vary over time. They added that there are two types of bricks, and then debated whether the wall cared about the type of brick each one was. The team concluded that if the wall was to create itself, then it would need to know the type of brick to be placed in each slot. However, after the bricks have been placed, the wall only needs to remember the number of remaining bricks. Therefore, other than when it is created, the wall does not need to know the type of any given brick. In fact, another member of the team noticed that a wall is an aggregate of brick1, . . ., brickn, where brick1 is a very tangable object, while brick and speed brick, though objects, are conceptual. This is a correct analysis of the game.

The playing field is considered the region where the ball is in play. The team had observed that it is bounded or defined by the three sides as well as by a fourth side, which is invisible. In fact, one of the team members pointed out that the requirement for "ball lost" is not stated properly. The ball really disappears when it goes out of the playing area. This is a correct analysis of the problem. Again, a common problem with requirements documents is that they do not say exactly what they mean.

If you think about a paddle as being able to move in any direction, this is a better analysis than the original idea of a ball being lost when it traverses behind the paddle. So the team came up with the idea that the ball is lost when it hits this fourth, invisible side, because this fourth side does not behave the same way as the other three sides to the service request "been_hit." The original three sides do nothing, while this fourth side will take the present ball out of play.

The brick-to-score link is a false link, as scoring is done via brick-to-player-to-score in their model. The player-to-paddle link is also a false link. The difficulty is that the word "player" is being used to represent two different things in the requirements document.[7] First, player refers to the real person who is moving the joystick/keyboard. Second (from the game's perspective), there is the concept of a player who owns the paddle

---

7   This is very common (and so are ambiguities) in the written document.

and the balls.[8] In this situation, player refers to the real person. From the problem domain's perspective, the mouse moves the paddle. This relationship from person-to-paddle is more accurately captured because the person controls the mouse, which controls the paddle. Most analysts will consider the real person to be outside of the application domain. Thus, this link is not captured.

Even though many object-oriented authors will argue against it, the aggregation of the Breakout game being assembled from parts is very useful. The team chose to use this concept. The game is an aggregate of a wall of bricks, a player, a score, a paddle, a playing field of four sides, and three balls.

The mouse-to-paddle link is a static link because it does not change over time. This link definitely needs to be captured in this model.

The ball-to-collision link and the collision-to-obstacles link are more complex; they capture a richer semantic. Here, the ball is using the collision object to determine its new direction and its final position when it needs to move. It really does not care what obstacles are in the way or what the obstacles do when they are hit. However, for collision to determine the new direction and final position of ball, it needs to know about all of the obstacles. Moreover, the collision is being used to encapsulate a sequence of function calls that are related to the fact that a collision occurred.

One of the team members, James, suggested that both links should be in the model. This seems very strange to the other team members because they are concerned about reusability. If ball has a link to collision and you want to reuse ball, you need to also use collision. Collision has links to all the obstacles, so you also have to include a list of all the obstacles.

Now we see why a lot of object-oriented authors argue that all relationships (aggregation, link, association, and inheritance) violate the encapsulation principle and should not be allowed. We have seen with abstraction that any simplification means that some information is ignored.

In order to build the sophisticated systems of tomorrow, developers need a richer set of mechanisms/constructs rather than the primitive constructs of today's programming languages. With the latter, we are forced to make those simplifications that eventually come back to haunt us. We will return to this issue in design.

There are ways in C++ to implement these links without losing the data semantics and retaining reasonable flexibility, maintainability, and decent performance. However, the team felt very uncomfortable with these links, so it decided that the ball should only create the collision object for the life of the move method of ball. Certainly, this is the only time it is used.

However, with that decision, the team created a problem with the obstacle-to-collision link. If the collision object is dynamic and destroyed at the end of ball's move method, every time a collision object is created it must be told what ball and what obstacles are involved in this iteration. Thus, the ball now also needs to know all of the obstacles. This, however, does not seem to be information that ball should be keeping.

---

[8] This kind of misunderstanding is very common. On many occasions, an analyst must be very careful about which meaning of a word is being used.

So who should keep the list of obstacles that are hitable by the ball? After lengthy discussion, the team concluded that the best object that should know what is hitable is the breakout object. This seems to make sense because it is the breakout object that contains all of the objects of the game. So ball move would require a list of hitable obstacles as an argument.

The reader should note that the two suggestions are not equal. In James' model, it is the collision that is required to have knowledge of obstacles. This is consistent with the actual specification of the methods because ball does not directly use any services of the obstacles.

In the team's model, ball is passed the list of obstacles as an argument. This implies that ball requires knowledge of the obstacles to perform the move service. This model gives the flexibility for ball to change or modify the list of obstacles that collision uses. This can be both good and bad. In James' model, ball cannot change or modify the list of obstacles. Again, this can be good or bad.

The key issue the team should have used to determine whether the consensus model or James' model is better is whether a list of obstacles reside outside or within ball's move method control. From the game's description, a strong case can be made that the obstacles are not within the ball move control, and James' model may capture the data semantics better than consenus model.

Unfortunately, these kinds of results by a team are common in object oriented-analysis and design. Any analysis and design based on consensus will have to cater to the lowest common denominator. In our opinion, many applications and systems built using object-oriented technology will not reach their fullest potential. It is not because it cannot be done for technical reasons; it just cannot be done with the people involved. If you ask developers who have been doing leading-edge development most of their lives, most will tell you that their most difficult issue was not the technology, but the resistance to and lack of in-depth knowledge of the new technology by both fellow workers and management.

The link between the hit_object and obstacle was eliminated because one of the team members suggested that the hit_objects are a subset of all the obstacles. Moreover, this subset does not exist for more than the life of the method. The method itself has the criteria for forming the subset (list) of obstacles that are hit_objects and that subset is not used by any other object.

The four links (player-to-regular brick, wall-to-regular brick, player-to-speed brick, and wall-to-speed brick) are needed to score points or to decrement the brick_count.

The ball-to-speed brick link appears to be needed to speed up the ball. However, there are some data semantics at issue here. This link is attempting to capture the speeding up of the ball that is actually in play. Capturing this using a link requires that every time a new ball is put into play, all the links would have to change to the new ball. This suggests that a link may not be a very good way of capturing this situation.

The team, remembering that there is a second way of getting a handle to another object, decides that the calling object should pass the handle to ball as anargument.

This now means that when the ball gets speeded up is determined by the caller. This frees speed brick from having a link to any ball. Thus, speed brick-to-ball is a false link.

The player-to-score link was kept for scoring. One of the members brought up the idea of making points_accumulated an attribute of player and getting rid of score so that the link does not have to be maintained. The team rejected the idea. The link and aggregation diagrams are shown in Figures 22-77 through 22-80. In the aggregation diagram, obstacles are not included because the team did not know what to do with them. These issues will be revisited in the next step.

In this step, team members made discoveries that caused them to modify the list of objects they created and the behaviors they specified in earlier steps. This is common

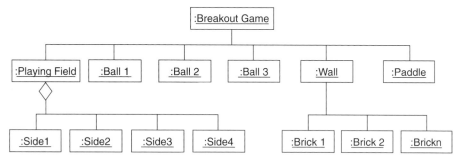

FIGURE 22-77   Object aggregation diagram for Breakout game.

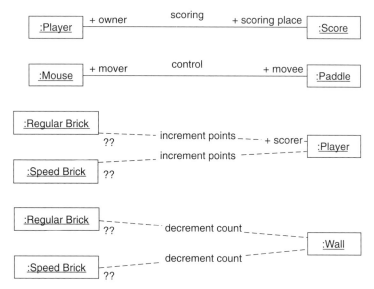

FIGURE 22-78   Object link diagram for Breakout game.

OBJECT NAME	Breakout Game
ATTRIBUTES	
To be defined	
SERVICES	
prototype: awake() // this is called by the system every 66.7 milliseconds	
{ // structured english definition	
ask paddle to update its position	
via move service of paddle.	
ask ball to update its position, direction, and speed	
via move service of ball.	
}	

FIGURE 22-79   CRC card for Breakout game.

OBJECT NAMES	side4
ATTRIBUTES	
length, width, position, not visible	
SERVICES	
prototype: getUL() // same as Side	
prototype: getLR() // same as Side	
prototype: inPath(hull) //same as Side	
prototype: been_hit()	
{ // this service should take the ball out of play	
//however, you have to be careful when you delete an object	
}	

FIGURE 22-80   CRC card for Side4.

practice in most methodologies. They made the changes shown in the following figures. This will work if there is only one paddle and one ball. However, as we know, this is not true. There are three balls; for the preceding service to work, BreakoutGame must know which ball is in play. Because balls are part of the game, it is not unreasonable for the game to keep track of which ball is in play.

The team recognized that there were a couple of problems with side4 taking the ball out of play. First, it is not natural for a side to have a relationship (link, aggregation, or inheritance) with the active ball or all the balls. Second, a side should not have the responsibility of taking a ball out of play, nor should it be the object that causes a new ball to be put into play.

If these are not responsibilities of side4, what object should have these responsibilities? After a lengthy discussion, the team concluded that taking the current ball out of play and determining the next ball to be in play, if any, is the responsibility of Breakout game. However, the team recognized that the event of the ball hitting side4 is the trigger for the preceding actions.

There are two ways to connect an event with its actions. In situations where the actions can be completed immediately, the event can cause the actions to occur as part of its method. For example, in our case, the been_hit method could either ask the active ball to become inactive or deleted, or ask game to put the next ball in play. If we did this, however, the active ball would immediately disappear. This would cause a technical problem. If you remember, this method is being called as part of the ball move for the active ball (i.e., ball move called collision's moveBall that called side4's been_hit service). So if we remove the ball now, collision's moveBall return path would be broken.

This means that we cannot perform all the actions associated with the response to the event immediately. Thus, we must use the second way of connecting events to actions. The second way is for the event recognizor (side4's been_hit service) to signal the object with the responsibilities that the event has occurred, and then it is the notified object's responsibility to ensure that the actions are taken at the appropriate time. This is the technique used by team 2. We have avoided the discussion of creating the new wall; this will be covered later.

Step 5: Refinement

THE following classes were identified after the first pass:

- Breakout Game
- Playing Field
- Paddle
- Ball
- Visible Side
- Invisible Side
- Wall

- Speed Brick
- Regular Brick
- Player
- Score
- Mouse

The class aggregations are as follows:

- Breakout Game with every Class
- Wall of Speed and Regular Bricks
- Playing Field of Visible and Invisible Sides

In this step, all of the object generalizations are converted to class generalizations and instances of a class are dropped. The results are shown in Figure 22-81 through Figure 22-83. Instances are created via the constructors and are not part of the generalization structure. All of the links are directly converted to associations. The generalization, aggregation, and association diagrams after the first pass are shown in Figure 22-84 through Figure 22-86.

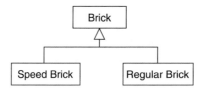

FIGURE 22-81   **Class inheritance diagram for classes derived from Brick.**

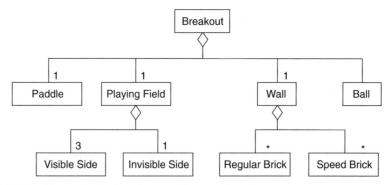

FIGURE 22-82   **Class aggregation diagram for Breakout game.**

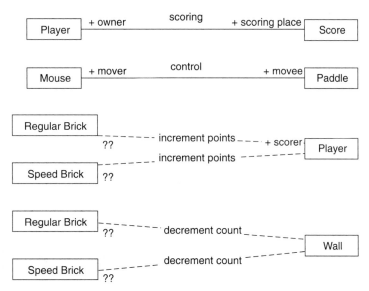

FIGURE 22-83 Class association diagram for Breakout game.

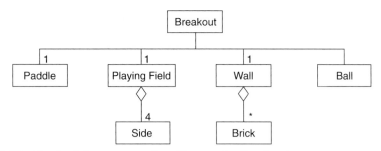

FIGURE 22-84 Revised class aggregation diagram for Breakout game.

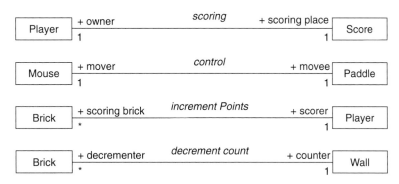

FIGURE 22-85 Revised class association diagram.

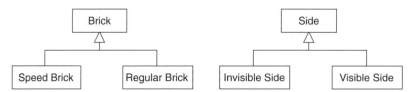

FIGURE 22-86 Revised class inheritance diagram.

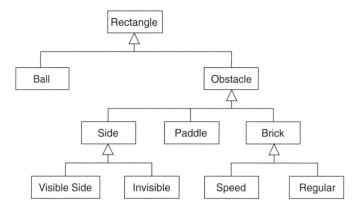

FIGURE 22-87 Final class inheritance diagram.

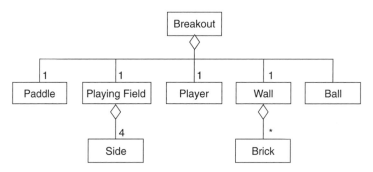

FIGURE 22-88 Final class aggregation diagram.

In the second pass, the team noticed that it could eliminate the funny relationship of Player and Wall to both Speed Brick and Regular Brick by using the superclass Brick to capture the relationship.

There was also a long discussion on whether the wall is a collection of bricks. This is confusing. Before being formed, the wall needs to know about the two types of bricks. When formed, however, the wall considers all of them bricks.[9] The new diagrams after the second pass are shown in Figure 22-87 through Figure 22-89.

The team continues to iterate. The complete class specifications are shown in Figure 22-90 through Figure 22-108.

---

[9] Wall does not use the fact that there are two types of bricks that make up the wall. Technically, the model should only reflect the steady state or static state of the model; as such, the better model is to make wall a collection of bricks. Changing of relationships as new superclasses are discovered is very common.

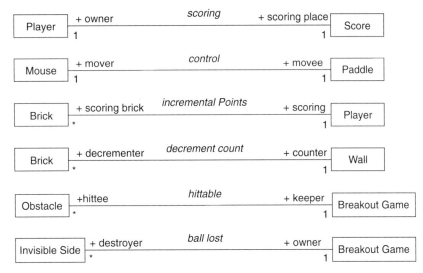

FIGURE 22-89   Final class association diagram.

CLASS NAME	Breakout Game
ATTRIBUTES	
ball_array[3], active_ball, lost_flag	
SERVICES	
prototype: start() // this is called at beginning of game	
{ // structured english definition	
set ball_array[1] to ball1.	
set ball_array[2] to ball2.	
set ball_array[3] to ball3.	
set active_ball to 1.	
set lost_flag to false.	
establish the members of the "hitable" association.	
}	

prototype: awake() // this is called by system every 66.7 milliseconds
{ // structured english definition
ask paddle to update its position
via move service of paddle.
ask ball_array[active_ball] to update its position, direction, and speed
via move service of ball.
if lost_flag is true,
then:
reset lost_flag to false.
// take active ball out of play
set active_ball to active_ball + 1.
if active_ball > 3,
then: //all three balls are played
end game.
else:
// initialize new ball to starting position.
endif:
endif:
}
prototype: ball_lost()   // this is called at beginning of game
{ // structured english definition
set lost_flag to true.
}

FIGURE 22-90 CRC card for Breakout game.

CLASS NAME	Rectangle
ATTRIBUTES	
length, width, position	
SERVICES	
prototype: getUL()	
{ // structured english definition	
return POSITION.	
// the position is the upper left corner	
}	
prototype: getLR()	
{ // lower right corner is position-x + width and position-y + length	
// we always assume that width is horizontal and length is vertical	
LR-x = POSITION-x + width.	
LR-y = POSITION-y + length.	
return LR.	
}	

FIGURE 22-91 CRC card for Rectangle.

CLASS NAME	Ball
SUPERCLASS	**Rectangle**
ATTRIBUTES	
velocity // plus all attributes of Rectangle	

SERVICES
prototype: move(elapsed_time, list_of_obstacles)
{
compute DELTA as
VELOCITY*ELAPSED_TIME.
compute hull as
if DELTA-y is positive,
then:
set hull's start POSITION to ball's POSITION.
else:
set hull's start POSITION to ball's POSITION + WIDTH.
endif.
set hull's end POSITION to   hull's start POSITION +DELTA.
ask collision to move me
via the moveBall service.
return
}
prototype: changeDirection (new_direction)
{
set DIRECTION to NEW_DIRECTION.
}

prototype: changePosition (new_position)
{
set POSITION to NEW_POSITION.
}
prototype: speed_increase(speedFactor)
{
set VELOCITY to VELOCITY*SPEEDFACTOR.
}

FIGURE 22-92   CRC card for Ball.

CLASS NAME	**Collision**
ATTRIBUTES	
none // this is a method that has been made into an object	
SERVICES	
prototype: moveBall(ball, hull, List_of_Obstacles)	
{ // this handles simultaneous hits.	
For each obstacle in the List_of_Obstacles:	
// ask each obstacle whether it is in the way.	
if obstacle->inPath(hull),	
then:	
hit_object is obstacle.	

endif:
endfor:
If hit_object(s) is not found,
then: // it can move unobstructed
ask ball to set its POSITION to POSITION + VELOCITY*ELAPSED_TIME via setPosition service.
else: // it has hit obstacle(s).
compute NEW_DIRECTION as   net effect of all the angles of reflection. (Details are left to design.)
ask ball to set its DIRECTION to NEW_DIRECTION via setDirection service.
For each obstacle that is hit:
ask the object to respond via its been_hit service.
endfor:
endif:
return
}

FIGURE 22-93   CRC card for Collision.

CLASS NAME	Obstacle
SUPERCLASS	**Rectangle**
ATTRIBUTES	
none // inherit attributes of rectangle	

SERVICES
prototype: inPath(hull)
{   // This is a geometric problem
if (the hull and the side occupy any space in common)
// the details on how to determine this is left to design
then: // there is an intersection
return true.
else:
return false.
endif:
}
prototype: getNorm()   //details deferred to design

FIGURE 22-94   CRC card for Obstacle.

CLASS NAME	Side
SUPERCLASS	Obstacle
ATTRIBUTES	
none // inherit attributes of rectangle and obstacle	
SERVICES	
none // inherit services from rectangle and obstacle	

FIGURE 22-95   CRC card for Side.

CLASS NAME	Visible Side
SUPERCLASS	Side

ATTRIBUTES
none   // inherit attributes of rectangle, obstacle, and side

SERVICES
none   // inherit services from rectangle, obstacle, and side

FIGURE 22-96   CRC card for Visible Side.

CLASS NAME	Invisible Side
SUPERCLASS	Side

ATTRIBUTES
none   // inherit attributes of rectangle, obstacle, and side

SERVICES
none   // inherit services from rectangle, obstacle, and side
prototype: been_hit()   // this overrides obstacle's method
{ // this service requires that we add   // a link between breakout game and side4.
tell breakout that ball is now lost
via ball_lost service.
}

FIGURE 22-97   CRC card for Invisible Side.

CLASS NAME	Paddle
SUPERCLASS	Obstacle

ATTRIBUTES

min-x, max-x   //inherit attributes of rectangle and obstacle

SERVICES

// inherit services from rectangle and obstacle

prototype: move()

{ // structured english definition

get DELTA from mouse object

via getDelta service of mouse.

// we assume that we can get to the mouse somehow

get DELTA-x from DELTA.

// Before the paddle can move, it must determine
if it is being asked to move outside of its range.

//check both left and right limits

if POSITION-x + DELTA-x is less than MIN-x,

then:

set POSITION-x to MIN-x.

else:

if POSITION-x + DELTA-x is greater than MAX-x,

then:

set POSITION-x to MAX-x.

else:

set POSITION-x to POSITION-x + DELTA-x.
endif:
endif:
// this has conceptually moved the paddle.
// when you get here, x value of POSITION has been changed.
// we need to redisplay the object at its new position;
// but this is actually an implementation issue.
// display self at new position (details left to design).
}

FIGURE 22-98   CRC card for Paddle.

CLASS NAME	Brick
SUPERCLASS	**Obstacle**
ATTRIBUTES	
pointValue // inherit attributes of rectangle and obstacle	
SERVICES	
none // inherit services from rectangle and obstacle	

FIGURE 22-99   CRC card for Brick.

CLASS NAME	Regular Brick
SUPERCLASS	**Brick**
ATTRIBUTES	
none // inherits attributes of rectangle, obstacle, and brick	

SERVICES
// inherit services from rectangle, obstacle, and brick
prototype: been_hit()
{   // This is now simple
ask Player to increment its value by pointValue
via add_points service of Player.
tell Wall that this brick has been removed
via brick_removed service
disappear.
}

FIGURE 22-100   CRC card for Regular Brick.

CLASS NAME	Speed Brick
SUPERCLASS	Brick

ATTRIBUTES
speedFactor   // inherits attributes of rectangle, obstacle, and brick

SERVICES
// inherits services from rectangle, obstacle, and brick
prototype: been_hit()
{   // This is now simple
ask Player to increment its value by pointValue
via add_points service of Player.
ask Ball to increase speed by SPEEDFACTOR

via speed_increase service.
tell Wall that this brick has been removed
via brick_removed service
disappear.
}

FIGURE 22-101   CRC card for Speed Brick.

CLASS NAME	Playing Field
ATTRIBUTES	
none // organizes the four sides	
SERVICES	
none	

FIGURE 22-102   CRC card for Playing Field.

CLASS NAME	Wall
ATTRIBUTES	
~~position~~, ~~length~~, ~~width~~, brickCount	
SERVICES	
prototype: brick_removed()	
{ // Assume that brick count keeps track of the number of bricks	
subtract 1 from brickCount	
}	

FIGURE 22-103   CRC card for Wall.

CLASS NAME	Player
ATTRIBUTES	
name, skill_level	
SERVICES	
prototype: add_points(points)	
{	
ask score to add POINTS via increment_score service.	
}	

FIGURE 22-104   CRC card for Player.

CLASS NAME	Score
ATTRIBUTES	
points_accumulated	
SERVICES	
prototype: increment_score(points)	
{	
add POINTS to POINTS_ACCUMULATED.	
}	

FIGURE 22-105   CRC card for Score.

CLASS NAME	Mouse
ATTRIBUTES	
previous location	
SERVICES	
prototype: getDelta()	
{ // structured english definition	
get CURRENT POSITION from mouse hardware.	
// the real hardware mouse knows where it is at	
compute DELTA	
as CURRENT POSITION minus PREVIOUS POSITION.	
return DELTA.	
// note: there was a discussion whether this object should just return delta x since the y value needs to be fixed as per our requirements.	
// This is a very subtle issue in reference to which object a constraint applies. The mouse is actually allowed to move in any direction that makes sense. In fact, what is being requested is that the paddle object interprets the deltas from the mouse in a manner where only the x values are changed.	
// The proper placing of requirements to the correct object also effects the reuse issue. If it returns delta y, it makes it easier for the paddle object to do its work. However, this is less flexible; what will happen when you want to use the mouse object in another application where you also want to get delta x?	
}	

FIGURE 22-106   CRC card for Mouse.

CLASS NAME	Wall
ATTRIBUTES	
position, length, width, brickCount	
SERVICES	
prototype: brick_removed()	
{ // Assume that brickCount keeps track of the number of bricks	
subtract 1 from brickCount	
}	
prototype: is_brickCount_zero( )	
{	
if brickCount is zero,	
then:	
return true.	
else:	
return false.	
endif:	
}	
prototype: create_new_wall( ) //left to design	
prototype; is_in_space( ) //left to design	
// we will discover that this and inPath are	
// the same function.	

FIGURE 22-107   CRC card for Wall.

CLASS NAME	Breakout Game

ATTRIBUTES
ball_array[3], active_ball, lost_flag

SERVICES
prototype: start()   // this is called at beginning of game
{ // structured english definition
set ball_array[1] to ball1.
set ball_array[2] to ball2.
set ball_array[3] to ball3.
set active_ball to 1.
set lost_flag to false.
establish the members of the "hitable" association.
}
prototype: awake()
{ // structured english definition
ask paddle to update its position
via move service of paddle.
ask ball_array[active_ball] to update its position, direction, and speed
via move service of ball.
if lost_flag is true,
then:
reset lost_flag to false.
// take active ball out of play
set active_ball to active_ball + 1.

if active_ball > 3,
then: //all three balls are played
end game.
else:
// initialize new ball to starting position.
endif:
endif:
ask Wall if brick count now zero
via is_brickCount_zero service.
if brickCount is zero,
then:
ask Wall if the ball is in its space
via is_in_space service.
if ball is not in Wall's space,
then:
ask Wall to create new wall
via create_new _wall service.
endif;
endif:
}
prototype: ball_lost()
{ // structured english definition
set lost_flag to true.
}

FIGURE 22-108   CRC card for Breakout game.

The team made a major addition to Breakout game's methods. In its start method, it now creates and maintains the list of obstacles that are hitable. This list is needed by Breakout game to use as one of the arguments to move the service of Ball.

Collision is not shown in any of the diagrams because it is a dynamic object/class. It is never kept over a time slice. The diagram in Figure 22-89 shows relatively static relationships between classes. Side is where the Playing Field-to-Side aggregation is established. So even though it has no additional attributes or methods, this class should be kept at least in analysis. It should be quite clear that Side is a useful concept in the application domain, and that by itself should be adequate reason to keep this class during analysis.

A case could be made to move the method for the been_hit service of Regular Brick to this superclass. The team felt that the method should stay with the class.

Now the team was ready for the two other aggregate classes, Playing Field and Wall. It is usually very difficult to determine aggregate type because many aggregates have all of the characteristics of the various types. However, when this aggregate was used in a specific application domain, it should always clarify the aggregate type.

The team addressed this issue as follows. First, one member suggested that Playing Field is defined when all four sides are defined. It has no attributes and provides no services directly, so this concept is not needed. This certainly is what the person had read in object-oriented books. It also would make the model have fewer classes and objects; thus, it must be good. This would be right, if the goal of object-oriented analysis/design is to make things as simple as possible.[10]

A second member of the team argues that Playing Field is a basic concept of the game. It was how the team came up with the fourth side. Another team member argues that it organizes the Game. If you do not have Playing Field, the four sides would all be part of Game and the concept that the sides form a boundary would be lost.

Now we have a very concrete example of how difficult it is to determine whether a concept is used or not used in an application domain. In any event, the team decided that Playing Field is a useful concept.

The wall seems easier because all of the team members considered it an assembly-parts type. In fact, the brickCount attribute is tied to it, being made from bricks. Even though it was recognized that the wall can be thought of as a rectangular region with position, length and width, this fact is not being used. Therefore, the attributes were dropped by the team. Then, the team adds the final three classes—Player, Score, and Mouse—for completeness.

Now, the team still had one more issue to resolve—creating a new wall. This can be done very simply. When brickCount, which Wall decrements, is zero, it is time to create a new wall. This decision just adds a few lines to the method brick_removed for Wall.

However, careful analysis by the team revealed two flaws. First, just like ball lost, there is a technical problem with creating a new wall within the method brick_removed;

---

[10] However, we think that is the wrong goal. It is our opinion that many of our problems come from trying to solve complex problems with constructs that are too simple to capture all the rich data semantics, procedural semantics, structural semantics, and declarative semantics of the application domain. We do not believe that developers intentionally write spaghetti code and forget to capture important information; instead, for years developers/programmers have been trying to build skyscrapers with a hammer and saw (simple to use), instead of the sophisticated tools that professional builders use. It is no wonder why so many software projects are failures.

the last brick has not been removed. Second, even without the technical problem, there is a business problem. The chances are that when the last brick is hit, the ball will be within the area that will be used to place the new set of bricks. If the application just places the wall back onto the playing surface, the ball would be trapped within the wall. This would make it very easy for the player to score points.

As usual, the requirements are not quite accurate. What the customer wants is for the ball to clear the area where the new set of bricks will be placed before the new wall is created. To handle this, the team decides that the best way to do this is for the Breakout game to handle testing for when a new wall will be created.

Wall will provide three new services: (1) is_brickCount_zero, which returns True when the brickCount is zero, (2) create_new_wall, which creates a new wall, and (3) is_in_space, which returns True if the object being passed as an argument is in the space of the wall. To be able to do this, the team needed to revive the attributes of position, length, and width for Wall.[11] The changes to Wall and Breakout game to handle creating a new wall are given in Figures 22-107 and 22-108.

Step 6: Design

IN the formation of subsystems, a starting point is to try to use existing subsystems. In the case study, three subsystems are made available to the team during design. Armed with these three subsystems of classes that it may be able to use, the team started to design its application.

The discussion went as follows: The mouse is very useful, and one team member suggested that the "main program" (i.e., the awake method of the Breakout game) should use the mouse getPoint service to get the new values and then pass it to Paddle as arguments. This is certainly the way most procedural programmers would have done it, so it must be so in object-oriented. However, another team member pointed out that knowledge of the mouse is not part of the game, but it is an implementation object that is needed only by Paddle.

By having the Breakout game get data from Mouse, the suggestion has broken the encapsulation principle. A third team member asked, "How can it be done without breaking the encapsulation principle?" After some thought, the second team member recognized that Mouse is actually a collaborator of Paddle in Paddle's performing its move service, and relationships with collaborators are usually captured by using associations. The second team member suggested that there needs to be an association between Paddle and Mouse that was already captured in the actual model.

This scenario is very common in projects. Even though the team has properly identified key concepts such as an association between Paddle and Mouse, it reverts back to a procedural way of implementing the application. This negates the benefits of having

---

[11] The team wanted to use the fact that the wall is both a rectangular region and an assembly of bricks. In object-oriented technology, this is done very easily. Consider how you would do this with conventional paradigms.

performed the object-oriented analysis and the application will not be able to realize the benefits of object-oriented technology.[12]

After recognizing that having Paddle use an association to access the mouse service is better object-oriented programming, the first team member decided that he can still use his prior experience to save the day. He notices that Displayable inherits from Rectangle and that Ball and Obstacle also need to inherit from Rectangle. Furthermore, both Ball and Obstacle are displayable. So he recommended that the team can take advantage of the fact that Displayable inherits from Rectangle by simply replacing Rectangle in its inheritance diagram with Displayable.

However, another team member had a problem with this. She raised the issue that Rectangle in a graphic subsystem must be in raster units of the display device, while the rectangle in the original model is in engineering units. They are not the same semantic rectangle, so the team should not be using the same rectangle to capture two semantically different concepts. Of course, the first team member argued that performance would be faster if the team just mentally converted everything to raster units because it will have to be done anyway.

Wisely, the team recognized that if it accepts the first team member's argument, it would not be free. In fact, there was a lot of maintainability and portability issues in this case. As a result, the team decided that it will sacrifice performance to preserve the semantic definitions.[13] Figure 22-109 shows the revised inheritance diagram for team 2.

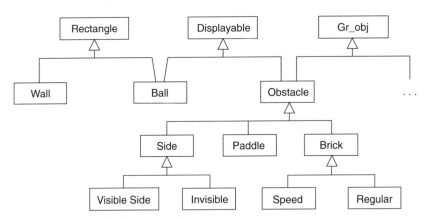

FIGURE 22-109   Revised inheritance diagram.

---

[12] It has been our experience that implementation constraints, especially when developers have to meet interfaces of legacy systems that are defined for procedural programming as well as having to meet performance constraints and language limitations, may compromise the main benefits (flexibility and maintainability) of moving to object-oriented technology. Unfortunately, it is not that object-oriented technology does not live up to its promises; it is more that developers/organizations have not made the changes necessary for it to happen.

[13] This is not a trivial issue. In real projects with performance constraints, every time independent classes are collapsed into one class for performance, the system is less flexible and harder to maintain. It is our recommendation that you should upgrade your hardware instead of collapsing the classes because hardware is getting cheaper faster than the cost of software maintenance and development.

Something very powerful happened here. The team is able to reuse the Rectangle class in two different semantic domains. Both Wall and Ball inherit directly from rectangle and Obstacle inherits from Gr_obj, which has embedded in it a rectangle.

These objects use Rectangle with application domain (engineering) units. These units could be miles, feet, meters, etc. However, all of the displayable objects also inherit from Displayable, which also inherits from Rectangle. However, the rectangle in Displayable is in raster units or the units of the display device. Here the team has used multiple inheritances very effectively to handle different semantic domains. This is a very powerful way to model objects/classes that operate in multiple semantic domains, when it seems natural for all of the attributes and services of the superclass to be part of the subclass.

However, in the case of the mouse and the paddle, it is not natural for a paddle to be a subclass of a mouse. In this instance, the team links the two classes together via a relationship. In this particular case, the team felt that this was a very weak relationship and represented it by an association.[14] Now the team was ready to look for opportunities to use polymorphism for handling of services. So the team started to look at the services of all the objects. The first service that the team found in common is the move service. Both Ball and Paddle have move services, and from the caller, Breakout game, perspective they have the same semantic meaning.

However, the signatures are quite different. The ball's move service has two arguments, while the paddle's move service has no arguments. Furthermore, both services are used only once in the application. Thus, in "good implementation judgment," the team decided to ignore the semantic commonality.[15]

The team had a very long discussion on the been_hit service of Invisible Side, Regular Brick, and Speed Brick. A team member said that from the caller's perspective, all three classes are providing the same service. In fact, the collision object that uses this service does not even know whether it has hit a brick, a side, or a paddle. However, another member said that they are not the same service because their methods (behaviors) are different. Furthermore, Visible Side and Paddle do not even have such a service. However, the first team member remembered very well how to solve these issues; she suggested that they define the service in the superclass and declare it as a no-op method for the superclass. Furthermore, any arguments differences can be handled by adding the missing argument to the signature and ignoring them in the method. Her suggestion was taken by the team. The revised class specifications are shown in Figures 22-110 through 22-116.

---

[14] Although it is rare that aggregation is used to integrate implementation classes/objects into the model, it should be considered when you are in the design stage.

[15] This is actually bad judgment. What happens when there are multitudes of moving objects?

CLASS NAME	Obstacle
SUPERCLASS	Rectangle

ATTRIBUTES
none   // inherit attributes of rectangle

SERVICES
prototype: inPath(hull)
{   // This is a geometric problem
if (the hull and the side occupy any space in common)
// the detail on how to determine this is left to design
then: // there is an intersection
return true.
else:
return false.
endif:
}
prototype: getNorm()   //details deferred to design
prototype: been_hit( )
{
// do nothing
}

FIGURE 22-110   CRC card for Obstacle.

CLASS NAME	Invisible Side
SUPERCLASS	Side

ATTRIBUTES
none // inherit attributes of Rectangle, Obstacle, and Side

SERVICES
none // inherit services from Rectangle, Obstacle, and Side
prototype: been_hit() // this overrides obstacle's method
{ // this service requires that we add   // a link between breakout game and side4.
tell breakout that ball is now lost
via ball_lost service.
}

FIGURE 22-111 CRC card for Invisible Side.

CLASS NAME	Regular Brick
SUPERCLASS	Brick

ATTRIBUTES
none // inherit attributes of Rectangle, Obstacle, and Brick

SERVICES
// inherit services from Rectangle, Obstacle, and Brick
prototype: been_hit() // this overrides obstacle's method
{ // This is now simple
ask Player to increment its value by pointValue
via add_points service of Player.
tell Wall that this brick has been removed.
via brick_removed service
disappear.
}

FIGURE 22-112 CRC card for Regular Brick.

CLASS NAME	Speed Brick
SUPERCLASS	Brick

ATTRIBUTES
speedFactor   // inherit attributes of Rectangle, Obstacle, and Brick

SERVICES
// inherit services from Rectangle, Obstacle, and Brick
prototype: been_hit()   // this overrides obstacle's method
{   // This is now simple
ask Player to increment its value by pointValue
via add_points service of Player.
ask Ball to increase speed by SPEEDFACTOR
via speed_increase service.
tell Wall that this brick has been removed
via brick_removed service
disappear.
}

FIGURE 22-113 CRC card for Speed Brick.

CLASS NAME	MouseX //library use Mouse

ATTRIBUTES
previous location

SERVICES
prototype: getDelta()
{ // structured english definition
get CURRENT POSITION from mouse hardware.

// the real hardware mouse knows where it is at
compute DELTA
as CURRENT POSITION minus PREVIOUS POSITION.
return DELTA.
}

FIGURE 22-114   CRC card for Mouse.

CLASS NAME	Breakout Game
ATTRIBUTES	
ball_array[3], active_ball, lost_flag	
SERVICES	
prototype: start() // this is called at beginning of game	
{ // structured english definition	
set ball_array[1] to ball1.	
set ball_array[2] to ball2.	
set ball_array[3] to ball3.	
set active_ball to 1.	
set lost_flag to false.	
establish the members of the "hittable" list.	
initialize the display (graphic) environment.	
}	
prototype: awake()	
{ // structured english definition	
ask paddle to update its position	
via move service of paddle.	

ask ball_array[active_ball] to update its position, direction, and speed
via move service of ball.
if lost_flag is true,
then:
reset lost_flag to false.
// take active ball out of play
set active_ball to active_ball + 1.
if active_ball > 3,
then: //all three balls are played
end game.
else:
// initialize new ball to starting position.
endif:
endif:
ask wall if brick count now zero
via is_brickCount_zero service.
if brickCount is zero,
then:
ask wall if the ball is in its space
via is_in_space service.
if ball is not in wall's space,
then:
ask wall to create new wall
via create_new _wall service.
endif;
endif:

}	
prototype: ball_lost()	
{ // structured english definition	
set lost_flag to true.	
}	

FIGURE 22-115 CRC card for Breakout game.

CLASS NAME	Wall
SUPERCLASS	**Rectangle**

ATTRIBUTES
brickCount

SERVICES
prototype: brick_removed()
{ // Assume that brick count keeps track of the number of bricks
subtract 1 from brickCount
}
prototype: is_brickCount_zero( )
{
if brickCount is zero,
then:
return true.
else:
return false.
endif:
}

| prototype: create_new_wall( )   // left to design |
| prototype: is_in_space( )   // left to design |
| // we will discover that this and inPath are |
| // the same function. |

FIGURE 22-116   CRC card for Wall.

Now the team was ready to address the associations. The team accepts the player-to-score, mouse-to-paddle, and brick-to-wall associations. In fact, the brick-to-wall association would be implemented using the aggregation relationship because the semantic meaning is consistent and compatible. However, the team had issues with the remaining three relationships. First, the team could not see it being natural for Brick to have a relationship with Player solely for the purpose of scoring.

A team member recognized that scoring is really not part of a service of Brick, but is really a result of collision. That person suggested that a point value be returned to collision by Brick instead of Brick doing the scoring. This means that Brick does not have to have an association with Player. However, collision must now know how to score. To create an association between collision and Player is still not natural, as one would not expect collision to know about a player. However, if the team created a new object call Scoreboard, scoring can be done by telling the scoreboard to update the score. This seems reasonable. In fact, now it seems plausible for either brick or collision to have this relationship.[16] Note that object-oriented technology does not force you to choose exclusively. You can implement both relationships. It is semantically very rich. In this case, the team decided that scoring is a property of collision.

Even with that decision, it still seems very awkward for collision to have access to a specific instance of a scoreboard. The problem is that scoring is not in the same semantic domain as collision. In fact, scoring, with its associated objects as Player, Score, and Scoreboard, is really another subsystem of its own. However, using an association to get to this subsystem services is a bit awkward. It would be nice to be able to access services of another subsystem without establishing an association. The answer is, obviously, there is a way.

By definition, a class is also an object; as such it has attributes and services. How does one access class services? In fact, every object has access to class services by knowing the class name, its service name, and its signature. This is the closest thing to a global service (or function). The collision or Brick objects can use a class service of Scoreboard to access the scoring service of the scoring subsystem. This very nicely separates the

---

[16] This is again another very common problem; the relationship is captured by the wrong object or at the wrong abstract class. So is it correct to have the relationship at Brick or at collision? The answer is that it all depends on the application. If scoring is the result of a collision, then the relationship belongs to the collision object. However, if scoring is really a property of the brick, then the relationship should be established for Brick. For example, if we decide that you can score the brick value by not hitting the brick for 50 seconds, then scoring is more a property of Brick than it is of collision.

issue of who should have points added to their score from the issue of when should scoring occurs.

There is a similar issue with the association between Obstacle and Breakout game. Again, this problem is solved differently. Here the library of classes from the collision subsystem removed our concerns. This again should seem correct to the reader, as this relationship is really part of the collision subsystem. The team recognized that the GO_formation object is, in fact, the list.

The discussion about the association between Invisible Side and Breakout game was very complex. A well-encapsulated resolution to this issue is to have Invisible Side notify collision that the ball is lost. Then, collision would notify Ball that it is lost, and finally, when game can delete the ball, it would ask Ball for permission. However, the team decided that this was very complex and difficult to follow. So it took advantage once again of the class services and made Ball Lost a class service of game.

Step 7: Implementation

For the most effective way to learn how to translate classes into C++, we will start with a simpler version of the Breakout game and then sucessively add more details to the code. In a real project, the team would have generally moved to the more direct implementation.

Implementing Class

We will start with a simple version of the Breakout game. This version, as shown in Figure 22-117, will have just four walls, the paddle, and one ball.

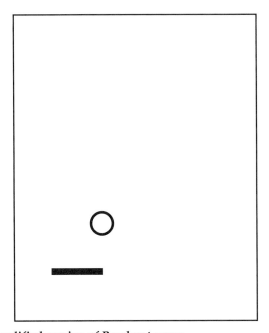

FIGURE 22-117   Simplified version of Breakout game.

In the process of doing detailed design, a team member decided that both the paddle and the wall are part of the field because the paddle and the wall use it as a boundary. The revised diagrams of aggregation, inheritance, and association are shown, along with any revisions, in Figure 22-118, Figure 22-119, and Figure 22-120. Figures 22-121 through 22-128 show the revised CRC cards for the necessary classes.

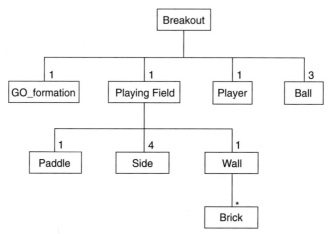

FIGURE 22-118   Class aggregation for simplified version of Breakout.

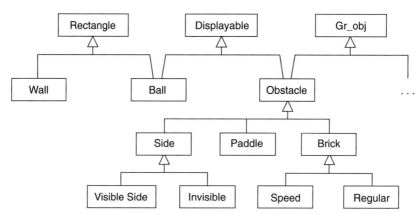

FIGURE 22-119   Inheritance diagram for simplified Breakout game.

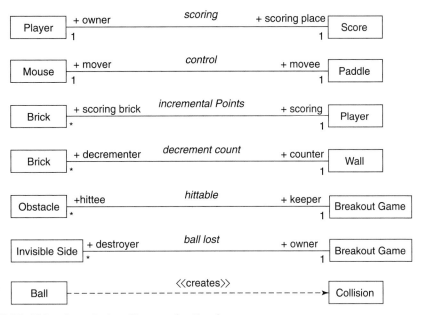

FIGURE 22-120   Association diagram for Breakout game.

CLASS NAME	Game
Responsibility	**Collaboration**
Provide "play the game" service to Main	GO_formation
Manage its aggregation	Scoreboard
	Field
	Players

METHODS	
Game( ) // create a game object	form
~Game( ) // destroy the game object	sb
void play_game( ) // play the game, see awake	fld

static Point convertGtoD(Point x) // conversion	plys
static Point convertDtoG(Point x) // conversion	

FIGURE 22-121 CRC card for Breakout game.

CLASS NAME	Obstacle
SUPERclasses	Gr_obj, Displayable
SUBclasses	Side, Paddle, Brick

Responsibility	Inheritance
Provide foundation object for hitable.	Gr_obj
Provide display capabilities.	Displayable
Provide link to GR_obj	

METHODS	Variables
Obstacle(GO_formation *f, Rectangle loc, char *name, Point p	
~Obstacle()	

virtual SpeedFactor respond_to_being_hit
       (Collision *c) // this is been_hit,
        // except that this returns a speed factor
        // this team has decided that speed up
        // is caused by the collision.
        // this has an advantage that if you hit two
        // speed bricks simultaneously,
        // the program can decide to speed up by,
        // say, 3 or anything you want.	

void *real_identity() //need by GO_collision	

FIGURE 22-122 CRC card for Obstacle.

CLASS NAME	Paddle
SUPERclass	**Obstacle**

Responsibility	Inheritance/Collaboration
Move itself as a movable.	Obstacle
Uses mouse to determine how it moves.	Mouse
Inherits it hit properties.	

METHODS	Variables
Paddle(GO_formation *f, Rectangle loc, Point P, int xmax, int xmin	mouse_prev_pos
~Paddle	mouse
void move()	Xmax
	Xmin

FIGURE 22-123   CRC card for Paddle.

CLASS NAME	Side
SUPERclass	**Obstacle**
SUBclasses	**ClosedSide, OpenSide**

Responsibility	Inheritance
Provide side abstraction	Obstacle

METHODS	Variables
// constructor	
// destructor	

FIGURE 22-124   CRC card for Side.

CLASS NAME	ClosedSide
SUPERclass	Side

Responsibility	Inheritance
Provide closed side abstraction	Side

METHODS	Variables
// constructor	
// destructor	

FIGURE 22-125 CRC card for ClosedSide.

CLASS NAME	Ball
SUPERclasses	Rectangle, Displayable

Responsibility	Inheritance
Provide ball abstraction	Rectangle
Provide "move" service given time-elapsed and the hitable formation	Displayable
Provide service to change velocity	
Provide service to change position	
Provide service to get velocity	
Provide service to get rectangle of ball	

METHODS	Variables
Ball(Point v, Point a, Point b);	
// destructor	

void move (int time_elapsed, GO_formation *form);	
void change_velocity(Point v);	
void change_position(Point new_position);	
Point get_velocity(); // { return velocity; }	
// Rectangle rect() const; // { return rectangle of ball }	

FIGURE 22-126   CRC card for Ball.

CLASS NAME	Collision
SUPERclass	**GO_collision**
Responsibility	Inheritance
Provide collision detection service	Private inheritance of
Provide scoring service to Hit_objects	GO_collision
METHODS	**Variables**
Collision(Rectangle init_projectile, Point motion, GO_formation *form)	
~Collision()	
void moveBall(Ball *ball)	
void incr_score(int score)	

FIGURE 22-127   CRC data for Collision.

CLASS NAME		Field	
Responsibility		**Collaboration**	
Manage its aggregation		Wall	
		ClosedSide	
		OpenSide	
		Paddle	

METHODS	**Variables**
// constructor to create object of type field	w
// destructor to destroy object of this type	top, left, right
getPaddle() // return a pointer to a paddle	bottom
getWall() // return pointer to a wall	pd

FIGURE 22-128 CRC card for Field.

Following are the header files (.h files) for the classes:

class.h file:

```
#ifndef _CLASS_H
#define _CLASS_H

// all forward declarations for classes
class Game;
class Field;
class Wall;
class Brick;
class Reg_brick;
class Speed_brick;
class Paddle;
class ClosedSide;
class OpenSide;
class Side;
class Obstacle;
class Ball;
class Collision;
class Scoreboard;
```

```
class Player;
class Players;
// library classes

class Point;
class Rectangle;
class GO_formation;
class Gr_obj;
class GO_collision;
class Displayable;
class Mouse;


#endif
```

Notice that the class.h file is use to capture all of the forward references. This has the advantage of making it easier for the programmer, so the programmer does not have to worry about forward declaration. All the programmer has to do is include the super-classes and any embedded classes. This comes at a price, however, as each new forward declaration you add to the class.h file will cause everything to recompile. For a large system, you may not want this to happen.

Ball.h file:

```
#ifndef _BALL_H
#define _BALL_H

#include   "Displayable.h"
#include       "Rectangle.h"
#include       "class.h"

typedef int    SpeedFactor;

class Ball : public Displayable, public Rectangle
{
    private:
        Point   velocity;
    public:
        Ball(Point v, Point a, Point b);
        ~Ball();
        void    move (int time_elapsed, GO_formation *form);
        void    change_velocity(Point v);
        void    change_position(Point new_position);
        Point   get_velocity();          // { return velocity; }
        //      Rectangle rect() const; // { return rectangle of ball}
};
#endif
```

There are two new public functions: Ball(...) and ~Ball(). The first function is called a **constructor** in C++, and the second function is called a **destructor**.

Paddle.h file:

```
#ifndef _PADDLE_H
#define _PADDLE_H

#include       "class.h"
#include       "Obstacle.h"

class Paddle: public Obstacle {
    private:
        Mouse *mouse;
        Point mouse_prev_pos;
        int Xmax;
        int Xmin;
    public:
        Paddle(GO_formation *f, Rectangle loc, Point P, int xmax,
               int xmin);
        ~Paddle();
        void move();
};
#endif
```

Field.h file:

```
#ifndef _FIELD_H
#define _FIELD_H

#include "class.h"

class Field {
    private:
        Side    *top, *left, *right, *bottom;
        Paddle  *pd
    public:
        Field(GO_formation *form);
        ~Field();
        Paddle *getPaddle();
};
#endif
```

Side.h file:

```
#ifndef _SIDE_H
#define _SIDE_H
```

```
#include          "class.h"
#include          "Obstacle.h"

class Side : public Obstacle {
    public:
        Side(GO_formation *f, Rectangle loc, char *name, Point p);
        ~Side();
};
#endif
```

Visible.h file:

```
#ifndef _CLOSEDSIDE_H
#define _CLOSEDSIDE_H

#include          "class.h"
#include          "Side.h"

class VisibleSide : public Side {
    public:
        VisibleSide(GO_formation *f, Rectangle loc, char *name,
                    Point P);
        ~VisibleSide();
};
#endif
```

Collision.h file:

```
#include          "class.h"
#include "GO_collision.h"

class Collision : private GO_collision {
    private:
    public:
        Collision(Rectangle init_projectile, Point motion,
                  GO_formation *form);
        ~Collision();
        void moveMe(Ball *ball);
};
```

Game.h file:

```
#ifndef _GAME_H
#define _GAME_H
```

```
#include   "class.h"

class Game {
    private:
        GO_formation *form;
        Field *fld;
    public:
        static bool ball_lost_flag;
    public:
        Game();
         ~Game();
        static void ball_lost();
        static Point convertGtoD(Point x);
        static Point convertDtoG(Point x);
};
#endif
```

Main.C file:
```
#include <iostream.h>
#include <new.h>
#include <assert.h>
#include <stdlib.h>
#include <string.h>
#include "GfxEnv.h"
#include "Game.h"

#include "IO.h"
#include "Breakout_Pak.h"

void free_store_empty() {
    static int i = 0;
    if(i++ == 0) {                    // guard against cerr allocating memory
        cerr << "Out of memory\n"; // tell user
        abort();  // give up
    }
}

static void init( const The& );
static void cleanup();
static Breakout_Pak bk_pak;

main ()
{
        // handle running out of memory
```

```
        set_new_handler(free_store_empty);
        cout << "here we go" << endl;
            // create the graphics environment
        GfxEnv ge( bk_pak );
        cout << "created ... " << flush ;
            // make the window for our game
        ge.makeWindow(Rectangle(5, 5, 805, 805));
        cout << "windowed ... " << flush ;
            // make sure everything is ok
        assert(ge.ok());
        cout << "OK'd ... " << flush ;
            // do some initialization
        init( ge.the() );
        cout << "init'd ... " << flush ;
            // Construct the breakout object here
            // and start things off
            //void test();
            //test();
            //cout << "hey this worked" << endl;
             /* Create game object */
        Game* game = new Game();
            /* Play game */
        game->play_game();
             /* Delete game object */
        delete game;
        cleanup();
        cout << "play over" << endl;
        return(0);
    }

#if 1
#    include "images/ScoreBoard"
#    include "images/Paddle"
#    include "images/Brick"
#    include "images/SpeedBrick"
#    include "images/SlowBrick"
#    include "images/Ball"
#    include "images/Side"
#    include "images/Top"
#    include "images/d0"
#    include "images/d1"
#    include "images/d2"
#    include "images/d3"
#    include "images/d4"
#    include "images/d5"
```

```
#     include "images/d6"
#     include "images/d7"
#     include "images/d8"
#     include "images/d9"
#endif

void
init( const The& )
{
#if 1
    // build Bitmaps from the data
    Pic_init bscoreboard(ScoreBoard_width, ScoreBoard_height,
                ScoreBoard_bits );
    Pic_init bbrick(Brick_width, Brick_height, Brick_bits );
    Pic_init bspbrick(SpeedBrick_width, SpeedBrick_height,
                SpeedBrick_bits );
    Pic_init bslbrick(SlowBrick_width, SlowBrick_height,
                SlowBrick_bits );
    Pic_init bball(Ball_width, Ball_height, Ball_bits );
    Pic_init bside(Side_width, Side_height, Side_bits );
    Pic_init btop(Top_width, Top_height, Top_bits );
    Pic_init bpaddle(Paddle_width, Paddle_height, Paddle_bits );
    Pic_init bboard(ScoreBoard_width, ScoreBoard_height,
                ScoreBoard_bits );
    Pic_init bd0(D0_R_18_width, D0_R_18_height, D0_R_18_bits );
    Pic_init bd1(D1_R_18_width, D1_R_18_height, D1_R_18_bits );
    Pic_init bd2(D2_R_18_width, D2_R_18_height, D2_R_18_bits );
    Pic_init bd3(D3_R_18_width, D3_R_18_height, D3_R_18_bits );
    Pic_init bd4(D4_R_18_width, D4_R_18_height, D4_R_18_bits );
    Pic_init bd5(D5_R_18_width, D5_R_18_height, D5_R_18_bits );
    Pic_init bd6(D6_R_18_width, D6_R_18_height, D6_R_18_bits );
    Pic_init bd7(D7_R_18_width, D7_R_18_height, D7_R_18_bits );
    Pic_init bd8(D8_R_18_width, D8_R_18_height, D8_R_18_bits );
    Pic_init bd9(D9_R_18_width, D9_R_18_height, D9_R_18_bits );

    // load pictures of objects
    PicTable& pt = GfxEnv::activeEnv()->pictures();
    pt.loadPic("Image_scoreboard", bscoreboard);
    pt.loadPic("Image_brick", bbrick);
    pt.loadPic("Image_speed_brick", bspbrick);
    pt.loadPic("Image_slow_brick", bslbrick);
    pt.loadPic("Image_ball", bball);
    pt.loadPic("Image_side", bside);
    pt.loadPic("Image_top", btop);
    pt.loadPic("Image_paddle", bpaddle);
```

```
        pt.loadPic("Image_zero", bd0);
        pt.loadPic("Image_one", bd1);
        pt.loadPic("Image_two", bd2);
        pt.loadPic("Image_three", bd3);
        pt.loadPic("Image_four", bd4);
        pt.loadPic("Image_five", bd5);
        pt.loadPic("Image_six", bd6);
        pt.loadPic("Image_seven", bd7);
        pt.loadPic("Image_eight", bd8);
        pt.loadPic("Image_nine", bd9);
#endif
}


void
cleanup() {
        // nothing to do yet!
}
```

Implementing Static Behavior

Following is the .C file for the classes for the simplified game:

Ball.C file:

```
#include "Ball.h"
#include "Collision.h"
#include "Game.h"


void
Ball::move(int time_elapsed, GO_formation *form) {
    Point a = Rectangle::upperLeft();
    Point b = Rectangle::lowerRight();
    Rectangle ball_rect(a,b);
    Collision c(ball_rect, time_elapsed*velocity, form);
    c.did_collision_occur(this);
    // c ceases to exist when function exits
}

void
Ball::change_velocity(Point v)
{
    velocity = v;
}
```

```
void
Ball::change_position(Point new_position)
{
    Rectangle::moveTo(new_position);
    Point p1 = Game::convertGtoD(new_position);
    Displayable::moveTo(p1,1);
}

Point
Ball::get_velocity()
{
    return velocity;
}
```

The .h file for the class is included so that the compiler can use the data member definitions. The .h files for other classes, Collision and Game, are included because the function calls functions that belong to these classes (i.e., the convert function of Game). The .h file of rectangle was not included in the .C file because the include of it is in the .h file.

Collision.C file:

```
#include "Collision.h"
#include "Ball.h"
#include "Hit_object.h"

void
Collision::moveBall(Ball *ball)
{
    ball->change_position(final_loc().upperLeft());
    int sf = 1;                 // speed factor
    for(int i=0; i<number_hit(); i++) {
        Obstacle *hitptr = (Obstacle *) obj(i)->real_identity();
        sf *= hitptr->respond_to_being_hit(this);
    }
    Point v = rebound(ball->get_velocity());
    if(v.X()==0 ) v.X(1);
    if(v.Y()==0 ) v.Y(-1);
    ball->change_velocity(sf*v);
}
```

Field.C file:

```
#include "Field.h"
#include "ClosedSide.h"
#include "Paddle.h"
Paddle *
```

```
Field::getPaddle()
{
    return (pd);
}
```

Obstacle.C file:

```
#include "Obstacle.h"

SpeedFactor
Obstacle::respond_to_being_hit(Collision *c)
{
    return(1);        // default SpeedFactor is 1
}
```

Paddle.C file:

```
#include "Paddle.h"
#include "Game.h"
#include "Mouse.h"

void
Paddle::move() {
    Point newpoint = mouse->getPoint();
    Point delta=newpoint - mouse_prev_pos;
        // convert to game coordinates
    Point game_delta = Game::convertDtoG(delta);
    if( (Gr_obj::upperLeft().X() + game_delta.X())< Xmin) {
        Gr_obj::moveto(Point(Xmin,Gr_obj::upperLeft().Y()));
    }
    else if ( (Gr_obj::lowerRight().X() + game_delta.X())> Xmax) {
        Gr_obj::moveto(Point(Xmax - Gr_obj::width(),
                    Gr_obj::upper-Left().Y()));
    }
    else {
        Gr_obj::move(Point(game_delta.X(), 0));
    }
    Displayable::moveTo(Gr_obj::upperLeft(),1);
    mouse_prev_pos = newpoint;
    }
}
```

In this implementation, the developer moves the mouse's previous position into the paddle. This is done for performance reasons because it is very expensive to call a representation of a mouse and the access the mouse library object. However, it is not for free; by making this change, the paddle now is less reusable because it is now more tightly tied to the library mouse class.

Instantiating Objects

Following is the .C file with constructors and destructors added for the classes in the simplified game:

Ball.C file:

```
#include "Ball.h"
#include "Collision.h"
#include "Game.h"

Ball::Ball(Point v, Point a, Point b) :Rectangle(a,b),
Displayable("Image_ball",Point(0,0))
{
    draw();
    Point p1 = Game::convertGtoD(a);
    Displayable::moveTo(p1,1);
    velocity = v;
}

Ball::~Ball()
{
}

void
Ball::move(int time_elapsed, GO_formation *form)
{
    Point a = Rectangle::upperLeft();
    Point b = Rectangle::lowerRight();
    Rectangle ball_rect(a,b);
    Collision c(ball_rect, time_elapsed*velocity, form);
    c.did_collision_occur(this);
        // c ceases to exist when function exits
}

void
Ball::change_velocity(Point v)
{
    velocity = v;
}

void
Ball::change_position(Point new_position)
{
    Rectangle::moveTo(new_position);
    Point p1 = Game::convertGtoD(new_position);
    Displayable::moveTo(p1,1);
}
```

```
Point
Ball::get_velocity()
{
    return velocity;
}
```

Collision.C file:

```
#include "Collision.h"
#include "Ball.h"
#include "Obstacle.h"

Collision::Collision(Rectangle init_projectile, Point motion,
                     GO_formation *form)
        :GO_collision(init_projectile, motion, *form)
{
}

Collision::~Collision()
{
}

void
Collision::did_collision_occur(Ball *ball)
{
    ball->change_position(final_loc().upperLeft());
    int sf = 1;                 // speed factor
    for(int i=0; i<number_hit(); i++) {
        Obstacle *hitptr = (Obstacle *) obj(i)->real_identity();
        sf *= hitptr->respond_to_being_hit(this);
    }
    Point v = rebound(ball->get_velocity());
    if(v.X()==0 ) v.X(1);
    if(v.Y()==0 ) v.Y(-1);
    ball->change_velocity(sf*v);
}
```

Obstacle.C file:

```
#include "Obstacle.h"

Obstacle::Obstacle(GO_formation *f, Rectangle loc, char *name, Point p):
            Gr_obj(*f,loc), Displayable(name,Point(0,0))
{
    Point p1;
    draw();
    p1 = Game::convertGtoD(p);  // convert to display coord.s
```

```
        Gr_obj::moveto(p);        // move Gr_obj to correct location
        Displayable::moveTo(p1,1);  // move to display coord.s and display
         attach();          // add to GO_formation list
}


Obstacle::~Obstacle()
{
}

SpeedFactor
Obstacle::respond_to_being_hit(Collision *c)
{
    return(1);        // default SpeedFactor is 1
}
```

Paddle.C file:

```
    #include "Paddle.h"
    #include "Game.h"
    #include "Mouse.h"

    Paddle::Paddle(GO_formation *f, Rectangle loc, Point p, int xmax,
                intxmin):Hit_object(f, loc, "Image_paddle", p) {
        mouse = new Mouse();
        mouse_prev_pos = mouse->getPoint();
        Xmax = xmax;
        Xmin = xmin;
    }


    Paddle::~Paddle()
    {
    }


    void
    Paddle::move()
    {
        Point newpoint = mouse->getPoint();
        Point delta=newpoint - mouse_prev_pos;
            // convert to game coordinates
        Point game_delta = Game::convertDtoG(delta);
        if( (Gr_obj::upperLeft().X() + game_delta.X())< Xmin)
            Gr_obj::moveto(Point(Xmin,Gr_obj::upperLeft().Y()));
        else if( (Gr_obj::lowerRight().X() + game_delta.X())> Xmax)
            Gr_obj::moveto(Point(Xmax - Gr_obj::width(),
                        Gr_obj::upperLeft().Y()));
        else
```

```
               Gr_obj::move(Point(game_delta.X(), 0));
          Displayable::moveTo(Gr_obj::upperLeft(),1);
          mouse_prev_pos = newpoint;
     }
```

Side.C file:

```
     #include "Side.h"

     Side::Side(GO_formation *f, Rectangle loc, char *name, Point p)
                   :Obstacle(f, loc, name, p)
     {
     }

     Side::~Side()
     {
     }
```

Field.C file:

```
     #include "Field.h"
     #include "ClosedSide.h"
     #include "Paddle.h"

      Field::Field(GO_formation *form)
     {
          top = new ClosedSide(form,Rectangle(Point(0,0),Point(500,15)),
                              "Image_top", Point(15,15));
          left = new ClosedSide(form,Rectangle(Point(0,0),Point(15,800)),
                              "Image_side", Point(15,15));
          right = new ClosedSide(form,Rectangle(Point(0,0),Point(15,800)),
                              "Image_side", Point(500,15));
          bottom = new ClosedSide(form,Rectangle(Point(0,0),Point(500,15)),
                              "Image_top", Point(15,790));
          pd = new Paddle(form, Rectangle(Point(0,0),Point(30,5)),
                              Point(250,775), 500, 30);
     }

     Field::~Field()
     {
          delete top;
          delete left;
          delete right;
          delete bottom;
          delete pd;
     }

     Paddle *
```

```
Field::getPaddle()
{
    return (pd);
}
```

Implementing Inheritance

In this next stage, the team simplifies the model so that we can effectively implement a version that is consistent with what we have been discussed so far. Specifically, we will replace the Player class with a Scoreboard class so that the points can be displayed. The scoring of points also moved from Brick to Collision, as now Collision provides an incr_score service for Brick. This says that scoring is a result of collision and brick has some point value that collision may use for scoring. Note that in the original model, the team concluded that scoring was a responsibility of brick. The revised diagrams and the new CRC cards are shown in Figures 22-129 through 22-137.

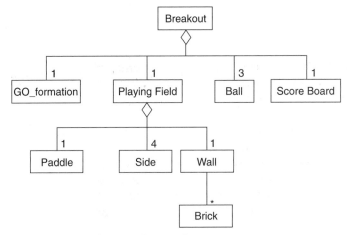

FIGURE 22-129   **Aggregation diagram for Breakout game.**

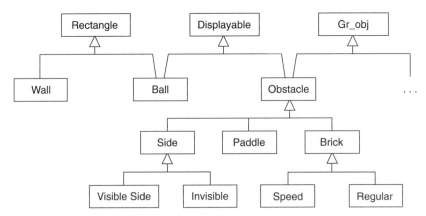

FIGURE 22-130   Inheritance diagram for Breakout game.

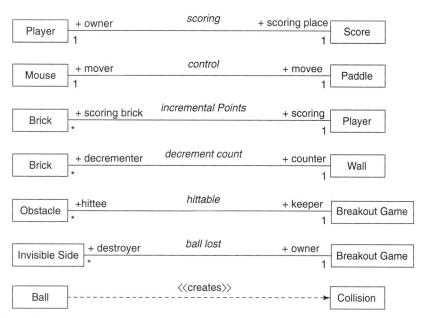

FIGURE 22-131 Association diagram for Breakout game.

CLASS NAME	Brick
SUPERclass	**Obstacle**
SUBclasses	**Reg_brick, Speed_brick**
Responsibility	**Inheritance/Collaboration**
Provide brick abstraction	Obstacle
Hold point value of brick	Is=part of Wall
METHODS	**Variables**
// constructor	visibility
// destructor	point_value
respond_to_being_hit(Collision *collision)	
regenerate_brick(GO_formation *f)	

FIGURE 22-132 CRC card for Brick.

CLASS NAME	Brick
SUPERclass	Obstacle

Responsibility	Inheritance
Provide open side abstraction	Side
Provide polymorphic service for respond to being hit	

METHODS	Variables
// constructor; how do we make it not visible	visibility
// destructor	point_value
respond_to_being_hit(Collision *c)	
{ tell game ball is lost; return 1 as speedfactor }	

FIGURE 22-133   CRC card for InvisibleSide.

CLASS NAME	Brick
METHODS:	
did_collision_occur(Ball *ball)	
{	
Detach this object from hitable list (GO_formation)	
Erase itself off screen	
Set visibility data member to FALSE	
Use collision's incr_score service	
Tell wall brick is no longer part of wall	
Return 1 as value	
}	

regenerate_brick(GO_formation *f)
{
Draw self
Set visibility data member to TRUE
Attach this object from hitable list (GO_formation)
}

FIGURE 22-134 CRC card for Brick.

CLASS NAME	Reg_brick
SUPERclass	Brick
Responsibility	**Inheritance**
Provide regular brick abstraction	Brick
METHODS	**Variables**
// constructor	
// destructor	

FIGURE 22-135 CRC card for Regular Brick.

CLASS NAME	Speed_brick
SUPERclass	Brick
Responsibility	**Inheritance**
Provide speed brick abstraction	Brick
Provide for speedfactor	

METHODS	Variables
// constructor	Speedfactor
// destructor	
respond_to_being_hit(Collision *collision	
{	
do standard brick response	
return a speedfactor via data member	
}	

FIGURE 22-136   CRC card for Speed Brick.

CLASS NAME	Wall
Responsibility	**Collaboration**
Provide wall abstraction	Rectangle
Provide number of bricks left	
Keep track of where bricks are	
METHODS	**Variables**
// constructor	num_left
// destructor	form
brick_off_wall( )	rectangle
	brick-array
void regenerate( )	
bool time_to_regenerate( )	
int intercept(Rectangle rect)	

FIGURE 22-137   CRC card for Wall.

CLASS NAME	Scoreboard
SUPERclass	**Displayable**

Responsibility	Inheritance/Collaboration
Provide scoreboard abstraction	Displayable
Provide for display of points	Digits
(version 2: keep score)	

METHODS	Variables
// constructor	score
// destructor	num_of_digits
display_score(int)	
incr_score(int n)	

FIGURE 22-138 CRC card for Scoreboard.

Following are the .h file and the .C file for these classes and the modified classes:

Brick.h file:

```
#ifndef _BRICK_H
#define _BRICK_H

#include     "class.h"
#include     "Hit_object.h"

typedef int    SpeedFactor;

  class Brick : public Hit_object {
     private:
          bool visibility;
          int     score;
          Wall *wall;
     public:
          Brick(GO_formation *f, Rectangle loc, Point p, bool vis,
               int pv, char *name, Wall *w);
          ~Brick();
          SpeedFactor respond_to_being_hit(Collision *collision);
          void regenerate_brick(GO_formation *f);
  };
#endif
```

Collision.h file:

```cpp
#include        "class.h"
#include "GO_collision.h"

class Collision : private GO_collision {
    private:
    public:
        Collision(Rectangle init_projectile, Point motion,
                    GO_formation *form);
        ~Collision();
        void did_collision_occur(Ball *ball);
        void incr_score(int score);
};
```

Field.h file:

```cpp
#ifndef _FIELD_H
#define _FIELD_H

#include        "class.h"
class Field
{
    private:
        Wall            *w;
        ClosedSide      *top, *left, *right;
        OpenSide        *bottom;
        Paddle          *pd;
    public:
        Field(GO_formation *form);
        ~Field();
        Paddle *getPaddle();
        Wall   *getWall();
};
#endif
```

Game.h file:

```cpp
#ifndef _GAME_H
#define _GAME_H

#include        "class.h"

class Game {
    private:
        GO_formation *form;
        Scoreboard *sb;
```

```
                    Field *fld;
                    int  ballno;
                    Ball * BALLS[5];
                    Ball * give_me_a_ball();
            public:
                    static bool ball_lost_flag;
            public:
                    Game();
                     ~Game();
                    void play_game();
                    static void ball_lost();
                    static Point convertGtoD(Point x);
                    static Point convertDtoG(Point x);
        };
        #endif
```

InvisibleSide.h file:

```
        #ifndef _OPENSIDE_H
        #define _OPENSIDE_H

        #include       "class.h"
        #include       "Side.h"

        typedef int SpeedFactor;

        class InvisibleSide : public Side
        {
            public:
                    InvisibleSide(GO_formation *f, Rectangle loc, char *name,
                            Point P);
                    ~InvisibleSide();
                    SpeedFactor respond_to_being_hit (Collision *c);
        };
        #endif
```

RegBrick.h file:

```
        #ifndef _REG_BRICK_H
        #define _REG_BRICK_H

        #include       "class.h"
        #include       "Brick.h"

        class Reg_brick : public Brick
        {
```

```
        private:
        public:
              Reg_brick(GO_formation *f, Rectangle loc, Point p, bool vis,
                        int pv, Wall *w);
              ~Reg_brick();
    };
    #endif
```

Scoreboard.h file:

```
    #ifndef _SCOREBOARD_H_
    #define _SCOREBOARD_H_

    #include "Displayable.h"
    #include "class.h"

    class Scoreboard : public Displayable
    {
        private:
              static int        point_scored;
        public:
              static Displayable      *score[10];
              static int              numdigits;
              static char       *digits[10];
              static void       drawscore(int);
        public:
              Scoreboard();
              ~Scoreboard();
              static void       display_score(int);
              static void       incr_score(int);
    };
    #endif
```

Notice that in Scoreboard, the incr_score function used by Collision is defined as a static function. This means that any function may access this service by prefixing the function with the class name and the scope operator. This is used in the Collision function definition, which is in Collision.C.

SpeedBrick.h file:

```
    #ifndef _SPEED_BRICK_H
    #define _SPEED_BRICK_H

    #include        "class.h"
    #include        "Brick.h"

    typedef int     SpeedFactor;
```

```
class Speed_brick : public Brick
{
    private:
        SpeedFactor speed_factor;
    public:
        Speed_brick(GO_formation *f, Rectangle loc, Point p, bool
                    vis, int pv, SpeedFactor sf, Wall *w);
        ~Speed_brick();
        int respond_to_being_hit(Collision *collision);
};
#endif
```

Wall.h file:

```
#ifndef _WALL_H
#define _WALL_H
#include        "class.h"
#include        "Rectangle.h"

const int MAX_BRICKS = 90;

class Wall
{
    private:
        Brick *bricks[MAX_BRICKS];
        int num_left;
        GO_formation *form;
        Rectangle bounds;
    public:
        Wall(GO_formation *f, Rectangle loc);
        ~Wall();
        void regenerate();
        void brick_off_wall();
        bool time_to_regenerate();
    int intercept(Rectangle rect);
};
#endif
```

Brick.C file:

```
#include        "Brick.h"
#include        "Wall.h"
#include        "Collision.h"

Brick::Brick(GO_formation *f, Rectangle loc, Point p, bool vis, int pv,
             char *name, Wall *w)
             :Hit_object(f, loc, name, p), visibility(vis),
                        score(pv), wall(w)
```

```
{
    if(visibility == FALSE)
        erase();          // if visibility false, created brick
                    //     is hittable, but not displayed
}

Brick::~Brick()
{
}
SpeedFactor
Brick::respond_to_being_hit(Collision *collision)
{
    Gr_obj::detach();
    erase();
    visibility = FALSE;
    collision->incr_score(score);
    wall->brick_off_wall();
    return(1);
}
void
Brick::regenerate_brick(GO_formation *f)
{
    draw();
    visibility = TRUE;
    Gr_obj::attach();
}
```

Collision.C file:

```
#include "Collision.h"
#include "Ball.h"
#include "Hit_object.h"
#include "Scoreboard.h"

Collision::Collision(Rectangle init_projectile, Point motion,
                    GO_formation *form)
        :GO_collision(init_projectile, motion, *form)
{
}

Collision::~Collision()
{
}

void
Collision::did_collision_occur(Ball *ball)
{
```

```
      ball->change_position(final_loc().upperLeft());
       int sf = 1;                    // speed factor
      for(int i=0; i<number_hit(); i++)
      {
            Hit_object *hitptr =  (Hit_object *) obj(i)->real_identity();
            sf *= hitptr->respond_to_being_hit(this);
      }
      Point v = rebound(ball->get_velocity());
      if(v.X()==0 ) v.X(1);
      if(v.Y()==0 ) v.Y(-1);
      ball->change_velocity(sf*v);
   }


void
Collision::incr_score( int score )
{       //  this is how you call a static function
      Scoreboard::incr_score ( score );
}
```

Notice that the function incr_score() of Collision calls the static function incr_score() of Scoreboard. Here, the scope operator is used for a class not in its hierarchy; thus, a static function is almost like a global function in that the program does not need a pointer to an instance of the class to use the function. However, unlike a global function, which is not tied to any class, to use a static function, the program must know what class to which it belongs.

Field.C file:

```
#include "Field.h"
#include "ClosedSide.h"
#include "OpenSide.h"
#include "Wall.h"
#include "Paddle.h"

Field::Field(GO_formation *form)
{
      top = new ClosedSide(form,Rectangle(Point(0,0),Point(500,15)),
                           "Image_top", Point(15,15));
      left = new ClosedSide(form,Rectangle(Point(0,0),Point(15,800)),
                           "Image_side", Point(15,15));
      right = new ClosedSide(form,Rectangle(Point(0,0),Point(15,800)),
                           "Image_side", Point(500,15));
      bottom = new OpenSide(form,Rectangle(Point(0,0),Point(500,15)),
                           "Image_top", Point(15,790));
      w = new Wall(form, Rectangle(Point(33, 65), Point(481,113)));
      pd = new Paddle(form, Rectangle(Point(0,0),Point(30,5)),
```

```
          Point(250,775), 500, 30);
     }

     Field::~Field()
     {
          delete top;
          delete left;
          delete right;
          delete bottom;
          delete w;
          delete pd;
     }
     Paddle *
     Field::getPaddle()
     {
          return (pd);
     }

     Wall *
     Field::getWall()
     {
          return(w);
     }
```

Game.C file:

```
     #include <stdio.h>
     #include "Game.h"
     #include "Scoreboard.h"
     #include "Field.h"
     #include "GO_formation.h"
     #include "Ball.h"
     #include "Paddle.h"
     #include "Wall.h"


     bool Game::ball_lost_flag = TRUE;

     Game::Game()
     {
          ball_lost_flag = TRUE;
          sb = new Scoreboard();
          form = new GO_formation();
          fld = new Field(form);

     }
```

```
Game::~Game()
{
    delete fld;   // field
    delete form;  // GO_formation
    delete sb;    // scoreBoard
}

void
Game::play_game()
{
    Ball *ball;
    Paddle *paddle;
    Wall *wall;
    paddle = fld->getPaddle();
    wall = fld->getWall();
    ballno = 0;
    for( int i=0; i < 5; i++) {
        BALLS[i] = new Ball(Point(1,1), Point(0,0), Point(16,16));
    }
    while( (ball =  give_me_a_ball()) != NULL) {
            // give ball initial velocity and position
        ball->change_velocity(Point(1,1));
        ball->change_position(Point(300,300));
        ball_lost_flag = FALSE;
        while(TRUE)
        {
            paddle->move();
            ball->move(1,form);
            if(wall->time_to_regenerate()) {
                if (wall->intercept((Rectangle) *ball))
                    ; // do nothing
                else
                    wall->regenerate();
            }
             if(ball_lost_flag == TRUE)
            {
                ball->erase();
                delete ball;
                break;
            }
        }        //end while(TRUE)
    }            // end while ( (ball= . . .) != NULL)
}

void
```

```
Game::ball_lost()
{
    ball_lost_flag = TRUE;
}


Point
Game::convertGtoD(Point x)
{
        // convert from game coordinates to display coordinates
    return(x);
}
Point
Game::convertDtoG(Point x)
{
        // convert from display coordinates to game coordinates
        return(x);
}


Ball *
Game::give_me_a_ball()
{
    if (ballno >= 5) return 0;
    else {
        Ball * rb = BALLS[ ballno++ ];
        return rb;
    }
}
```

InvisibleSide.C file:

```
#include "OpenSide.h"
#include "Game.h"

InvisibleSide::InvisibleSide(GO_formation *f, Rectangle loc,
                             char *name, Point p)
            :Side(f, loc, name, p)
{
    erase();
}

InvisibleSide::~InvisibleSide()
{
}

SpeedFactor
InvisibleSide::respond_to_being_hit(Collision *c)
```

```
{
    Game::ball_lost();
    return(1);        // default SpeedFactor is 1
}
```

RegBrick.C file:

```
#include        "Reg_brick.h"

Reg_brick::Reg_brick(GO_formation *f, Rectangle loc, Point p, bool vis,
                     int pv, Wall *w)
        :Brick(f, loc, p, vis, pv, "Image_slow_brick", w)
{
}

Reg_brick::~Reg_brick()
{
}
```

Scoreboard.C file:

```
#include <stdlib.h>
#include <unistd.h>
#include "Scoreboard.h"

unsigned sleep(unsigned);

char *Scoreboard::digits[] = {
    "Image_zero",
    "Image_one",
    "Image_two",
    "Image_three",
    "Image_four",
    "Image_five",
    "Image_six",
    "Image_seven",
    "Image_eight",
    "Image_nine"
};

int Scoreboard::numdigits = 10;
int Scoreboard::point_scored = 0;

Displayable* Scoreboard::score []= {
    0,
    0,
    0,
```

```
        0,
        0,
        0,
        0,
        0,
        0,
        0
};

Scoreboard::Scoreboard() :
        Displayable("Image_scoreboard", Point(530, 15))
{
    draw();          // Displayable::draw();
    for (int n = 0; n < 10; n++)
    {
        score[n] = new Displayable("Image_zero");
        score[n]->move(Point((700 - n * 18), 40));
    }
    sleep(1);
    drawscore(0);
}

Scoreboard::~Scoreboard()
{
    for(int n=0; n<10; n++) delete score[n];
}

void
Scoreboard::display_score(int n)
{
    drawscore(n);
}

const int XBUF = 15;
const int YBUF = 30;

void
Scoreboard::drawscore(int n)
{

    while(numdigits-- > 0) {
        score[numdigits]->erase();
      }
        // build new score in loop, each time update position
    numdigits = 0;
```

```
                        // if score is 0, just display "0"
            if (n == 0) {
                delete score[numdigits];
                score[numdigits] = new Displayable(digits[0]);
                score[numdigits]->move(Point((700 - numdigits * 18), 40));
                score[numdigits]->draw();
                numdigits++;
            }
            while (n) {
                int rem = n % 10;
                delete score[numdigits];
                score[numdigits] = new Displayable(digits[rem]);
                score[numdigits]->move(Point((700 - numdigits * 18), 40));
                score[numdigits]->draw();
                n /= 10;
                 numdigits++;
            }
        }
        void
        Scoreboard::incr_score( int n ) {
            point_scored += n;
            drawscore( point_scored );
        }
```

SpeedBrick.C file:

```
        #include         "Speed_brick.h"

        Speed_brick::Speed_brick(GO_formation *f, Rectangle loc, Point p,
                             bool vis, int pv, SpeedFactor sf, Wall *w)
                :Brick(f, loc, p, vis, pv, "Image_speed_brick", w),
        speed_factor(sf)
        {
        }

        Speed_brick::~Speed_brick()
        {
        }


        SpeedFactor
        Speed_brick::respond_to_being_hit(Collision *collision)
        {
            Brick::respond_to_being_hit(collision);
            return(speed_factor);
        }
```

Wall.C file:

```
#include "Wall.h"
#include "Rectangle.h"
#include "Speed_brick.h"
#include "Reg_brick.h"


Wall::Wall(GO_formation *f, Rectangle loc)
        :bounds(loc), form(f)
{
    int max_row = bounds.height()/16;
    int max_col = bounds.width()/32;
    for(int row=0; row<max_row; row++)
    {
        for(int col=0; col<max_col; col++)
        {
            Point new_pos;
            new_pos=bounds.upperLeft() + Point(col*32, row*16);
            if (col == row) {  // make a speed brick
                bricks[(row*max_col) + col] =
                new Speed_brick(f,
                Rectangle(Point(0,0),Point(32,16)),
                new_pos, TRUE, 20, 2, this);
            }
            else    {    // make a regular brick
                bricks[(row*max_col) + col] =
                new Reg_brick(f,
                Rectangle(Point(0,0),Point(32,16)),
                new_pos, TRUE, 10, this);
            }
        }
    }
    num_left = max_row * max_col;
}

Wall::~Wall()
{
    int max_row = bounds.height()/16;
    int max_col = bounds.width()/32;
    for(int row=0; row<max_row; row++)
      {
        for(int col=0; col<max_col; col++)
        {
            delete bricks[(row*max_col) + col];
        }
```

```
        }
    }

    void
    Wall::regenerate()
    {
        // redraw each brick
        // reattach each brick to form
        int max_row = bounds.height()/16;
        int max_col = bounds.width()/32;
        for(int row=0; row<max_row; row++) {
            for(int col=0; col<max_col; col++) {
                bricks[(row*max_col) + col]->regenerate_brick(form);
            }
        }
        num_left = max_row * max_col;
    }

    void
    Wall::brick_off_wall()
    {
        num_left -= 1;
    }

    bool
    Wall::time_to_regenerate()
    {
        if( num_left == 0)
            return(TRUE);
        else
            return(FALSE);
    }

    int
    Wall::intercept(Rectangle rect)
    {
        return(bounds.intersectsWith(rect));
    }
```

Implementing Relationships

To help us understand static functions and associations better, the game is changed so that there can be multiple players. First, we will add two new classes: Players and Player. Then, we will modify the incr_score() function to handle multiple players. Figures 22-139 through 22-142 show the modified diagrams and class descriptions for the new classes.

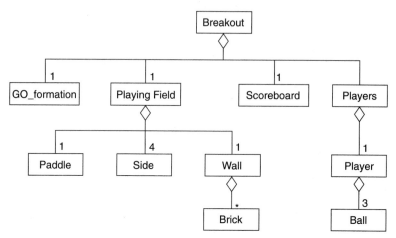

FIGURE 22-139   Aggregation diagram for Breakout game.

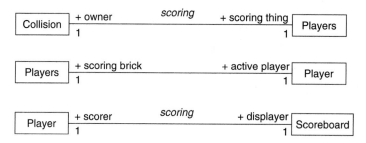

FIGURE 22-140   Association diagram for Breakout game.

CLASS NAME	Players	
Responsibility	**Collaboration**	
Provide players abstraction	Player	
Provide list of players		
Keep track of number of players and next player		
METHODS	**Variables**	
// constructor	list of players	

// destructor	next_player
static void increment_score(int points)	max_num
void respond_to_ball_lost( )	active-player
Ball *give_me_a_ball( )	

FIGURE 22-141   CRC card for Players.

CLASS NAME	**Player**
Responsibility	**Collaboration**
Provide individual player abstraction	Players
Keep track of player's balls	Ball
Keep track of player's score	
METHODS	**Variables**
// constructor	score
// destructor	list of balls
void update_score(int)	max_num
Ball *give_me_a_ball()	current_ball
int get_score() cons	
bool any_balls_left() const	

FIGURE 22-142   CRC card for Player.

Following are the .h and .C files for Players and Player, and the .C file for Collision with the modified code for incr_score() function, and the modified code for Game::play_game() function.

Players.h file:

```
#ifndef _PLAYERS_H
#define _PLAYERS_H
```

```
#include        "class.h"

class Players {
private:
    Player* List_of_p[5];    // list of players
    int nextplayer;
    int maxnum;
public:
    static char *p_names[];
    static Player *active_player;
public:
    Players(int n);
    ~Players();
    static void increment_score(int points);
    void respond_to_ball_lost();
    Ball *give_me_a_ball();
  };
#endif
```

Players.C file:

```
#include <stdio.h>
#include <stdlib.h>
#include "Players.h"
#include "Player.h"
#include "Ball.h"
#include "Scoreboard.h"

Player * Players::active_player=NULL;

char *Players::p_names[] = { "Player A",
                             "Player B",
                             "Player C",
                             "Player D",
                             "Player E"
};

Players::Players(int n)
{

    if(n>5)
        maxnum=5;
    else
        maxnum=n;
    for(int i=0; i<maxnum; i++) {
        List_of_p[i]  = new Player(p_names[i], 6, 0,
                                Point(530, 300 + i*20));
```

```
                        // put new player on list
        }
                        // active_player to first one
        active_player = List_of_p[0];
            // set next player pointer
        nextplayer = 1;
}


Players::~Players()
{
            // Delete All Players in List
        for(int i=0; i<maxnum; i++) {
            delete List_of_p[i];
        }
}


void
Players::increment_score(int points)
{
        active_player->update_score(points);
        int score = active_player->get_score();
        Scoreboard::display_score(score);
}


void
Players::respond_to_ball_lost()
{
}


Ball *
Players::give_me_a_ball()
{
        Ball *newBall;
        if(active_player->any_balls_left())
            newBall = active_player->give_me_a_ball();
        else {
            if(nextplayer == maxnum) newBall = NULL;
            else {
                active_player = List_of_p[nextplayer++];
                newBall = active_player->give_me_a_ball();
                sleep(5);
            }
        }
        return(newBall);
}
```

Player.h file:

```
#ifndef _PLAYER_H_
#define _PLAYER_H_

#include "class.h"
#include "Ball.h"

class Player
{
    private:
        char*    p_name;
        int      score;
        int curball;
        int maxball;
        Ball* BallPtrList[50];
    public:
        Player(char*, int, int, Point);
         ~Player();
        void     update_score(int);
        Ball     *give_me_a_ball();
        char*    get_name() const;
         int              get_score() const;
        bool any_balls_left() const;
};

#endif
```

Player.C file:

```
#include <stdio.h>
#include "Player.h"
#include "Ball.h"
#include "Point.h"

Player::Player(char* nm, int init_num_balls, int init_score,
               Point ball_disp)
         : p_name(nm), score(init_score), curball(0)
{
    if (init_num_balls > 50 ) init_num_balls = 50;
    maxball = init_num_balls;
    for(int i=0; i< init_num_balls; i++)
    {
        Ball *pb;
        Point pos = ball_disp + Point(i*20,0);
        pb = new Ball(Point(0,0), Point(0,0), Point(16,16));
        pb->change_position(pos);
```

```
            BallPtrList[i] = pb;    // save ball pointer
        }
}

Player::~Player()
{
    Ball *b;
    while(curball < maxball-1) {
        b = BallPtrList[curball];
        delete b;
        curball++;
    }
}

void
Player::update_score(int n)
{
    score += n;
}

char*
Player::get_name() const
{
    return p_name;
}

int
Player::get_score() const
{
    return score;
}

bool
Player::any_balls_left() const
{
    return (( curball < maxball ) ? TRUE : FALSE);
}

Ball *
Player::give_me_a_ball()
{
    Ball *b;
    if(curball == maxball) {
        b = NULL;
    }
```

```
    else {
        b = BallPtrList[curball];
        curball++;
    }
    return b;
}
```

Collision.C file:

```
#include "Collision.h"
#include "Ball.h"
#include "Hit_object.h"
#include "Players.h"

Collision::Collision(Rectangle init_projectile, Point motion,
                 GO_formation *form)
            :GO_collision(init_projectile, motion, *form)
{
}


Collision::~Collision()
{
}


void
Collision::did_collision_occur(Ball *ball)
{
    ball->change_position(final_loc().upperLeft());
    int sf = 1;              // speed factor
    for(int i=0; i<number_hit(); i++) {
        Hit_object *hitptr =  (Hit_object *) obj(i)-
>real_identity();
        sf *= hitptr->respond_to_being_hit(this);
    }
    Point v = rebound(ball->get_velocity());
    if(v.X()==0 )  v.X(1);
    if(v.Y()==0 ) v.Y(-1);
    ball->change_velocity(sf*v);
}


void
Collision::incr_score(int score)
{
    Players::increment_score(score);
}
```

The reader should note the use of static function to separate the scoring from the actual playing of the game. Also, by using the Players abstraction, you can add rules for scoring that are independent of Collision. This is a very powerful concept.

Game.C file:

```
#include <stdio.h>
#include "Game.h"
#include "Scoreboard.h"
#include "Field.h"
#include "Players.h"
#include "GO_formation.h"
#include "Ball.h"
#include "Paddle.h"
#include "Wall.h"

bool Game::ball_lost_flag = TRUE;

Game::Game()
{
    ball_lost_flag = TRUE;
    sb = new Scoreboard();
    form = new GO_formation();
    fld = new Field(form);
    plys = new Players(2);
}

Game::~Game()
{
    delete plys;   // players
    delete fld;    // field
    delete form;   // GO_formation
    delete sb;     // scoreBoard
}

void
Game::play_game()
{
    Ball *ball;
    Paddle *paddle;
    Wall *wall;
    paddle = fld->getPaddle();
    wall = fld->getWall();
    while( (ball=plys->give_me_a_ball()) != NULL)
    {
        // give ball initial velocity and position
```

```
            ball->change_velocity(Point(1,1));
            ball->change_position(Point(300,300));
            ball_lost_flag = FALSE;
            while(TRUE) {
                paddle->move();
                ball->move(1,form);
                if(wall->time_to_regenerate()) {
                            //if (wall->intercept((Rectangle) *ball))
                    if (wall->intercept( *ball ) )
                            ;  // do nothing
                    else
                            wall->regenerate();
                }
                if(ball_lost_flag == TRUE) {
                    plys->respond_to_ball_lost();
                    ball->erase();
                    delete ball;
                    break;
                }
        }        //end while(TRUE)
        }  // end while ( (ball= . . .) != NULL)
}

void
Game::ball_lost()
{
    ball_lost_flag = TRUE;
}

Point
Game::convertGtoD(Point x)
{
        // convert from game coordinates to display coordinates
    return(x);
}

Point
Game::convertDtoG(Point x)
{
        // convert from display coordinates to game coordinates
    return(x);
}
```

CHAPTER

23

Case Study:
Microwave Oven

I N this chapter, we show a complete version of a very simple case study on the microwave oven. This should give the reader an opportunity to see how all of the techniques described in the book are used together to produce an application. Three separate approaches for the microwave oven described by the requirements presented in Chapter 21 are examined. The three approaches differ in terms of the sophistication of the solution achieved by the development team. The three solutions presented here are representative of the solutions achieved by novices, experienced practitioners, and experts, respectively. The critical point of this chapter is to show that all of the principles of object-oriented design must be applied to ensure a well-designed system that is flexible, extensible, and maintainable.

Solution 1 is developed by a novice team. Team members applied only the encapsulation principle. The major drawback of their approach is that it produces a "GOD" object that contains all of the business logic. Thus, essentially this will have all of the problems of a traditional procedural program. One will not realize any of the benefits of OO design and implementation.

Solution 2 is developed by an experienced team of practitioners. The team applied both the encapsulation principle and the delegation principle (distribution of responsibility). The result is a model in which the responsibilities are distributed across objects better, but it has the drawback that there is high coupling among objects. This is due to the fact that the delegation principle usually creates a lot of interdependencies. This has been one of the major complaints about OO technology.

Solution 3 is developed by a team of experts. The team applied all three principles (encapsulation, delegation, and separation of interface from implementation). The result is a highly flexible and extensible model with distributed responsibility that is easily maintained. In the process, the team employs two common design patterns—the publish-subscribe pattern and the adapter pattern.

Although all three approaches are valid solutions, each is unique with respect to cost of extension, maintenance, and performance. After a course in C++ programming, it is expected that the reader will usually generate the first solution. After learning OO design and experience, the reader should be able to generate the second solution. However, the final solution presented here takes years of experience to achieve, as it brings into play very advanced concepts and practices. From our perspective, we believe this is one of the major difficulties in the usage of this technology in reaching its fullest potential.

Use Cases[1]

ALL three of our teams begin in the same way. They all establish high-level primary essential use cases describing the normal operation of the microwave oven. Three use cases are sufficient to establish the normal usage of the microwave oven. These cases are:

1. Cook without interruption
2. Cancel cooking
3. Interrupt cooking

While it might appear that the latter two use cases represent secondary use cases, they are actually integral operations of the microwave oven. There is nothing exceptional about a user removing the food early or canceling cooking. Consistent with our recommendation in Chapter 4, we do not address the boundary use case—namely plugging the microwave oven into the wall socket and initializing the software. At this point in time, we really don't know (or care) what that involves.

Use Case 1: Cook Without Interruption

Description: The user sets the microwave oven to cook for a set number of minutes and allows the microwave oven to finish its complete cook cycle.

Includes: None

Extends: None

Actors: User

Preconditions: The oven is off, the door is closed, and the oven light is off.

Details: See Figure 23-1 for details.

Postconditions: The oven is off, the door is closed, and the oven light is off.

Exceptions: None

Constraints: None

Variants: None

Comments: None

---

[1] See Chapter 4 for the steps to follow in creating use cases. Choosing the most useful set of use cases is a tricky matter. You want to capture all of the use cases that are of value to the customer/user; but at the same time, you do not want to capture use cases that will not add value to the design. However, if you are also using use cases for testing, you may want to have your testers generate all use cases.

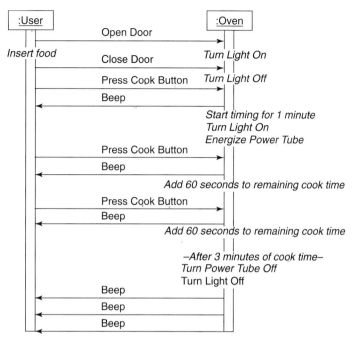

FIGURE 23-1 Sequence diagram for use case 1.

This use case covers the situation in which a user puts food in the oven and then cooks it for 3 minutes. The dialog described here is very simple:

1. The user opens the door;
2. The user closes the door;
3. The user presses the cook button;
4. The oven beeps the user;
5. The pressing of the button by the user and beeping by the oven are repeated twice; and
6. The oven finally beeps the user three times.

The details of this use case, as presented in the sequence diagram, are a direct result of the requirements document. Opening the door by the user is accompanied by turning on the light. This is dictated by the first requirement, which states that the light must be on when the door is open. Inserting food into the microwave oven is not explicitly identified in the requirements, but this act is integral to the purpose for which the oven is being used.[2] Closing the door by the user turns the light off as dictated by the first requirement. The user then initiates cooking by pressing the cook button. This causes a

---

[2] For this particular microwave oven, the placing of food in the oven is not essential for the proper operation of the oven.

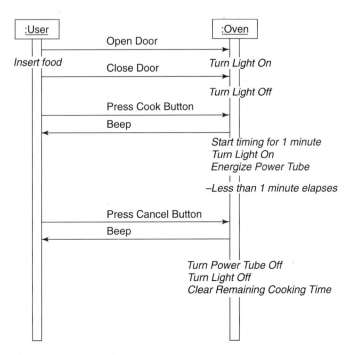

FIGURE 23-2   Sequence diagram for use case 2.

beep to be sounded as dictated by requirement 8; starts timing the cooking activity for 1 minute as dictated by requirement 3; the light is turned on as dictated by requirement 1; and the power tube is energized as a result of requirement 3. The next two presses of the user button sound a beep as dictated by requirement 8 and the cooking time is increased by 1 minute as dictated by requirement 4. After 3 minutes of cooking time, requirement 5 dictates turning off the power tube; turning off the light, and generating three beeps.

Use Case 2: Cancel Cooking

Description: The user sets the microwave oven to cook for a set number of minutes but then interrupts the microwave oven before the cook time elapses by pressing the cancel button.

Includes: None

Extends: None

Actors: User

Preconditions: The oven is off, the door is closed, and the oven light is off.

Details: See Figure 23-2 for details.

Postconditions: The oven is off, the door is closed, and the oven light is off.

Exceptions: None

Constraints: None

Variants: None

Comments: None

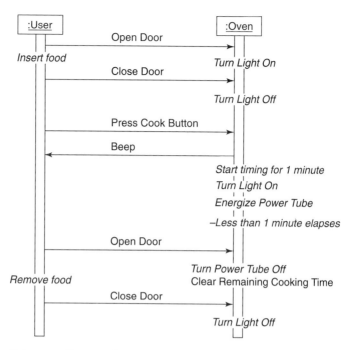

FIGURE 23-3 Sequence diagram for use case 3.

This use case follows the same sequence as the first use case except that the cancel button is pushed after having pushed the cook button once. At that point the use cases diverge. Once the cancel button is pushed, the oven informs the user of the event by beeping as dictated by requirement 8. The 7th requirement dictates that the oven turn off the power tube, turn off the light, and clear the remaining cooking time.

Use Case 3: Interrupt Cooking

Summary: The user sets the microwave oven to cook for a set number of minutes but then interrupts the microwave oven before the cook time elapses by opening the oven door.

Includes: None

Extends: None

Actors: User

Preconditions: The oven is off, the door is closed, and the oven light is off.

Description: See Figure 23-3 for details.

Postconditions: The oven is off, the door is closed, and the oven light is off.

Exceptions: None

Constraints: None

Variants: None

Comments: None

This use case follows the same sequence as the first use case except that the door is opened after having pushed the cook button once and before the first minute of cooking has completed. At that point the use cases diverge. Once the door is opened, the 6th requirement dictates that the oven turn off the power tube and clear the remaining cooking time. The light must remain on because of requirement 1, which states that the light must be on when the door is open.

Solution 1: The Controller Class Design

THIS solution is generated by a novice team that only applies the encapsulation principle. The following sections outline the steps the team performed in generating its design.

Step 1: Finding the Objects

This step requires reading through the problem charter and the requirements document and writing all of the nouns as potential candidates on a sheet of paper. The requirements presented in Chapter 21 are repeated here with the nouns underlined.

1. Whenever the <u>oven</u> is cooking, the <u>light</u> inside the <u>oven</u> must be on to allow the <u>cook</u> to see the <u>food</u>. The <u>light</u> should also go on when the oven <u>door</u> is opened. At all other times, the <u>light</u> must be off.
2. <u>Cooking</u> can only be initiated when the <u>door</u> is closed.
3. <u>Cooking</u> is initiated by pressing the <u>cook button</u>. Pressing it once results in the <u>oven</u> cooking (by energizing the <u>power tube</u>) for 1 <u>minute</u>.
4. Pressing the <u>cook button</u> while the <u>oven</u> is cooking extends the cooking <u>time</u> by 1 <u>minute</u>. <u>One</u> can then press the <u>cook button</u> any number of <u>times</u> during cooking to add as many <u>minutes</u> as desired.
5. When the <u>oven</u> completes cooking, the <u>power tube</u> and the <u>light</u> are turned off. The <u>oven</u> will then alert the <u>cook</u> by beeping three times.
6. While the <u>oven</u> is cooking, opening the <u>door</u> will interrupt cooking. Any remaining <u>cooking time</u> is cleared and the <u>oven</u> will not beep.
7. Pressing the <u>cancel button</u> while the <u>oven</u> is cooking will cancel cooking. The <u>light</u> is turned off and any remaining <u>cooking time</u> is cleared. The <u>oven</u> does not beep three times for this cooking <u>interruption</u>.
8. Each time the <u>cancel button</u> or the <u>cook button</u> is pushed, a single <u>beep</u> is issued so that the <u>cook</u> knows that the <u>oven</u> has acknowledged the pushing of the <u>button</u>.
9. If the <u>cook button</u> is pressed while the oven <u>door</u> is open, nothing happens except a single <u>beep</u>.
10. If the <u>cancel button</u> is pressed when the <u>oven</u> is not cooking, nothing happens except a single <u>beep</u>.
11. The microwave <u>oven</u> has no requirement to display the <u>cooking time</u>.

The nouns identified from the requirements are shown in Table 23-1. It is common for the same individual item to be referred to by different names in the requirements document. This is the case here; cook and the noun 'one' are referring to the same person. In

TABLE 23-1   List of Nouns

oven	light	food
cook	door	beep
cook button	minute	~~one~~
power tube	cancel button	time
interruption	button	times
cooking		

TABLE 23-2   List of Classes

oven	light	~~food~~
button	door	beeper
timer	power tube	

this case, we will eliminate the noun 'one.' We also recognize that the cook refers to the "user" actor in our use cases.

Next, we identify classes utilizing the nouns identified in the previous substep. We will write all of the nouns that are classes on the CRC cards. The list of classes identified during this step appears in Table 23-2.[3]

In examining the list of nouns, we quickly recognize that a beep is not an object, but the sound produced by a device. Our actual object is the beeper, which produces the beep. In the same way, a minute and time are not objects, but are measured by a timer. The noun 'times' is a count rather than an object, and we dispose of it.

There are three different ways in which buttons are mentioned: cook button, cancel button, and button. After much discussion, the team decided that a cook button and a cancel button are both buttons that activate different functions rather than having intrinsic differences. Thus, the team has only one class to represent all three buttons.[4]

Step 2: Identifying Responsibilities

In this step we will allocate responsibilities to the classes. Normally, we would read through the documents (problem charter and requirements) and assign responsibilities by using the verbs in sentences. The action verbs define the responsibilities of the object of the sentence and not the subject. In this example, this step can be simplified because the use cases contain the "white box" sequencing. The results are shown in Figure 23-4 through Figure 23-10.

The Timer class is responsible for keeping track of the remaining cook time. It has to add 60 seconds to the time to cook and set the time remaining to zero. We add an attribute representing the time remaining to cook.

---

[3] We will not draw the CRC cards for this step.

[4] Determinations of specialized class are very difficult in the early stages of analysis. This is one reason why we recommend that you do not throw away rejected CRC cards.

Class Name: Timer	
Attributes	
timeRemaining	
Responsibilities (External Services)	Collaborators
add60secToTime()	
setTimeToZero()	

FIGURE 23-4   CRC card for the Timer.

The Oven class is the controller for the system. It handles all events and handles all sequencing and business logic.[5]

Class Name: Oven (GOD object)	
Responsibilities (External Services)	Collaborators
handle all external events:	
doorOpen(), doorClose()	
cookButtonPressed(), cancelButtonPressed()	
timerExpired()	

FIGURE 23-5   CRC card for the Oven.

The Light class is responsible for illuminating the inside of the oven while "cooking" or when the door is open.

Class Name: Light	
Responsibilities (External Services)	Collaborators
turnOn()	
turnOff()	

FIGURE 23-6   CRC card for the Light.

---

[5] This is how to do procedural programming within an OO wrapping. Most of us consider this very poor design unless there is some good business reason to have centralization of code.

From an application perspective, the power tube is used to cook the food in the oven. Thus, the Power Tube class is to heat the food in the oven.

Class Name: Power Tube	
Responsibilities (External Services)	Collaborators
turnOn()	
turnOff()	

FIGURE 23-7   CRC card for the Power Tube.

The Beeper class is to alert the user of the oven when cooking has completed and to signal that each button press has been received.

Class Name: Beeper	
Responsibilities (External Services)	Collaborators
beep()	

FIGURE 23-8   CRC card for the Beeper.

The Door class is responsible for opening and closing the door. The actual responsibility of the door should be to allow the user to take food out when it is safe and to keep itself closed when the power tube is on.

Class Name: Door	
Responsibilities (External Services)	Collaborators
open()	
close()	
isOpen()	

FIGURE 23-9   CRC card for the Door.

The Button class is to allow the user to start cooking, extend cooking, or cancel cooking.

Class Name: Button	
Responsibilities (External Services)	Collaborators
press()	

FIGURE 23-10   CRC Card for the Button.

Step 3: Specifying Behavior

In practice, you would now look at the services to be provided by the system[6] and determine how to provide those services by distributing the work to the objects within the system. In determining how we distribute the work, we recommend using sequence diagrams.

In our case study, we have already identified the actions that must be performed for each system service. They are the logic in italic.[7] Thus, for this exercise, we only need to draw the "white box" sequence diagram for the system services. This forces us to assign services to the classes and help find the helpers (collaborators). An example is given here for the "white box" logic for pressing the cook button. The white box logic states:

- Oven beeps the user
- Start timing for 1 minute
- Turn light on
- Energize power tube

The corresponding sequence diagram for this is given in Figure 23-11. The check for the state of the door is included so that it won't violate the requirements that the oven won't cook when the door is open. As can be seen from the sequence diagram, the oven has to collaborate with the door, timer, power tube, beeper, and light, while the cook button collaborates with the oven.

After generating all of the "white box" sequence diagrams, we can identify the collaborations that are occurring. We add this information to our CRC cards. The results are shown in Figure 23-12 through Figure 23-15. Only the CRC cards for which collaborators have been identified are given.

---

[6] In case you have forgotten, these services were determined by the use cases!

[7] The italic portion of the use case sequence diagram is technically not part of a proper UML diagram, as this is "white box" logic! But in practice, we need to do this high-level, white box thinking to determine the proper sequence of interaction at the black box level.

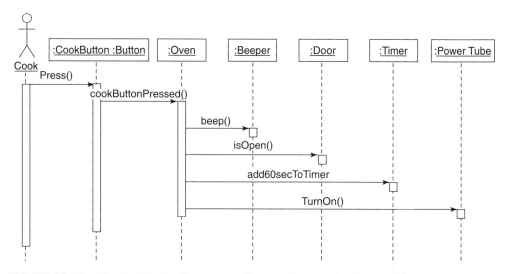

FIGURE 23-11 The "white box" sequence diagram for pressing the cook button.

The Timer class has to collaborate with the oven so that the oven will know when cooking has completed.

Class Name: Timer	
Responsibilities (External Services)	Collaborators
add60secToTime()	Oven
setTimeToZero()	

FIGURE 23-12 CRC card for the timer with collaborators identified.

The Oven class is the controller for the system. It handles all events and handles all of the sequencing and business logic. The Oven class has to know about the timer so that it can set the time, the door so that it can check the door state, the power tube to turn it on and off, the light to turn it on and off, and the beeper to tell it to beep.

Class Name: Oven (GOD object)	
Responsibilities (External Services)	Collaborators
handle all external events:	Timer
doorOpen(), doorClose()	Door
cookButtonPressed(), cancelButtonPressed()	Power Tube

FIGURE 23-13 CRC card for the Oven with collaborators identified.

Class Name: Oven (GOD object)	
timerExpired()	Light
	Beeper

FIGURE 23-13 CRC card for the Oven with collaborators identified. (Continued)

The Door class is responsible for opening and closing the door.

Class Name: Door	
Responsibilities (External Services)	Collaborators
open()	Oven
close()	
isOpen()	

FIGURE 23-14 CRC card for Door with the collaborators identified.

The Button class collaborates with the oven to initiate cooking, add to the cooking time, and to cancel cooking.

Class Name: Button	
Responsibilities (External Services)	Collaborators
press()	Oven

FIGURE 23-15 CRC card for the Button with the collaborators identified.

We show a complete use case in Figure 23-16 for the convenience of the reader. At this point in our process, we would normally generate such use case scenarios to allow us to validate the services found and to help us identify if we have missed any service. We have already taken these use cases into account in allocating services.

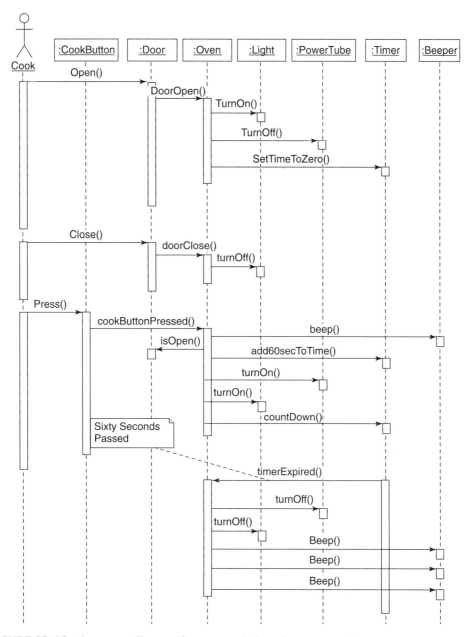

FIGURE 23-16 Sequence diagram for a scenario based on use case 1.

FIGURE 23-17   State diagram for the Door.

Many of the objects exhibit state. We can develop the state diagrams for our classes. The state diagram for the door is given in Figure 23-17. Similar diagrams can be constructed for the light and power tube.

Step 4: Specifying Relationships

The dependency diagram for this system is shown in Figure 23-18. There are seven dependencies that exist among the six objects. We have to capture these dependencies in some fashion. Because all of the objects interact with the oven, we will do this by introducing aggregation. This is consistent with the business semantics, namely that an oven is made of parts.

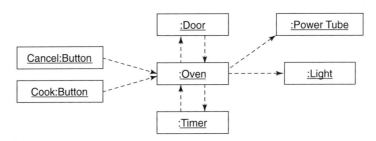

FIGURE 23-18   Dependency diagram for the objects.

The oven in this model is an aggregate of its parts. Those parts are: the light, the beeper, the door, the power tube, the timer, and two buttons. The aggregation diagram for the oven is shown in Figure 23-19.

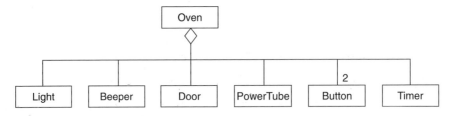

FIGURE 23-19   Aggregation diagram.

Step 5: Refinement

After examining the sequence diagrams for all of the use cases, it becomes clear that the oven doesn't require refinement. This is often the case when one captures all of the business logic in one class and introduces a number of simple classes that are slavishly driven by the controller. In this example, the principal function of the light, door, and button classes is to provide software interfaces to hardware functions.

Discussion

This solution has very high reuse and very low coupling! However, this solution is like procedural programming: All of the (domain and application) semantics is captured in the Oven logic. The result is that we are not managing complexity any better than with procedural programming.

Solution 2: Distributed Responsibility with High Coupling

IN this solution, a team of experienced object-oriented technologists emphasizes two of the basic object-oriented principles: encapsulation and delegation. This team's solution differs significantly from the previous solution.

Step 1: Identify the Objects

In this solution the team has arrived at the same set of classes, with one exception—it has eliminated the oven. The decision to eliminate the oven was in recognition of the fact that there is no need to put some major control object between the generator of an event and the processor of the event. The set of classes selected here is given in Table 23-3.

Step 2: Identifying Responsibilities

The elimination of the oven object forces a redistribution of responsibilities. The CRC cards generated for the classes identify the responsibilities as allocated to the classes. However, there is a major restructuring of the collaborators to account for the fact that we don't have an oven class coordinating message passing.

    The Door class is responsible for allowing the user to take food out when it is safe and to keep itself closed when the power tube is on. The CRC card is shown in Figure 23-20.

TABLE 23-3   List of Classes

cancel button	light	timer
cook button	door	beeper
power tube		

Class Name: Door (Controller)	
Responsibilities (External Services)	Collaborators
open()	
close()	
isOpen()	

FIGURE 23-20   CRC card for Door.

The Cook button class is responsible for getting the "food" cooked. The CRC card is shown in Figure 23-21.

Class Name: Cook Button (Controller)	
Responsibilities (External Services)	Collaborators
press() {semantic meaning- cook}	

FIGURE 23-21   CRC card for the Cook Button class.

The Cancel button class is responsible for stopping cooking and putting the microwave in a safe condition for the user to open the door. The CRC card is shown in Figure 23-22.

Class Name: Cancel Button (Controller)	
Responsibilities (External Services)	Collaborators
press() {semantic meaning- stop cooking}	

FIGURE 23-22   CRC card for the Cancel Button class.

The Timer class is responsible for controlling the power tube. The CRC card is shown in Figure 23-23.

Class Name: Timer (Technology)	
Responsibilities (External Services)	Collaborators
add60secToTime()	
setTimeToZero()	
timeExpired()	

FIGURE 23-23   CRC card for the Timer class.

The Light class is responsible for illuminating the inside of the oven while "cooking" or when the door is open. The CRC card is shown in Figure 23-24.

Class Name: Light (Model)	
Responsibilities (External Services)	Collaborators
turnOn()	
turnOff()	

FIGURE 23-24   CRC card for the Light class.

The Power Tube class is to heat the food in the oven. The CRC card is shown in Figure 23-25.

Class Name: Power Tube (Model)	
Responsibilities (External Services)	Collaborators
turnOn()	
turnOff()	

FIGURE 23-25   CRC card for the Power Tube class.

The Beeper class is to alert the user of the oven when cooking has completed and to signal that each button press has been received. The CRC card is shown in Figure 23-26.

Class Name: Beeper (View)	
Responsibilities (External Services)	Collaborators
beep()	

FIGURE 23-26   CRC card for the Beeper class.

Step 3: Specifying Behavior

Team members used their expertise in the domain of being a user of microwave ovens to identify the responsibilities. They then use the use cases to check for completeness. The example for pressing the cook button is presented in Figure 23-27.[8]

---

[8]   The reader may want to compare this diagram against the diagram in Figure 23-11.

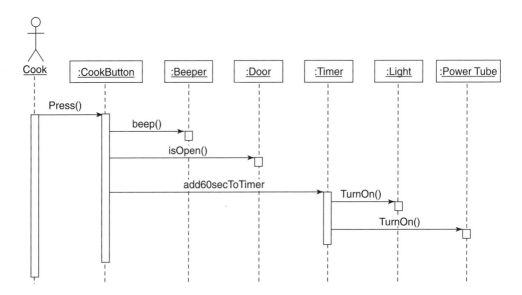

FIGURE 23-27 The "white box" sequence diagram for pressing the cook button.

The Door collaborates with the timer (so that it can inform the timer when it is opened), with the light (so that the light can turn on or off when the door is opened or closed), and with the power tube (so that it can inform the power tube to turn off when the door is opened during cooking) as a safeguard. The CRC card is shown in Figure 23-28.

Class Name: Door (Controller)	
Responsibilities (External Services)	Collaborators
open()	Timer
close()	Light
isOpen()	Power Tube

FIGURE 23-28 CRC card for Door.

The Cook button collaborates with the timer (so that it can add 60 seconds to the time remaining to cook), the beeper (so that it can inform the user that the button has been pressed), and the door (so that it can make sure that the door is closed before activating the power tube). The CRC card is shown in Figure 23-29.

Class Name: Cook Button (Controller)	
Responsibilities (External Services)	Collaborators
press() {semantic meaning- cook}	Timer
	Beeper
	Door

FIGURE 23-29   CRC card for the Cook Button class.

The Cancel button collaborates with the timer (so that it can reset the time to zero) and the beeper (so that it can provide feedback to the user). The CRC card is shown in Figure 23-30.

Class Name: Cancel Button (Controller)	
Responsibilities (External Services)	Collaborators
press() {semantic meaning- stop cooking}	Timer
	Light
	Beeper

FIGURE 23-30   CRC card for the Cancel Button class.

The Timer class collaborates with the power tube (so that it can turn it on and off), the light (so that it can turn it on and off), and the beeper (so that it can signal the completion of cooking). The CRC card is shown in Figure 23-31.

Class Name: Timer (Technology)	
Responsibilities (External Services)	Collaborators
add60secToTime()	Power Tube
setTimeToZero()	Light
timeExpired()	Beeper

FIGURE 23-31   CRC card for the Timer class.

Another example of a scenario of a use case is given in Figure 23-32.

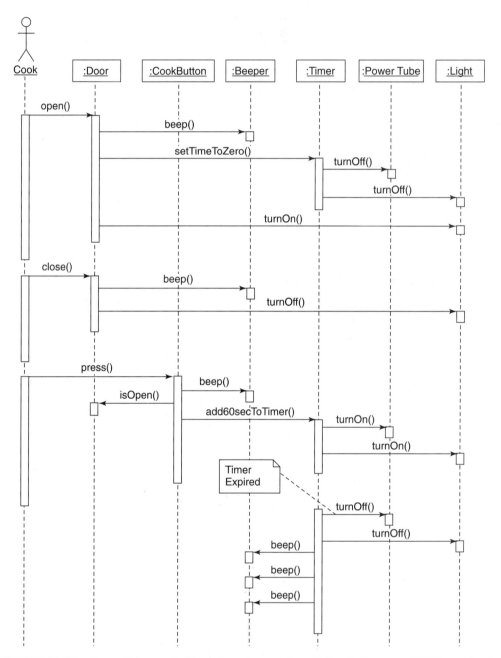

FIGURE 23-32 Scenario generated based on use case 1 verifying that responsibilities and collaborations have been allocated proportionately.

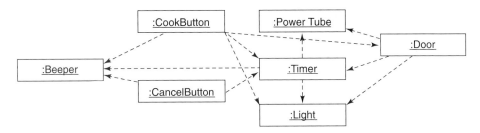

FIGURE 23-33   Dependency diagram for solution 2.

The state diagrams for the various classes in this model are identical to those developed in the first solution. The light has two states (off and on), the power tube has two states (off and on), and the door has two states (open and closed). Note that their actions are very different in some of the classes.

Step 4: Specifying Relationships

Taking into account of all the collaborators, we can generate a dependency diagram. The dependency diagram for this system is given in Figure 23-33. Comparison of this diagram with the dependency diagram in Figure 23-18 illustrates the more complicated nature of the interactions between objects.

Unlike solution 1, in which a universal object (the oven) coordinated all of the interactions, this solution does not possess such an object. This means that we will not have an aggregation. Instead, all of the objects that depend upon each other must use associations to capture the dependencies. Because the dependencies are all unidirectional, the associations will be unidirectional as well. The association diagram is shown in Figure 23-34.

Step 5: Refinement

An experienced team will often stop at this point.

Discussion

If you look at the dependency diagram for this model, you see that this model has very high coupling: thus, also less reuse![9] Many purists will tell us that this solution is more OO-like (this is more responsibility-driven) than the "GOD object" solution; i.e., solution 1. From a superficial analysis, it appears as if solution 1 is better. However, solution 1 is like procedural programming; nearly all the (domain and application) semantics are captured in the Oven logic and the reuse is of class with no business logic or semantic. So we are not managing complexity any better than with procedural programming. In

---

[9]   Some OO professionals, including one of the authors, believe that reuse is like fool's gold and will not be achieved whether you use OO or any other modeling paradigm. Many of us believe the lower of cost of development of software will come from the development of "frameworks" and the proper development of "service-level" components consistent with the framework.

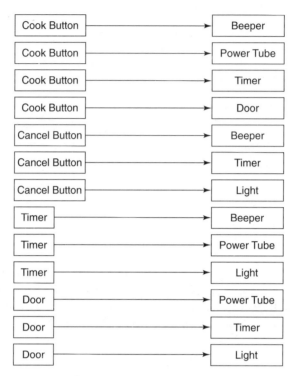

FIGURE 23-34   Association diagram for the microwave oven.

solution 3, we will show how to solve the coupling issue and still have distributed business logic.

Solution 3: Distributed Responsibility Using the Observer Mechanism

Do the limitations of the previous two solutions mean that OO is not useful? NO! It means that OO is very difficult to do properly because there is a lot more to OO than what is taught in any introductory book or class. We will now present a more balanced OO solution (using the observer mechanism) that lowers coupling and increases reuse without losing the ability to distribute the domain responsibilities (true bedrock of OO) in solution 3.

In solution 3, the team not only applies the first two principles:

1. Encapsulation
2. Delegation

But also applies the following additional OO principles and concepts:

1. Abstraction
2. Separation of interfaces from implementation
3. Use of patterns

To abide by all three principles, the development team finds that it has to introduce abstractions into the solution that are not identified in the requirements.

In solution 3, the team took the same identical approach taken by team 2, up to step 5. At this point, the experts introduce an abstraction that removes the strong coupling between all of the objects. Hence, this discussion begins with step 5.

Step 5: Refinement

The solution presented previously has a major failure in two parts: One is that the classes are highly coupled and the second is that the interfaces are not separated from the implementation. An expert will address both of these problems.

We begin by examining the dependencies upon the cancel button. In particular, we see that the beeper and timer both respond to the cancel button getting pushed. The diagram for this is illustrated in Figure 23-35.

One approach for decoupling dependencies of this nature is to employ the publish-subscribe pattern (also called the Observer pattern). This pattern has the advantage that it separates the implementation from the interface. This fact makes the publish-subscribe pattern very popular among experts. This pattern introduces the idea of a subject object and a set of observers. The observers are actually interfaces (i.e., a pure abstract class) that tie the subject to an implementation of that interface. The UML diagram for the publish-subscribe pattern is shown in Figure 23-36.

The CRC card for a publisher (or subject) class is shown in Figure 23-37. In the case of our cancel button, we can incorporate the attributes and responsibilities into the CRC card for the button.

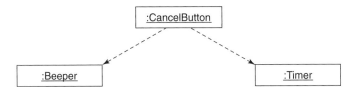

FIGURE 23-35 Dependencies between the cancel button and the beeper, timer, power tube, and light.

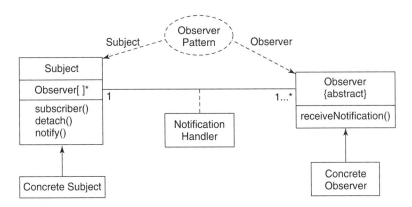

FIGURE 23-36 Publish-subscribe pattern.

Subject
List of observers (listeners)
subscribe (Object observer) {attach observer to the list of observers }
unsubscribe(Object observer) {detach observer to the list of observers }
notify ( ) { call the notify service of every observer on the list }

FIGURE 23-37   CRC card for a subject in the publish-subscribe pattern.

The subject class is the template or definition of an object in which a number of other objects express an interest in knowing about events that it can generate. These interested parties are the observers. Rather than hard-coding each observer, we allow the observer to indicate its interest by subscribing to the subject. When the subject determines that it is time to signal an event, it goes to the list of subscribed observers and notifies them of the event.[10]

The subscribers to a subject are observers. Every observer must, at a minimum, support the same interface. However, each observer can have customized code so that it can exhibit the appropriate behavior. The CRC card for the observer class[11] appears in Figure 23-38.

Observer (Subscriber)
receiveNotification ( ) { do your customized thing }

FIGURE 23-38   CRC card for the Observer Class.

With the publish-subscribe mechanism, we do not have to capture the collaborators from the CRC as either arguments or as persistent relationships (associations). We have reduced the degree of coupling with a flexible, albeit transitory, relationship. Any object can be an observer by inheriting from the observer class and implementing (providing the code) the pure virtual function: receiveNotification. To actually activate itself as an observer, it must also put itself on the notification list by using the subscribe service of the subject. An object can unsubscribe from the notification at any time by using the unsubscribe service of the subject.

We observe that both the cook button and the cancel button have a common service— pressed(). However, there is a significant difference. The behavior of the overall system is the

---

[10] This is an example of using late binding. The subject does not know about or care how the events that it generates are being handled.

[11] An observer class is actually an interface. At some point in time, often at initialization, the subscriber must subscribe to the subject.

same for pressing the cancel button regardless of the state of the system, while pressing the cook button leads to different behaviors depending upon whether the door is open or closed.

There seems to be a challenge here. The cook button appears to have to query the door to determine the state of the door. The most obvious solution is to establish an association between the cook button and the door. However, this solution still couples the button and door, which reduces the reusability of both. An alternative is to have the cook button subscribe to door events and allow the cook button to have an active and an inactive state. Opening the door will cause the cook button to transition into the inactive state. Closing the door will transition the cook button into the active state. In the active state, the button will perform the notifications, while in the inactive state it will not.

There remains one minor challenge. Requirement 10 states that the beeper will beep when the cook button is pressed when the door is open. If the beeper subscribes to a stateful button, then pressing the button means that it will not perform the notifications. However, it can be argued that having the button beep when it doesn't initiate cooking is misleading. We can renegotiate this requirement. This allows the button with state to have a consistent behavior with respect to subscribers. An alternative is to provide subscriptions to both active and inactive states. For the sake of brevity, we will assume the requirement has been renegotiated.

What does this mean in terms of our solution? It means that we will have a base button class that defines the basic button operations (press, subscribe, and unsubscribe) and attributes (set of subscribers). We will add two subclasses, stateless button and stateful button. The stateful button will add two operations (activate and deactivate) and a state variable. The behavior of the press operation will be based on the state. If the button is in the active state, all of the subscribers will be notified that the button was pressed. However, if the button is in the inactive state, then pressing the button will be ignored. The CRC cards for these classes are shown in Figures 23-29 through 23-42.

Class Name: BaseButton
Responsibilities {External Service}
notify() {tell all subscribers button pressed}
subscribe() {attach observer to the list of observers }
unsubscribe() {detach observer to the list of observers }

FIGURE 23-39   CRC card for BaseButton.

Class Name: ButtonObserver
Responsibilities {External Service}
recieveButtonNotification() {this is pure virtual}

FIGURE 23-40   CRC card for ButtonObserver.

Class Name: RegularButton Inherits BaseButton
Responsibilities {External Service}
// This is done a lot for completeness and consistency
// No addtitional methods or overridden methods

FIGURE 23-41   CRC card for Regular Button.

Class Name: StatefulButton Inherits BaseButton
State variable = {inactive,active}
Responsibilities {External Service}
notify() {{if state=active then super.notify; return;}
activate() {state = active; return;}
deactivate() {state = inactive; return;}

FIGURE 23-42   CRC card for StatefulButton.

This solution has a certain elegance to it. If we need a button, we can reuse the appropriate subclass of button without modification. Anything that is activated by a button can subscribe to it. No matter how many different buttons our microwave oven (or any other device) may have in the future, we can use the three button classes and the button observer class without needing to introduce any other kinds of buttons. These classes must be captured in a package because we want them to be used as a package and not as individual classes.

We have a similar situation with respect to the door and the timer classes. We apply the publisher-subscriber pattern to those classes as well. However, the door generates more than one event, namely a door close event and a door open event. We have two choices: (1) we can implement a single subscription and have every object that subscribes get notified of every event, or (2) we can implement a subscribe and unsubscribe operation for each event that can be generated. For our purposes, we will use the second choice.[12] We end up with three highly reusable packages: the button package, the door package, and the timer package. These are illustrated in Figure 23-43 through Figure 23-45.

---

[12] The actual analysis required to select one option over the other can be quite complex and exceeds the scope of this book. The reasons why we chose as we did will become clear later in this example.

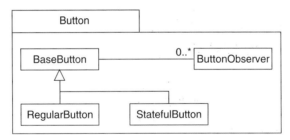

FIGURE 23-43   **Button package containing button classes and a Button Observer class.**

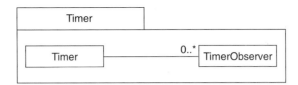

FIGURE 23-44   **Timer package containing the Timer class and the timer observer.**

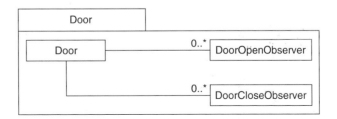

FIGURE 23-45   **Door package containing the Door class and two observer classes.**

There remains one major problem to be solved: connecting the classes associated with our microwave oven with the observer classes that have been introduced. There are many approaches to connecting an implementation class to an observer class.[13] We will use the observer class as a virtual base class from which subscriber-specific observer classes are derived.

---

[13] There are at least four different ways that are supported by C++. We can have all potential subscribers be specializations of the observer class. We can have explicitly coded in our observer class all possible classes that can subscribe. We can pass the address of the method that is supposed to be invoked as an argument of the subscribe method. We can create specializations of the observer class that are tailored to specific subscribers. The first two ways are maintenance nightmares. The third approach is just plain scary. The fourth approach actually gives us significant flexibility.

An example for the Timer class observing the Button is shown in Figure 23-44. In this figure, we have two subclasses of the ButtonObserver class. An instance of the Timer_CancelButtonObserver Class is used by the timer to subscribe to the cancel button. Pressing the cancel button will generate a button-pressed event message to an instance of the Timer_CancelButtonObserver. This message is then forwarded to the light via the association. An instance of the Timer_CookButtonObserver class is used by the light to subscribe to the cook button. Pressing the cook button generates a button-pressed event to that instance. The message is then forwarded to the light via the association.

There remains two design challenges: The timer doesn't respond to a button-pressed event—it expects other messages. Second, the timer needs to respond to two different buttons using the same service (function proptotype), namely, recieveButton-Notificiation.

A simple solution to both challenges lies in another design pattern—the adapter Pattern. In this pattern a class is introduced that transforms a generated message into a form that can be handled by the intended receiver. An instance of this class is placed between the sender and intended receiver to map the message. The UML diagram for the adapter pattern is shown in Figure 23-46.

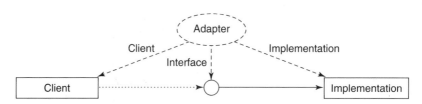

FIGURE 23-46   The adapter pattern.

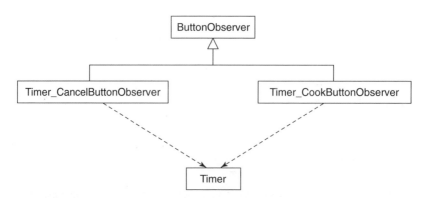

FIGURE 23-47   Subclassing the Button Observer class so that a light can get notified of button presses.

In our case, we will use a combination of inheritance, delegation, and the adapter pattern to meet the challenge. First, the inheritance mechanism will be used to implement two subclasses that implement different behaviors for the button pressed function, receiveButtonNotification. The inheritance diagram is shown in Figure 23-47.

Now we will use the adapter pattern plus delegation via collaboration to complete our solution. We already have a class that exists between the client (generator of an event) and the implementation (receiver of the event), namely the observer class. We shall use the observer classes as the interface adapters. The CRC cards for our Button observer classes are shown in Figures 23-48 through Figure 23-50.

Class Name: ButtonObserver	
Responsibilities (External Services)	Collaborators
recieveButtonNotification() { pure virtual function}	Button

FIGURE 23-48   CRC card for Button Observer.

Class Name: Timer_CancelButtonObserver	**Superclass: ButtonObserver**
Responsibilities (External Services)	Collaborators
recieveButtonNotification() { set timer to zero}	Timer

FIGURE 23-49   CRC card for Timer_CancelButtonObserver.

Class Name: Timer_CookButtonObserver	**Superclass: ButtonObserver**
Responsibilities (External Services)	Collaborators
recieveButtonNotification() { add 60 seconds to timer and start timing}	Timer

FIGURE 23-50   CRC card for Timer_CookButtonObserver.

Introducing the adapter pattern via collaboration (which will be implemented by an association) into our observers is very simple. The Timer_CancelButtonObserver will map the button pressed message into a set timer to zero message for the timer. The Timer_CookButtonObserver will map the button pressed message into an add 60 seconds to timer message for the timer.[14]

---

[14] Note that we could have also solved the design challenge by using multiple inheritance. In that case, Timer would inherit from both subclasses: CancelButtonObserver and CookButtonObserver. They again will override each function with the appropriate code.

We extend this approach for all of our publishers and their subscribers. The necessary classes are shown in the CRC cards shown in Figure 23-51 through Figure 23-61.

Class Name: Beeper_ButtonObserver	SuperClass: Button Observer
Responsibilities (External Services)	Collaborators
recieveButtonNotification() { invokes beep on beeper}	beeper

FIGURE 23-51 CRC card for the Beeper_ButtonObserver.

Class Name: PowerTube_TimerOnObserver	Superclass: TimerObserver
Responsibilities (External Services)	Collaborators
on() {turn on power tube}	PowerTube

FIGURE 23-52 CRC card for the PowerTube_TimerOnObserver.

Class Name: Light_TimerOnObserver	Superclass: TimerObserver
Responsibilities (External Services)	Collaborators
on() {turn on light}	Light

FIGURE 23-53 CRC card for Light_TimerOnObserver.

Class Name: Light_TimerOffObserver	Superclass: TimerObserver
Responsibilities (External Services)	Collaborators
off() {turn off light}	Light

FIGURE 23-54 CRC card for Light_TimerOffObserver.

Class Name: Beeper_TimerExpiredObserver	Superclass: TimerObserver
Responsibilities (External Services)	Collaborators
timeExpired() {Beep 3 times}	Beeper

FIGURE 23-55 CRC card for Beeper_TimerExpiredObserver.

Class Name: PowerTube_TimerOffObserver	Superclass: TimerObserver
Responsibilities (External Services)	Collaborators
off() {Turn off power tube}	PowerTube

FIGURE 23-56 CRC card for PowerTube_TimerOffObserver.

Class Name: Light_TimerOffObserver	Superclass: TimerObserver
Responsibilities (External Services)	Collaborators
timeExpired() {turn off light}	Light

FIGURE 23-57 CRC card for Light_TimerOffObserver.

Class Name: PowerTube_DoorOpenObserver	Superclass: DoorOpenObserver
Responsibilities (External Services)	Collaborators
open() {turn off power tube}	PowerTube

FIGURE 23-58 CRC card for PowerTube_DoorObserver.

Class Name: Timer_DoorOpenObserver	Superclass: DoorOpenObserver
Responsibilities (External Services)	Collaborators
open() {set time remaining to zero}	Timer

FIGURE 23-59 CRC card for Timer_DoorOpenObserver.

Class Name: Light_DoorOpenObserver	Superclass: DoorCloseObserver
Responsibilities (External Services)	Collaborators
open() {turn off light}	Light

FIGURE 23-60   CRC card for Light_DoorObserver.

Class Name: Light_DoorCloseObserver	Superclass: DoorOpenObserver
Responsibilities (External Services)	Collaborators
close() {turn on light}	Light

FIGURE 23-61   CRC card for Light_DoorCloseObserver.

The CRC cards for our microwave related classes are given in Figure 23-62 through Figure 23-69. One will notice that there are no interdependencies among these classes. The collaborators are observer classes that serve to decouple these classes.

Class Name: Timer	
Attributes	Collaborators
time-remaining	TimerObserver
Responsibilities {External Service}	
add60secToTime()	
setTimeToZero()	
timeExpired()	
on()	
off()	
subscribe()	
unsubscribe()	

FIGURE 23-62   CRC card for Timer.

Class Name: Door	
Responsibilities {External Service}	Collaborators
open() {tell all subscribers door opened}	DoorOpenObserver
close() {tell all subscribers door closed}	DoorCloseObserver
subscribeDoorOpen()	
subscribeDoorClose()	
unsubscribeDoorOpen()	
unsubscribeDoorClose()	

FIGURE 23-63   CRC card for Door.

Class Name: BaseButton	
Responsibilities {External Service}	Collaborators
pressed() {tell all subscribers button pressed}	ButtonObserver
subscribe()	
unsubscribe()	

FIGURE 23-64   CRC card for BaseButton.

Class Name: RegularButton	Superclass: BaseButton
Responsibilities (External Services)	Collaborators

FIGURE 23-65   CRC card for RegularButton.

Class Name: StatefulButton	Superclass: BaseButton
Responsibilities (External Services)	Collaborators
activate()	
deactivate()	

FIGURE 23-66   CRC card for StatefulButton.

Class Name: Beeper	
Responsibilities {External Service}	Collaborators
beep()	

FIGURE 23-67   CRC card for Beeper.

Class Name: Light	
Responsibilities {External Service}	Collaborators
turnOn()	
turnOff()	

FIGURE 23-68   CRC card for Light.

Class Name: PowerTube	
Responsibilities {External Service}	Collaborators
turnOn()	
turnOff()	

FIGURE 23-69   CRC card for PowerTube.

We can generate the state diagrams for these classes, recognizing that the Light, PowerTube, Timer, and Door all have state. This is left as an exercise for the reader.

One area that has not been addressed to this point is when instances of the classes are created and when those instances subscribe to the appropriate publishers. There are three basic approaches that are commonly taken: (1) perform all of these functions during program start-up within the main routine; (2) create the objects in the main and use the constructors of the objects to perform the subscriptions; and (3) create an oven object that functions as a factory (the factory creates all of the instances and establishes the subscriptions).

The first option is perfectly satisfactory for the microwave oven. We only have one oven that has to be created. Placing the logic about constructing the objects in the main routine is perfectly reasonable. Instances of each of the classes are created and then the subscriptions are performed.

The second option requires that each constructor has the logic for subscribing to the publishers encoded within it. Such an approach limits the reusability of the classes. Each class must capture within its definition knowledge about the other objects of the oven. This makes it more difficult to reuse these classes for other purposes.

The third option is a powerful approach that promotes reusability. The idea is that we have an object that serves as a factory. The same logic that would be encoded in the main routine for the first option is encoded within a method of the factory object. The value of this approach is that the factory can produce as many ovens as needed. For the purposes of this program, such an approach is overkill—we only need a single oven.

Discussion

This solution is very elegant and has major advantages over the other two solutions.[15] We have split our business domain into two components: the business entities and the business policies. The entities in a business are relatively stable (devices).[16] The business policies specific how these entities are to interact (the observer-adapters). Business policies are subject to more frequent changes than business entities. By splitting our model of the microwave oven into those two parts, we end up with a major proportion of our code (business entities) that is stable, extensible, and reusable.

We have localized our knowledge about the devices comprising the oven in individual classes. If we need to modify some aspect of the timer or power tube, we only have one location where that information is captured. We can add new components to our business, such as a voice module. We can extend existing components to provide additional capabilities, such as adding different tones to our beeper.[17] The localization of information about our devices has increased the cohesion of our model without increasing coupling.

For a specific kind of microwave oven, the dependencies between these devices represent business policies. That is, this particular microwave oven uses three beeps to indicate that cooking has completed. The next version of the product might use a voice module to state that cooking has completed. Because we have separated the business policy from the business entities, the alterations in our software are relatively straightforward. We introduce another component, a voice module, in the new microwave oven and introduce a new observer connecting it to the timer. The observer-adapter class that was used by the beeper to subscribe to the timer is removed or ignored because the old beeper does not subscribe to the timer. Instead, the voice module does. Every other aspect of the oven can remain the same. We've reused (without modification) over 95% of our code!

---

[15] Our solution is still not optimal. In actuality, experts would have revisited the business entity classes and removed some of the hardcoded aspects. The add60secToTime would have been replaced by an addTime that takes an argument stating the amount of time to be added. In fact, the timer would have probably been totally redesigned to have a method to clear the timer, suspend the timer, and start the timer. One might argue that such features were not called for in the requirements and, hence, represent wasted work, but an expert will work a little harder now to save significantly more effort later.

[16] There are probably only a half dozen different kinds of power tubes used in microwave ovens despite the fact that there are hundreds of different kinds of microwave ovens on the market.

[17] Backward compatibility can be maintained by keeping legacy interfaces to our classes.

Unified Modeling Language

UML is a modeling language for documenting and visualizing the artifacts that we have specified and constructed in the analysis and design of a system. This appendix gives a broad understanding of what is UML and what is not UML.

Introduction

UML is a generic syntax for creating a logical model of a system. It is normally used to describe a computer system as it is understood at various points during analysis and design. The syntax was defined originally by Jim Rumbaugh and Grady Booch to contain all of the constructs available in each of their own methods, but with a common graphical representation. Later they were joined by Ivar Jacobson, who added syntax for defining requirements with use cases, and the language was finalized by a committee of OO experts.

The syntax has been designed to be independent of any particular target language, software process, or tool, but is sufficiently generic and flexible that it can be used customized using user-defined extensions to accommodate almost all language, tool, or process requirement. Although the syntax itself is well-defined and reasonably easy to understand, to apply it to a particular project is much less easy to define. This requires the definition of a set of semantics that are appropriate for a particular architecture and software process. This is left to the users.

What Is the Unified Modeling Language?

UML is a language that unifies the best engineering practices for modeling systems:

- It is a language for capturing knowledge (partial semantics) and for expressing that knowledge (syntax).
- Its purpose is for modeling of systems.

- It is used for documenting in a visual manner that models.
- It is a collection of best practices.
- It is used to produce a set of artifacts that can be delivered.
- It has world-wide support.

What Is Not UML?

UML is **not:**

- A visual programming language
- A tool or repository specification
- A process

What Are the Goals of UML?

The stated goals of UML are to:

- Be an expressive, visual modeling language that is relatively simple and extensible.
- Have extensibility and specialization mechanisms for extending, rather than modifing, the core concepts.
- Be independent of any programming language.
- Be process-independent.
- Support high-level concepts (framework, patterns, and components).
- Address recurring architectural complex issues using the high-level concepts.
- Be scaleable and widely applicable (over many domains).

Why Use UML?

We produce products and services that address customer needs and requirements. Requirements may be considered the *problem* and the products and/or services may be considered the *solution*. The problem and solution occur within some domain (space or context). For a good solution to be produced, first, the problem must be understood. The solution must also be understood for it to be constructed and used. Furthermore, the solution must be organized (architecture) in order to facilitate its realization and adhere to the constraints of the domain. Thus, to solve problems, the appropriate knowledge of the problem and solution must be captured (modeled), organized (architecture), and depicted (diagrams) using some mechanism that enables communication and leverage of our knowledge. UML is the mechanism of choice of industry.

What Are the Diagrams of UML?

UML has the following diagram types:

- Use case diagrams
- Static structure diagrams

- ■ Object diagrams
- ■ Class diagrams
- ■ Interaction diagrams
  - ■ Sequence diagrams
  - ■ Collaboration diagrams
- ■ Statechart diagrams
- ■ Activity diagrams
- ■ Implementation diagrams
  - ■ Component diagrams
  - ■ Deployment diagrams

Each of these diagrams is defined in the following sections.

What Are the Most Important UML Diagrams?

The most important models in the UML syntax are:

- ■ Use case diagrams

  Use cases are used to capture the way in which the users want to use the system. They form an outside-in definition of the requirements for the computer system in a way that can be understood by users and developers.

- ■ Class diagrams

  Class diagrams are used to define the static structure model of the system. The static structure model identifies the objects, classes, and relationships among them.

- ■ Interaction diagrams (usually sequence diagrams)

  Interaction diagrams are used to capture the functional requirements. They are used as a tool to help in deciding how the functionality required to support the use cases will be distributed across the classes (objects). They can also be used as a mechanism for mapping the required system functionality onto the objects in a way that produces functionally coherent, maintainable, reusable, and extensible classes.

- ■ Statechart (dynamic) diagrams

  Statechart diagrams are used to capture the dynamic view of the system. The state diagrams that make up the model show the dependence of the functionality on the state of the system. They also show the system functionality from an object-centric point of view (rather than the use case-centric point of view). This helps in detailed design to ensure the correct coding of the conditionality of the operations. It also allows a maintainable, coherent, and robust coding of a class that encapsulates the dynamics. To ignore this view totally is to miss an in-depth understanding of the functionality of each individual class.

UML Diagrams

UML defines nine types of diagrams: class, object, use case, sequence, collaboration, statechart, activity, component, and deployment diagrams. In all of the diagrams, concepts are depicted as symbols, and relationships among concepts are depicted as paths (lines) connecting symbols. Each of these elements may also have a name.

Use Case Diagram

A use case diagram describes the functionality and users (actors) of the system. It is used to show the relationships between the actors that use the system and the use cases they use (and also the relationship between use cases). A single use case can also be thought of as a procedure by which an external actor can use the system. Taken together, the use cases define the full functionality of the system from an outside-in perspective and can be used as a basis from which to develop system tests.

The two concepts in a use case diagram are:

- Actor

  Represents users of the system, including human and other systems

- Use case

  Represents services or the functionality provided by the system to the users

A use case is represented by an oval. The name of the use case can appear within or below the oval.[1] A description of the use case is attached to the use case as an attribute. It describes in prose (or a sequence diagram) the sequence of interactions across the system boundary that make up the procedure by which the system is used. The use case is attached to at least one actor, represented by a stick man, by a line called a 'communicates' relationship. It shows which actor or actors outside the system are involved in the use case. An example is shown in Figure A-1.

A use case can be related to another use case by either an 'include' or an 'extend' relationship. An 'include' relationship indicates that the procedure of the used use case is part of the procedure of the using use case. The arrow is, in effect, an unconditional call to the procedure in the used use case. An example of the include relationship is illustrated in Figure A-2, in which use case 1 includes use case 2.

If the procedure of the use case is an alternative or partial alternative course to a defined in another use case, then an 'extend' relationship is used from the 'extending' use case to the 'extended' use case. The procedure in the 'extending' use case then replaces all or part of the procedure in the 'extended' use case under conditions specified in the 'extending' use case. This is illustrated in Figure A-2, in which use case 3 extends use case 2.

Include and extend relationships allow all possible procedures to be specified without duplication.

---

[1]   The majority of UML tools place the name of the use case below the oval.

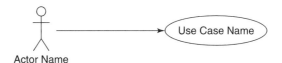

FIGURE A-1   Use case diagram.

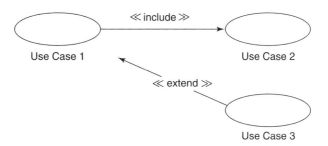

FIGURE A-2   The extend and include relationships among use cases.

The boundaries of the system are illustrated in a use case diagram as a boundary rectangle that includes the use cases with the actors outside of it. The name of the system appears at the top of the rectangle. A typical use case diagram incorporating the boundary rectangle appears in Figure A-3.[2]

Associated with a use case diagram is usually the corresponding use case details. The details may be captured as either a sequence diagram or in a textual description. Use cases are discussed in Chapter 4.

Class Diagram

A static structure diagram describes the static structure[3] of a system. In other words, it describes how the system is structured instead of how it behaves. It describes "what things are" and their static relationships with other things. To describe all of the objects in a system would be rather tedious, as many of them have similar characteristics, and in any case, some of them will be created and destroyed as a program proceeds. Class diagrams are therefore used more often than object diagrams to show this view.[4]

Classes define the types of objects that exist within the system. Classes can have attributes that are usually primitive data members of objects, and operations that define methods that can be performed on the object. The visibility of attributes and operations

---

[2]   It should be noted that many books on UML and UML tools do not incorporate the boundary rectangle in use case diagrams. The assumption is that the boundaries are well known and the rectangle is redundant.

[3]   Object diagrams describe actual objects and their relationships; class diagrams describe types of objects and their relationships.

[4]   Actual objects become important when they interact with other objects, so it is more useful to view them in interaction diagrams.

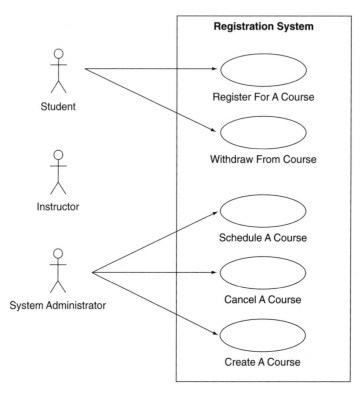

FIGURE A-3   Use case diagram for a registration system.

to other objects can be defined, as can their signatures including types, default values, parameters, parameter types, and return types.

Object relationships between classes show what links can exist between objects and define constraints on those links including the relative quantity of instances linked by an association. Class diagrams can also show packages that group classes, dependencies between classes, and dependencies between the packages that contain them. Generalization/specialization relationships that relate classes in a supertype/subtype relationship can also be included.

A typical static model will usually consist of many class diagrams that, taken together, define the static structure of the system. How they are organized depends largely on the architecture of the system.

The concepts and paths in this diagram are:

- Class
  - Object
  - Class
  - Parameterized class
  - Constraints
  - Packages

FIGURE A-4   Common representational elements across UML diagrams.

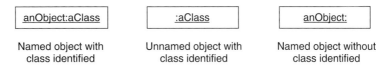

FIGURE A-5   UML notation for objects.

- ■ Relationship
  - ■ Association
  - ■ Associative object (association class)
  - ■ Aggregation
  - ■ Composition
  - ■ Generalization
  - ■ Dependency
  - ■ Interfaces

Some key diagrammatic elements are common across all UML diagrams. These are illustrated in Figure A-4. The note with the dashed line connecting to another UML element is a mechanism for attaching textual comments in the diagram. Constraints are illustrated as comments within curly braces. The comment can contain anything. Stereotypes are used to create a new type of UML element (this is how one extends UML).

Class. A class represents entities with common characteristics and behaviors (i.e., attributes, services, rules, and relationships.) The following paragraphs describe how objects, classes, and parameterized classes are documented in UML.

Figure A-5 illustrates how objects are represented in UML. An object is illustrated as a rectangle with the name underlined. The full name of an object is the object name and the class name separated by a colon. In some cases, either the object name or class name is not present. In all cases (and in diagrams illustrating objects), the name of the object is underlined to distinguish it from a class.

It is recognized in UML that a class may appear in multiple diagrams. One result of this possibility is that different diagrams may suppress all or some attributes or operations. If a single attribute or operation is given, the rectangle for the class is partitioned into three sections. An empty section does not mean that there are no attributes or operations associated with the class, only that they have not been shown in that diagram. Figure A-6 illustrates two ways in which classes (as opposed to templated classes) are represented in UML diagrams. The first example illustrates how a class is represented

Class Name

Class Name
Attributes
Operations

Class with attributes and
operations suppressed

Class with attributes and
operations represented

FIGURE A-6 UML representations for classes.

when the attributes and operations associated with the class are suppressed. The second example illustrates a class with the attributes and operations represented. In the second example, the name of the class appears in the top section, the attributes in the middle section, and the operations in the bottom section.

Attributes are specified according to the following notation:

visibility name: type = default-value

where

- *visibility* is public (+), protected (#), or private (-)[5]
- *name* is a string by which the attribute is identified
- *type* is the attribute type
- *default-value* is a value assigned to the attribute unless specified otherwise

At a minimum, the name of the attribute must be specified. The other fields are optional.[6] A derived attribute, one that is computed rather than stored, is indicated by a '/' before the attribute declaration.

Operations are specified according to the following notation:

visibility name (parameter-list) : return-type [property-string]

where

- *visibility* is public (+), protected (#), or private (-)
- *name* is a string by which the operation is identified
- *parameter-list* contains comma-separated parameters whose is given by

  direction name: type = default-value

---

[5] The visibility parameter does not have rigorous semantics in UML. In fact, the interpretation of this parameter is usually locally defined based on the semantics of visibility employed by the programming language used in implementation. Hence, a C++ oriented development organization and a Smalltalk oriented development organization may use the same visibility for an attribute, but may mean different things by it.

[6] We should not be concerned with identifying the type associated with an attribute during analysis, as that is a design decision. Because class diagrams are used during analysis and design, UML must support documenting our model with the appropriate levels of detail.

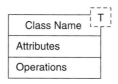

FIGURE A-7 A parameterized class.

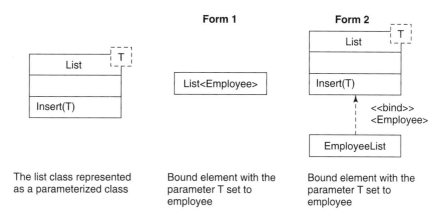

FIGURE A-8 Two forms of bound elements.

- *direction* indicates if the parameter is for input (in), output (out) or both (inout)
- *name* is the name of the parameter
- *type* is the type of the parameter
- *default-value* identifies the default value of the parameter
- *return-type* is a comma-separated list of return types
- *property-string* indicates property values that apply to the operation

As was the case with attributes, only the name of the operation must be specified; the other fields are optional.

Figure A-7 illustrates the notation for a parameterized class. A parameterized class (templated class) is a class in which the type specified for one or more attributes (or parameters and/or return-values in operations) is specified as a formal argument of the class specification. In this example, the formal parameter is 'T' and serves as placeholder for type information within the class specification.

A use of a parameterized class is called a bound element. It creates a new class with the formal parameters bound to the argument. There are two forms for illustrating a bound element, which appear in Figure A-8. The first form uses what can be considered C++ semantics for specifying a bound element in a template. In this case, the class name is the parameterized class name with the name of the bound class within angle brackets. The second form uses a dependency arrow (the dashed arrow) with a dependency prototype of bind shown in doubled angle brackets and the binding for the parameter shown in single angle brackets.

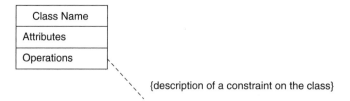

FIGURE A-9   Attaching a constraint to a class.

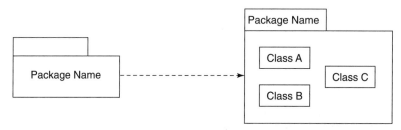

FIGURE A-10   Package diagram.

Figure A-9 illustrates how a constraint can be attached to a class. Anything may appear within the braces identifying the constraint. Most practitioners use a textual description of the constraint. However, UML does provide a formal language, Object Constraint Language, that can be used to document constraints.

Figure A-10 shows a package diagram. According to the UML specification, a package is illustrated using a folder style icon. When the classes contained within the package are suppressed, the name of the package goes in the center of the folder. When the classes are present, the name of the package goes in the tab portion of the folder. Dependencies between packages are illustrated as a dashed arrow pointing in the direction of the dependency.

Relationships. Relationships can exist between instances of classes or between classes. Associations and aggregations are relationships that relate two or more other instances of classes (association and aggregation). Generalization and specialization are relationship between two classes.

Figure A-11 illustrates the basic representation of an association in UML. An association is drawn as a line connecting two classes. The line is labeled with the name of the association, the multiplicities of the two classes (number of objects of the given class) participating in the association, and the roles that an instance of each class takes within the association. All of these labels are optional.

The multiplicity associated with one end of an association can be given in any of the forms identified in Table A-1.

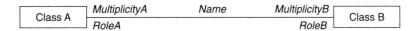

FIGURE A-11 Associations in UML.

TABLE A-1 Multiplicity Keys and Their Interpretation

Key	Interpretation
*	Any number of objects (including none)
1	Exactly one object
n	Exactly *n* objects (*n* is an integer)
0..1	Zero or one (indicates the assocation is optional)
n..m	Range from *n* as minimum to *m* as maximum (*n* and *m* are integers)
2,4	Discrete combinations (as in two doors or four doors)

FIGURE A-12 Unidirectional traversal across an association is indicated by an arrow.

The default assumption about an association is that it can be traversed by an object at either end of the association. In many cases, this assumption is not valid. To indicate unidirectional traversal, the line connecting the two classes is replaced by an arrow pointing in the direction of traversal. This is illustrated in Figure A-12.

Figure A-13 illustrates how an association class is expressed. The association class is connected to the link between the two classes participating in the association by a dashed line. The association class can have attributes and operations associated with it.

Figure A-14 shows an association class that has been promoted to a full class. A derived association has been introduced to capture the fact that there is an association between Class A and Class B. The derived association is denoted through the use of a '/' in front of the association name.

Figure A-15 illustrates the diagram for a qualified association. Qualifiers can be used to denote key lookup in a map.

Figure A-16 illustrates the use of constraints on relationships. There are two cases, one in which the constraint is on the association itself and one in which the constraint is across two relationships. The constraint is expressed in the same fashion as constraints on classes (as a condition within curly braces).

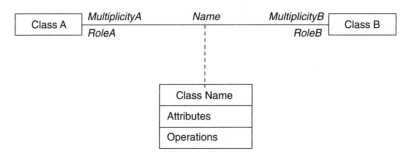

FIGURE A-13   Association class.

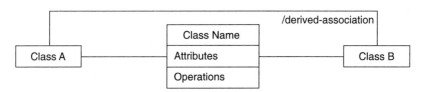

FIGURE A-14   Promoting an association class to a full class and introducing a derived association.

FIGURE A-15   Qualified association.

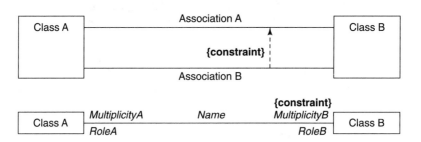

FIGURE A-16   Use of constraints on relationships.

Figure A-17 illustrates how aggregation and composition are documented. Unidirectional navigation across the aggregation or composition is illustrated using an arrow in the same manner as for associations. Constraints can be anything and must appear in curly braces. Multiplicity is denoted in the same fashion as done for associations.

Figure A-18 shows generalization and specialization. The generalization is indicated as the class with the point tof theriangle pointing at it. Subclass 1 illustrates single generali-

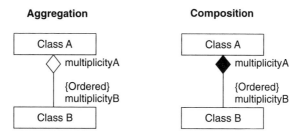

FIGURE A-17 Aggregation and composition.

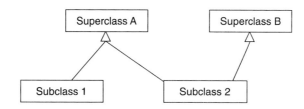

FIGURE A-18 Generalization and specialization.

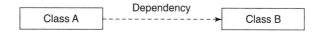

FIGURE A-19 Dependency.

zation, while Subclass 2 illustrates multiple generalization. Generalization can have a discriminator that distinguishes between different kinds of generalizations.[7]

Figure A-19 illustrates how dependencies between classes are documented. Dependencies are typically associations that are created dynamically.

Figure A-20 illustrates how an interface can be specified using classes. The dashed line with the triangle at the end is used to indicate that the implementation class realizes the interface. An alternative way of documenting interfaces uses a lollipop style icon to represent the interface, as shown in Figure A-21.

Typical class diagrams illustrating the static structure of the Breakout game are illustrated in Figure A-22 through Figure A-24.

---

[7] This diagram can be used to express multiple and dynamic classification. For this diagram, one employs a discriminator to establish which combinations are legal. Classification is different than inheritance, in the sense that multiple classification allows multiple types for an object without defining a specific type for that purpose.

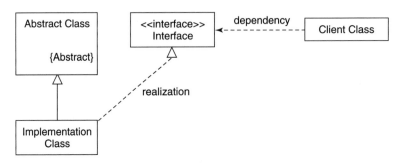

FIGURE A-20   Interface diagram using classes.

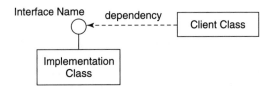

FIGURE A-21   Alternative form for representing interfaces.

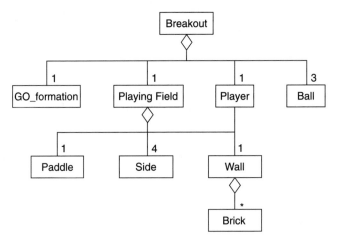

FIGURE A-22   Class aggregation for simplified version of Breakout game.

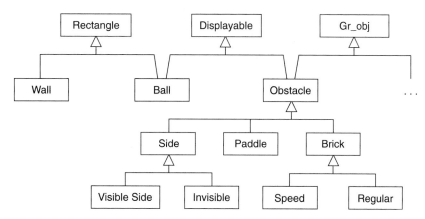

FIGURE A-23   Inheritance diagram from simplified Breakout game.

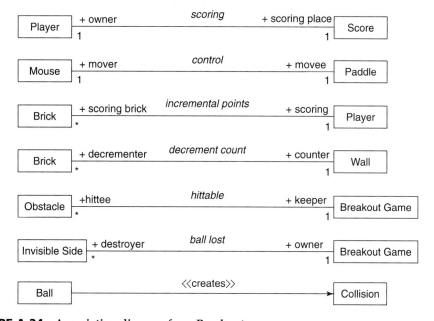

FIGURE A-24   Association diagram from Breakout game.

Sequence Diagram

Sequence diagrams capture the interaction between objects. These interactions are modeled as exchanges of messages. These message exchanges will result in some desired behavior. It can show the interactions that take place, both across the system boundary, and between objects inside the system, in order to fulfil the requirements defined for one or more paths through a use case.

The concepts and paths in this diagram are:

■ Object of a particular type (class or interface)
  Represents the role that the object plays in the interaction

■ Lifeline
  Represents the existence of the object over a period of time

■ Activation
  Represents the time when an object is performing some method

■ Message
  Represents communication between objects

A sequence diagram is a diagram that shows actual objects and interactions between objects in the horizontal direction and sequence in the vertical direction. The vertical dotted lines represent the lifetime of the object and horizontal arrows represent the interactions or messages between objects. These messages can represent any kind of message (specifically a call to an operation on the target object). Messages can include sequence numbers, operation names, and actual parameters. Narrow elongated boxes on the object lifelines represent the "activation" of the object when interactions are sequential and represent calls to operations. The operation remains active until all of the sequential operations that it calls have completed and returned; thus allowing it to return control to its caller. A basic sequence diagram is shown in Figure A-25.

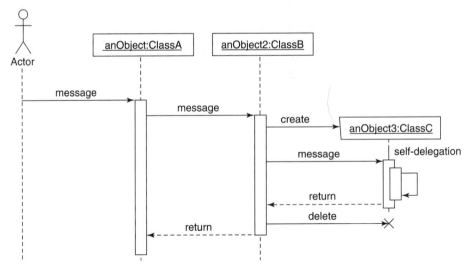

FIGURE A-25 Sequence diagram.

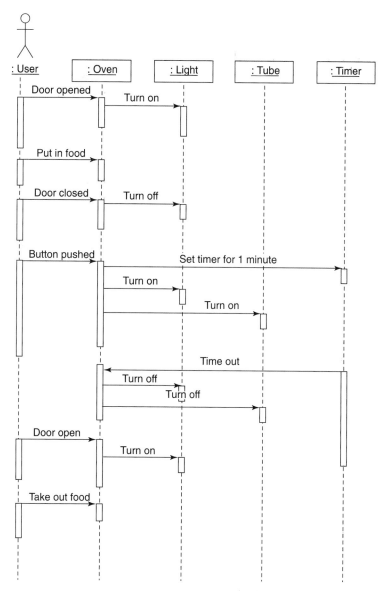

FIGURE A-26   Sequence diagram for microwave oven in scenario 2.

Figure A-26 shows a typical sequence diagram taken from the microwave oven example in Chapter 8.

Collaboration Diagram

A collaboration diagram captures the interactions among objects. These interactions are modeled as exchanges of messages. These message exchanges will result in some desired behavior.

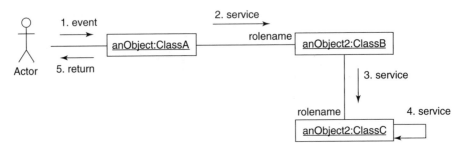

FIGURE A-27 Collaboration diagram.

A collaboration diagram is functionally equivalent to a sequence diagram, with two exceptions:

- It shows actual links between objects along which messages can flow, whereas only the messages are shown in a sequence diagram.
- The order of the messages can only be seen in their numbering, as the vertical dimension is used to show static relationships along with the horizontal dimension.[8]

A collaboration diagram is used to show how groups of objects work together to perform a piece of functionality required for one path through a use case.[9]

The concepts and paths in this diagram are:

- Object of a particular type (class or interface)
  Represents the role that the object plays in the interaction

- Relationship rule
  Represents the role that the link may play within the interaction

- Message
  Represents communication between objects

Figure A-27 illustrates a collaboration diagram. The service request is of the form:

sequence-number : [condition] : message (arglist)

where

- *sequence-number* identifies the order in which the service request was dispatched
  - * is used to indicate iteration (for example, 2* indicates that the second service request repeats)

---

[8]   This makes the collaboration diagram effectively an object diagram with messages on the links.

[9]   Sequence diagrams are better for fully specifying a use case because they can include conditional functionality in various ways without confusing the order of the messages.

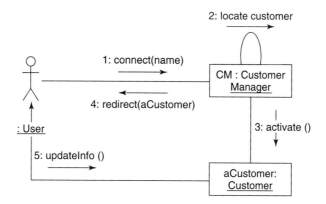

FIGURE A-28 UML notation for a collaboration diagram.

■ sequence numbers can be sequential integers or can be based on a decimal scheme

■ *condition* is an optional condition that is to be evaluated to determine if the request is sent

■ *message* is a string identifying the service request

■ *arglist* is a list of arguments formatted in the same fashion as the arglist for an operation

Figure A-28 shows a collaboration diagram from Chapter 11.

Statechart Diagram

A statechart diagram describes how the functionality of an object depends upon its state and how its state changes as a result of the events that it receives. It is used to show the dependency of operations upon the order of their calling (i.e., upon the state of the object when a call to an operation arrives at the boundary of an object).[10]

The concepts and paths in this diagram are:

■ State

Represents an abstraction of the attribute values of an object. It represents a period between events during which the object is stable. If an object has many internal states, the state model can be simplified by using "nested states" within a simpler state model.

■ Event

Represents a condition that can be detected by the object. Events can cause a transition to another state and/or they can cause one or more actions to be triggered. An incoming event, normally a call to one of the object's public operations, will

---

[10] Those familiar with structured methods may recognize them as "Entity Life Histories."

cause a different response by the object depending on its current state. Operations will be coded such that their response is conditional upon the state of the object.

■ Transition

Represents a response by an object to an event received by it. The response produces a change in the object, which can constitute a change in state. The mechanism for identifying if a change in state occurs is a *guard condition*. A guard condition is a Boolean expression in terms of event parameters and the state variables and functions of the object to which the state diagram belongs. When an event triggers the transition, the value of the guard condition is evaluated. If the value evaluates to true, the transition occurs; otherwise, the transition does not occur. Not all transitions have an associated guard condition.

■ Action

Represents a set of operations that is done inside of a state or on a transition.

In UML, three additional constructs are added: *history state*, *activity*, and *timing mark*. A *history state* is used to capture the concept that a state must "remember" its substate when it is exited and be able to enter the same substate on subsequent reentry into the state. An *activity* is an operation or set of operations within a state that takes time to complete. Thus, it is not instantaneous and can be interrupted. Some activities continue until they are terminated by an external event (usually a state change) and others terminate on their own accord. A *timing mark* construct is used to capture real-time constraints on transition. The most common use of a timing mark is to capture the maximum limits on the elapsed time between events.

Figure A-29 illustrates a simple state diagram. States are represented by rounded boxes. Transitions are represented by arrows between states. An event/action block on the transition defines the event that causes the transition, any conditions that qualify the event, and any actions that take place. Event/action blocks can also be contained within states. These can be used to define what actions take place on entry into or exit from the

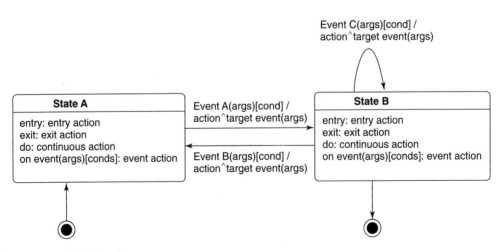

FIGURE A-29　Simple state diagram.

state or when the object receives an event while in that state that does not require it to change state.

More complex state models will incorporate nested states (i.e., substates). The UML diagram for illustrating a nested state diagram is illustrated in Figure A-30. The transition from the nested solid circle identifies the entry substate. Actions are associated with the nested states rather than the encompassing state.

Figure A-31 is from Chapter 8. This example illustrates how the nested concurrent states are represented.

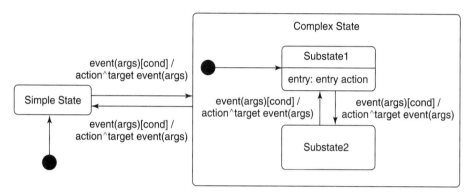

FIGURE A-30   Nested state diagram.

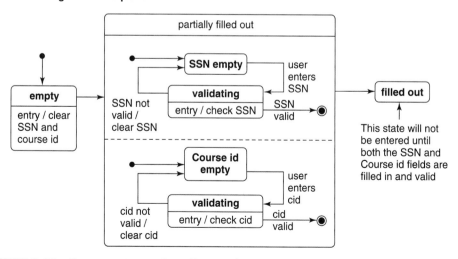

FIGURE A-31   Concurrent state chart diagram for a course registration request.

Activity Diagram

An activity diagram can be used anywhere in the model to show a flow of activity. However, it is usually reserved for defining the flow of business level events outside the scope of the system.[11]

In some methods, an activity diagram is used to describe activities that are either:

- Within an object (i.e., capturing state and its relationship with an interaction), or
- Between objects (i.e., capturing state dependencies across objects).

  The concepts and paths in this diagram are:

- Swimlane

  Represents responsibilities of one or more objects for actions within an overall interaction.

- Action state

  Represents atomic, or noninterruptible, actions of an entity

- Action Flow

  Represents relationship between different action states of an entity

- Object flow

  Represents the utilization of objects by action states and the influence of these states on the object

An activity diagram is similar to a state diagram in that both represent sequences of activity. But activity diagrams are closer in semantics to flowcharts in allowing action states. Swimlanes allow activities associated with action states to be assigned to business-level actors.

Figure A-32 shows a basic activity diagram. The solid circle at the top indicates the start point. The rounded rectangles (sausages) identify activities. The arrows represent a transition. Conditional behavior is identified by branches and merges. A diamond represents a branch point if one arrow enters and multiple arrows exit, or a merge if several arrows enter and one arrow exits. Concurrent behavior is identified by forks and joins. A dark bar represents a fork if one arrow enters and multiple arrows exit, or a join if multiple arrows enter and a single arrow exits.

Figure A-33 is an activity diagram from Chapter 7 that illustrates the use of swim lanes.

---

[11] It was introduced in order to provide some syntax for business process modeling that is separate from the model of the system requirements, the use cases, and the model of the internal system architecture defined by all of the other diagram types.

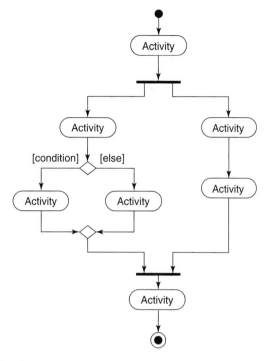

FIGURE A-32 Activity diagram.

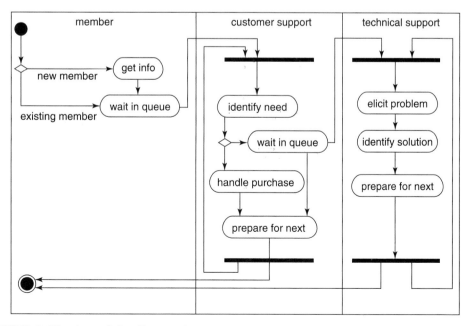

FIGURE A-33 An activity diagram for a customer support system.

Component Diagram

A component diagram describes the organization and dependencies among software implementation components. It shows the structure of actual software components that will be used to implement the system. These components can include source files, relocatable code, and executable code.

Figure A-34 illustrates a component diagram. The concepts and paths in this diagram are:

- Component
  Represents distributable physical units such as source code, object code, or executable code

- Dependency
  Represents the dependency between components

If a group of classes forms a component, we may define another way in which other components use it by applying a special UML construct: an interface. The interface allows components to be designed for use by other components without any knowledge of the internal structure of the used component. Thus, the using component depends upon the interface to the used component, not upon its implementation. This makes it possible to design components that are polymorphic (i.e., substitutable for one another).

Figure A-35 is a component diagram from Chapter 12.

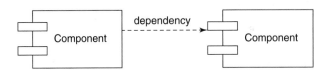

FIGURE A-34   Component diagram.

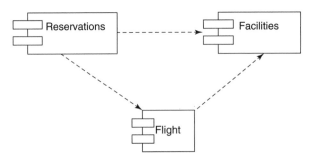

FIGURE A-35   Component diagram for a flight reservations system.

Deployment Diagram

A deployment diagram describes the configuration of processing elements and the mapping of the software implementation components to the processing elements. It shows instances of processor nodes, their interconnection, instances of the components that will run on them, and the dependence between the instances.The concepts and paths in this diagram are:

■ Component
  Represents distributable physical units such as source code, object code, or executable code

■ Node
  Represents a processing or computation resource

Figure A-36 illustrates a deployment diagram. It consists of two processors with a single component on each. The processors are connected by TCP/IP. There is a dependency between the GUI component on CPU 2 with the myComponent on CPU 1.

Figure A-37 is an example deployment diagram taken from Chapter 12 that shows a physical device (TicketPrinter) connected to a CPU (the AgentTerminal).

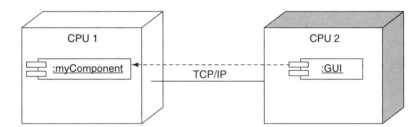

FIGURE A-36   Deployment diagram.

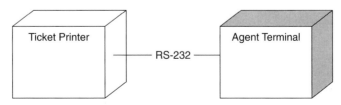

FIGURE A-37   Deployment diagram.

UML Glossary

TABLE A-2   Glossary of UML Terms

Term	Definition
action	An operation or a set of operations that is done inside of a state or on a transition. It cannot be interrupted.
action flow	Represents relationships between different action states of an entity.
action state	Represents atomic, or noninterruptible, actions of an entity.
activation	The time when an object is performing some method.
activity	An operation or set of operations within a state that takes time to complete. Thus, it is not instantaneous and can be interrupted.
activity diagram	A diagram of state behavior in which each individual state is a sequence of steps representing the operations of an interaction. The interaction is typically the service of a given class, and the activity diagrams describes the serial events that take place within it.
actor	An entity outside of a system that interacts with it. An actor's activities are described by a use case.
adornment	A graphical element used to denote some particular property or state.
aggregation	A hierarchy containment relationship in which the part(s) can exist without the container.
association	A peer-to-peer relationship between objects.
associative object	Special case of an object relationship in which the attributes (information) of the relationship need to be kept
attribute	An inherent property of a class. It has a name and a type.
class	A descriptor for a set of objects with identical attributes, behaviors, rules, and relationships.
class diagram	Describes the static structure of a system.
collaboration diagram	Captures the interaction between objects.
compartment	A visual display area that can take part of or all of a UML element. For example, a UML class shows the class name, services, and attributes in separate compartments.
component	A distributable physical unit, usually of software.
component diagram	Describes the organization and dependencies among software implementation components.
composition	A hierarchy containment relationship in which the part(s) cannot exist without the container.

Term	Definition
constraint	A semantic relationship between the model elements that describes conditions that must be maintained as true. If the constraint is violated, then the model is considered semantically invalid.
dependency	A semantic relationship between two or more model elements. It shows that one element would be affected by the change or absence of another element.
deployment diagram	Describes the configuration of processing elements and the mapping of the software implementation components to the processing elements.
element	Any UML concept.
event	A noteworthy occurrence that, in a state diagram, may trigger the transition from one state to the next.
export	In the context of packages, it makes an element accessible outside its enclosing namespace by adjusting its visibility
generalization/ specialization	An hierarchal relationship between classes in which the subclass (child class) inherits all the attributes, operations, rules, and object relationships (association and aggregation) of its superclasses.
history state	Remembers its substate when it is exited and is able to enter the same substate on subsequent reentry into the state.
inheritance	A mechanism for implementing generalization/specialization in some programming languages. Also used in UML as equivalence of G/S.
interaction diagram	A UML diagram that describes how a group of objects collaborate in some behavior, typically by exchanging messages. Sequence diagrams and collaboration diagrams are the different kinds of interaction diagrams.
interface	Makes the using component depend upon the interface to the used component, not upon its implementation.
lifeline	In a sequence diagram, it shows the lifetime of the object in the given interaction.
message	Represents an interaction between objects.
multiplicity	Shows the allowable numeric range of values that a given UML element has with another element.
node	Represents a processing or computation resource.
note	Shows textual information with regard to a UML model element
Object Constraint Language (OCL)	A text language for specifying constraints and queries using expressions, guard conditions, actions, preconditions, postconditions, assertions, etc.
object diagram	Describes actual objects and their relationships. Rarely used.

Term	Definition
object flow	Represents the utilization of objects by action states and the influence of these states on the object
object relationship	Association or aggregation or composition.
operation	A service or function of an instance of a class that can be requested to perform. An operation consists of a name and a list of parameters.
package	A mechanism for organizing model elements into groups. Packages may be nested. Inner packages can see elements in enclosing packages without imports.
package diagram	A class diagram that shows the packages within a system, their interfaces plus the dependency between packages and other packages or their interfaces.
realize	To provide the implementation for a specification element. This is shown using a dotted generalization relationship.
refinement	Specifies that a model element is a more refined version of a generalized element. (i.e., generalization/specialization).
relationship	Relates two or more other instances of classes (association and aggregation) or relates two classes (generalization and specialization).
sequence diagram	Captures the interaction between objects. These interactions are modeled as exchanges of messages.
state	A condition or interaction that satisfies a condition during the lifetime of an object. This is depicted in UML state and activity diagrams as a rectangle with rounded corners
statechart diagram	Describes how the functionality of an object depends upon its state and how its state changes as a result of the events that it receives.
static structure diagram	Either a class diagram or an object diagram
stereotype	Used to create a new type of UML element. This is how one extends UML.
subsystem	A package with one or more interfaces that is designed to representation a component that is the implementation of the subsystem.
swimlane	Represents responsibilities of one or more objects for actions within an overall interaction
timing mark	Used to capture real-time constraints on transition. The most common use of a timing mark is to capture the maximum limits on the elapsed time between events.
transition	A relationship between two states that indicates that an object will progress from the first state to the second when a specified event takes place

Term	Definition
use case	A meaningful unit of functionality provided by a system or class instance that is visible to one or more actors.
use case diagram	Describes the functionality and users of the system.
visibility	A designation that describes the scope of access for a particular attribute or operation. In UML, this is public (+), private (-), and protected (#).

BIBLIOGRAPHY

These are some of the references used in creating the material of the course. Unfortunately, this is a rapidly evolving field and there is no one book that will give you in-depth coverage of all the topics that we introduced to you in the course. The references are given in alphabetical order by authors, and does not represent the importance of the respective books.

Blaha, Michael, and Wiliam Premerlani. *Object-Oriented Modeling and Design for Database Applications*, Prentice-Hall, 1998.

Bloor Research Group. *CASE & Methods Based Development Tools: An Evaluation and Comparison*, United Kingdom, 1994.

Booch, Grady. *Object Oriented Design with Applications*. Benjamin/Cummings, 1991.

Booch, Grady. *Software Engineering with Ada*, Benjamin/Cummings Publishing Co., Menlo Park, California, 1983.

Booch, Grady. "Object-oriented Development." *IEEE Trans. on Software Engineering*, vol. SE-12, no. 2, pp. 211–21, February 1986.

Booch, Grady, James Rumbaugh, and Ivar Jacobson. *The Unified Modeling Language User Guide*, Addison-Wesley, 1998.

Brooks, F. P. *The Mythical Man-month: Essay on Software Engineering*, Addison-Wesley, 1982.

Brooks, F. P. "The Silver Bullet, Essence and Accidents of Software Engineering." *Information Processing '86*. Ed H. J. Kugler, Elsevier Science Publishers B. B. (North-Holland), 1986.

Chen, Peter. "The entity-relationship model—Toward a unified view of data." *ACM Trans. on Database Systems*, 1(1) March 1976.

Coad, Peter, and Edward Yourdon. *Object-Oriented Analysis*, Yourdon Press, 1991.

Coad, Peter, and Edward Yourdon. *Object-Oriented Design*. Yourdon Press, 1991.

Cockburn, A. Writing Effective Use Cases (Draft 3), Addison Wesley Longman, 2000.

Codd, E. "Entending the database relational model to capture more meaning," *ACM Trans. on Database Systems*, 4(4), December 1979.

Embley, David W., Barry D. Kurtz, and Scott N. Woodfield. *Object-Oriented System Analyis: A Model-Driven Approach,* Yourdon Press, 1992.

Entsminger, Gary. *The Tao of Objects: A Beginner's Guide to Object-Oriented Programming,* Yourdon Press, 1992.

Fowler, M. and K. Scott. *UML Distilled A Brief Guide To The Standard Object Modeling Guide (2nd Edition),* Addison Wesley Longman, Inc., 1999.

Goldstein, N. and J. Alger. *Developing Object-Oriented Software for the Macintosh Analysis, Design, and Programming,* Addison-Wesley, 1992.

Graham, Ian. *Object-Oriented Methods,* Addison-Wesley, 1991.

Jacobson, I., M. Christerson, P. Jonsson, and F. Overgaard. *Object-Oriented Software Engineering—A Use Case Approach,* Addison-Wesley, Wokingham, England, 1992.

Jacobson, I., G. Booch, and J. Rumbaugh. *The Unified Software Development Process,* Addison-Wesley, 1999.

Josuttis, Nicolai M. *The C++ Standard Library: A Tutorial and Reference,* Addison-Wesley, 1999.

Kernighan, B. W. and D. M. Ritchie. *The C Programming Language,* Prentice-Hall, Englewood Cliffs, New Jersey, 1978.

Khoshafian, Setrig, and Razmik Abnous. *Object Orientation: Concepts, Languages, Databases, User Interfaces,* John Wiley, 1990.

Kuhn, T. *The Structure of Scientific Revolution (2nd edition),* University of Chicago Press, 1970.

Lippman, Stanley B. *C++ Prime,* Addison Wesley, 1991.

Martin, James, and James Odell. *Object-Oriented Analysis and Design,* Prentice Hall, 1992.

McMenamin, S. M. and J. F. Palmer. *Essential System Analysis,* Yourdon Press, 1984.

Meyer, Bertrand. *Object-Oreinted Software Construction,* Prentice-Hall International (UK) Ltd., Cambridge, UK, 1988.

Musser, David R., and Atul Saini. *STL Tutorial and Reference Guide C++ Programming with the Standard Template Library,* Addison Wesley, 1996.

Page Jones, Meilir. *Fundamentals of Object Oriented Design in UML,* Addison Wesley, 2000

Plauger, P. J. *The Draft Standard C++ Library,* Prentice-Hall, 1995.

Quillian, M. Ross. "Semantic Memory." In Marvin Minsky (Ed.), *Semantic Information Processing* (216–269). Cambridge, Mass, 1968.

Ross, D., "Applications and extensions of SADT." *IEEE Computer,* April 1985.

Rumbaugh, J., M. Blaha, W. Premerlani, F. Eddy, and W. Lorensen. *Object-Oriented Modeling and Design,* Prentice-Hall, 1992.

Rumbaugh, J., "Getting Started: Using Use Cases To Capture Requirements," *Object-Oriented Programming*, September, 1994.

Rumbaugh, J., I. Jacobson, and G. Booch. *The Unified Modeling Language Reference Manual*, Addison-Wesley, 1999.

Shlaer, Sally, and Stephen Mellor. *Object-Oriented Systems Analysis: Modeling the World in Data*, Yourdon Press, 1988.

Shlaer, Sally, and Stephen Mellor. *Object Lifecycles: Modeling the World in States*, Yourdon Press, 1992.

Stevens, Perdita, and Rob Pooley. *Using UML Software Engineering with Objects and Components*, 2000.

Stein, L. A., H. Lieberman, and D. Ungar. "A shared view of sharing: The Treaty of Orlando." *Object-Oriented Concepts, Databases, and Application.* Eds., W. Kim and F. H. Lechosky, ACM Press, New York, 1989.

Stroustrup, Bjarne. *The C++ Programming Language*, Addison-Wesley, 1991.

Walden, Kim, and Jean-Marc Nerson. *Seamless Object-Oriented Software Architecture Analysis and Design of Reliable Systems*, Prentice-Hall, 1995.

Winston, M. E., R. Chaffin, and D. Herrmann. "A taxonomy of part-whole relations." *Cognitive Science*, 11:417–44, 1987.

Wirfs Brock, Rebecca. *Designing Object-Oriented Software* Prentice-Hall, 1990

Yourdon, E. M. and L. L. Constatine. *Structured Design: Fundamentals of a Discipline of Computer Program and Systems Design*, Prentice-Hall, Englewood Cliffs, New Jersey, 1979.

ACKNOWLEDGMENTS

Preface

Keats, John. "Letter to J. H. Reynolds." May 3, 1918.

Chapter 1

Shakespeare, W., *Macbeth.*

Bloor Research Group. *CASE & Methods Based Development Tools: An Evaluation and Comparison*, United Kingdom, 1994.

Chen, Peter. "The entity-relationship model—Toward a unified view of data." *ACM Trans. on Database Systems*, 1(1) March 1976.

Codd, E. "Extending the database relational model to capture more meaning." *ACM Trans. on Database Systems*, 4(4), December 1979.

Hughes DoD Composite Software Error History.

Yourdon, E. N. and L. L. Constatine. *Structured Design: Fundamentals of a Discipline of Computer Program and Systems Design*, Prentice-Hall, Englewood Cliffs, New Jersey, 1979.

The Standish Group International, Inc. "Chaos Report," *http://standishgroup.com/visitor/chaos.html*, 1995.

Chapter 2

Goldsein, N. and J. Alger. *Developing Object-Oriented Software for the Macintosh Analysis, Design, and Programming*, Addison-Wesley, 1992.

Brooks, F. P. *The Mythical Man-month: Essay on Software Engineering*, Addison-Wesley, 1982.

Chapter 3

Brooks, F. P. "The Silver Bullet, Essence and Accidents of Software Engineering." *Information Processing '86*. Ed., H. J. Kugler, Elsevier Science Publishers B.B. (North-Holland), 1986.

Kuhn, T. *The Structure of Scientific Revolution (2nd edition)*, University of Chicago Press, 1970.

Chapter 4

Wordsworth, *The Recluse*, 1850.

Booch, G., J. Rumbaugh, and I. Jacobson. *The Unified Modeling Language User Guide*, Addison-Wesley, 1999.

Jacobson, I., G. Booch, and J. Rumbaugh. *The Unified Software Develoment Process*, Addison-Wesley, 1999.

Rumbaugh, J., I. Jacobson, and G. Booch. *The Unified Modeling Language Reference Manual*, Addison-Wesley, 1999.

Cockburn, A., Writing Effective Use Cases (Draft 3), Addison Wesley Longman, 2000.

Rumbaugh, J. "Getting Started: Using Use Cases To Capture Requirements," J. Object-Oriented Programming, September, 1994.

Chapter 5

King, R. "My Cat is Object-Oriented." *Object-Oriented Concepts, Databases, and Applications*. Eds. Won Kim and Fredrick H. Lochosky, ACM Press and Addison Wesley, 1989.

Booch, G. *Software Engineering with Ada*, Benjamin/Cummings Publishing Co., Menlo Park, California, 1983.

Booch, G. "Object-Oriented Development." *IEEE Trans. on Software Engineering*, vol. SE-12, no. 2, pp. 211-21, February 1986.

Meyer, B. *Object-Oriented Software Construction*, Prentice-Hall International (UK) Ltd., Cambridge, UK, 1988.

Wirfs-Brock, R. *Designing Object-Oriented Software*, Prentice-Hall, 1990.

Coad, P. and E. Yourdon. *Object-Oriented Analysis*, Yourdon Press, 1991.

Schlaer, S., and S. Mellor. *Object-Oriented Systems Analysis: Modeling the World in Data*, Yourdon Press, 1988.

Ross, D. "Applications and extensions of SADT." *IEEE Computer*, April 1985.

Chapter 6

Wordsworth. *The Prelude*, 1850.

Coad, P., and E. Yourdon. *Object-Oriented Analysis*, Yourdon Press, 1991.

Schlaer, S., and S. Mellor. *Object-Oriented Systems Analysis: Modeling the World in Data*, Yourdon Press, 1988.

Wirfs-Brock, R. *Designing Object-Oriented Software*, Prentice-Hall, 1990.

Chapter 7

McMennin, S. M. and J. F. Palmer. *Essential System Analysis*, Yourdon Press, 1984.

Chapter 8

Jacobson, I., M. Christerson, P. Jonsson, and F. Overgaard. *Object-Oriented Software Engineering—A Use Case Approach*, Addison-Wesley, Wokingham, England, 1992.

McMennin, S. M. and J. F. Palmer. *Essential System Analysis*, Yourdon Press, 1984.

Schlaer, S., and S. Mellor. *Object Lifecycles: Modeling the World in States*, Yourdon Press, 1992.

Chapter 9

Lamb, C. *Last Essays of Elia*, 1833.

Winston, M. E., R. Chaffer, and D. Herrmann. "A taxonomy of part-whole relations," *Cognitive Science*, 11:417–44, 1987.

Chapter 10

Kant, E. *Logic*, (Trans.) Robert S. Hartman and Wolfgange Schwarz, Dover, 1988.

Martin, J. and J. Odell, *Object-Oriented Analysis and Design*, Prentice-Hall, 1992.

Meyer, B. *Object-Oriented Software Construction*, Prentice-Hall International (UK) Ltd., Cambridge, UK., 1988.

Quillian, M. Ross, "Semantic Memory." In Marvin Minsky (Ed.), *Semantic Information Processing* (216–269). Cambridge, Mass, 1968.

MIT Press.

Chapter 11

Paine, T. *The Age of Reason*, Pt. ii, par 56, 1795.

Fowler, M., and K. Scott, *UML Distilled A Brief Guide To The Standard Object Modeling Guide (2nd Edition)*, Addison Wesley Longman, Inc, 1999.

Schlaer, S. and S. Mellor. *Object-Oriented Systems Analysis: Modeling the World in Data*, Yourdon Press, 1988.

Rumbaugh, J., M. Blaha, W. Premerlani, F. Eddy, and W. Lorensen. *Object-Oriented Modeling and Design*, Prentice-Hall, 1992.

Booch, G., J. Rumbaugh, and I. Jacobson. *The Unified Modeling Language User Guide*, Addison Wesley, 1998.

Jacobson, I., Booch, G, and J. Rumbaugh, *The Unified Software Development Process*, Addison-Wesley, 1999.

Rumbaugh, J., I. Jacobson, and G. Booch. *The Unified Modeling Language Refernce Manual*, Addison Wesley, 1999.

Chapter 12

Stein, L. A., H. Lieberman, and D. Ungar. "A shared view of sharing: The Treaty of Orlando." *Object-Oriented Concepts, Databases, and Applications*. Eds., W. Kim and F. H. Lechosky, ACM Press, New York, 1989.

Lieberman, H. First Conference on Object-Oriented Programming Languages, Systems, and Applications. [OOP-SLA-86], ACM SigCMI, Portland, Oregon, September 1986.

Chapter 13

Stroustroup, B. *The C++ Programming Language*, Addison-Wesley, 1991.

Kernighan, B. W., and D. M. Ritchie. *The C Programming Language*, Prentice-Hall, Englewood Cliffs, New Jersey, 1978.

Chapter 14

Peirce, C. S. "How to Make Our Ideas Clear." *Charles S. Peirce: Selected Writings (Values in a Universe of Chance)*. Ed., Philip P. Wiener, Dover, 1966.

Chapter 15

Shakespeare, W. *The Tempest*.

Plauger, P. J. *The Draft Standard C++ Library*, Prentice Hall, 1995.

Musser, David R., and Atul Saini. *STL Tutorial and Reference Guide C++ Programming with the Standard Template Library*, Addison Wesley, 1996.

Josuttis, Nicolai M. *The C++ Standard Library: A Tutorial and Reference*, Addison-Wesley, 1999.

Chapter 16

Aristotle. "Zoology." *Aristotle*, (Trans.) Philip Wheelwright, The Odyssey Press, 1951.

Chapter 17

Orwell, G., *1984*.

Chapter 18

Alfonso the Wise (Attributed)

Chapter 19

Donne, J. *Devotions Upon Emergent Occasions*, 1624.

Chapter 20

Solemnization of Matrimony, The Book of Common Prayers.

Appendix A

Fowler, M., and K. Scott. *UML Distilled: A Brief Guide to the Standard Object Modeling Guide (2nd Edition)*, Addison-Wesley-Longman, Inc, 1999.

Booch, G., J. Rumbaugh, and I. Jacobson. *The Unified Modeling Language User Guide*, Addison-Wesley, 1998.

Booch, G., J. Rumbaugh, and I. Jacobson. *The Unified Software Development Process*, Addison-Wesley, 1998.

Booch, G., J. Rumbaugh, and I. Jacobson. *The Unified Modeling Language Reference Manual*, Addison-Wesley, 1999.

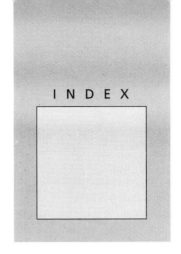

INDEX